D1559209

Marriages

of

Loudoun County, Virginia

1757-1853

Marriages

of

Loudoun County,

Virginia

1757-1853

Compiled by

MARY ALICE WERTZ

GENEALOGICAL PUBLISHING CO., INC.

Note to the Reader

LOUDOUN COUNTY was formed from Fairfax County, which was primarily Truro Parish, in 1757. In October 1748, Truro was divided at Difficult Run and the upper part became Cameron Parish. When Loudoun was created, its boundaries were essentially those of Cameron Parish: on the north it was bounded by the Potomac River; on the south by Prince William County (which later became Fauquier); on the east by Difficult Run; and on the west by the Blue Ridge Mountains. In 1770, Shelburne Parish was created from the western part of Cameron and included, generally, the land west of Goose Creek running to the Blue Ridge.

Key

Shel. - Shelburne Parish
Cam. - Cameron Parish
    Where known the name of the parish is included at the end of
    each entry.
FeeBk. - Fee Book. These are kept in the Office of the Clerk of the
    Circuit Court, Leesburg, Va., to record any monies received.
    FeeBk 1 - 1764 - Clerk's Office
    FeeBk 2 - 1765 - Clerk's Office
    FeeBk 3 - 1762 - Clerk's Office
    FeeBk 4 - 1761 - Loudoun Museum, Leesburg, Va.
MarReg - Marriage Register. These are kept in the Clerk's Office
    and begin in 1850, the last year bonds were required.
OB - Order Book. These start in 1757 and concern matters brought
    before the court.
MB - Minute Book. These continue the records begun in the order
    books.
DB - Deed Book. Deed records are kept from 1757.
ParReg - Parish Register. All churches were checked for records
    of marriages. The Virginia State Library has some parish
    records but none includes marriages. St. James Episcopal
    Church, Leesburg, has recently discovered its early minutes
    are in Richmond but, at this writing, the church has received
    no copy of them. As far as known, these are the only extant
    records for the period prior to 1854:
    ParReg A - New Jerusalem Evangelical Lutheran Church,
        Lovettsville. The original records have been sent to the
        Lutheran Theological Seminary Library, Gettysburg, Pa.
        A copy of the minutes, kept at New Jerusalem, was trans-
        lated from the German in 1970.
    ParReg B - Emmanuel Episcopal Church, Middleburg, Va.
FFMM - Fairfax Monthly Meeting. These records of the Society
    of Friends were extracted by Robert R. Walker, Oct.,
    1924, at his request as Custodian of Records of Fairfax
    Monthly Meeting, Waterford, from early minutes of the
    Society. A copy is kept at the Clerk's Office.
        Some early FFMM records are kept at the Thomas Balch
    Library, Leesburg.

Where bonds were not found, ministers' returns were checked to
secure marriage records. These were records returned to the
court by ministers performing the ceremony and may be found at
the Clerk's Office. Last names of ministers are found at the end
of each entry before the name of the parish. A complete listing
of ministers who returned records is given in the Appendix.

Section 1

____, Adam, free man of colour & Kitty Hardin, free woman of
    color. m. 24 April 1823. Dunn. Cam.
____, Ben & Sophy (   ), people of color. m. 20 March 1808.
    Littlejohn.
____, Tom, servant of Mr. Moss & Lizzie (   ), servant of Miss
    M. Hereford. m. 5 April 1849. ParReg B.
____ous, George & Mary Bayer, of Maryland. m. 29 Sep. 1833.
    ParReg A.
____ter(?), William & Catharina Geist, both single. By license.
    m. 31 Dec. 1818. ParReg A.
Abbot, William R. & Eleanor I. Harris, dau. of Samuel B. Harris,
    bm. 6 May 1833. m. 7 May 1833. Dorsey.
Abbott, Jeremiah & Theny Eaton. m. 10 Jan. 1800. Littlejohn.
Abel, Conrad & Mary Shriver. m. 1807-1808. Mines.
Abel, George & Nanzy Blieker, both single. By license. m. 25 March
    1824. ParReg A.
Abel, George F. & Margaret J. Derry, dau. of Christian Derry, who
    proves groom's age, bm. 14 June 1852. m. 17 June 1852.Holland.
Able, Christopher & Sarah Blakley. m. 21 March 1808. Littlejohn.
Abraham, John & Mary Wenner, dau. of Magdalena Frazier. Adam Karn,
    bm. 4 June 1831. Wit: Thomas J. Marlow. m. 4 June 1831.
    Dorsey.
Abrams, Carl & Maria Blahn, both single. By license. m. 8 Oct.
    1821. ParReg A.
Acha, Martin & Elizabeth Davis. m. 28 Feb. 1805. Jefferson.
Acres, James & Nancy Taylor. m. 15 April 1801. Littlejohn.
Acres, Walters & Ann Cunningham. m. 1807-1808. Mines.
Adam, Matthew & Susannah Triplet. m. 27 Sep. 1804. Williamson.
Adam, William F. & Adelaide Osburn, dau. of Joel Osburn, bm.
    1 Dec. 1834. Shel.
Adams, Charles & Julia A. Gibson. m. 3 May 1852. George W. Gibson
    proves bride's age. Hirst.
Adams, Daniel & Susanna Smith. Levi Winegarner proves bride's age,
    bm. 9 Sep. 1833. m. 12 Sep. 1833. Hauer.
Adams, Francis T. & Martha L. Rousseau. Beverly Rousseau attests
    ages, bm. 9 March 1850. m. 14 March 1850. T. D. Herndon. Cam.
Adams, Georg & Christina Wirtz, dau. of Peter Wirtz; both single.
    By license. m. 25 Dec. 1814. ParReg A.
Adams, Henry & Ann Tillett. m. 25 Feb. 1805. Littlejohn.
Adams, Henry & Duana Magahy, in Maryland. m. 7 Aug. 1843.ParReg A.
Adams, Henry, widower & Mary McGaha, dau. of David McGaha, bm.
    13 Jan. 1836. m. 19 Jan. 1836. Hauer. Shel.
Adams, James & Abigal Compher. m. 10 April 1808. Saunders.

1

Adams, James & Jane S. Cranwell, dau. of John ( ) Cranwell.
Daniel Ott attests bride's age, bm. Acknowledged 8 May 1834.
Shel.
Adams, James & Mary Dulaney. m. 20 May 1816. Littlejohn.
Adams, John & Amelia Norton. m. 27 Nov. 1793. Littlejohn.
Adams, John & Eleanor Watkins, dau. of Ann Brown. Bernard Watkins,
bm. 11 Aug. 1834. m. 14 Aug. 1834. Dorsey. Shel.
Adams, Joseph & Winefred Bready. m. 2 Jan. 1814. Henkle.
Adams, Josias & Mary Ann Hill. Thomas C. Durall attests bride's
age. William McClosky, guardian of groom, bm. 9 Feb. 1829.
m. 10 Feb. 1829. Tippett.
Adams, Richard & Anna Dyer. Charles G. Eskridge, bm. 10 April
1837. Shel.
Adams, Richard & Rebecca Ellgin. m. 16 Dec. 1807. Littlejohn.
Adams, Thomas & Anna Spring, both single. By license. m. 2 Nov.
1813. ParReg A.
Adams, Thomas B. & Latitia Marge. m. 6 Oct. 1818. Dunn. Shel.
Adams, William & Elizabeth Hendrick. m. 28 July 1803. Littlejohn.
Adams, William & Linney Willet. William Willet attests bride's
age, bm. 1 Jan. 1799. Littlejohn. Shel.
Adams, William & Mahala Wolford, dau. of William Wolford, who
proves groom's age, bm. 26 Feb. 1839. Shel.
Adams, William & Margaret Harra. m. 25 July 1822. T. Littleton.
Adams, William & Nancy Robartson. m. 24 Dec. 1816. T. Littleton.
Adams, William & Sally Bennet. m. 22 Aug. 1801. Littlejohn.
Addison, Anthony & Mary (Juliet) Thompson, dau. of William M.
Thompson, at house of M. Fayette Ball, Leesburg. m. 4 June
1833. Adie. Shel.
Adie, George, Rev. & Mrs. Mary E. Powell, dau. of Cuthbert Powell,
by Revd. Charles W. Andrews, at Llangollen, residence of her
father. m. 22 Dec. 1835. Adie. Shel.
Adie, Samuel F. & Gustavia B. Wilson, at St. James Church,
Leesburg. m. 1 June 1848. Adie.
Aduddell, Cabel & Ann Wilson, dau. of Edward Wilson, bm. William H.
Francis attests groom's age. 29 Dec. 1834. Shel.
Akers, John & Stelly Swarts. John Palmer attests ages, bm. 3 Aug.
1835. Shel.
Akers, Walter & Rutha Gill. m. 24 Jan. 1805. Littlejohn.
Alabough, Jacob & Elizabeth Law. m. 1807-1808. Mines.
Albaugh, Eli C. & Sarah Ann Gray, dau. of Phela Gray. John A.
Moore, bm. 28 April 1837. Shel.
Alder, Albert & Mary Catharine Locker. Gerard Locker attests ages,
bm. 11 Feb. 1839. Shel.
Alder, George & Margaret Miller. Samuel Cordell attests groom's
age, bm. George Alder, guardian of bride. 11 March 1829.
Alder, ·George H. & Jane Nichols. m. 1821-1822. Mines.
Alder, Isaac & Mary S. (F.) Smith, dau. of Mary Smith. 14 Jan.
1851. MarReg. m. 21 Jan. 1851. Startzman.
Alder , James & Hester Reed. m. 13 Sep. 1802. Littlejohn.
Alder, James, Jr. & Amanda E. Marshall. m. 27 May 1841. R. N.
Herndon.
Alder, John, son of John Alder & Elizabeth Collins (Collings),dau.
of Levi Collins (Collings), bm. 20 Dec. 1830; both single.
m. 23 Dec. 1830. ParReg A. Shel.

2

LOUDOUN COUNTY MARRIAGES

Alder, Joseph M. (W.) & Lucy A. Alder. Albert Alder attests ages,
    bm. 17 Oct. 1836. m. 17 Oct. 1836. White.
Alder, Sanford Mason & Maria (Mary) A. Marshall. Francis M.
    Bradfield attests ages, bm. 16 May 1849. m. 24 May 1849.
    Eggleston. Shel.
Alder, William Silcott & Margaret E. Birkitt (Birkett). William
    Birkitt attests ages, bm. 14 Aug. 1848. m. 15 Aug. 1848.
    Eggleston.
Aldridge (Aldrige), John & Mary Ellen Moffett (Moffit), at house
    of her father, Loudoun. Robert D. Moffett, bm. 4 Jan. 1844.
    m. 16 Jan. 1844. Adie.
Alender, Elias J. & Lucinda Fox. Wit: George K. Fox, Sr. 11 Feb.
    1852. MarReg.
Alender, Jacob & Eliza Ann Stuart. m. 26 July 1846. ParReg A. Shel.
Alexander, David & Elizabeth McMullin. Andrew McMullin attests
    bride's age, bm. 10 May 1813.
Alexander, David & Sarah Susannah Brabham, dau. of Mary Brabham.
    Richard Alexander, bm. 9 Aug. 1842.
Alexander, Gerard & Eleanor Lee. m. 29 May 1806. Dunn.
Alexander, James & Lydia Jane Boggess, dau. of Mary Anne Carlisle.
    Mahlon Baldwin attests groom's age, bm. 19 March 1849. m.
    22 March 1849. Dodge. Shel.
Alexander, John Thomas & Mary Jane Power. Wit: Their fathers.
    18 March 1851. MarReg.
Alexander, Richard & Mary E. Brabham. William Alexander attests
    ages, bm. 18 Feb. 1841. Shel.
Allder, James, Jr. & Amanda E. Marshall, dau. of Ruse Marshall.
    Joseph Allder attests groom's age. Joseph W. Allder, bm.
    19 May 1841. Shel.
Allder, William & Jane Ann Orr. Francis M. Bradfield attests
    ages, bm. 3 April 1847. Shel.
Allen, David & Elisabith Massee. m. 29 May 1821. T. Littleton.
Allen, Edmund (Edmond) & Margaret B. Jenkins. John Butler,
    guardian, bm. 13 Feb. 1832. m. 8 March 1832. Green. Shel.
Allen, Jacob, son of James Allen & Sarah Derry. Joseph L.
    Russell attests bride's age. James Allen, bm. 27 Dec. 1845.
    Shel.
Allen, James & Martha Hughes. m. 2 Jan. 1822-21 March 1822. Mines.
Allen, William & Nancy Cornell. Thomas Ashby attests ages, bm.
    25 June 1831. m. 30 June 1831. Green. Shel.
Allender, Jacob & Eliza Ann Steward. Charles E. Speaks attests
    ages, bm. 23 July 1846. Shel.
Aller, Georg & Margretha Philler, both single. By license. m.
    20 March 1829. ParReg A.
Alt, Johannes, son of late William Alt and wife & Maria Juliana
    Springin, dau. of Andreas Springin and wife. By license.
    m. 7 May 1818. ParReg A.
Alt, William & Sussanna Ulm, both single. By license. m. 20 Aug.
    1815. ParReg A.
Amblar, Lewis & Sally Hutchison, dau. of John Hutchison. Vincent
    Hutchison, bm. 1 April 1799.
Amiss, John L. & Mary Jane Dagg. m. 7 Dec. 1824. Dagg.
Anders, John & Susan Beavers. Silas Garrett, guardian of both,
    bm. 14 Sep. 1835. m. 20 Sep. 1835. Trott. Shel.

3

Anders, William & Mary Griffith, widow. Joseph McDonald attests
groom's age. John Bazzell, bm. 10 Aug. 1829.
Anderson, Abram & Catherine Butcher. m. 23 Dec. 1802. Littlejohn.
Anderson, Andrew & Eleanor Hixon. m. 1820-1821. Mines.
Anderson, Charles F., son of Eleanor Anderson & Mary Frances
Hough. Benjamin Hough, bm. 15 Jan. 1842. m. 18 Jan. 1842.
Phelps. Shel.
Anderson, Eli & Nancy Pile. m. 25 March 1824. Rozell.
Anderson, Eli & Sarah Frances Stillings, dau. of Benjamin
Stillious. Jefferson Anderson attests groom's age, bm. 10 May
1841. Shel.
Anderson, Eliakim & Mary Barby. m. 21 May 1807. Littlejohn.
Anderson, George & Catherine Wildman. James M. Carr attests ages,
bm. 7 March 1848. Shel.
Anderson, Harrison, son of Elijah Anderson & Catherine Anderson.
Elijah Anderson, bm. 2 April 1832. m. 10 April 1832. Green.
Shel.
Anderson, Jacob & Rachel Lafaber. William Lafaber attests ages,
bm. 10 Feb. 1832. Cam.
Anderson, James S. & Emma Reed. Wit: Father of girl who proves
groom's age. 18 Dec. 1852. MarReg. m. 21 Dec. 1852. Greer.
Anderson, John E. & Amanda M. Carpenter, dau. of Elizabeth
Carpenter. John A. Beavers attests groom's age, bm. 25 Nov.
1843.
Anderson, Joseph & Jane Ross. m. 1815. Littlejohn.
Anderson, Marcus & Mary Ann Brown, dau. of William P. Brown, who
proves groom's age, bm. 11 April 1837. Shel.
Anderson, Richard & Mary E. Milbourne. Jonathan Milbourne attests
ages, bm. 13 May 1847. Shel.
Anderson, Robert & Melia Lacey. m. 27 Jan. 1812. J. Littleton.
Anderson, Smith, son of Nancy Anderson & Frances A. Moore. Seth
Smith attests bride's age. John Wornall, bm. 14 Feb. 1848. m.
19 Feb. 1848. Hayes. Shel.
Ankers, Samuel & Henrietta B. Edwards. William M. Moran attests
ages, bm. 31 Oct. 1849. Cam.
Ansel, Leonard & Susannah Fry. m. 1 March 1803. Littlejohn.
Ansel, Michal & Catherine Fioccoats. m. 28 March 1796. Littlejohn.
Ansel, Peter, son of Leonhard Ansel & Elisabeth Freyin, dau. of
Nicolaus Frey. By license. m. 13 Aug. 1793. ParReg A.
Armistead, George G. & Alice Virginia Fontaine. William Noland,
bride's guardian, bm. 1 Nov. 1831. m. 28 Nov. 1831. Cuttler.
Armstrong, Amos & Margaret Vanhorne. m. 20 Feb. 1803. Dunn.
Armstrong, James & Mary Vanhorne. m. 12 Feb. 1793. Littlejohn.
Arnell, Adam & Catherine Boges. m. 1 May 1810. Littlejohn.
Arnet, John & Mary E. Reed. Moses Arnet attests ages, bm. 2 Nov.
1840. Shel.
Arnet, Samuel & Ann E. Cummins. Wit: George W. Noland. 1 Feb. 1853.
MarReg. m. 3 Feb. 1853. Greer.
Arnett, Moses & Ruth Hannah Gibson. Jonas Janney attests ages,bm.
13 Dec. 1837. Shel.
Arnold, Edward & Ann Procter. 13 Aug. 1794. Littlejohn.
Arnold, Jacob & Maria Hemrich, dau. of Jacob Hemrich; both single.
By license. m. 2 Dec. 1813. ParReg A.
Arnold, John & Elizabeth Case. Samuel Case attests ages, bm.
20 May 1844. m. 23 May 1844. ParReg A. Shel.

4

Arnold, Jonathan & Margaret A. Compher. Wit: Michael Arnold
    proves ages. 9 Dec. 1851. MarReg.
Arnold, Joseph & Martha A. Matthias. Simon Arnold attests ages,
    bm. 28 Dec. 1846. m. 28 Dec. 1846. ParReg A. Shel.
Arnold, Martin Lewis & Elizabeth Smith, dau. of Jacob Smith, who
    attests groom's age, bm. 24 Feb. 1848. m. 2 March 1848.
    Shuford. Shel.
Arnold, Michael & Elizabeth C. Souder. Wit: George P. Souder
    proves ages. 1 March 1852. MarReg.
Arnold, Michael & Polly Fry. m. 2 Jan. 1822-21 March 1822. Mines.
Arnold, Noah & Emeline Filler, dau. of Jacob Filler who attests
    groom's age, bm. 13 Nov. 1838. m. 15 Nov. 1838. Hauer. Shel.
Arnold, Simon & Catharine Frey, dau. of Michael Frey, bm.
    31 March 1845. m. 3 April 1845. ParReg A. Shel.
Arnolt, John & Mary Millburn. m. 27 Nov. 1796. Littlejohn.
Arundell, Joseph & Honour Lafaber. William Jacobus attests
    groom's age, bm. 7 June 1837. Cam.
Arundle (Arundell), Franklin & Mary E. Houser. James Wiley
    attests ages, bm. 17 Feb. 1847. Cam. m. 17 Jan. 1847. Gover.
Ash, John & Patty Ashton. m. 12 May 1806. Littlejohn.
Ashby, Enoch R. & Delila Cline. m. 2 Jan. 1823. Frye.
Ashby, Nimrod & Mary Agnes Smallwood, dau. of John Wesley
    Smallwood, who acknowledges groom's age, bm. 15 Sep. 1840.
    m. 14 Dec. 1840. Sheras. Shel.
Ashen, William & Mary McCarthy. m. 29 Aug. 1793. Littlejohn.
Ashton, John & Sarah Burgoine. m. 16 Jan. 1808. Littlejohn.
Ashton, John A. & Emily Mills, dau. of William Mills. Wit: William
    Mills and Alfred Wright who proves groom's age. 14 April 1851.
    MarReg. m. 15 April 1851. Gover.
Ashton, Joseph & Mary Herrick. m. 21 Nov. 1796. Littlejohn.
Askins, Samuel & Fanny Pool. m. 26 May 1795. Littlejohn.
Athey, George & Sarah Moffett. m. 30 Aug. 1811. Littlejohn.
Athey, John M. & Ann E. Edwards. John S. Edwards attests groom's
    age, bm. 14 April 1842. Shel.
Athey, Levi & Agnes Coats. Walter Brabham attests bride's age, bm.
    23 Jan. 1835. m. 1 Feb. 1835. Broaddus. Shel.
Athey, Thomas & Mary Thompson, dau. of Benjamin Thompson. French
    Thompson attests groom's age, bm. 15 Feb. 1833. m. 27 Feb.
    1834. Baker. Shel.
Athey, Wilford & Nancy Legg. m. 7 March 1805. Littlejohn.
Athey, William & Elizabeth Bridges. m. 6 Feb. 1806. Littlejohn.
Athy, Benjamin & Sarah Oden. m. 1809-1810. Mines.
Atkin, William & Elizabeth P. Clark. Thomas Hensey attests ages,
    bm. 28 April 1848. m. 25(?) April 1848. Krebbs. Shel.
Atkinson, Archibald & Elizabeth A. Chilton. William Powell, bm.
    20 April 1829. m. 23 April 1829. Williamson.
Atwell, Bernard R. & Jane A. Hammerly. John A. Klein attests ages,
    bm. 27 Nov. 1834. Shel.
Atwell, Ewell & Mary A. Simpson. A. K. Peisor, bm. 15 March 1847.
    m. 7 April 1847. Gover. Shel.
Atwell, Jesse & Mary Peugh, widow. Charles Binns, bm. 9 Aug. 1836.
    m. 11 Aug. 1836. Trott. Shel.
Atwell, Thomas H. & Rebecca J. Havenner. Wit: Father of bride, who
    attests groom's age. 26 May 1851. MarReg. m. 24(?) May 1851.
    Gover.

5

Atwell, Thompson & Nancy Cumming. m. 20 Jan. 1825. Dunn.

Auchslein, Daniel, son of David Auchslein and wife & Catharina
  Schaffer, dau. of Johannes Schaffer and wife; both single.
  By license. m. 17 Dec. 1818. ParReg A.

Auchslein, Emanuel, son of David Auchslein and wife, Eva &
  Sussana Schaffer, dau. of Mjohannes Schaffer and wife; both
  single. By license. m. 7 Sep. 1820. ParReg A.

Auchslein, Johannes, son of Johannes Auchslein & Christina
  Bockern, dau. of Samuel Bocker; both single. By license.
  m. 24 March 1812. ParReg A.

Ault, John, son of William Ault & Mahala Campbell, dau. of John
  Campbell. William Ault, John Campbell, bm. 5 June 1838.

Ault, William & Nancy Thomas, widow. Charles Binns, bm. 2 Aug.
  1836. Shel.

Austin, William & Ann Sanders. m. 2 March 1805. Littlejohn.

Axline, David & Catharine Sarah Coe (Cole). John Prince attests
  ages, bm. 21 March 1846. m. 26 March 1846. ParReg A. Shel.

Axline, Henry, son of John Axline & Catharine Ross. John Axline
  attests bride's age, bm. 26 Dec. 1809. m. 26 Dec. 1809.
  Littlejohn.

Ayres, Charles M. & Mary J. Dennis, dau. of Mrs. Matilda Carter.
  Giles Jackson attests groom's age, bm. 3 Feb. 1845. m. 6 Feb.
  1845. Massey. Cam.

Ayres, George S. & Mary Ann Benton, dau. of William Benton, who
  attests groom's age, bm. 23 April 1841. Shel.

Ayres, Thomas W. & Mary C. Hogeland. Wit: John J. Hogeland.
  31 May 1852. MarReg. m. 1 June 1852. Nixon.

Baarn, William F. & Mary Jane Tucker. m. 17 May 1849. Gover.

Baffington, Joshua & Mary Morell. m. 1807-1808. Mines.

Bagent, Jacob & Ellenora McGathen; both single. By license.
  m. 28 Nov. 1828. ParReg A.

Bagent, James & Sarah Wigginton. Benjamin Wigginton, bm. 23 July
  1849. Cam.

Bagent, William & Nancy Keist. Joseph Keist attests ages, bm.
  13 Aug. 1832. m. 16 Aug. 1832. Hauer. Shel.

Bagerly, Levi & Kessiah Guy. James Lewis attests ages, bm.
  24 Dec. 1799.

Bagly, William & Catharina Sahrbach; both single. By license.
  m. 4 Dec. 1818. ParReg A.

Bailes, William & Jane Venander. m. 19 Dec. 1812. Dunn.

Bailis, Joshua C. & Mary Ann Harkin. m. 16 Nov. 1848. Gover.

Baker, Conrad & Mary Will. m. 1807-1808. Mines.

Baker, Daniel & Lydia Ann Bitzer, dau. of William Bitzer, who
  attests groom's age, bm. 24 Aug. 1846. m. 6 Sep. 1846.
  Massey. Shel.

Baker, Edwin & Elizabeth R. Biscoe. Harrison Pool attests groom's
  age. James B. Biscoe attests bride's age, bm. 13 April 1833.
  Shel.

Baker, George William & Martha Ann Ball, dau. of Samuel Ball.
  1 June 1852. MarReg. m. 3 June 1852. Holland.

Baker, John & Mary Elizabeth Spring, dau. of John Spring, who
  attests groom's age, bm. 11 Jan. 1845. m. 4 Jan. 1845.
  Shaull. Shel.

Baker, John W. & Julia Ann Wells. Wit: John W. Virts proves ages.
  8 Dec. 1851. MarReg.

Baker, Joseph C. & Mary Jane Coe (Cole), dau. of Peter Coe, bm. Groom's brother attests his age. 8 Nov. 1847. m. 11 Nov. 1847. Williard. Shel.

Baker, Richard & Mary Ann Baggot. William Tavener affirms bride's age, bm. 3 April 1832. Shel.

Baker, Samuel & Elisabeth Virts. Samuel C. Luckett attests ages, bm. 5 June 1848. Shel.

Baker, Samuel & Sarah Shriver. Jacob Shriver attests ages, bm. 2 Nov. 1820 (1829). G. Frye.

Baker, Solomon & Catherine Amick, in Maryland. m. 18 March 1835. ParReg A.

Baker, Solomon & Susan Prince. m. 2 March 1845. ParReg A.

Baldwin, John, Jr. & Mary (Polly) Vanhorne. John Whitacre attests ages, bm. "He is also the Grandfather and Guardian before me. J.A. Binns." 13 July 1831. m. 22 July 1831. Green. Shel.

Baldwin, Joseph & Eliza H. Benton. Richard H. Benton attests ages, bm. 1 Oct. 1849. m. 3 Oct. 1849. Dodge. Shel.

Baldwin, Stacy & Margaret McVeigh. m. 22 Aug. 1805. Williamson.

Bales (Bailes), Joshua C. & Mary A. Harper, dau. of Catherine Harper. John Johnson attests groom's age, bm. Catherine Harper, bm. 13 Nov. 1848. Shel.

Bales, Thomas & Catharine Ballenger. John Ballinger attests bride's age, bm. 23 Oct. 1839. Shel.

Ball, Alfred & Sarah C. Carter. m. 27 May 1828. White.

Ball, August William & Permelia Meirs. m. 24 Feb. 1820. Littleton.

Ball, Erasmus & Elizabeth Chilton. John T. Muliken attests ages, bm. 26 Feb. 1835. Shel.

Ball, Henry & Jane Ratikin. m. 29 April 1807. FFMM.

Ball, Henry A. & Elizabeth Anne Thrift. Wesley S. McPherson, guardian, bm. 16 June 1834. m. 17 June 1834. Dorsey. Shel.

Ball, James & Mary Brown. m. 8 Aug. 1770. FFMM.

Ball, James F. & Maria Louisa Luckett, dau. of Horace Luckett. Asher W. Gray attests groom's age, bm. 9 Dec. 1846. m. 10 Dec. 1846. ParReg B.

Ball, Samuel & Catharine McPherson, dau. of Sebastian McPherson, bm. 29 Feb. 1832. Cam.

Ball, Stephen & Mary Bradon (Braden). Mahlon Janney, Jr. affirms bride's age, bm. 14 April 1809. m. 10 April 1809. Saunders.

Ball, William & Anna Davis, dau. of George Davis. Wit: Thomas Davis, William Davis, James Davis. Thomas Davis, bm. 3 Dec. 1832. Shel.

Ball, William & Rachel Bradfield. m. 28 Oct. 1824. T. Littleton.

Ball, William & Rachel Reed. m. 27 Feb. 1805. Littlejohn.

Ball, William & Sarah Ellen Lee, dau. of Joshua Lee, bm. William Shreve attests groom's age. 17 Dec. 1838. m. 18 Dec. 1838. Herndon. Cam.

Ball, William W. & Dorothy H. McCabe, dau. of John H. McCabe. S. M. Ball attests ages, bm. 6 May 1834. m. 7 May 1834. Dorsey. Shel.

Ballenger, Harrison & Caroline E. Brackenridge. Her father consents. Richard Ballenger attests groom's age, bm. 16 May 1846. m. 17 May 1846. Gover. Shel.

Ballenger, Leroy & Elizabeth Ann Gibson, dau. of Solomon Gibson. Thomas Hatcher attests groom's age. Guilford Gregg, bm. 3 Nov. 1829.

7

Ballenger, Troy & Margaret Ann Brackenridge. John Ballenger, bm. 22 Jan. 1846. m. 22 Jan. 1846. Gover. Shel.

Balman, William & Mary Tucker. m. (June) 1797. Littlejohn.

Balthrop, Jeremiah & Margaret E. Eidson, dau. of J. Eidson. W. H. Eidson, bm. 30 Dec. 1844. Shel.

Balthrope, Charles A. & Mary Ann Dawes, ward of Eli Crupper. James E. Dawes attests groom's age, bm. 13 Feb. 1838. Shel.

Banks, Samuel & Ann Jury. m. 8 Feb. 1816. T. Littleton.

Bantz, John & Susan Owings, with Maryland license. m. 13 Aug. 1833. ParReg A.

Baracraft, John & Mary Laycock. m. 1809-1810. Mines.

Barden, Miles & Mary Hughely. m. 13 Nov. 1798. Littlejohn.

Bardit, Sanford & Catherine Loveless. m. 9 Aug. 1821. Dunn. Shel.

Barker, John & Mary Elizabeth Spring. m. 14 Jan. 1845. Shaull.

Barker, Samuel & Rebeckah Bazill, dau. of John Bazill. Joseph Eidson, bm. 15 Jan. 1834. Shel.

Barker, William & Mary Janney. m. 17 April 1765. FFMM.

Barlow, Benjamin R. & Priscilla D. Smith, dau. of James Smith, who proves groom's age. 22 Jan. 1851. MarReg. m. 23 Jan. 1851. Whaley.

Barnehouse, John & Sarah Margaret Johnson, dau. of John Johnson, bm. 13 Dec. 1841. m. 13 Dec. 1841. Gover. Shel.

Barnehouse, Randolph & Elizabeth Ann Newton. Wit: John Newton. MarReg. m. 11 Jan. 1853. Gover.

Barnhouse, Caleb & Sarah Ann Thomas. George Thomas attests ages, bm. 3 June 1839. Shel.

Barnhouse, Joseph & Margaret Jane Barnhouse. William D. Drish attests bride's age, bm. 19 Nov. 1849. Shel.

Barr, Adam & Mary Beatty. David Beatty, bm. 27 July 1829.

Barr, Adam & Priscilla Holmes. m. 11 Oct. 1808. Williamson.

Barr, George & Mary Coe. William M. Herrick attests bride's age, bm. 29 Oct. 1833. Shel.

Barr, Lott & Nancy Chinn. m. 9 Nov. 1826. Williamson.

Barrett, John H. (W.) & Mary C. Reeder. Wit: Her father; his mother consents. 8 March 1853. MarReg. m. 10 March 1853. Smith.

Barrett, Robert & Martha Moffett. m. 25 July 1822. Gilmore.

Barrett, Thomas D. & Hannah McDaniels. Coleman R. Brown attests ages, bm. 12 Dec. 1829.

Barry, William & Catherine Mason. m. March 1812. Dunn.

Barsheers, Colman & Ann Tignor. m. 5 Aug. 1803. Littlejohn.

Barsheers, James & Mary Thomas. m. 11 Jan. 1803. Littlejohn.

Bartholomew, Moses & Elizabeth Sagar, dau. of George Sagar, bm. 22 Oct. 1796. m. 22 Oct. 1796. Littlejohn.

Bartlet (Barttel?), Jacob & Elizabeth Everhart; both single. By license. m. 30 Sep. 1830. ParReg A. Shel.

Bartlett, John & Sarah Compher, dau. of John Compher, bm. 19 March 1836. m. 22 March 1836. ParReg A. Shel.

Bartlett, Johnson & Ann H. Tracey. Evritt (Evert) Tracey, bm. 29 Sep. 1849. Shel.

Barton, Bailey & Sarah **Wornall,** dau. of James Wornall, who attests groom's age, bm. 14 March 1831. Shel.

Barton, Benjamin & Harriet G. Fletcher, dau. of Joshua Fletcher. Samuel Richards, bm. 11 Jan. 1836. Shel.

Barton, Benjamin C. & Mary E. Monroe, dau. of William Monroe, bm.
   20 Sep. 1845. Shel.
Barton, Joseph & Rachel Richards. m. 22 March 1796. Littlejohn.
Barton, Levi & Sarah Chinn. m. 20 Nov. 1817. Williamson.
Barton, Thomas & Sarah McMorris. m. 13 May 1808. Davis.
Bascue, James S. & Sarah C. Hummer. Thomas Hummer attests ages,
   bm. 28 Aug. 1843. Shel.
Bascue, John L. (S.) & Matilda Hummer, dau. of Thomas Hummer, who
   attests groom's age, bm. 21 Dec. 1840. m. 22 Dec. 1840. Larkin.
Basford, Mahlon & Elizabeth Near, dau. of John Near, bm. 9 Dec.
   1833. m. 12 Dec. 1833. Hauer. Shel.
Bassett, Rensselaer & Eliza A. Cranwell, dau. of Susan Cranwell.
   John W. Shipley, bm. 11 March 1845. Shel.
Bates, Humphrey & Hannah Powell. m. 12 March 1804. Littlejohn.
Bates, Leander & Maria Louisa Waters, dau. of Levi Waters, who
   proves groom's age. 26 May 1852. MarReg. m. 27 May 1852.
   Coombs.
Bates, Thomas & Zilphia Queen. m. 14 May 1804. Littlejohn.
Bates, William H. & Hannah Lee, dau. of Joshua Lee, bm. 22 Nov.
   1847. Cam.
Battaile, Laurence & Ann M. Fitzhugh. m. 15 Sep. 1819. Dunn. Shel.
Battefeld, Adam, son of Adam Battefeld & Eva Margareth Schaka, dau.
   of Georg Schaka; both single. m. 11 April 1790. ParReg A.
Bauer(?), Jacob, widower & Margreth Altemus. By license. m.
   31 Dec. 1812. ParReg A.
Bauer, Johannes & Elisabeth Stier; both single. By license. m.
   19 Dec. 1811. ParReg A.
Baugh, Jacob & Mary Kephart. m. 28 Jan. 1795. Littlejohn.
Baughman, Aquila & Emily Campbell, dau. of John Campbell, who
   attests groom's age, bm. 31 Jan. 1843. Shel.
Baughman, James A. & Mary Elizabeth Spring. Casper Spring, bm.
   23 Nov. 1849. Shel.
Baughman, Mr. & Miss Spring. m. 20 Nov. 1849. ParReg A. Shel.
Baylis, Isaac T. & Sarah A. Piles. Alexander D. Lee, bm. 10 Jan.
   1845. m. 14 Jan. 1845. Massey. Cam.
Bayly, Thomas P. & Mary Elizabeth Bayly. Robert Bayly attests ages,
   bm. 7 Oct. 1844. Cam.
Bayne, Lawrence P. & Delia Elizabeth Rust, dau. of Bushrod Rust.
   A. M. Gibson, bm. 6 July 1837. m. 10 July 1837. Broaddus. Shel.
Bazill, James & Mary Frances Hales, dau. of Warner Hales. Joseph E.
   Bazill attests groom's age, bm. 21 March 1848. m. 23 March
   1848. Gover. Shel.
Beach, John W. B. & Susan A. E. Higdon. James D. McPherson attests
   groom's age, bm. 17 Nov. 1845. Shel.
Beal, Samuel & Rebecca Cummins. m. 23 March 1803. Littlejohn.
Beal, Thomas & Margaret Jacobs. Jacob Jacobs, bm. 11 May 1813.
Beale, Benjamin C. & Laney Ann Richards. m. 21 July 1853. Rodgers.
Beale, Thomas & Ann Cunnard, in meeting house at Hillsboro. m.
   27 May 1802. FFMM.
Beales, Benjamin C. & Laney Ann Richards. Wit: Jonah Orrison,
   bride's guardian who proves groom's age. 20 July 1853. MarReg.
Beales, David L, son of Elisabeth Beales & Catharina A. Wynkoop.
   Samuel C. Wynkoop attests bride's age, bm. 31 March 1843. Shel.

Beall, David L. & Luclemma E. Gibson, dau. of Rebecca Gibson.
Levi G. Ewers attests groom's age, bm. 25 May 1838. m. 29 Aug.
1838. T. Herndon. Shel.
Beall, Robert E. & Susan Wright. Alfred Wright affirms ages, bm.
6 March 1832. Shel.
Beall, Smith & Mrs. Eliza Lowry, with Maryland license. m. 30 July
1835. ParReg A.
Beamer, George & Catherine Hickman. m. 8 Oct. 1810. Littlejohn.
Beamer, George & Elizabeth Dixon. Samuel Cordell, bm. 26 April
1833. m. 2 May 1832(?). Hauer. Shel.
Beamer, James William & Mary Elizabeth Goodhart, ward of J. W.
Goodhart, who proves groom's age. 21 April 1852. MarReg. m.
22 April 1852. Startzman.
Beamer, Michael & Julian Morrison. Edward Morrison attests ages,
bm. 15 Jan. 1844. m. 23 Jan. 1844. ParReg A.
Beamusdaffer, John & Nancy Alexander, dau. of James Alexander, who
attests groom's age. Mahlon Baldwin, bm. 17 June 1844. Shel.
Beans, Absalom & Maria Gooden. David Reece, bm. 15 Dec. 1834. Shel.
Beans, Absalom & Ruth Dillon. m. 23 Feb. ___. Janney, Clerk.
Beans, Amos & Elizabeth Ann Lacock, dau. of Joseph Lacock, bm.
Older brother proves groom's age. 25 March 1850.
Beans, Isaiah & Sophronia Morris, ward of John Hesser, bm. 15 Sep.
1836.
Beans, Isaiah B. & Elizabeth Moss. Carter Moss attests bride's age,
bm. 9 March 1829.
Beans, Isaiah B. & Hannah Humphrey. m. 25 May 1820. Dagg.
Beans, John & Rosh. McKimmey. m. 12 Aug. 1805. Littlejohn.
Beans, Joseph & Rachel Brumley. m. 28 Dec. 1805. Littlejohn.
Beans, Levi & Letitia Taylor. m. 17 March 1807. Littlejohn.
Beans, Mahlon & Sarah Hiatt. m. 1821-1822. Mines.
Beans, Moses & Letty Vermillion. m. 1820-1821. Mines.
Beans, Samuel & Harriet Newhouse. Enos Purcel attests bride's age,
bm. 22 Sep. 1842. Shel.
Beans, Samuel & Pleasant Adams. m. 8 April 1823. C. Frye.
Beans, Seth & Elizabeth Edwards. m. 27 March 1802. Littlejohn.
Beans, Timothy & Mary Randall. m. 19 Nov. 1793. Littlejohn.
Beans, William & Winefred Lee. m. 22 March 1810. Dunn.
Beard, Benjamin B. & Eleanor Frere, dau. of Barrow Frere. James
Keene attests groom's age. 23 June 1841. Cam.
Beard, David & Mary Ann Beach. James P. Wright attests groom's age.
John Beach, bm. 6 March 1833. Shel.
Beard, Edward & Dolly Ann Leachman. William Leachman, bm. 10 Feb.
1829.
Beard, Joseph & Mary Lewis. 8 Jan. 1798. Littlejohn.
Beard, Stephen & Orphy Lacey, dau. of Joseph Lacey. Meshec Lacey,
bm. 4 Nov. 1799. Littlejohn.
Beatty, David & Dicey Polen. Adam Barr attests bride's age, bm.
2 Nov. 1829.
Beatty, John & Frances C. Chinn. m. 4 Jan. 1852. Eggleston.
Beatty, Thomas B. & Catherine M. Marye. m. 4 Nov. 1819. Dunn. Shel.
Beatty, Washington & Elizabeth Beatty. m. 10 Oct. 1822. Dagg.
Beatty, William & Catherine Eliza Smith, dau. of Jacob Smith, bm.
17 May 1836. Shel.
Beatty, William & Rebecca Todd. m. 1 June 1820. Williamson.

Beaty, James & Sarah Brown. m. 22 Nov. 1813. Henkle.
Beaty, John & Frances C. Chinn. R. S. Chinn proves ages. 2 Jan.
    1852. MarReg.
Beaumont, Edward & Lucy Ellen Shipman. Ellen Shipman, bm. 21 March
    1850. Cam.
Beaumont, James & Caroline Elizabeth Johnson, dau. of Amos W.
    Johnson, bm. 12 Jan. 1837. m. 15 Jan. 1837. T. Herndon. Shel.
Beavers, Abraham & Pleasant Barton. m. 7 Dec. 1820. T. Littleton.
Beavers, John A. & Christiana Anderson. Washington Beavers
    attests ages, bm. 23 Sep. 1837. Shel.
Beavers, Joseph & Anna Barnett Swarts, dau. of Barnet Swarts.
    Willis Legg, bm. 20 April 1799. Cam.
Beavers, Richard F. & Sarah Francis Richards, dau. of Barton
    Richards, who proves groom's age. 27 Dec. 1850. MarReg.
    m. 31 Dec. 1850. Leachman.
Beavers, Samuel & Hannah Fulton. Price Jacobs attests bride's age,
    bm. 12 Jan. 1832. m. 16 Feb. 1832. Green. Shel.
Beavers, Samuel & Martha M. Moulden. Joseph Beavers attests ages,
    bm. 21 Dec. 1844. Cam.
Beavers, Samuel & Sarah Hough. Samuel B. F. Caldwell, bm.
    26 Dec. 1833. Shel.
Beavers, Thomas & Delelia Jenkins. John Beavers attests ages, bm.
    2 March 1830.
Beavers, Thomas & Sarah Spencer m. 12 Feb. 1798. Littlejohn.
Beavers, Washington, son of Samuel Beavers & Delila Anderson.
    Alfred Anderson attests bride's age. John Asbury Beavers
    attests groom's age, bm. 25 Nov. 1835. m. 1 Dec. 1835.
    Morgan. Shel.
Beck, Isaiah E. & Phebe Massey. Samuel Massey gives permission.
    Levi Massey attests groom's age, bm. 17 March 1830.
Beck, Vivian & Emily Huffman, dau. of John Huffman, bm. 3 Dec.
    1834. Shel.
Beckwith, Lewis & Matilda Carter. m. 22 Dec. 1808. Dunn.
Bedenger, Henry & Margaret E. Rust. George Rust, Jr., bm.
    1 Jan. 1839. Shel.
Beech, Lial T. & Charlotte E. M. Ball, dau. of Mary Ball.
    Joseph Hough, bm. 12 Oct. 1835. Shel.
Beech, Presley & Frances Lane, dau. of Mary Thiare. Abel Orrison
    attests groom's age, bm. 23 April 1838. Shel.
Beemer, George & Elizabeth Dixon. m. 2 May 1833. ParReg A.
Bekny(?), Georg , widower & Maria Bantzin, widow. By license.
    m. 13 Feb. 1823. ParReg A.
Bell, John William & Mary Catharine Jones. Seth Robertson attests
    ages, bm. 3 March 1840. m. 12 March 1840. Hauer. Shel.
Bell, William & Nancy Cunning. 14 Dec. 1812. Littlejohn.
Belmain, Andrew & Amey Ellen Denham. Charles T. Denham attests
    bride's age, bm. 6 Feb. 1839. Shel.
Belt, George William & Cassandra Virginia Russell. Wit: Samuel A.
    Tillett, Jr. proves ages. 10 July 1851. MarReg. m. 15 July
    1851. T. Herndon.
Bemusdaffer, Joseph V. & Mary E. Hardy, dau. of John Hardy.
    John G. Lester attests groom's age, bm. 2 Jan. 1841. Shel.
Benedict, William B. & Henrietta Henderson. Samuel K. Jackson,
    bm. 18 July 1849. m.18 July 1849, at house of her sister
    Rebeca A. Gray. Adie. Shel.

Benedum, Charles E. & Martena K. Boss, dau. of Samuel M. Boss,
    bm. 19 Feb. 1849. Shel.
Benedum, Henry & Elizabeth Yantus. m. 22 June 1815. Littlejohn.
Benedum, James H. & Sarah A. Hammatt. Edward Hammett, bm. 2 Sep.
    1841. Shel.
Benham, Jacob & Barthana Floyd. m. 30 Sep. 1812. Littlejohn.
Benjamin, James & Ann Wilson Hardy. John P. Dickey attests ages,
    bm. 20 Jan. 1840. Shel.
Benjamin, William & Jane Costolow. m. 10 June 1811. Littlejohn.
Bennett, Hudson & Lucy Moseley. Lucian Fitzhugh attests ages, bm.
    11 April 1839. Cam.
Bennett, John H. & Hannah Ann Frank. Thomas J. Marlowe, bm.
    11 April 1837. Shel.
Bennett, John H. & Mary Isabella White. James McIlhany, guardian,
    gives permission. John R. White, bm. 22 Sep. 1830. Shel.
Bennett, Josiah & Elizabeth Ann Lowe. Joseph Wood attests bride's
    age, bm. 19 Dec. 1836. Shel.
Bennett, Richard & Nancy Grubb, dau. of John Grubb. Reed Poulton
    attests groom's age, bm. 19 Oct. 1839. Shel.
Bennett, Sydnor & Mary M. Silcott. James Silcott attests bride's
    age, bm. 15 Nov. 1847. m. 16 Nov. 1847. Dulin. Shel.
Bennett, Sydnor & Sarah E. Russell. Henry Russell, bm. 25 Oct.
    1841. m. 26 Oct. 1841. Phelps. Shel.
Bently, Edgar L. & Helen Mary Wilson, dau. of Charlotte F. Wilson.
    George Rickard, bm. 8 Sep. 1841. Shel.
Bently, Richard Montgomery & Ann Catharine Drake. Wit: Bride's
    father. 30 April 1851. MarReg. m. 30 April 1851, at house of
    her father, Dr. Drake, in Leesburg. Adie.
Benton, Benjamin H. & Margaret J. (T.) Gulick, dau. of William
    Gulick. William Benton attests groom's age, bm. William
    Gulick, bm. 12 Aug. 1839. m. 10 Sep. 1839. T. Herndon. Shel.
Benton, Richard H. & Martha Ann Skillman. Certif. from bride's
    mother filed; groom's age "taken for granted". 21 Jan. 1852.
    MarReg. m. 5 Feb. 1852. Eggleston.
Berch, Feilder & Sarah Smith. m. 14 Dec. 1816. Littlejohn.
Berchett, William & Catherine Davis. m. 13 Nov. 1811. Littlejohn.
Berkeley, Jaquetin A. & Mary B. Fontaine. William Noland attests
    ages, bm. 8 June 1829.
Berkeley, Lewis & Frances Noland. m. 27 Sep. 1821. Dunn. Cam.
Berkley, George & Susanna Bartlett. Bailey Donaldson attests
    bride's age. John Linton, bm. 31 Dec. 1799. Cam.
Bernardaffer, Joseph & Elizabeth Robartson. m. 26 Sep. 1816.
    T. Littleton.
Berrick (Barrick; Barrett), Thomas B. & Hannah McDaniels.
    Coleman R. Brown attests ages, bm. 12 Dec. 1829.
Berry, Fielding & Elizabeth McPherson. m. 19 Feb. 1818. Williamson.
Best, Albert & Elizabeth Goodheart, dau. of Jacob Goodheart, bm.
    22 Oct. 1831. Shel.
Best, Enos & Hannah Potts. m. 4 Nov. 1806. Littlejohn.
Best, James & Rosanah M. Janney. Mahlon Janney attests groom's
    age, bm. 4 Feb. 1832. m. 4 Feb. 1832. Dorsey. Shel.
Best, Jonas M. & Nancy Young. David Young attests ages, bm.
    27 Dec. 1841. Shel.
Beveridge, Andrew & Rebecca H. L. Race. John W. Race, bm. 14 June
    1830. Cam.

Beveridge, Samuel R. & Harriet C. Moffett. Carter Moss attests
 ages, bm. 13 Feb. 1832. Cam.
Beveridge, William R. & Margaret Whitmore, dau. of Michael
 Whitmore, bm. m. 23 Dec. 1830. Littlejohn. Shel.
Beverley, William & Frances H. Gray, dau. of William H. Gray,
 Esq., wit. Groom's age "taken for granted". 15 Nov. 1852.
 MarReg. m. 16 Nov. 1852, Locust Hill, Gray's residence. Adie.
Biegel, Friederick, son of David Bugel (Biegel) & Maria
 Kittelmeyer, dau. of Martin Kittelmeyer; both single. By
 license. m. 1 Nov. 1795. ParReg A.
Biggs, William & Ann Rhodes. m. 1807-1808. Mines.
Binley, James & Margeret Bradley. m. 27 Aug. 1804. Littlejohn.
Binns, John Alexander & Mary Maria Rose. m. 3 Nov. 1818. Griffith.
Birch, Francis & Harriet P. Newton. Wit: Bride's father. 13 Dec.
 1852. MarReg. m. 21 Dec. 1852. Gover.
Birch, Jonathan T. & Lucinda J. Franklin. George W. Hummer
 attests ages, bm. 30 June 1844. Cam.
Birdsall, Benjamin & Deborah B. Hough. Wit: William T. Hough
 proves ages. 11 Oct. 1851. MarReg. m. 22 Oct. 1851. FFMM.
Birkett, Henry & Elizabeth Young. m. 25 March 1795. Littlejohn.
Birkly, Thomas W. & Susan Ratie. Wit: Benjamin D. Rathie. 1 Nov.
 1852. MarReg. Duncan.
Bishop, Aquilla & Jemima Violett. m. 4 March 1824. Dagg.
Bishop, Hamilton & Juliann Neuswanger, dau. of John Neuswanger.
 m. 2 Dec. 1834. ParReg A.
Bishop, Henderson & Elizabeth Campbell. Henry Clapper attests
 ages, bm. 25 June 1846. Shel.
Bishop, Henderson & Juliann Nisewanger, dau. of John Nisewanger,
 bm. 1 Dec. 1834. Shel.
Bisit, Daniel & Nancy Conner. m. 20 Dec. 1804. Littlejohn.
Bitzer, Harmon & Catherine Franklin. Benjamin T. Franklin attests
 ages, bm. 21 Jan. 1847. Cam.
Bitzer, James Harvey & Mary Jane Gochnauer. "James Harvey Bitzer
 was appointed guardian of Mr. Bitzer's children at Sept.
 Court 1839." David Gochnauer attests bride's age, bm.
 8 Aug. 1840.
Bitzer, John & Amanda C. Lovett. Wit: Mortimer C. Lovett proves
 bride's age. 9 Nov. 1852. MarReg. m. 10 Nov. 1852. Hirst.
Bitzer, William & Sarah Reed. m. 4 July 1824. Baker.
Bitzger, James H. & Mary J. Gochanauer. m. 11 Aug. 1840. R.
 Herndon.
Blair, Montgomery & Caroline R. Buckner, dau. of Ariss Buckner.
 Spencer A. Buckner, bm. 12 July 1836. Cam.
Blakeley, John & Jane Torbert. m. 6 March 1821. Dagg.
Blakely, William & Emily A. Nichols. Nathaniel Nichols, bm.
 24 Nov. 1842.
Blakely, William & Letitia Russell. m. 30 Jan. 1797. Littlejohn.
Bletscher, Johannes, son of Henrich Bletscher and wife & Elisabeth
 Steinbrenner, dau. of Peter Steinbrenner and wife; both
 single. By license. m. 16 Feb. 1815. ParReg A.
Blieker, Marck & Maria Schuhmacher, both single. By license.
 m. 13 Sep. 1827. ParReg A.
Blincoe, Henry Corbin & Mary Ann Solomon, dau. of William
 Solomon, bm. 15 Jan. 1836. Cam.

Blincoe, Joseph & Lucinda Jones. George W. Hunter attests bride's age, bm. 16 April 1832. Cam.

Blincoe, Joseph & Mary Thomas. Augustus Stonestreet attests groom's age. Thomas L. Hoskinson attests bride's age, bm. 11 Jan. 1845. Cam.

Blincoe, Sampson & Mary S. Jones. m. 21 March 1808. Littlejohn.

Blockley, Jesse & Manda E. Beaninger, dau. of Henry W. Beaninger. John H. Beaninger, bm. 4 May 1844. m. 19 May 1844. Massey.

Bloxham, Ephraim & Clarissa Fred. Joseph Fred consents. Joseph H. Fred attests groom's age, bm. 26 Jan. 1835. m. 29 Jan. 1835. Baker. Shel.

Bloxham, James A. & Malinda Jury. Joseph Fredd attests bride's age, bm. 9 Dec. 1831. m. 15 Dec. 1831. Baker. Shel.

Board, John William & Margaret Ann Ramsey, dau. of John R. Ramsey. Samuel C. Ramsey attests ages, bm. 6 March 1848. Shel.

Board, Norris & Emily Orum. Henry Orum attests groom's age, bm. 11 March 1829.

Boarn, William H. & Mary Jane Tucker. Elijah P. Myers attests ages, bm. 15 May 1849. Shel.

Bocker, Adam & Sarah Kiefer; both single. By license. 24 Nov. 1825. ParReg A.

Bocker, Georg, son of Samuel Bocker and wife & Anna Wertzin, dau. of Peter Wertz and wife; both single. By license. 23 Jan. 1816. ParReg A.

Bocker, Johannes, son of Samuel Bocker's wife, Clare & Catharina Kuntz, dau. of Adam Kuntz and wife. By license. 9 April 1812. ParReg A.

Bodine, John W. & Margaret Ann Power, dau. of Robert Power, wit. 7 Feb. 1852. MarReg.

Boger, Johannes, son of late Friedrich Boger and wife & Margretha Heckmanin, dau. of Peter Heckman and wife; both single. By license. m. 12 May 1822. ParReg A.

Boger, Michael, son of Michal Boger, Sr. & Catharina Wentzel, dau. of Georg Wentzel; both single. By license. 23 Oct. 1817. ParReg A.

Boger, Michael & Elisabetha Brennerin, dau. of Philip Brenner. m. 13 April 1785. ParReg A.

Boger, Samuel & Mary Shafer. John Shafer attests ages, bm. 26 Nov. 1839. m. 29 Nov. 1839. Hauer. Shel.

Boges, David & Catherine Wine. m. 13 Aug. 1806. Littlejohn.

Boggess, Samuel & Eliza Jane Rust, dau. of Bushrod Rust. R. W. Latham attests ages, bm. 30 March 1840. Shel.

Boggess, William & Abigail Lewellin. m. 3 Aug. 1807. Dunn.

Boggus, Samuel & Elizabeth Rust. m. 2 April 1840. Broaddus.

Bogguss, William & Jane McVicker. m. 25 July 1796. Littlejohn.

Bogsel, Herwey & Maria Wentzel, dau. of Johannes Wentzel and wife. By license. m. 13 Jan. 1820. ParReg A.

Bogue, John & Francis Stewart. m. 8 Nov. 1800. Littlejohn.

Bolden, John & Mary Garrett. m. 17 Aug. 1814. Littlejohn.

Bolen, Edward & Gracie Fox. m. 12 June 1825. Dunn. Shel.

Boley, Beverly & Sarah Ann (Jane) Figgins (Feggins). "Boley is well known to be more than that (21 years) age." Huziah Figgins (Feagans) attests bride's age, bm. 7 March 1849. m. 8 March 1849. T. Herndon. Shel.

Boley, John & Nancy Rhodes. m. 27 Feb. 1821. Dagg.
Bolon, Alfred & Sarah Roach. Henry S. Taylor affirms bride's age.
    Ferdinando Bolon, bm. 5 June 1832. Shel.
Bolon, Ferdinando & Harriett Bradfield, dau. of Amy W. Bradfield.
    Charles Taylor, William Vanhorn, bm. 28 Jan. 1833. Shel.
Bolon, William & Mary Ann Whitacre, ward of Thomas Gregg, bm.
    Amos Whitacre, bm. 13 April 1830. Shel.
Bolton, Amos & Fanny Thornton Mott. m.13 Oct. 1810. Davis.
Bomcrots (Bomerots), John & Christiana Emery. Adam Emery attests
    bride's age, bm. 28 Nov. 1809. m. 1808-1809. Mines.
Bonce, David & Carolina McArter. m. 28 Aug. 1828. Tippett.
Bond, Asa & Sarah Alice Taylor. m. 24 March 1831. Taylor, Clerk.
Bond, Clauson & Susannah C. Rowles. Amos Janney attests ages, bm.
    3 Feb. 1835. m. 3 Feb. 1835. ParReg A.
Bond, Edward & Eliza Schooley, with Maryland license. m. 5 Nov.
    1833. ParReg A.
Bond, Joseph, son of Samuel and Thomzin Bond, both deceased,
    Frederick Co., Va. & Elizabeth Moore, Jr., dau. of Thomas
    and Elizabeth Moore. m. 31 Dec. 1794. FFMM.
Bond, Joseph, Waterford & Rachel B. Littler. 4 June 1817. FFMM.
Bontz, Jacob & Ann Prince, dau. of Mathias Prince, bm. 30 Dec.
    1833. m. 2 Jan. 1834. ParReg A.
Bontz, John & Mary Merchant, dau. of James Merchant, bm. 11 Oct.
    1840. m. 18 Oct. 1840. Larkin. Shel.
Booth, James, Jr. & Sarah Arnold. m. 19 Nov. 1833. ParReg A.
Booth, John & Catharine Venander. m. 1809-1810. Mines.
Boothe, James, Jr. & Sarah Arnold, ward of Philip Boger, who
    attests groom's age, bm. 8 Nov. 1833. Shel.
Boothe, John & Emily Jane Owens. Edward Owens attests groom's age,
    bm. 17 Dec. 1846. m. 17 Dec. 1846. Shuford. Shel.
Boren, David & Elizabeth Sixlin (Sexton). Edward Hooper attests
    ages, bm. 28 Dec. 1836. m. 30 Dec. 1836. Hauer. Shel.
Bornhaus, Christoph & Rosina Rollerin. m. 11 Aug. 1784. ParReg A.
Bornhaus, Johannes & Margretha Mollin; both single. By license.
    m. 9 Aug. 1814. ParReg A.
Boss, David & Eliza Hoskins. m. 17 June 1819. Littlejohn.
Boss, Samuel M. & Elizabeth Fox. m. 29 July 1819. Littlejohn.
Boteler, Washington & M. E. Cordell. Presley Cordell, bm. 2 Dec.
    1830. Shel.
Bottenfield, Samuel & Mary Bottenfield. m. 1806. Mines.
Bottenfield, Truman W. & Margaret Jane Verts, dau. of Conrad
    Virts, who proves groom's age, wit. 3 Dec. 1851. MarReg.
Botton, Joseph & Ann Spates. m. 11 Aug. 1798. Littlejohn.
Botts, Charles & Peggy Connalley. m. 12 March 1810. Littlejohn.
Bounn, William H. & Mary Jane Tucker. m. 17 May 1849. Gover.
Bowen, Alexander & Sarah French. m. 24 Feb. 1803. Dunn.
Bowensmith, Jacob & Matilda Jenkins. m. 20 July 1815. Dunn.
Bowers, Adam & Malinda Triplett. 26 June 1816. Frye.
Bowersett, John & Elizabeth Rickards. m. 16 Dec. 1806. Littlejohn.
Bowie, Robert G. & Julia A. H. Wilson. Charles G. Eskridge, bm.
    23 June 1846. m. 24 June 1846, St. James Church. Adie.
Bowie, Watson & Lucinda Iden. m. 4 Dec. 1821. Dagg.

Bowles, Isaac G. & Ann Young, dau. of William Young, bm. 6 Sep. 1833. Shel.

Bowles, James & Elizabeth Gibson. m. 13 Feb. 1803. Dunn.

Bowles, James & Nancy Updike. Thomas Rogers attests ages, bm. 8 March 1841. Shel.

Bowles, Samuel & Amelia Wildman. John Wornal attests ages, bm. 16 June 1831. Shel.

Bowman, Charles & Catharine Kyle. 21 June 1818. Williamson.

Bowman, Robert C. & Hannah Glascock, dau. of Uriel Glascock. William H. Francis, bm. 22 Sep. 1841. Shel.

Boxwell, Joseph & Elenor Chamblin. "My brother Joseph Boxwell was bound to Mr. Noland of Winchester to serve to the Age of Twenty-one years he has served out that time and taken up his Indenture, and I heard them read. Nancy Boxwell." John Chamblin, guardian, bm. 8 March 1830. Shel.

Boyd, Daniel (David) & Catharine Minor (Mercer). Charles G. Eskridge attests age. Nathan Wisener, bm. 12 Dec. 1842. Mercer. Shel.

Boyd, Robert & Elizabeth A. Palmer. William Palmer attests ages, bm. 2 March 1846. m. 3 March 1846. Massey. Shel.

Boyd, William & Mary Frame. m. 13 Oct. 1800. Littlejohn.

Bozzael, George H. & Emily Elgin. James A. Foster attests ages, bm. 18 Dec. 1843. Shel.

Brabham, Francis M. & Mary E. Etcher. Richard Alexander proves bride's age, wit. 24 May 1851. MarReg.

Brabham, Thomas & Elizabeth Dewar . m. 14 Oct. 1824. T. Littleton.

Brabham, Thomas Jefferson & Martha Stephenson, dau. of James Stephenson. James Whitacre attests groom's age, bm. 20 Aug. 1840. Cam.

Brabham, Wesley & Elizabeth Orr. Harrison Knight attests ages, bm. 11 Dec. 1829.

Brabham, William & Sush. Wicuff. m. 25 Nov. 1807. Littlejohn.

Brackenridge, Samuel T. & Nancy A. Wildman. Joseph Wildman proves bride's age, wit.; "the male taken for granted". 12 Oct. 1852. MarReg.

Brackett, Russell & Frances Ann Jenkins. Washington Jenkins attests ages, bm. 17 Sep. 1833. Shel.

Braden, John & Mary D. Stevens. m. 7 Jan. 1806. Littlejohn.

Braden, Noble S. & Mary Ann Pusey, dau. of Joshua Pusey, bm. 29 Jan. 1834. m. 30 Jan. 1834. Dorsey. Shel.

Braden, Robert & Elizabeth Stephens. m. 28 Jan. 1795. Littlejohn.

Braden, Rodney C. & Eliza A. Vandeventer. Gabriel Vandeventer, guardian, bm. 3 Feb. 1835. Shel.

Bradfield, Benjamin & Drucilla King. m. 30 Jan. 1817. T. Littleton.

Bradfield, Francis M. & Elizabeth Keen. m. 9 Jan. 1851. Chenoweth.

Bradfield, George W. & Matilda E. Klein. James J. Love attests ages, bm. 12 Jan. 1846. Shel.

Bradfield, John & Ann Nicholds. m. 29 Sep. 1816. T. Littleton.

Bradfield, John E. & Mary M. (A.) Hesser, both of Snickersville. Wit: Creighton Hesser. 3 June 1853. MarReg. m. 7 June 1853. McGee.

Bradfield, Jonathan & Nancy McNight. Uriah Wright, bm. m. 12 Nov. 1804. Littlejohn. Shel.

16

Bradfield, William & Elizabeth Allder. m. 4 April 1816.
T. Littleton.
Bradley, John & Mary Vanhorn. m. 15 Jan. 1821. Dagg.
Bradshaw, Walter R. & Rebecca W. Ayres. Wit: John J. Hogeland.
18 July 1853. MarReg. m. 21 July 1853. Duncan.
Brady, Edward & Margaret O. Lowe. George W. Dorrell attests
bride's age, bm. 24 April 1845. Cam.
Brady, John & Reba. Moore. m. 26 July 1805. Littlejohn.
Brady, Malcolm & Sarah Ann Pierce. Wallace Brady, bm. 31 March
1837. Shel.
Brady, Peyton & Frances Stewart. Presley Saunders, bm. 12 May
1845. Shel.
Brady, Wallace & Mahala Harper, dau. of Enoch Harper, free
people of colour, bm. "Wallace Brady is free _ and about
24 years of age." 27 Sep. 1830. Shel.
Brandon, James P. & Catharine H. Williams, dau. of Hiram Opie
Williams, bm. 12 Sep. 1844. Shel.
Brawner, James W. & Sarah Rosseau. Samuel C. Rose attests ages,
bm. 5 Aug. 1834. m. 7 Aug. 1834. Furlong. Cam.
Breckenridge, Samuel S. & Nancy A. Wildman, in Leesburg. m.
21 Oct. 1852. Adie.
Breitenbagh, Samuel & Maria L. Kline, dau. of John Nicholas
Kline, bm. 16 June 1834. m. 16 June 1834, at home of William
Kline, Leesburg. Adie.
Brent, Willis & Emsey Hansford. m. 3 April 1804. Williamson.
Breward, James L. & Margaret Shoemaker (Shumaker). Col. Leslie
proves ages, wit. 9 Dec. 1850. MarReg. m. 24 Dec. 1850.
ParReg A.
Brewer, John & Nancy Milholland. 1796. Littlejohn.
Bridges, Benjamin, Jr. & Lucy A. Elgin. Bride's father consents
and proves groom's age, wit. 12 Dec. 1853. MarReg. m. 13 Dec.
1853, at Francis Elgin's. Smith.
Bridges, David & Nancy Hummer. m. 8 Feb. 1813. Littlejohn.
Bridges, Dennis & Violinda Athey. m. 1804. McPherson.
Bridges, Hardage & Margaret Ann Lee, dau. of Alexander D. Lee,
bm. 19 Feb. 1846.
Briel, John & Mrs. Sally Filler (Fuller), widow of Henry Filler,
this county. George Vinsell attests ages, bm. 22 July 1833.
m. 23 July 1833. ParReg A.
Briggs, Newman & Sarah Jane Jones. Henderson Bishop attests
bride's age, bm. 22 Sep. 1845. Shel.
Briscoe, William H. & Eliza H. Harris. m. 3 Oct. 1816. Littlejohn.
Broadwater, Charles H. & Emily Ann Smith. m. 18 Oct. 1835. White.
Broadwater, Guy & Mary Piles. m. 30 Dec. 1809. Littlejohn.
Brocchas, Benjamin M. & Isabella G. Armistead. John Graham attests
bride's age, bm. 24 March 1834. m. 26 March 1834, at her
mother's near Aldie. Adie.
Brodie, Alexander M. & Janette A. Lamarque, ward of David E.
Graham, who proves groom's age, wit. 27 July 1853. MarReg.
"Mrs. Brodie resides in Aldie, Loudoun Co." m. 5 Aug. 1853.
Hirst.
Brohard, John & Mary Randall. m. 17 Dec. 1796. Littlejohn.
Bronaugh, P.H.W., Dr. & Eleanor A. Wildman, dau. of Jane D.
Wildman. Francis W. Luckett, bm. 10 Oct. 1836. m. 11 Oct.
1836. Adie. Shel.

17

Brookbank (Brookebank), Charles & Hannah Hughs (Hughes). John Wynn attests ages, bm. 8 Aug. 1809. m. 2 Aug. 1809. Littlejohn.

Brooke, James, Frederick Co., Md. & Hannah Janney. m. 13 Oct. 1759. FFMM.

Brookes, Aron & Alice Stephens. m. 11 Feb. 1793. Littlejohn.

Brookes, Elijah & Mary Fouch. m. 27 March 1793. Littlejohn.

Brooks, Alexander & Susan A. Love. James D. McPherson attests ages, bm. 13 Jan. 1848. m. 14 Jan. 1848. Gover. Shel.

Brooks, Charles & Phobe W. Caldwell. Samuel B.T. Caldwell attests ages, bm. 22 Oct. 1844. Shel.

Brooks, Ebenezer & Edith Young, dau. of David Young. John Young, bm. 2 March 1835. m. 3 March 1835. Baker. Shel.

Brooks, John A. & Elizabeth McMullen, dau. of Mary McMullen, widow of Cobert McMullen. John Smith attests groom's age, bm. 10 Nov. 1840. m. 26 Nov. 1840. ParReg A. Shel.

Brooks, Joseph M. & Virginia L. Prall. S. Ans' Buckner proves groom's age; bride's guardian consents. 3 Aug. 1852. MarReg. m. 4 Aug. 1852. Fowles.

Brooks, Philip & Mary Lamb. Samuel Lamb attests ages, bm. 6 Dec. 1847. m. 9 Dec. 1847. Shuford. Shel.

Brooks, Thomas W. & Sarah H. Saunders. Thomas Saunders consents. Archibald Kittzmiller, bm. 7 Nov. 1832. Shel.

Brown, Abram & Cathrine Tiller. m. 31 Oct. 1805. Littlejohn.

Brown, Benjamin & Sarah Brown. m. 1809-1810. Mines.

Brown, Benjamin & Sarah E. White. John Brown proves groom's age; bride's father consents, wit. 21 Feb. 1853. MarReg. m. 24 Feb. 1853. Smith.

Brown, Burr & Mary Ellenor Nichols. Jonah Nichols attests groom's age, bm. 20 Feb. 1846. m. 20 Feb. 1846. Massey.

Brown, Bushrod & Cecilie H. Taylor. m. 21 Feb. 1850. Taylor,Clerk.

Brown, Coleman & Mary Sinclair. m. 19 Feb. 1818. Williamson.

Brown, Daniel & Sarah Ann Smith. William Wright attests bride's age, bm. 20 Sep. 1834. m. 21 Sep. 1834. Trott. Shel.

Brown, David & Kezziah Wiley. John Brown attests ages, bm. 1 Feb. 1834. Shel.

Brown, Edward & Sarah Ann Smith. Bride's father consents, wit. 10 Nov. 1851. MarReg. m. 25 Nov. 1851. Taylor, Clerk.

Brown, Edwin C. & Elizabeth Channel. m. 10 Aug. 1819. Littlejohn.

Brown, George & Rhoda Rhodes. m. 14 April 1800. Littlejohn.

Brown, George M., Dr. & Eliza Bruce Gibson, dau. of Mahlon Gibson. John C. Murray, bm. 8 June 1846. Shel.

Brown, Isaac & Christina Kyle. m. 8 Jan. 1818. Williamson.

Brown, Isaac, son of Richard and Elizabeth Brown & Mary Esther Pierpoint, dau. of Joseph and Rue Ann Pierpoint. m. 17 April 1850. FFMM.

Brown, Isaac, Jr. & Sarah Burson. m. 26 May 1784. FFMM.

Brown, Issachar & Margaret Griffith. Thomas C. Gregg attests bride's age, bm. 22 Nov. 1830. Shel.

Brown, James & Margaret Clark. m. 6 May 1813. Littlejohn.

Brown, James & Ruth Clewes. m. 12 March 1810. Littlejohn.

Brown, Joel, son of Issachar Brown & Mahala Barr. Thomas C. Gregg, bm. 28 Dec. 1830. Shel.

LOUDOUN COUNTY MARRIAGES

Brown, John & Catherine Sample. m. 10 Aug. 1812. J. Littleton.
Brown, John & Elizabeth Davis. Moses Dowdell attests ages, bm.
    12 June 1809.
Brown, John & Lydia Burson. 9 Dec. 1793. Littlejohn.
Brown, John & Margeret Davis. m. 8 June 1805. Littlejohn.
Brown, John & Margaret Whiting. William Brown attests bride's age,
    bm. 10 Jan. 1837. Shel.
Brown, John, son of Henry and Esther Brown & Martha Ball.
    m. 10 April 1776. FFMM.
Brown, John & Mary Rhodes, widow. m. 8 Feb. 1775. FFMM.
Brown, John & Sarah Bond. m. 22 Oct. 1806. Littlejohn.
Brown, John H., son of John and Ann Brown & Mary Esther Schooley.
    m. 19 March 1834. FFMM.
Brown, John V. & Aseneth Stocks. S.S. Stocks attests bride's age,
    bm. 12 Feb. 1850. Shel.
Brown, John V. & Harriet Umbaugh, dau. of John Umbaugh, bm. 8 Dec.
    1845. m. 9 Dec. 1845, house of her father. Adie.
Brown, Jonah T. & Alcey Jane Olley, dau. of Mary Olley. Benjamin
    Stevens attests groom's age, bm. 8 July 1845. Shel.
Brown, Joseph & Margaret Philips. m. 1809-1810. Mines.
Brown, Joseph John & Emily Boling. Joseph Hope attests ages, bm.
    20 Oct. 1830. Shel.
Brown, Josiah, son of William and Mary Brown of Fred. Co., Va.
    (mother deceased) & Mary M. Scott, dau. of Mahlon and Mary
    Hough, Alexandria. m. 17 Jan. 1827. FFMM.
Brown, Mason & Malinda Graham. m. 18 Sep. 1823. Dagg.
Brown, Nathan & Nancy Holms. m. 14 June 1805. Littlejohn.
Brown, Nathan & Sarah A. Phillips. Edmund Phillips attests bride's
    age, bm. 11 Jan. 1847. Shel.
Brown, Nixon G. & Hannah P. Wilson, dau. of William Wilson, wit.
    9 May 1853. MarReg. m. 12 May 1853. Brown, Clerk.
Brown, Richard, son of William Brown & Elizabeth Davis. William
    Brown attests bride's age, bm. 25 Sep. 1809. m. 25 Sep. 1809.
    Littlejohn.
Brown, Richard & Elizabeth Piggott. m. 24 Jan. 1828. Taylor, Clerk.
Brown, Richard, son of William and Elizabeth Brown & Sarah Cox,
    dau. of Joseph and Sarah Cox. m. 11 Jan. 1786. FFMM.
Brown, Samuel & Mary Jane Bradfield. John Brown, groom's father,
    and William Bradfield, bride's father, bm. 31 Oct. 1836.Shel.
Brown, Thomas, son of Isaac and Martha Brown & Ann Beck, dau. of
    Edward and Ann Beck, the former deceased. m. 26 Jan. 1780.
    FFMM.
Brown, Thomas & Louisa Whiting. George Brown attests ages, bm.
    14 Aug. 1837. Shel.
Brown, Thomas & Rachel Pottet. m. 29 June 1804. Williamson.
Brown, William & Sarah Tomlinson. m. Jan. 1807. Dunn.
Brown, William & Sarah Walters. Samuel Gregg attests bride's age,
    bm. 13 April 1809. m. 13 April 1809. Littlejohn.
Brownly (Brumley), William & Elizabeth Gray, dau. of John G. Gray.
    George Craig attests groom's age, bm. John G. Gray, bm.
    m. 1 Jan. 1834. Dorsey.
Bryerly, Samuel & E. T. Harrison. m. 13 May 1827. Kennerly.
Bryme, Ewell N. & Hannah P. Jeffries. B. P. Jeffries attests ages,
    bm. 15 Feb. 1843. Shel.

Buck, Mason, Warren Co., Va. & Amanda Fitzallen Adams, dau. of
    Henry Adams. Alexander Adams, bm. 17 Jan. 1850. m. 24 Jan.
    1850. Dulin. Shel.
Buck, Samuel & Mary P. Bayly. m. 1806. Mines.
Buckey, John & Elizabeth Tawner. m. 6 April 1797. Littlejohn.
Buckmaster, Corbin W. & Catherine Davis. m. 28 Nov. 1822.
    C. Frye.
Buckner (Bucknor), Norvall (Norban), alias Jones & Ellen Stewart,
    alias Jones, free persons of colour. Ramey G. Saunders, bm.
    19 Aug. 1839. m. 22 Aug. 1839, in Leesburg. Adie.
Buffington, George & Nancy Panten. Edward Panten (Panter),
    father of bride, bm. 4 March 1816.
Buffington, John & Ann Hessos (Hessor). m. 10 Sep. 1798.
    Littlejohn.
Buffington, Samuel & Mary (Nancy) Ann Wheatley. Joseph Wheatley
    attests ages, bm. 14 Jan. 1832. m. 19 Feb. 1832. Doup. Shel.
Bugent, Jacob & Sarah Snoots. m. 24 Dec. 1846. Shuford.
Bugly, Christian & Maria Eva Reutenbachin, Friederich Reutenbach's
    surviving widow. m. 15 Dec. 1784. ParReg A.
Bumcrots, John (William) & Catharine Cooper. Jacob Bamcrots
    attests groom's age,bm. 5 Jan. 1837. m. 10 Jan. 1837.ParReg A.
Bunk, James & Mary Brook. m. 18 July 1810. T. Littleton.
Bunnel, Samuel & Elizabeth Davis, dau. of Samuel Davis, wit.
    29 Aug. 1851. MarReg.
Bunnell, Daniel & Nancy Thomas, ward of William Harned, bm.
    13 Nov. 1809.
Bunnell, Jonathan & Ruth Millbourne. 24 Dec. 1807. Littlejohn.
Bunnell, William & Ann Milburn. Jonathan Bunnell (Bonnell)
    attests ages, bm. m. 31 Dec. 1811. Littlejohn.
Burch, William, son of Barbary Burch, widow of James Burch &
    Ann Lawson Butler. Landon Jones attests bride's age, bm.
    28 Oct. 1839. Shel.
Burchett, Josiah & Sarah Ann Burchett, dau. of William Burchett,
    bm. Eli Janney affirms groom's age. 7 April 1832. Shel.
Burgess, William & Martha A. Campbell. John Stephens attests ages,
    bm. 19 Feb. 1844. Shel.
Burgoyne, Joseph & Ann McGeath. m. 29 Feb. 1808. Littlejohn.
Burk, James & Sarah Vanhorn. Bernard Vanhorne attests bride's age,
    bm. 24 July 1834. Shel.
Burk, William & Reba. Dillon. m. 9 March 1807. Littlejohn.
Burke, Israel & Elizabeth Garner. James H. Chamblin attests
    groom's age. Mary Hains attests bride's age. John A. Binns,
    bm. 1 Oct. 1832. Shel.
Burke, Jonah & Lucinda Davis. Joseph Davis attests ages, bm.
    28 Jan. 1839. Shel.
Burke, Samuel & Sarah Siddler. m. 24 Sep. 1803. Littlejohn.
Burke, William & Mahala Wright. William G. Wright, bm. 23 Sep.
    1841. Shel.
Burnes, Thomas & Sarah Ann Waller, dau. of George Waller, bm.
    7 April 1841. Cam.
Burnhouse, George & Sush. Fox. m. 21 March 1805. Littlejohn.
Burns, Frederick & Barbara Hardy. m. 21 Jan. 1793. Littlejohn.
Burrell, Lewis & Syntha Peake. m. 7 Dec. 1805. Littlejohn.

Burson, Aaron & Kitty Burson, dau. of Joseph Burson. Moses Wilson, bm. 7 March 1799. Littlejohn.

Burson, Benjamin, son of Joseph Burson & Ann Roberts. m. 23 Oct. 1760. FFMM.

Burson, Benjamin & Elizabeth Kile. m. 27 Jan. 1820. Dagg.

Burson, Benjamin, son of George and Sarah Burson & Hannah Young, dau. of Hercules and Sarah Young. m. 8 Jan. 1772. FFMM.

Burson, Benjamin & Polly Humphrey. m. 22 June 1817. T. Littleton.

Burson, Cyrus & Ansey Thompson. Presley Saunders, bm. 4 Jan. 1838. m. 4 Jan. 1838. Tapler.

Burson, Cyrus & Phobe Bales. m. 26 April 1812. Dunn.

Burson, James & Hannah Spencer. 22 Feb. 1803. Littlejohn.

Burson, Jehue & Anna Kent. Thomas Kent, bm. 18 Feb. 1799. Shel.

Burson, Moses & Catherine Swick. m. 27 June 1803. Littlejohn.

Burton, Bazil T. F. & Ann Squire, in Maryland. m. 13 Aug. 1843. ParReg A.

Bussard, Persander L. & Caroline Amanda Sheid, dau. of Martin B. Hummer. Newton Keene attests groom's age, bm. 11 Nov. 1839. Cam.

Bussell, George & Sarah Moore. Jacob Stump attests bride's age, bm. 21 June 1799.

Butler, Ferdinand & Lydia Cloud. Asa Brown attests ages, bm. 11 May 1835. Shel.

Butler, Henson & Alice Williams. m. 14 Jan. 1829. Tippett.

Butler, Jacob & Sarah Dawson. m. 29 June 1794. Littlejohn.

Butler, John & Sarah Hamilton. Thomas Littleton attests ages, bm. 26 March 1841. Shel.

Butler, William & Harriet Dailey. L. T. Beach attests ages, bm. m. 29 Dec. 1849. Eggleston.

Butts, Isaac & Lydia Ann Hart. Colin C. Campbell attests ages, bm. 15 July 1844. m. 18 July 1844. Massey. Shel.

Butts, Oliver G. & Mary C. Everhart. Nelson B. Everhart proves ages, wit. 8 Dec. 1851. MarReg.

Byrne, George F. & Eliza Frances Bogue, dau. of Elizabeth B. Bogue. John R. Skinner attests groom's age, bm. 8 Sep. 1849. Cam.

Byrne, James & Henrietta South. m. 20 Nov. 1823. Dagg.

Byrne, John & Eliza Mathews. Simon Mathews attests bride's age, bm. 9 Sep. 1831. Shel.

Byrne, John & Elizabeth Barton, dau. of Joseph Barton. Abraham H. Beavers attests groom's age, bm. 4 Nov. 1830.

Cadel, Adam & Sussana Blotzer; both single. By license. m. 13 Dec. 1825. ParReg A.

Cadwalader, Thomas & Jane Daniel. m. 31 March 1785. FFMM.

Calvert, George & Elizabeth Carr. m. 17 May 1819. Williamson.

Calvert, Solomon, son of Vincent Calvert & Elizabeth Willis, dau. of William Willis. William Davis, bm. 15 Oct. 1832. Shel.

Camble, James & Elizabeth Eveland. m. 27 May 1804. Littlejohn.

Camble, John & Elizabeth Beason. m. 28 Dec. 1794. Littlejohn.

Camble, John & Mary Fictcher. m. 26 June 1804. Littlejohn.

Camble, William & Margaret Reed. m. 24 March 1798. Littlejohn.

Cammel, James & Elizabeth Reed. m. 15 April 1819. Griffith.

Cammeron, Thomas & Mary Crupper. m. 27 Dec. 1806. McPherson.

Camp, Isaac & Sarah Newhouse. Andrew Copeland attests bride's age, bm. 1 Jan. 1829. m. 4 Jan. 1829. Tippett.

Campbell, Addison, son of Margret Campbell & Susan Snoots, dau.
of Mary Snoots. Christian Compher, bm. 5 June 1841. m.
10 June 1841. ParReg A. Shel.
Campbell, Andrew & Martha Ann Campbell. John Campbell attests
groom's age, bm. 15 Jan. 1838. Shel.
Campbell, James & Mary Jackson. John Jackson, Jr. attests bride's
age, bm. 20 Feb. 1799. Littlejohn. Shel.
Campbell, James Madison, son of Sarah Campbell & Margaret
Wynkoop, dau. of Joseph Wynkoop. Samuel C. Wynkoop, Thomas
Smitson, bm. 17 Aug. 1839. Shel.
Campbell, John & Sarah Ann Saunders. John Saunders attests ages,
bm. 31 March 1834. Shel.
Campbell, John B. & Rachal Ann Grubb. Archibald Morrison attests
ages, bm. 9 Aug. 1847. m. 17 Aug. 1847. Dulin. Shel.
Campbell, Joseph & Ruth Thomas, dau. of Eleanor Thompson who
attests groom's age, bm. 19 May 1843. Shel.
Campbell, Robert & Martha Ellen Curry, dau. of Robert Curry who
attests groom's age, bm. 23 April 1849. m. 24 April 1849.
Gover. Shel.
Campbell, William, son of Andrew Campbell & Jane Wynkoop, b. 19
Dec. 1787, dau. of Cornelius Wynkoop. Garrad Wynkoop attests
bride's age, bm. 26 Jan. 1809.
Campher, Peter & Catharina Phillern, both single. By license.
m. 19 March 1816. ParReg A.
Campher, William & Maria Spring, dau. of Friedrich Spring and
wife; both single. By license. m. 27 May 1817. ParReg A.
Canby, Benjamin Hough, son of Samuel and Elizabeth Campher,
mother deceased & Sarah Taylor, dau. of Thomas and Caleb
Taylor. m. 26 Dec. 1792. FFMM.
Canby, Joseph & Mary Hughes. m. 26 Feb. 1829. Taylor, Clerk.
Canby, Samuel & Ann Shene. m. 1 Sep. 1779. FFMM.
Canby, Samuel & Elizabeth Hough. m. 28 Feb. 1770. FFMM.
Canby, Samuel T. & Julietta Cookus. John G. Hogue attests ages, bm.
3 Nov. 1834. Shel.
Cardel, Samuel & Catharina Kerns; both single. By license.
m. 10 Sep. 1815. ParReg A.
Carlisle, David & Mary Ann Boggess. Reed Poulton attests ages, bm.
14 Aug. 1843. m. 24 Aug. 1843. Jones. Shel.
Carlisle, James & Emily Wiley. John Wiley attests ages, bm.
7 Feb. 1848. Shel.
Carlley, John Z. & Eveline Warr. Jesse L. Rice attests ages, bm.
12 Feb. 1848. Shel.
Carlyle, James & Elizabeth Beatey. m. 5 Aug. 1794. Littlejohn.
Carlyle, Robert & Catherine Brown. m. 4 Nov. 1806. Littlejohn.
Carnehan, George & Jane Wilkins. m. 27 July 1816. Littlejohn.
Carneš, Daniel & Anna E. Everhart, dau. of Michael Everhart, bm.
Groom "shows himself above the age of 21 years". 23 Feb.
1847. Shel.
Carnes, James & Mary Scatterday. m. 19 Nov. 1813. Littlejohn.
Carnes, Peter & Salley Greenwall. m. 20 Nov. 1847. Gover.
Carnes, Samuel Lawson & Sarah Margaret Fry, dau. of Peter Fry who
proves groom's age, wit. 13 Dec. 1850. MarReg. m. Dec. 1850.
Martin.
Carney, John & Mary Cartnail. m. 26 Sep. 1810. Littlejohn.

LOUDOUN COUNTY MARRIAGES

Carns, Daniel & Ann Elizabeth Everhart. m. 25 Feb. 1847. ParReg A.
Carpenter, Charles & Elizabeth Vanhaun (Vanhorn). m. 3 July 1817.
T. Littleton.
Carr, James M. & Elizabeth Costs, dau. of Mary Costs. Peter Costs,
bm. 10 March 1838. Shel.
Carr, John & Jane Means. m. 1821-1822. Mines.
Carr, John & Prudence Collins. C. Binns, Jr., bm. 24 Jan. 1799.
Littlejohn. Shel.
Carr, Joseph & Martha Ann Carr. James M. Carr attests ages, bm.
3 Oct. 1837. Shel.
Carr, Joseph & Mary Hale (Hall). William Hall attests bride's age,
bm. 5 Sep. 1831. Shel.
Carr, Peter & Mary Minner. m. 23 July 1796. Littlejohn.
Carr, Peter & Polly Wilson. m. 12 March 1798. Littlejohn.
Carr, Samuel & Elizabeth Brocon. James Williams attests ages, bm.
6 Feb. 1843. Shel.
Carr, Thomas & Priscilla Wade. Thomas Carr, Robert Wade, bm.
28 Jan. 1801.
Carr, William & Mary Hughes. m. 11 Aug. 1810. Littlejohn.
Carrington, Timothy & Margrit Chew. m. 9 Nov. 1820. T. Littleton.
Carroll, James & Esther Ann Grubb, dau. of Curtis Grubb. 30 Sep.
1850. MarReg. Return dated 30 Sep. 1850. Wit: Thomas Boland,
Miss Schooley. Plunkett.
Carruthers, John & Malinda E. Nixon, dau. of Joel Nixon, bm.
3 March 1835. Shel.
Carruthers, William & Louisa White, dau. of Adin White, bm.
16 Nov. 1841. Shel.
Carson, Jacob & Elizabeth Susan Scott, dau. of Gilbert Scott, wit.
17 Feb. 1851. MarReg. m. 20 Feb. 1851. Carter.
Carson, James H. & Catharine A. R. Saunders, dau. of Th. R.
Saunders, bm. 20 Feb. 1850. Wills.
Carter, Abner & Martha E. Carter, dau. of Martha E. Carter. Wit:
R. K. Littleton, Landon Carter. Richard Littleton, bm.
12 April 1830. Cam.
Carter, Asa & Cynthee Parker. m. June 1797. Littlejohn.
Carter, Benjamin F. & Rebecca M. Wright. Robert L. Wright, bm.
17 May 1837. m. May 1837. Campbell. Shel.
Carter, Eden & Susannah Hann. m. 15 Dec. 1803. Williamson.
Carter, Elihu & Frances Jenkins. m. 1809-1810. Mines.
Carter, Ephraim & Elizabeth Reed. m. 1809-1810. Mines.
Carter, Ferdinand A. & Pammelia (Parmelia) Jane Swart, dau. of
Elizabeth Swart. Samuel Swart, bm. 7 Nov. 1838. m. 13 Nov.
1838. Herndon.
Carter, George & Mrs. Elizabeth O. Lewis, at Clifton, her residence
near Upperville. Jesse Timms, bm. 30 Oct. 1835. m. 12 Nov.
1835. Adie.
Carter, George & Helen Ewers. m. 9 March 1807. Littlejohn.
Carter, George & Jane Updyke. m. 13 Dec. 1808. Littlejohn.
Carter, George W. & Orra M. McIlhany. Wit: Bride's father. 11 Dec.
1850. MarReg. m. 12 Dec. 1850. Blackwell.
Carter, James & Mary Howell. m. 20 Nov. 1806. Littlejohn.
Carter, James & Rachel Jenkins. m. 12 Oct. 1820. Dagg.
Carter, James S. & Jemima Leath. m. 31 May 1825. Evans.

23

LOUDOUN COUNTY MARRIAGES

Carter, John A. & Richardetta T. DeButts, dau. of Louisa F. Hall.
John P. Dulaney testamentary guardian for bride by will of
Mary DeButts, from Reg. Wills, Alexandria. Robert McIntyre,
bm. 11 Feb. 1834. m. 12 Feb. 1834. Furlong. Shel.
Carter, Jonathan & Nancy Ball. m. 19 March 1818. Dagg.
Carter, Joseph & Martha Ann, alias Martha Ann Lucas. Stephen
Gregg, bm. 6 Sep. 1837. Shel.
Carter, Joseph & Mary Wilson. m. 22 May 1810. Littlejohn.
Carter, Landon C. & Mahala Battson, ward of Landon C. Carter.
Jacob F. Humphrey attests groom's age. John Wornal, bm.
9 March 1829. Shel.
Carter, Leander & Elizabeth Beatty, dau. of Susan Beatty. Enos
Updike attests bride's age. Joshua Pancoast, bm. 6 Sep. 1841.
Shel.
Carter, Legard L. & Elizabeth Lee. m. 6 Oct. 1808. Dunn.
Carter, Oswell & Emily Combs (Cool). Thomas Powell attests ages,
bm. 8 Oct. 1838. m. 10 Oct. 1838. Broadus.
Carter, Peter & Mary Ann Harrison, dau. of James Harrison, bm.
24 Dec. 1840. m. 29 Dec. 1840. Herndon. Shel.
Carter, Richard, son of Henry Carter & Deborah Newlan. Jesse
Newlan attests bride's age, bm. 17 April 1809. Shel.
Carter, Richard & Lavina Craven. Charles Carter attests bride's
age, bm. 23 Sep. 1833. Shel.
Carter, Richard H., son of Edward Carter & Mary DeButts, ward of
John P. Dulany; both under 21 years. Samuel W. DeButts, bm.
25 April 1837. Shel.
Carter, Samuel & Elizabeth Ann Barton (Batson). Samuel West
attests bride's age. Enos Updike attests groom's age, bm.
12 March 1832. m. 29 March 1832. Baker. Shel.
Carter, Samuel & Jane Rivers. Thomas Phillips, bm. 12 Dec. 1842.
m. 5 Jan. 1843. ParReg A. Shel.
Carter, Samuel & Matilda Dennis. James E. Stonestreet attests
bride's age, bm. 5 Feb. 1842. Cam.
Carter, Thomas & Sarah Pyott, dau. of John Pyott. James Pyott
attests groom's age, bm. 30 Jan. 1809. Littlejohn.
Carter, William & Margeret Updyke. m. 2 Oct. 1804. Littlejohn.
Carter, William & Susanah Woodford. m. 29 Jan. 1810. T. Littleton.
Cartis, Ambrose D. & Nancy Vanander. m. 10 Sep. 1804. Littlejohn.
Cartwright, Nicodemus & Ann Taylor. John Smith, bm. 6 Nov. 1849.
m. 8 Nov. 1849. Gover.
Cartzendoffer, Johannes & Sophia Crabel; both single. By license.
m. 13 Feb. 1817. ParReg A.
Caruthers, Thomas & Martha Myers. m. 18 Sep. 1812. J. Littleton.
Casa, William & Sarah V. Perry. m. 25 April 1842. Gover.
Case, Benjamin & Ann Oden, dau. of Thomas Oden, bm. 9 July 1833.
Shel.
Case, John & Christena (Christiana) Crim (Krime), dau. of Charles
Crim, bm. 6 April 1809. m. 1808-1809. Mines.
Casey, John & Hannah Warner, dau. of George Warner. Jeremiah Clouts,
bm. 16 Jan. 1809. m. 1808-1809. Mines. Shel.
Casey, Leven & Elizabeth Perry. m. 21 Nov. 1810. Littlejohn.
Casey, William & Ann E. Edwards. m. 15 Jan. 1827-5 Feb. 1827.
Burch.

Casey, William & Sarah V. Perry. John D. Perry, bm. 26 April
1842. Shel.
Cassady, William H. & Mary Jane Denham. David B. Denham attests
bride's age, bm. 1 March 1837. m. 2 March 1837. Broaddus.
Castle, Eli S. & Rowena E. Drish. Joel L. Nixon, bm. 19 June
1850. Wills.
Castleman, Charles M. & Eveline Elizabeth Francis. Wit: William
H. Francis. 13 June 1853. MarReg. m. 15 June 1853. Hirst.
Castleman, Henry W. & Mary E. Sinclair, at Mrs. Sinclair's
tavern, Leesburg. David J. Castleman attests groom's age, bm.
8 Nov. 1848. m. 9 Nov. 1848. Adie.
Catlett, Alfred & Catharine Garett. m. 14 Sep. 1813. McPherson.
Cavan, Patrick,& Sarah Baker. m. 1 March 1798. Littlejohn.
Cavans (Cavins), Robert & Ann Todd Marr. 15 Dec. 1764. Lic.
FeeBk 1.
Cerdell (Cordell), Alexander & Dienna Wilsen, niece and ward of
Sanford Ramey. Order Bk. 4, p. 290, Sanford Ramey appointed
bride's guardian, orphan of James Wilson late Culpepper Co.,
now Madison County. Permission to marry. 21 June 1813.
Chamberlain, Stephen T. & Susanna Marmaduke. m. 17 Nov. 1836.
Broaddus.
Chamblin, Albert G. & Evelina B. Maddux. John Francis attests
bride's age, bm. 19 Dec. 1837. Shel.
Chamblin, Burr Peyton & Mary V. Purcell. Valentine V. Purcell
attests ages, bm. 14 March 1831. m. 17 March 1831. Baker.
Chamblin, Elisha & Mahala Romine. Lawson Osburn attests ages, bm.
11 Sep. 1837. Shel.
Chamblin, George & Mary Davis, dau. of Samuel Davis. Van Davis,
bm. 21 Aug. 1799. Shel.
Chamblin, James Heaton & Octavia Kepler (Kippler). Samuel Keppler
attests bride's age. Charles G. Eskridge, bm. 2 March 1839.
m. 4 March 1839. Shel.
Chamblin, John L, ward of Leven P. Chamblin & Mary Ann Baldwin,
ward of Mahlon Baldwin. Leven P. Chamblin, Mahlon Baldwin,
bm. 13 Feb. 1832. m. 23 Feb. 1832. Baker. Shel.
Chamblin, Leven P. & Juliann Furr. m. 1 June 1840. Cadden.
Chamblin, Mason & Duanna Vandeventer. m. 16 Feb. 1825. Tuston.
Chamblin, Norval & Sarah Vandeventer. m. 7 Dec. 1824. Tuston.
Chamblin, Stephen T. & Susannah Marmaduke, ward of Alfred G.
Chamblin, bm. 15 Nov. 1836. Shel.
Chance, Samuel & Mary Smallwood. m. 1807-1808. Mines.
Chancellor, Lorman & Margaret E. Smith. Rufus Smith attests
bride's age, bm. 6 Sep. 1847. m. 7 Sep. 1847. ParReg B.
Chandler, George, Frederick Co., Md. & Deborah Brooke. m. 27 Aug.
1783. FFMM.
Chann, Zachariah T. & Mary S. Rust, dau. of Bushrod Rust.
Bushrod Rust, Jr., bm. 10 May 1845. Shel.
Chappell, Addison & Mary Anderson. Jonah Steere attests bride's
age, bm. 5 Oct. 1835. m. 6 Oct. 1835. Monroe. Shel.
Chappell, James & Susan Slack, dau. of Tunis Slack, bm. 18 Aug.
1832. m. 19 Aug. 1832. Baker. Shel.
Chapple, James & Elizabeth Thompson. m. 15 Jan. 1824. Dagg.
Charlton, Bernard & Mary Mills, dau. of Chloe McDuffy. Thomas
Cornelle attests groom's age, bm. 8 March 1841. Shel.

25

Check, George Washington & Elizabeth Umbaugh, dau. of John
Umbaugh, bm. 3 April 1849. m. 3 April 1849. Gover. Shel.
Chenoweth, James B. & Eliza Davis. David J. Eaton attests ages,
bm. 2 Jan. 1830.
Chew, Richard & Mary Grady. m. 13 Oct. 1818. Dagg.
Chew, Robart & Daucaus Osburn. m. 6 March 1821. T. Littleton.
Chew, Roger & Sarah W. Aldridge, house of her father, old glebe.
Joseph W. Aldridge, bm. 25 March 1835. m. 2 April 1835.
Adie. Shel.
Chichester, William McCarty Bains & Francis Barnett. m. 29 Sep.
1815. Littlejohn.
Chick, William & Jemima Evans. m. 4 June 1801. Littlejohn.
Chilton, Henry & Nancy Ellis. m. 15 April 1806. Littlejohn.
Chilton, James & Margeret Jinkins. m. 8 Dec. 1807. Littlejohn.
Chilton, Richard & Dewanner S. Bennett. m. 1807-1808. Mines.
Chinn, Benjamin T. & Edmonia R. Carter. Alfred Ball attests ages,
bm. 26 Jan. 1838. Cam.
Chinn, Charles E. & Rebecca Elgin. William Card, Jr. attests
bride's age, bm. 6 June 1839. Shel.
Chinn, R. Shetchly (Stretchley) & Sally Beaty. John M. Orr proves
ages, wit. 22 Feb. 1851. MarReg. m. 4 March 1851. Eggleston.
Chinn, Samuel & Amelia Myres. m. 31 Oct. 1816. Williamson.
Chunn, Zachariah T. & Mary S. Rust. m. 15 May 1845. Dodge.
Church, James & Delila Triplett. m. 21 Sep. 1813. Littlejohn.
Cimmins, Joseph & Polly Custor. m. 3 Oct. 1810. Littlejohn.
Claggett, Zachariah & Margaret E. Peugh. Abraham Peugh proves
bride's age, wit. 17 March 1851. MarReg. m. 18 March 1851.
Jones.
Clapper, Henry & Zillah Copeland. Craven A. Copeland attests ages,
bm. 28 Nov. 1831. Shel.
Clapsaddle, Ferdinand & Mary Ann Glasgow, dau. of Catharine
Glasgow; at house of her mother, Leesburg. F. M. Weadon
attests groom's age, bm. 9 March 1841. m. 11 March 1841. Adie.
Clare, John & Elizabeth Hall. Eleanor Thompson attests bride's
age, bm. 15 June 1843. Shel.
Clark, John & Malinda Thompson. m. 24 Sep. 1824. Dagg.
Clarke, James & Martha J. Hunt (Hart), dau. of Jonathan Hunt, who
attests groom's age, bm. 22 Aug. 1842. m. 23 Aug. 1842. Phelps.
Clarke, John & Nancy Clayton. m. 10 April 1817. T. Littleton.
Clarke, John F. & Effa Tillett. m. 1820-1821. Mines.
Clarke, Orson D. & Mary E. Chamblin. Samuel J. Chamblin proves
ages, wit. 15 July 1850. MarReg. m. 15 July 1850. Smith.
Clarke, William F. & Abigal Morgin. m. 11 May 1824. T. Littleton.
Claspy, Nimrod & Mary Orum, dau. of Henry Orum, who attests
groom's age, bm. 19 June 1834. Shel.
Claxton, Thomas & Caroline Fichter. George Fichter, bm. 6 Feb.
1840. Cam.
Clem, alias Clem Watson & Betsy Warrick. m. 21 Nov. 1807.
Littlejohn.
Clemens, Alfred & Matilda Payne. m. 2 Jan. 1820. Dunn.
Clements, Charles W. & Sarah Ann Filler. Jacob Smith attests ages,
bm. 20 Dec. 1847. m. 23 Dec. 1847. Williard. Shel.
Clements, Hezh. & Martha Templar. m. 23 Dec. 1800. Littlejohn.
Clemmons, Samuel & Elizabeth Sewell. m. 27 June 1810. Williamson.

Clemons, Ozzy & Ann Cavens. m. 24 Dec. 1798. Littlejohn.
Clendening, William & Ruth Russell, dau. of William Russell.
Thomas Russell attests ages, bm. 20 March 1809. m. 28 March
1809. Littlejohn.
Clendening, William, Jr. & Elizabeth Ann Thompson. Samuel P.
Thompson attests bride's age, bm. 16 Nov. 1841. Shel.
Clendenning, Samuel & Elizabeth Thomas. James W. Nixon attests
ages, bm. 22 March 1842. Shel.
Clerk, John W. A. & Margeret O'Niel. m. 8 Jan. 1803. Littlejohn.
Clewes, Joseph & Mary Vanclevender. m. 19 Aug. 1805. Littlejohn.
Clewes, Thomas & Ann Smither. m. 4 Jan. 1802. Littlejohn.
Clifford, Obediah & Betsy Cowper (Couper), dau. of Alexander
Couper of Leesburg. James Hamilton, bm. 16 Sep. 1799.
Littlejohn.
Cline, John T. & Marion V. Cockran (Cochran). William Pickett
proves ages, wit. 29 Sep. 1852. MarReg. m. 30 Sep. 1852.
Rodgers.
Cline, Lewis & Elizabeth Connard. m. 1806. Mines.
Cline, William & Margaret Anna Boss. Samuel M. Boss, bm. 9 March
1844. Shel.
Cline, William & Margaret Carr. Thomas Carr attests bride's age,
bm. 4 July 1809. m. 1808-1809. Mines.
Clothier, John & Margaret Ann Iden. John Iden attests ages, bm.
11 May 1846. m. 27 May 1846. H. Herndon. Cam.
Cloud, Jeremiah & Sidney Brown. Mahlon Janney affirms groom's
age, bm. 17 April 1809. Littlejohn.
Coad, William & Barbara Tauperman. m. 27 Jan. 1825. Williamson.
Coale, Lewis, son of Samuel and Lydia Coale & Phebe Steer, dau.
of Isaac and Phebe Steer. m. 4 Oct. 1820. Mendenhall, Clerk.
Coals, William T. & Mary E. Taleaferro. m. May 1831. Dorsey.
Coats, Calvin & Elizabeth Robey, dau. of Jane Robey. Abel Jones,
bm. 10 April 1837. Shel.
Cochran, Adison & Sarah James, ward of Robert James, bm. 14 Jan.
1848. m. 18 Jan. 1848. Dulin.
Cochran, Edward & Emily Iden. Samuel Iden, bm. 26 Jan. 1830.
m. 28 Jan. 1830. Williamson. Shel.
Cochran, Elijah & Susannah Richardson. m. 27 Nov. 1817.
T. Littleton.
Cochran, John T. & Elizabeth Lodge. Nathan Lodge proves ages, wit.
15 March 1852. MarReg. m. 23 March 1852. Eggleston.
Cochran, Tholemiah (Jorlemiah) & Hannah James. Asa James attests
ages, bm. 27 Jan. 1847. m. 28 Jan. 1847. Massey. Shel.
Cochran, William B., Dr. & Catharine M. P. Noland, dau. of Lloyd
Noland, at house of her father, Loudoun. m. 5 Nov. 1835. Adie.
Cocke, William C. & Lucy Ann Hines, dau. of Hester Hines. John
Riley, bm. 21 March 1838. m. 22 March 1838. Hauer. Shel.
Cockerell, James & Sarah J. Verts. m. 23 Dec. 1845. Massey.
Cockerell, Robert & Prudence Tally. m. 1809-1810. Mines.
Cockerill, Alexander, of Fairfax & Catharine F. Rose. B. D.
Cockerell attests groom's age, bm. George W. Rose attests
bride's age. 14 Dec. 1842. m. 15 Dec. 1842. Trott.
Cockerill, Harley & Harriet Craig. Alfred H. Shields attests ages,
bm. 9 Oct. 1837. Shel.
Cockerill, Hiram & Eleanor Talley. Isaac Talley attests ages.
Amos Harvey, bm. 18 Sep. 1834. Shel.

Cockerill, James & Sarah Jane Verts, dau. of Jacob Verts, bm.
19 Dec. 1845. Shel.
Cockerill, Joseph & Jane Fulton, ward of George Briscoe, bm.
14 Dec. 1829.
Cockerill, Mortimore & Sarah Ann Evans, dau. of Jesse Evans, who
attests groom's age, bm. 15 June 1840. Shel.
Cockerill, Reuben & Mary E. Coe, dau. of Mary Coe, bm. John L.
Tillett attests groom's age. 3 June 1833. Shel.
Cockerill, Sandford & Nancy Schryock. Presley Saunders, bm. 9 Feb.
1835. Cam.
Cockran, Nathan & Mary P. McGavick. William Graham attests ages,
bm. 28 March 1831. Shel.
Cockrill, John & Tamer Combs. m. 3 Jan. 1805. Williamson.
Cockrille, Lee & Delilah Hepburne, ward of Mahlon Roach, bm.
Elias Cockrille attests groom's age. 16 Nov. 1809. m. 11 Nov.
1809. Littlejohn.
Cockrill, Sanford & Nancy Evans. m. 12 Oct. 1807. Littlejohn.
Coe, Ebenezer & Jane Grubb. Richard J. Grubb attests bride's ages,
bm. 16 Sep. 1844. m. 17 Sep. 1844. Shel.
Coe, Elijah & Adaline Smallwood. William Smallwood attests bride's
age, bm. 10 Feb. 1843. m. 14 Feb. 1843. ParReg A.
Coe, Hezekiah & Barbara Neer. m. 18 Jan. 1812. J. Littleton.
Coe, Horatio & Catherine Grubb. m. 3 Aug. 1811. Littlejohn.
Coe, Orin & Ruth Nicholds. m. 6 Sep. 1821. T. Littleton.
Coe, Robert & Elizabeth Coe. m. 28 Dec. 1813. Littlejohn.
Coe, Samuel & Elizabeth Herron. m. 2 Aug. 1806. Littlejohn.
Coe, William & Catherine Coe. m. Oct. 1803. Dunn.
Coe, William & Elizabeth Copeland. m. 27 March 1804. Littlejohn.
Coffee, John & Rachel Pidgeon, Jr. m. 8 Dec. 1784. FFMM.
Coghlan, Edward & Bridget Boland. Patrick Boland attests bride's
age, bm. 19 Aug. 1830. Shel.
Cohl, William, widower & Prisilia Roller, dau. of Conrad and
Elisabetha Roller. By license. 19 Oct. 1823. ParReg A.
Colbert, Jesse & Christena Verts, dau. of Mrs. Susan Ann Verts.
Robert E. Beall attests groom's age, bm. 24 Dec. 1847. m.
29 Dec. 1847. Bryan. Cam.
Cole, John & Catherine Kephart. m. 25 Oct. 1815. Littlejohn.
Cole, Thomas & Elizabeth Cole, dau. of Peggy Cole, bm. 29 Aug.
1837. Shel.
Cole, William & Hannah Razor. m. 29 Jan. 1810. Littlejohn.
Cole, William T. & Mary E. Taliaferro. Sampson Hutchison attests
bride's age, bm. 23 May 1831. Cam.
Cole, Wilmon P. & Mary E. Cox, dau. of Samuel Cox. J. F. Newlon,
bm. 6 June 1842. m. 9 June 1842. Trott. Shel.
Collett, James, son of William Collett & Mary Carter. Levi
Whaley attests bride's age. William Collett, bm. 16 Feb. 1809.
m. 16 Feb. 1809. Littlejohn.
Collier, John & Rhoda Clerk. m. 30 Dec. 1802. Littlejohn.
Collier, William & Mary Styles. Columbus Hickman attests ages, bm.
4 June 1840. Shel.
Collins, John & Elizabeth Binley. m. 25 July 1798. Littlejohn.
Collins, John & Nancy Evans. m. 28 Nov. 1816. J. Frye.
Collins, Levi & Elizabeth Fawley. Joseph Allder attests bride's
age, bm. 2 April 1832. Shel.

Collins, Levi & Susah. Binley. m. 10 Jan. 1804. Littlejohn.
Collins, Thomas & Effamah (Effannah) Harper, dau. of Thomas
    Harper. Valentine Ford attests groom's age, bm. 27 Jan. 1809.
Collins, William & Elizabeth Scrivener. m. 15 Aug. 1795. Littlejohn.
Colston, Raleigh & Gertrude Ann Powell. B. P. Noland, bm. 17 May
    1845. Shel.
Colvert, Jeremiah & Priscilla Smithers. m. 18 April 1816.
    Littlejohn.
Combs, Andrew & Abigail Oden. m. Feb. 1811. Dunn.
Combs, Henson & Maria Tarperman. Cageby Jones attests ages, bm.
    26 Aug. 1830. Shel.
Combs, Israel & Jane Bolling. m. 9 Feb. 1815. Dunn.
Combs, James & Ann Orrison. m. 12 March 1804. Littlejohn.
Combs, Joseph & Nancy J. Brabham, dau. of Thomas Brabham,who
    attests groom's age, bm. 19 Dec. 1831. Shel.
Combs, Robert & Nancy Sears. m. 31 Oct. 1804. Williamson.
Combs, William & Barbara E. McCray. Joshua Nichols attests ages,
    bm. 14 Sep. 1835. Shel.
Comfer, Peter & Susanna Stonebonner, dau. of Peter Stonebonner,
    bm. 20 March 1799. Shel.
Compher, John & Elizabeth Ault. m. 25 April 1808. Littlejohn.
Compher, John & Elizabeth M. Grubb, dau. of Ebenezer Grubb, who
    proves ages, wit. 16 Jan. 1851. MarReg. m. 21 Jan. 1851.
    Startzman.
Compher, John & Esther Ann Grubb. Ebenezer Grubb attests groom's
    age, bm. 28 Jan. 1846. m. 3 Feb. 1846. ParReg A. Shel.
Compher, John & Margeret Razor. m. 1 Jan. 1802. Littlejohn.
Compher, John & Susan (Susanna) Fawley. Henry Fawley, bm. 14 Feb.
    1837. m. 16 Feb. 1837. Hauer. Shel.
Compher, John, Jr. & Margaret Spring. m. 24 March 1808. Littlejohn.
Compher, Jonas J. (I.) & Mary C. Wade. Wit: John H. Minor.
    17 Jan. 1852. MarReg. m. 15 Jan. 1852. ParReg A. Shel.
Compher, Joseph & Susan Smith, dau. of Jacob Smith, who attests
    groom's age, bm. 10 Jan. 1842. m. 12 Jan. 1843. ParReg A. Shel.
Compher, Peter & Mary D. Hooe, dau. of Howson L. Hooe, bm.
    22 May 1849. Shel.
Compher, Samuel & Hannah Williams, dau. of Israel Williams, who
    attests groom's age, bm. 28 Oct. 1839. m. 31 Oct. 1839. Hauer.
Compher, William & Mary Fawley, dau. of Henry Fawley, bm. 22 Feb.
    1836. m. 25 Feb. 1836. Hauer.
Comphor, Peter, Jr. & Mary Dale Hoe. m. 24 May 1849. Eggleston.
Conard, Abner & Mary C. Axline. m. 15 Nov. 1838. ParReg A.
Conard, Abner A. & Ann S. Neer. Jesse Neer attests groom's age,
    bm, 24 Feb. 1846.
Conard, Archibald & Emily Gulick. m. 16 Nov. 1824. Tuston.
Conard, John & Eleanor Gregg, dau. of George Gregg. Andrew S.
    Anderson attests groom's age, bm. 2 May 1829.
Conard, John W. & Mary Ann Nisewanger. m. 28 Feb. 1850. Eggleston.
Conard (Conrad), John William & Susan Ann Grubb, dau. of William
    Grubb, bm. 30 Oct. 1848. m. 7 Nov. 1848. Eggleston. Shel.
Conard (Conrad), Joseph M. & Mary J. D. Potts, dau. of Ezekiel
    Potts, who attests groom's age, bm. 4 Sep. 1848. m. 12 Sep.
    1848. Dulin. Shel.

LOUDOUN COUNTY MARRIAGES

Connard, John & Eleanor Gregg, dau. of George Gregg. Andrew S.
    Anderson attests groom's age, bm. Wit: Matilda Jacobs.
    2 May 1829. Shel.
Connard, Jonathan, son of Sarah Connard, yeoman & Jane Potts,
    dau. of David Potts. m. 18 April 1764. FFMM.
Conner, David & Elizabeth E. Anderson. Robert S. Anderson attests
    ages, bm. 8 Sep. 1838. Shel.
Conner, David & Jane Ann Merchant, dau. of William Merchant, bm.
    9 Nov. 1835. Shel.
Conner, David & Martha Williams. m. 20 Dec. 1803. Littlejohn.
Conner, John & Lucinda Rice. James Thomas attests ages, bm.
    10 Feb. 1834. Shel.
Conner, John & Susan Lyne. Levi G. Ewers attests ages, bm. 5 Aug.
    1837. Shel.
Conner, Joseph & Elizabeth Cline. m. 20 Sep. 1805. Littlejohn.
Conner, Timothy & Pleasant R. Dailey, dau. of John Dailey.
    Dailey's consent carried by John Potter, Waterford; he "is
    sick and is not able to go down" and "is my nearest neaghbour."
    John S. Edwards attests groom's age. John A. Moore, bm.
    16 Nov. 1829.
Connerd, David & Elisabetha Wertzin, dau. of Jacob Wertz; both
    single. By license. m. 29 Feb. 1816. ParReg A.
Conrad (Conard), Abner & Mary C. Axline. David Axline attests
    bride's age, bm. Jacob Filler attests groom's age, bm. 13 Nov.
    1838. m. 15 Nov. 1838. Hauer. Shel.
Conrad, David P. & Amanda M. Saffer. John W. Saffer attests
    groom's age, wit. Bride's mother consents in writing. 24 Feb.
    1852. MarReg. m. 26 Jan. 1852. Smith.
Conrad, Johannes & Maria Eberhard; both single. By license. m.
    7 Dec. 1820. ParReg A.
Conrad, Johathan & Rahel Grubb; both single. By license. m.
    13 Jan. 1825. ParReg A.
Conrad, Joseph & Maria Grubb (Grubbs). By license. m. 9 March
    1826. ParReg A.
Conrad, Luther E. & Amanda Bazzell. m. 21 Jan. 1830. Baker.
Conrad, Robert Y. & Elizabeth W. Powell, dau. of Burr Powell.
    George C. Powell, bm. 8 Dec. 1829. m. 10 Dec. 1829.Williamson.
Conwell, Josiah, son of Loveless Conwell & Mary Ann Porter.
    Isaac Conwell attests bride's age, bm. 31 March 1830. Shel.
Cooke, Edward E. & Margaret L. Harrison. Wilson C. Selden, Jr.,
    bm. 19 Feb. 1831. m. 15 Feb. 1831. Cutler. Shel.
Cooke, Peyton & Mary A. Lacey. m. 8 June 1818. Dunn. Shel.
Cooke, Samuel & Susannah Love. m. 26 March 1806. Jefferson. Shel.
Cooke, William & Elizabeth Staddler. m. 16 Jan. 1810. Littlejohn.
Cooke, William & Maria E. Lacey. m. 31 May 1808. Littlejohn.
Cooksey, John & Elizabeth Ann Curry. Father of bride consents.
    " - the man no doubt of his being upwards of 21 years of age."
    Oscar F. Reed, bm. 11 Aug. 1845. m. 27 Aug. 1845. Gover.
Cooksey, William & Elizabeth Oden. m. 15 Jan. 1808. Littlejohn.
Cooksey, William & Mary C. Shrigley. George W. Mock attests ages,
    bm. 16 Jan. 1847. Shel.
Coombs, John N., Revd., of Baltimore Conference, age 26 years 6
    mos. & Sallie A. Hatcher, 20 years. Bride's mother consents in
    writing. Groom's age "taken for granted". 9 Nov. 1853. MarReg.
    Chenoweth.

30

Cooper, Adam & Harriet Edwards, dau. of Charles G. Edwards, bm.
3 Dec. 1832. m. 6 Dec. 1832. Hauer.
Cooper, Adam & Mary Jane McGahee, in Maryland. m. 16 March 1835.
ParReg A.
Cooper, Daniel & Elizabeth Sanders. John Bumerouts attests ages,
bm. 12 Aug. 1809.
Cooper, Eli F. & Susanna Commerell, dau. of William Commerell, bm.
15 Jan. 1837. Shel.
Cooper, Elias & Margaret Cooper. John Crim attests ages, bm.
27 Dec. 1835. m. Dec. 1835. Campbell. Shel.
Cooper, George & Milly Spring, dau. of Jacob Spring, bm. 2 June
1829.
Cooper, John & Catherine Cooper. m. 28 Oct. 1841. ParReg A.
Cooper, John & Nancey Mercer. m. 27 Oct. 1810. T. Littleton.
Cooper, John & Sally Ann McGachen; both single. m. 17 March 1831.
ParReg A.
Cooper, Jonathan & Mary Ann Myres. Mahlon Myres attests ages, bm.
5 Nov. 1833. Shel.
Cooper, Joseph & Catharine Aslinger. A.T.M. Scott attests bride's
age. John Jones, Jr., bm. 10 May 1847. m. 11 May 1847.
Williard. Shel.
Cooper, Michael & Mary Ann Hunter. William Hunter, bm. 14 March
1842. m. 17 March 1842. Hauer. Shel.
Cooper, Noah & Eliza Ann Cooper. Wit: Peter Cooper. 22 March 1852.
MarReg. m. 25 March 1852. Gover.
Cooper, Peter & Elizabeth Pickerill. Richard Ballenger proves
ages, wit. 28 Oct. 1851. MarReg. m. 30 Oct. 1851. Gover.
Cooper, Peter & Rachel Myers, dau. of Mahlon Myers, bm. 27 July
1835. Shel.
Cooper, Philip & Elizabeth Addleman. George Cooper attests ages,
bm. 5 Nov. 1799.
Cooper, Samuel & Mary Umbaugh. John Umbaugh attests groom's age,
bm. 15 Feb. 1842. m. 24 Feb. 1842. Hauer. Shel.
Cooper, Solomon & Emiline Titus. Tunis Titus, bm. 4 Nov. 1839.
m. 7 Nov. 1839. Hauer. Shel.
Cooper, William F. & Lydia Schooley, with Maryland license. m.
7 Oct. 1851. ParReg A.
Copeland, Andrew & Jane Copeland. m. 17 March 1825. Tuston.
Copeland, Charles & Anna McNight. m. 29 Aug. 1807. Littlejohn.
Copeland, Craven A. & Cynthia M. Cunnard. George N. Tracy attests
bride's age, bm. 16 Sep. 1843. Shel.
Copeland, David & Mary Cooper. m. 13 March 1813. Littlejohn.
Copeland, James R. & Ann Preston. George Preston proves ages, wit.
4 Jan. 1851. MarReg. m. 7 Jan. 1851. Herndon.
Copeland, Jonathan & Polly Gillow. m. 10 May 1802. Littlejohn.
Copeland, Mahlon & Tamison Buckhannan. m. 1821-1822. Mines.
Copeland, Richard & Elizabeth Roach. m. 29 Nov. 1797. Littlejohn.
Copeland, William & Lydia Brown, dau. of James and Christiana
Brown, who also give permission for Jeremiah Cloud to marry
their daughter, Sidney Brown. Mahlon Janney, Jr., bm. 17 April
1809. Littlejohn.
Copeland, William & Nancy McKinney. m. 10 May 1800. Littlejohn.
Corbin, Silas & Miriam Schooley, dau. of John Schooley, Jr., who
proves groom's age, wit. 5 April 1852. MarReg. m. 6 April 1852.
Gover.

Cordell, Adam A., son of Adam and Susannah Cordell, aged about
24, carpenter & Sarah Ann Fawley, dau. of Henry and Christena
Fawley, aged about 25. Wit: Joseph Fawley. 14 Nov. 1853.
MarReg. m. 17 Nov. 1853. Martin.

Cordell, Martan & Martha Combs. m. 23 May 1804. Littlejohn.

Cordell, Martin & Roseanah Hough. m. 13 March 1803. Littlejohn.

Cordell, Presley & Amelia Conner. m. 16 Sep. 1802. Littlejohn.

Cordell, Presley & Ressy Wilson. m. 14 April 1801. Littlejohn.

Cornelle, Thomas & Harriet Ann Hawes, dau. of Asa Hawes. Thomas P.
Matthews, Bernard Charlton, Thomas Mills, who attests groom's
age, bm. 8 March 1841. Shel.

Correll, Abraham & Nancy Strider. 9 Jan. 1824. G. Frye.

Corts, Peter & Mary Gross. m. 13 June 1808. Littlejohn.

Cost, Jacob F. & Amanda Davis. James M. Carr attests ages, bm.
16 March 1844. Shel.

Cost, Jacob F. & Mary P. Powell. Bride's father consents and
proves groom's age, wit. 8 Nov. 1853. MarReg.

Costello, Robert, son of James Costello & Mary Ann Triplett, dau.
of Lucy Gray. Jesse Fleming, bm. 9 March 1841. Shel.

Cotton, William, Jr. & Frances Taylor, spinster. 23 Sep. 1765.
FeeBk 2.

Couk, ____ & ____ ____. m. 1846. Gover.

Counard, Anthony & Nancy Gregg. m. 1821-1822. Mines.

Cowgill, Isaac & Martha Goodwin. m. 29 Jan. 1805. Littlejohn.

Cowper, Jacob & Bara. Shoemaker. m. 25 Sep. 1796. Littlejohn.

Cox, James A. & Lydia Garner. Eli Tavenner attests ages, bm.
20 Dec. 1838. Shel.

Cox, Johannes & Margretha Demery; both single. By license. 8 Nov.
1817. ParReg A.

Cox, Richard S. & Mary Lewis Berkeley. Major William Noland proves
ages, wit. 17 Nov. 1851. MarReg. m. 18 Nov. 1851. Adie.

Cox, Samuel & Sarah Chamblin. m. 9 Jan. 1823. Dagg.

Coxs, Benjamin & Cathrine Thatcher. m. 9 Oct. 1797. Littlejohn.

Cragg, James & Reba. Titus. m. 21 March 1803. Littlejohn.

Craidler, Andrew W. & Rachel J. Smallwood. m. 13 June 1840. Gover.

Craig, James & Louisa Gulick. John Gulick attests ages, bm. 7 Jan.
1839. Shel.

Craig, Norval & Frances Dristle. William Gore proves ages, wit.
21 April 1851. MarReg.

Craig, Samuel & Ann M. Gulick. James D. McPherson attests ages.
William S. G. Craig, bm. 15 July 1844. Cam.

Craig, Samuel & Mary Hughs. m. 13 Oct. 1796. Littlejohn.

Craig, William T. J. & Martha Ann Cockerell. John Cockerell
(Cockrill), bm. 7 April 1848. Shel.

Crain, Bailey & Huldah Cockerill. Luther O. Sullivan attests
bride's age, bm. 16 June 1838. m. 17 June 1838. Herndon.

Crain, John & Elizabeth Wornell. John Wornall, bm. 11 April 1836.
Shel.

Crain, Philo R. & Catharine Jane Jett. James Leith proves ages,
wit. 1 July 1852. MarReg. m. 8 July 1852. Hirst.

Crane, Peter & Maria Margretha Beltz, dau. of Peter Beltz. By
license. m. 7 July 1811. ParReg A.

Cranwell, John S. & Susan Newton, ward of Joseph T. Newton, bm.
18 Feb. 1809. Littlejohn.

Craven, Abner & Sarah Sinclair. Samuel Sinclair consents. George
    Sinclair attests bride's age, bm. 9 Nov. 1799. Littlejohn.
Craven, Alfred & Eliza Ann Mahony (Mahany). "The above persons
    are coloured and both their freedom and ages are recorded
    in this office and are according thereto entitled to license.
    P. Saunders." Presly Saunders, bm. 21 July 1849. m. Aug.
    1849. Gover. Shel.
Craven, Cornelius & Peggy Crookes. m. 1807-1808. Mines.
Craven, John & Caty Dulin. m. 25 Sep. 1797. Littlejohn.
Craven, John & Elizabeth Dorrell. m. 8 March 1800. Littlejohn.
Craven, John & Mary Carlisle. "Father in the bond." David
    Carlisle, bm. 6 Feb. 1799.
Craven, Joseph & Hannah Steers. m. 22 Oct. 1804. Littlejohn.
Craven, Josiah & Elizabeth Shepherd. m. 13 Aug. 1804. Littlejohn.
Craven, Mahlon & Hannah Iden. m. 8 March 1810. Littlejohn.
Craven, Rodney & Sarah E. Jones. John Jones attests bride's age.
    Alexander Johnson, bm. 26 June 1843. Shel.
Craven, William L. & Eleanor H. Craven. Craven Sinclair attests
    ages, bm. 16 Feb. 1830. Shel.
Creamer, Bernard & Jona. Virts. m. 25 Jan. 1798. Littlejohn.
Crebs, Berry & Lucy J. Wilson. m. 31 Jan. 1826. Williamson.
Creiner, Christian, widower & Maria Lance. By license. 1 Oct.
    1820. ParReg A.
Crenshaw, John B., Henrico Co. & Rachel Hoge. m. 12 Sep. 1844.
    Bond, Clerk.
Crider, John & Elizabeth Taylor. m. 19 Nov. 1812. Littlejohn.
Cridler, Andrew M. & Rachel Jane Smallwood. Joseph H. Bodine
    attests ages, bm. 13 June 1840. Shel.
Cridler, John & Rebecca Gibbins. George Survick attests bride's
    age, bm. 22 June 1843. Shel.
Crim, Abraham & Rosannah Roller. m. 1809-1810. Mines.
Crim, Charles F. & Mary McCartor. m. 5 Dec. 1851. Chenoweth.
Crim, George F. & Matilda Filler. Jacob Filler attests groom's
    age, bm. 2 Jan. 1838. m. 11 Jan. 1838. Hauer.
Crim, Jacob & Susanna Abel. George Abel, bm. 24 May 1809. m. 1808-
    1809. Mines.
Crim, John & Catharine Everhart. William Carroll attests bride's
    age, bm. 28 June 1842. m. 3 July 1842. Hauer. Shel.
Crim, John H. & Mary Hickman. Martin L. Arnold attests ages, bm.
    7 Feb. 1842. m. 15 Feb. 1842. Hauer. Shel.
Crim, Peter & Mary Wolfe, ward of Jacob Shriver, who attests
    groom's age, bm. 15 Nov. 1831. Shel.
Crim, Peter & Susannah Water. John Smith attests bride's age, bm.
    29 July 1848. Shel.
Crim, Samuel & Amanda White. m. 22 Aug. 1843. ParReg A.
Crim, William & Celia White, with Maryland license. m. 10 June
    1841. ParReg A.
Crimm, Daniel, son of Carl Crimm & Maria Bagert; both single.
    By license. m. 22 Feb. 1816. ParReg A.
Criss, James & Elizabeth Lowe, dau. of Henry Lowe, who attests
    groom's age, bm. 29 Jan. 1840. Cam.
Crissey, Frederick J. & Mary Elizabeth Surghnor, dau. of John
    Surghnor, bm. James H. Benedum attests groom's age. 23 June
    1840. Shel.

LOUDOUN COUNTY MARRIAGES

Cronaan, Timothy & Julia Sullivan. Michael Moriorty proves ages,
    wit. 20 Oct. 1851. MarReg.
Crook, Samuel & Margret Lyden. m. 10 Dec. 1817. T. Littleton.
Cross, Hamilton & Matilda Brown, dau. of Fielding Brown, bm.
    5 Feb. 1839. Shel.
Cross, Harrison & Catherine Sutherland, dau. of William
    Sutherland, who attests groom's age, bm. Wit: James Hamilton.
    8 June 1830. Cam.
Cross, Henry & Betsey Costs. m. 17 Dec. 1807. Saunders.
Cross, James T. & Kitty Jackson, "coulard people". " - he produced
    his free papers and she recorded in clerk's office." 14 Sep.
    1853. MarReg. m. 14 Sep. 1853. Gover.
Cross, John & Elizabeth Burgess. Daniel Ackers attests ages, bm.
    3 Sep. 1838. Cam.
Cross, John W., son of Susan Cross, who attests groom's age &
    Margaret A. Harper. William Harper, bm. 14 May 1844. Shel.
Cross, William, Dr. & Mary James. Robert James proves bride's age,
    bm. 12 June 1848. m. 14 June 1848, at home of bride's mother.
    Adie. Shel.
Crumbach, Johannes, single & Catharina Rahlerin. By license. m.
    31 Jan. 1813. ParReg A.
Crumbach, Solomon & Catharina Stautzenbergern, both single. By
    license. m. 3 March 1812. ParReg A.
Crupper, John T. & Cora Ann Beatty (Beaty). George W. Norris
    attests groom's age. William Beatty, bm. 12 Oct. 1846. m.
    20 Oct. 1846. Massey.
Crushen, Jacob & Sarah Russ, both single. By license. m. 12 Jan.
    1826. ParReg A.
Crusin, Samuel & Amanda White. Jacob Crusin attests groom's age.
    Thomas White attests bride's age, bm. 14 Aug. 1843. Shel.
Cullen, John & Winifred H. McCarthy. m. 21 May 1853. Eidson.
Cullihan (Cullahan), Peter & Catherine Specht (Speckt), widow.
    Andrew Henderson, bm. 25 July 1796. Littlejohn.
Culverhouse, James & Fanny Battson. m. 31 Dec. 1807. Williamson.
Cumings, James & Mary Bodine. m. 5 Jan. 1793. Littlejohn.
Cummar, John & Penelope Evans. m. 7 March 1815. Littlejohn.
Cummings, George H. & Harriett Haislip, ward of Thomas Coffer.
    Clerk of Fairfax Co. court certified that at Aug. Court 1835
    Thomas Coffer was appointed bride's guardian. William H.
    Brown attests groom's age, bm. 10 Jan. 1845. Shel.
Cummings, Gidion & Sarah Edwards. m. 13 Aug. 1805. Littlejohn.
Cummings, Harrison & Ansey Cummings. William Lyons attests ages,
    bm. 26 Nov. 1836. Shel.
Cummings, John & Margaret Emerson. m. 12 April 1813. Littlejohn.
Cummings, Norman & Hannah Urton. Jesse Lewis attests ages, bm.
    10 Aug. 1829.
Cummings, Robert & Mary Carter. Bride made choice of groom as her
    guardian 9 Jan. 1809. Thomas Carter, bm. m. 30 Jan. 1809.
    Littlejohn.
Cummings, William & Elenor Miller. m. 10 Feb. 1810. Williamson.
Cummins, John T. & Hannah Elizabeth Hains. Sanford Cockerill
    proves groom's age; bride's father consents, wit. 25 April
    1853. MarReg. m. 28 April 1853. Gover.
Cunard, John, son of Sarah Cunard & Elizabeth Potts, dau. of
    David Potts. m. 16 Dec. 1762. FFMM.

34

Cunnard, Luther C. & Amanda Bazzell, ward of John Chamblin.
11 Jan. 1830. Shel.
Cunningham, Robert & Elizabeth Settle. William Saffer attests
groom's age, bm. 14 Sep. 1829.
Currell, John J. & Armelia Humphrey. m. 1 Feb. 1820. Dagg.
Currie, Ellison A. & Sarah Frances Luckett, dau. of Horace
Luckett. Asher W. Gray Attests ages, bm. 24 May 1848. Shel.
Curry, John & Elizabeth Graham, dau. of Andrew Graham, bm.
1 March 1832. Shel.
Curry, Joseph & Nancy Wildman. m. 1821-1822. Mines.
Curry, Joseph A. & Leah Ann Conard. David Conard attests groom's
age, bm. 19 June 1843. m. 4 July 1843. ParReg A.
Curry, William & Elizabeth Taylor. m. 11 July 1815. Littlejohn.
Curtis, Thomas & Fanny Sinclair, ward of Hamilton Rogers, bm.
Alijah Sands, bm. 9 Jan. 1809.
Dagg, Samuel D. & Elizabeth Dutro. m. 10 April 1817. Williamson.
Dagmud, John & Betsey Garret. m. 4 Aug. 1818. Williamson.
Dah, Johannes & Maria Schnal(?); both single. By license. m.
15 Jan. 1827. ParReg A.
Dailey, John & Elizabeth Smith. m. 5 Sep. 1803. Littlejohn.
Dailey, John W. & Frances J. Green, dau. of Thomas Green, bm.
m. 11 Dec. 1847. Shel.
Dailey, Samuel & Harriet R. Tucker. Landon W. Worthington attests
ages, bm. 30 June 1847. Shel.
Daniel, James, son of William Daniel & Hannah Seybold, dau. of
Jasper Seybold. m. 15 April 1778. FFMM.
Daniel, James & Rachel Carter. m. 24 Nov. 1803. Williamson.
Daniel, John H. & Catherine E. Rogers, dau. of Edwin Rogers, who
proves groom's age, wit. 13 Jan. 1853. MarReg. m. 18 Jan.
1853. Marders.
Daniel, Joseph & Tacy Humphrey. m. 22 Oct. 1795. Littlejohn.
Daniel, Lemuel & Frances A. Gouchenour, dau. of Elisabeth
Gouchenour. John R. Hibbs, bm. 24 Feb. 1845. Shel.
Daniel, Richard N., Fairfax Co. & Missouri Catherine Ann Cross,
dau. of Harrison Cross. S. S. Hodgson, bm. 12 Jan. 1848. Cam.
Daniel, Samuel & Frances A. Gouchehaur. m. 28 Feb. 1845. Herndon.
Daniel, Samuel & Sarah Hunt. m. 1 March 1806. Littlejohn.
Daniel, Stephen & Catharine McGeath. William Wright, bm.
20 March 1813.
Daniel, William & Nancy Hobbs. m. 1807-1808. Mines.
Daniel, William & Sarah Garrett. m. 29 Nov. 1821. Gilmore.
Danner, Joseph & Mary McKinley. m. 18 Dec. 1800. Littlejohn.
Darne, James T. & Mary Jane Havener. Thomas A. Havener proves
ages, wit. 6 Dec. 1852. MarReg. m. 7 Dec. 1852. Gover.
Darne, James W. & Emily Adiline Nichols. John W. Nichols attests
bride's age, bm. 1 Dec. 1845. m. 1 Dec. 1845. Gover. Shel.
Darnes, William & Barbara Saunders. m. 12 Feb. 1808. Saunders.
Darr, Enos & Emily Violette Speaks. James H. Sanders attests ages,
bm. 14 April 1845. m. 17 April 1845, in Maryland. ParReg A.
Darr, Lenard & Mary Musgrove. m. 1 Sep. 1810. Littlejohn.
Darr, Samuel & Margaret Shoemaker. Samuel Cooper attests groom's
age. George W. Shoemaker attests bride's age, bm. 8 June
1836. m. June 1836. Campbell. Shel.
Darr, Steward & Tabitha Ann Collins. Thomas Davis attests ages, bm.
19 Feb. 1840. Shel.

35

Darry, David & Nancy Wartman (?); both single. By license. m.
12 Jan. 1826. ParReg A.
Darry, Georg & Elisa Watson; both single. By license. m. 18 Nov.
1824. ParReg A.
Davason, John & Jane Helaffer. m. 27 Jan. 1820. Dagg.
Davidson, Frederick A. & Elizabeth D. Weekes. m. 18 May 1832.
G. Frye.
Davidson, Theodore N. & Sarah Rogers. Asa Rogers attests ages.
Charles G. Eskridge, bm. 14 March 1831. Shel.
Davis, Benjamin, son of Howell Davis & Sarah White, ward of Levi
White, bm. 25 Oct. 1830. Shel.
Davis, David & Patsey Edwards. m. 4 Feb. 1815. Littlejohn.
Davis, Edward & Elizabeth Triplett. m. 8 Aug. 1798. Littlejohn.
Davis, Edward & Mary Tillet, dau. of Giles Tillet, bm. 22 Nov.
1809. m. 1808-1809. Mines.
Davis, Edward P. & Elizabeth Klein. M. C. Klein attests groom's
age, bm. 16 Feb. 1844. Shel.
Davis, Elias & Charlotte Everheart (Everhart). Philip Everhart,
bm. 22 Oct. 1838. m. 25 Oct. 1838. Hauer. Shel.
Davis, Elijah & Peggy Pryley. m. 12 March 1808. Littlejohn.
Davis, Gidion & Ann Hughes. m. 14 Feb. 1803. Littlejohn.
Davis, Henry M. & Cathrine Ansell. m. 25 Jan. 1806. Littlejohn.
Davis, Hezekiah & Francis Brooks. Sampson Harper attests ages, bm.
2 June 1841. Shel.
Davis, Jacob, son of Thomas Davis & Susannah Beamer. Thomas Davis
attests bride's age, bm. 13 Feb. 1809. Littlejohn.
Davis, James & Mary Kile. m. 23 March 1807. Littlejohn.
Davis, Jeremiah & Catharine Weadon (Weedon). Ashton Weadon
attests ages, bm. 31 Dec. 1832. m. 3 Jan. 1833. Baker.
Davis, Johannes & Maria Kiefer; both single. By license. m.
13 Jan. 1829. ParReg A.
Davis, John & Elizabeth Hess. m. 11 March 1811. Littlejohn.
Davis, John & Malinda Davis. Presley Davis attests ages, bm.
6 Aug. 1838. m. 7 Aug. 1838. Hauer. Shel.
Davis, John & Martha Spring, widow. John Vincell attests groom's
age, bm. 19 Jan. 1846. m. 20 Jan. 1846. Shuford. Shel.
Davis, John & Sarah Hampton. m. 22 Aug. 1801. Littlejohn.
Davis, John M. & Ann Sweaney. 1793. Littlejohn.
Davis, Jonathan & Betty Keen. 18 Dec. 1764. Lic. FeeBk 1.
Davis, Joseph & Amey Powell. Benjamin Davis attests groom's age,
Peyton Powell, bm. 20 Nov. 1837. Shel.
Davis, Joseph & Permelia Longly. m. Feb. 1802. Davis.
Davis, Morris & Sarah Russel. m. 10 Nov. 1796. Littlejohn.
Davis, Norvell, Register No. 1252 & Elizabeth Thomas, Register No.
1061, dau. of Richard Thomas, bm.; both colored. 7 Oct. 1840.
Cam.
Davis, Peyton & Lydia Carlisle, dau. of Robert Carlisle, bm.
17 Jan. 1844. Shel.
Davis, Presley & Mary Ann Gladhill. John Griffith attests ages,
bm. 12 Jan. 1832. m. 19 Jan. 1832. ParReg A.
Davis, Samuel & Sally Marker. m. 1809-1810. Mines.
Davis, Solomon & Mary McIlhany. m. 1806. Mines.
Davis, Soloman & Rachel Hixon. m. 12 May 1800. Littlejohn.

Davis, Thomas & Barbara Kitzer (Kizer). Samuel McCutchen attests
bride's age, bm. 12 Jan. 1844. m. 18 Jan. 1844. ParReg A.
Davis, Thomas & Eve Firestone. m. 24 May 1800. Littlejohn.
Davis, Thomas & Lea Baal, dau. of Earlieg(?) Ball. By license.
m. 6 Jan. 1796. ParReg A.
Davis, Thomas & Mrs. Sarah Collins, widow. m. 30 March 1836.
ParReg A. Shel.
Davis, Thomas, Sr., widower & Elisabetha McGreth, single. By
license. m. 3 March 1814. ParReg A.
Davis, Thomas S. & Margaret A. Davis. John L. Davis attests ages,
bm. 6 Jan. 1845. Shel.
Davis, William & Catharine Betzer (Bitzer). Harmon Betzer, bm.
13 March 1809. m. 16 March 1809. Williamson.
Davis, William & Darcus Preston. Benjamin Shreve, Jr. attests ages,
bm. 19 Sep. 1837. Shel.
Davis, William, son of Gary Davis & Elizabeth Gaunt, dau. of
Samuel Gant. Wit: John Gaunt, Rachel Ann Gaunt. J. Binns, bm.
10 Dec. 1833. Shel.
Davis, Zepheniah & Polly Grey. m. 1 Feb. 1813. Littlejohn.
Davison, Nathaniel & Nancy McIlhany, dau. of James McIlhany.
Note says groom "is a stranger in this county". Charles
Binns, bm. 30 Sep. 1799.
Davisson, Frederick A. & Eliza D. Wickes, dau. of William Wickes,
bm. 18 May 1832. Shel.
Dawes, James & Sarah Saunders. m. 2 Dec. 1816. Littlejohn.
Dawis, Thomas, widower & Elisabeth Liemer, single. By license.
m. 20 Sep. 1820. ParReg A.
Dawson, James & Mary Hewit. m. 16 July 1800. Littlejohn.
Dawson, Richard & Winifred Allison. m. 1809-1810. Mines.
Dawson, Robert & Harriett Leedom. Isaac Leedom attests groom's
age, bm. 14 March 1842. Cam.
Dawson, William M. & Mary F. Dawson. James H. Gulick proves ages,
wit. 27 Oct. 1851. MarReg.
Day, John & Cathrine Booth. m. 23 April 1805. Littlejohn.
Daymud, John & Sarah Allison. m. 24 Aug. 1815. Williamson.
Daymude, Jacob & Eleanor Marsteller. m. 24 Dec. 1826. Williamson.
Daymude (Daymode), John H. & Catherine Wiley, dau. of Nancy
Crusur (Crusus), whose first husband is dead. 3 Oct. 1850.
MarReg. m. 3 Oct. 1850. Smith.
Deakins, Daniels & Mary Smith. m. 27 Oct. 1812. Littlejohn.
Dean, John W. & Sarah Skinner. Benjamin F. Skinner proves ages,
wit. 10 Feb. 1851. MarReg. m. 14 Feb. 1851. Eggleston.
Deaver, Daniel & Catharine Ritchie. m. 30 Oct. 1834. Hauer.
Deaver, Richard & Magreth Wild. By license. m. 18 July 1811.
ParReg A.
DeButts, Samuel W. & Julia A. Dulany, dau. of John P. Dulany, bm.
13 Sep. 1834. m. 16 Sep. 1834. Furlong. Shel.
Dedricks, Daniel & Elizabeth Murray. Samuel Jinkins attests bride's
age, bm. 29 Dec. 1849. Shel.
Deerborrow, James R. & Margaret Elizabeth Marlow, dau. of Thomas
Marlow. Draco Marlow, son of Thomas J. Marlow, attests groom's
age, bm. 21 Sep. 1849. Shel.
DeHaven, Jacob & Nancy Bell. m. 12 June 1797. Littlejohn.
Denagh, James & Keziah Jinkins. m. 26 June 1794. Littlejohn.

Denning, William H. & Margaret A. French. James W. Mankins proves
bride's age; "the other taken for granted". 1851-1853. MarReg.
Dennis, James B. & Harriet McAtee, dau. of Harrison McAtee.
Andrew Beveridge, bm. 19 Oct. 1829.
Dennis, Lewis & Oliva F. Dennis, dau. of William A. Dennis, who
attests groom's age, bm. 28 April 1831. Cam.
Dennis, Thomas & Ellice (Lettice) Downs. m. 14 Feb. 1805.
Williamson.
Densman, William & Sarah Hough, dau. of Garrett, who attests
groom's age, bm. 1 June 1831. Shel.
Derbin, Jesse & Lucinda Purcell. Wit: Burr S. Walker. 31 Jan.
1852. MarReg. m. 24 Feb. 1852. Nixon.
Derry, A. R. & Mary Derry. Lewis W. Derry proves ages, wit.
27 Nov. 1851. MarReg.
Derry, Jacob & Mary Ann Sarah Badgett, with Maryland license.
m. 13 March 1834. ParReg A.
Derry, Michael & Anna Barbary Kalb. m. 10 Aug. 1819. Keyes.
Derry, Peter & Elisha Wertz, dau. of Jacob Wertz. m. 4 March
1819. ParReg A.
Derry, Philip & Margaret Everhart. m. 30 Nov. 1796. Littlejohn.
Derry, Philip & Mary Elizabeth Painter, dau. of Jonathan Painter,
who attests ages, bm. 7 Jan. 1850. m. 10 Jan. 1850. Eggleston.
Shel.
Derry, Philip & Rachel Dowling, ward of bride who attests groom's
age, bm. 31 Jan. 1848. m. 3 Feb. 1848. Dulin. Shel.
Derry, Solomon & Maria Derry, dau. of William Derry. George
Derry attests ages, bm. 18 June 1834. m. 19 June 1834. Hauer.
Shel.
Derry, William, son of Jacob Derry & Barbara Rapp, dau. of Widow
Rapp; both single. By license. m. 26 March 1812. ParReg A.
Devers, Daniel & Catherine Ritchie. John Filler attests ages, bm.
29 Oct. 1834. Shel.
Dewein, William & Maria Bough; both single. By license. m. 8 Sep.
1815. ParReg A.
Dickey, John P. & Eliza Ann Mosbury. Otho Riggs attests ages, bm.
7 Feb. 1842. m. 7 Feb. 1842. Gover. Shel.
Diedricks, Daniel & Elizabeth Murray, at house of Mrs. Muse. m.
11 Jan. 1850. Adie.
Diggs, Whiten & Maria Ross. Special permission. m. 24 Jan. 1833.
ParReg A.
Dilloe, John & Elizabeth Darflinger, dau. of Frederick Darflinger
who attests groom's age, bm. 24 June 1809. m. 1808-1809.
Mines.
Dillon, Abner & Mary Oxley. m. 14 March 1796. Littlejohn.
Dillon, James & Ann Hatcher. m. 7 April 1785. FFMM.
Dillon, William & Sarah Bollen. m. 30 July 1814. Littlejohn.
Dimmy, Mortimer, "for age - see Register 1221" & Jane Fox,
Register 929; colored persons. Thomas W. Edwards, bm. 29 May
1841. Shel.
Dishman, Marcus & Mary Ann Violett, dau. of John Violett.
Thomas M. Winn, bm. 12 Dec. 1836. m. 15 Dec. 1836. Broaddus.
Shel.
Dishman, William & Esther Sinclair. m. 3 Jan. 1821. Dagg.
Divine, Aron & Nancy Surgenor. m. 11 May 1805. Littlejohn.

LOUDOUN COUNTY MARRIAGES

Divine, Bonham & Hanh. Burgoynon. m. 11 Sep. 1793. Littlejohn.
Divine, Charles William & Ann Noland Hurdell. George W. Hough
    attests bride's age. P. Saunders attests groom's age.
    Robert E. Divine, bm. 6 Feb. 1849. m. 8 Feb. 1849.Eggleston.
    Shel.
Divine, D. Mortimer & Susan Ann Birkit. Bride's father consents
    in writing. Groom's age "taken for granted". 9 Dec. 1852.
    MarReg.
Divine, George H. & Eliza Hough. Samuel Gover attests ages, bm.
    27 Aug. 1849. m. 28 Aug. 1849. Gover. Shel.
Divine, George H. & Tacey Myers. William W. Myers attests ages,
    bm. 7 Dec. 1844. Shel.
Divine, Jacob & Elizabeth Dodd. L. Dodd attests bride's age, bm.
    25 April 1831. Shel.
Divine, Jacob & Judith Rougue. m. 20 May 1811. Littlejohn.
Divine, James F. & Hannah E. Towner. Middleton Smith attests
    bride's age, bm. Aaron Divine, bm. 22 Jan. 1838. Shel.
Divine, Robert E., son of Jacob Divine & Emily Johnson, dau. of
    William Johnson. Alexander Johnson, bm. 29 Sep. 1845. Shel.
Divine, William & Cathrine Cremor. m. 26 March 1803. Littlejohn.
Divine, William W. & Eliza Ann Orrison, dau. of Catharine Orrison.
    William Milbourn attests groom's age, bm. 12 Feb. 1840. Shel.
Dixon, Joseph & Sarah Peacock, dau. of William Peacock, bm.
    14 Nov. 1831. Shel.
Dixon, Samuel & Eliza (Elizabeth) Smitley, dau. of Jane Smitley.
    Jacob Stontsenberger attests groom's age. Henry S. Williams,
    bm. 13 April 1840. m. 14 April 1840. Gover. Shel.
Dixon, Thomas & Milly Gladhill. m. 20 Nov. 1805. Littlejohn.
Dobson, Thomas & Sarah McClenan. Thomas Jefferson Stedman attests
    ages, bm. 12 Jan. 1850. Wills. Shel.
Dodd, James B. & Delila B. Fox. Dr. Joseph B. Fox attests bride's
    age. Samuel Dodd, bm. 23 Jan. 1832. Shel.
Dodd, James W. & Elizabeth F. McClenahan. Charles A. Ware attests
    ages, bm. 15 Dec. 1847.
Dodd, Jesse & Agnest Tribbe. m. 26 Aug. 1814. Littlejohn.
Dodd, John W. & Rachel Young. Ludwell Luckett consents for groom.
    John Young, bm. 26 Nov. 1834. Shel.
Dodd, Samuel & Catherine Smith. m. 27 Aug. 1812. J. Littleton.
Dodd, Thomas & Sarah Sample. m. 29 July 1760. FFMM.
Dodd, William & Hannah Pancoast. John Dodd, Jr. attests bride's
    age, bm. 12 Oct. 1799. Littlejohn.
Dodd, William & Martha Best. m. 2 Jan. 1804. Littlejohn.
Dodd, William & Mary Hunt. Ramey G. Sanders, bm. 11 Feb. 1830.
    Shel.
Donaldson, George R. & Patience Beans, ward of David Reece, bm.
    William McDonaugh proves groom's age. 23 Oct. 1847. m.
    28 Oct. 1847. Shuford. Shel.
Donaldson, Stephen & Nancy Littleton. m. 4 April 1795. Littlejohn.
Donham, Amos & Anna Gheen. m. 23 Nov. 1803. Dunn. Cam.
Donohoe, George & Sarah Tillett. Thomas Moss, guardian, bm.
    13 Dec. 1830. Cam.
Donohoe, Stephen & Rachel Harper. m. 1 June 1807. Littlejohn.
Dornon, Andrew & Anna Parker. License: 24 Dec. 1810. m. 30 Dec.
    1810. T. Littleton.

Dorrell, George William & Mary Ann Bozell, dau. of Susan Bozell. John A. Binns, bm. 25 July 1836. Shel.

Dorrell, John & Margaret Dulaney. m. 23 June 1794. Littlejohn.

Dorsey, Alfred I. & Eleanor Moon. Isaac W. Moon attests bride's age. Allen M. Dorsey attests groom's age, bm. 7 Dec. 1833. Shel.

Dorsey, Presley K. & Hannah Reed. Allen M. Dorsey attests ages, bm. 22 Dec. 1834. Shel.

Douglass, Jonathan E. & Anna M. Moore. Wit: John Moore. 18 Jan. 1853. MarReg. m. 19 Jan. 1853. Hargrave.

Douglas, Levi & Jane Vanhorne. m. 23 Aug. 1803. Williamson.

Douglas, Patrick Hume & Evelyn Bird Lee. m. 1806. Mines.

Douglass, John & Sarah Piles. m. 31 Jan. 1793. Littlejohn.

Dove, William & Elizabeth Whaley, ward of William Whaley, bm. 11 Nov. 1833. Shel.

Dowall, Elisha & Ann Bitzon. m. 14 March 1803. Littlejohn.

Dowdell, Micajah & Elizabeth Simpson. m. 1 Aug. 1811. Dunn.

Dowden, Horace W. & Eleanora Smallwood. Thomas Lloyd Jones attests ages, bm. 22 May 1834. Shel.

Dowell, Albert B., son of C. Dowell & Ann E. Matthias. C. Dowell, wit. Col. N. Osburn proves bride's age, wit. 3 Nov. 1851. MarReg. m. 5 Nov. 1851 at Col. Osburn's Hotel. Adie.

Dowling, Daniel & Kitty McCabe. m. 19 June 1802. Littlejohn.

Dowling, Edward & Mary Demory. Edward Harding attests bride's age, bm. 1 July 1831. Shel.

Dowling, Henry M. & Harriet J. Haslett. David Ogden attests bride's age, bm. 13 April 1831. Shel.

Down, William & Ellender Archer. m. 10 Dec. 1820. Williamson.

Downer, James & Elizabeth Poston. m. 23 Nov. 1817. T. Littleton.

Downey, Samuel S. & Nancy Fiechter, dau. of George Fiechter, bm. 7 Sep. 1836. Cam.

Downs, Charles Fenton & Hester Daniel. Eli Pierpoint attests ages, bm. 25 Aug. 1832. Shel.

Downs, Henry & Cynthia Beans. Jesse Downs attests groom's age. James Beans, bm. 11 Dec. 1809. m. 28 Dec. 1809. Dunn.

Downs, James & Elizabeth McFarlen. m. 11 May 1801. Littlejohn.

Downs, Jesse & Sarah Swick. m. 21 Feb. 1813. McPherson.

Downs, John & Lydia Dulaney. m. 18 Aug. 1822. Chapman.

Downs, Noah & Mary Jane Hains, dau. of Edward Hains, who attests groom's age, bm. 6 March 1847. m. 9 March 1847. Gover. Cam.

Downs, Stephen & Mary Ann Ault. Presley Saunders attests ages, John Ault, bm. 23 March 1846. m. 24 March 1846. Gover.

Downs, Walter & Fornetta Wilson. m. 20 March 1813. McPherson.

Doyle, Charles & Nancy Combs. m. Nov. 1802. Dunn.

Dreher, Ludwig, son of Michael Dreher & Ann Maria Belz, dau. of Andreas Belz. By license. m. 5 Dec. 1798. ParReg A.

Drew, Dolphen & Abegail Hicks. m. 11 March 1810. T. Littleton.

Drish, Horatio & Elizabeth Weadon. Frederick Weadon attests ages, bm. 15 Nov. 1833. m. 19 Nov. 1833. Baker. Shel.

Drish, William & Barbara Stoneburner. m. 16 Jan. 1819. Griffith.

Dudgeon, James A. & Sarah Buffington. William B. Grubb proves ages, wit. 3 Sep. 1850. m. 4 Sep. 1850. Chenoweth.

Dulaney, Israel & Catharine Miller. George Miller attests ages, bm. 2 Aug. 1838. m. 5 Aug. 1838. Hauer. Shel.

LOUDOUN COUNTY MARRIAGES

Dulany, William & Rachel Wright. m. 18 Dec. 1807. Littlejohn.
Dulin, Alfred & Margaret Beveridge. Edward Hammett, bm. 13 Sep.
  1843. m. 14 Sep. 1843. Gover. Shel.
Dulin, Edward & Nancy Ellgin. m. 2 April 1804. Littlejohn.
Dulin, John & Reba. Elbin. m. 8 Dec. 1796. Littlejohn.
Duncan, Elzey & Emily D. Eidson, dau. of Jos. Eidson. " - said
  Duncan elderly." 5 Dec. 1850. MarReg. m. 5 Dec. 1850.
  Eggleston.
Duncan, John & Mary C. Spencer. Wit: John Wilsen. 28 Aug. 1852.
  MarReg. m. 31 Aug. 1852. L. Nixon.
Dunkin, John & Rachel Day. m. 20 Jan. 1822. T. Littleton.
Dunkin, William & Phebe Gibson. m. 14 May 1820. Williamson.
Dunn, Patrick & Elizabeth McKenney. Francis McKimmi (McKimeny)
  attests bride's age, bm. 12 Nov. 1799. Littlejohn.
Durham, Lee & Catey A. Binns. m. 29 Sep. 1796. Littlejohn.
Dusk, John & Ruth Dyer. m. 29 Dec. 1803. Williamson.
Dutton, John B. & Emma Schooley. T. M. Bond attests ages, bm.
  1 Sep. 1838. Shel.
Duval, Wilson C. & Harriet Jennings, dau. of Betsey Jennings;
  colored persons. John A. Binns, bm. 10 June 1834. m. 12 June
  1834. Dorsey. Shel.
Easton, James & Laura Ambrose, dau. of Robert Ambrose, bm. James
  McNeally attests groom's age, bm. 15 Aug. 1848. m. 17 Aug.
  1848. Gover. Shel.
Eaton, David J. & Mary J. (E.) Dailey. William Dailey attests ages,
  bm. 18 July 1832. m. 18 July 1832. Dorsey. Shel.
Ebel, George & Catharina Rollerin, dau. of Joh. Roller. m. 3 Jan.
  1785. ParReg A.
Eberhard, Daniel, son of Phillip E. and Scharlotta Eberhard &
  Catharine Wentzel, dau. of Johannes Wentzel and wife; both
  single. By license. m. 11 March 1819. ParReg A.
Eberhard, Jacob & Sarah Stock; both single. By license. m. 5 May
  1825. ParReg A.
Eberhard, Johannes & Sarah Printz; both single. By license. m.
  10 March 1825. ParReg A.
Eberhard, Joseph & Lidia Stock; both single. By license. m.
  2 May 1826. ParReg A.
Eberhardt, Jacob & Charlotta Baurin. m. 17 May 1786. ParReg A.
Eberhart, David & Elisabetha Haushaltern; both single. By license.
  m. 13 Feb. 1823. ParReg A.
Eberhart, William, widower & Susanna Nichkan, widow. By license.
  m. 14 Jan. 1817. ParReg A.
Eblin, Isaac & Elizabeth Wilson. m. 4 March 1806. Littlejohn.
Echart, Casper & Ann Gregg. m. June 1796. Littlejohn.
Edmonds, Sanford & Margaret Peirpoint. m. 26 Aug. 1816. Littlejohn.
Edward, Joseph & Elisabeth Conrad; both single. By license. m.
  13 Jan. 1814. ParReg A.
Edwards, Alpheus L. & Mary S. Washington. Presly Saunders, bm.
  2 Feb. 1848. Shel.
Edwards, Jacob & Elizabeth Vickers. m. 8 April 1819. Keyes.
Edwards, John & Catherine Cline. m. 25 Nov. 1816. Littlejohn.
Edwards, John & Jane Cummings. m. 23 Jan. 1796. Littlejohn.
Edwards, John & Susan W. McPherson. m. 8 May 1838. Tapler.
Edwards, Joseph & Lydda Dent Prim. m. 1809-1810. Mines.

41

Edwards, Joseph & Mary Dove. William Dove attests bride's age, bm.
11 Feb. 1850. Cam.
Edwards, Richard H. & Ann E. Edwards. Charles G. Edwards, bm.
2 March 1840. Shel.
Edwards, Samuel M. & Ann Saunders. m. 10 April 1811. Littlejohn.
Edwards, Thomas W. & Sarah E. Chichester, at St. James Church,
Leesburg. Charles B. Tebbs, bm. 1 Nov. 1843. m. 2 Nov. 1843.
Adie.
Egtcher, Cornielous & Mary Slack. m. 17 Oct. 1803. Littlejohn.
Ehmich, Johannes, widower & Anna Maria Sauder, dau. of late
Phillip Sauder and wife, Susanna. By license. m. 15 June
1823. ParReg A.
Eidson, Joseph & Francis Blincoe. m. 7 Nov. 1808. Littlejohn.
Eidson, Joseph & Nancy Skinner. Gabriel Skinner attests bride's
age, bm. 13 Aug. 1838. Shel.
Elder, Latimore & Catherine Silcot. m. 8 Feb. 1808. Littlejohn.
Elderkin, James K. & Sarah E. W. Conrad, at house of her father,
in Waterford. David P. Conrad attests ages, bm. 31 Aug.
1849. m. 1 Sep. 1849. Adie. Shel.
Elemmens, Sanford & Sarah Dickson; both single. By license. m
10 April 1825. ParReg A.
Elgin, Charles H. & Edmonia F. Swart. Both fathers consent in
writing. 20 Nov. 1851. MarReg. m. 20 Nov. 1851. Eggleston.
Elgin, Francis C. & Mary Fouch, dau. of Amos Fouch. William
Ball, bm. 4 June 1836. m. 16 June 1836, at house of bride's
father. Adie. Shel.
Elgin, Francis & Mary Jane Rogers, at house of her father,
Prince William Co., Va. m. 7 Aug. 1832. Adie.
Elgin, Gustavus, Jr. & Elizabeth Cross, dau. of James Cross, bm.
Wit: James Hamilton. 6 Nov. 1830. Shel.
Elgin, Joseph & Maria Walters.Thomas L. Hoskinson proves groom's
age. Bride's mother consents in writing. 24 Sep. 1852.
MarReg. Duncan.
Elgin, Robert & Margaret Elizabeth Currell (Curl), dau. of
Parmelia C. Lynn. Bride's an infant under 21 years. Charles
G. Eskridge, bm. 15 June 1846. m. 25 June 1846. Trott. Cam.
Elgin, William & Phobe Taylor, dau. of Mandly Taylor. Isaac
Harris, bm. 10 April 1797.
Eliason, Talcott, Dr. & Sallie Chunn. m. 5 Oct. 1848. ParReg B.
Elliett, Henson & Catharine Heskett. m. 2 Oct. 1831. Baker.
Elliott, Henson & Catharine D. Heskett. L. C. Cunnard, bm.
23 Sep. 1831. Shel.
Elliot, John, Jr. & Reba. Camble. m. 13 Feb. 1798. Littlejohn.
Elliot, Mathew & Elizabeth Vanskiver. 9 Jan. 1823. Dorsey.
Elliott, George & Elizh. Merrick. m. 20 Sep. 1805. Littlejohn.
Ellis, Elizer & Sarah McKinley. m. 9 April 1800. Littlejohn.
Ellis, Henry & Jane Combs. m. May 1815. Dunn.
Ellis, John & Nancy Humphries (Humphrey), dau. of John Humphreys.
John Ellis, Sr., bm. 7 Dec. 1799. Littlejohn.
Ellis, Samuel & Effee Ann McKim, dau. of James McKim, bm. 7 Feb.
1837. Shel.
Ellis, William R. & Rebecca Skinner. Alexander Skinner attests
bride's age, bm. 19 Aug. 1833. Cam.
Ellis, Zachr. & Elizabeth Loveless. 9 Dec. 1804. Littlejohn.

Ellmane, William & Maria Lenon. m. 25 Feb. 1842. Gover.
Ellmore, Charles, son of John Ellmore & Mary Rose. Richard Rose
    attests bride's age. John Ellmore, bm. 11 Feb. 1841. Cam.
Ellmore, Edward & Elizabeth Hatton, dau. of Benjamin Hatton.
    William L. Timms, bm. 21 June 1834. Cam.
Ellmore, Edward & Nancy Speaks. Boly Speaks, bm. 19 March 1799.
    Cam.
Ellmore, John & Elizabeth Ann Rose, dau. of George Rose, bm.
    13 April 1833. Cam.
Ellmore, John W. & Elizabeth Mills. Bride's father consents, wit.
    Charles W. Ellmore proves groom's age, wit. 10 Nov. 1851.
    MarReg. m. 11 Nov. 1851. Gover.
Ellmore, William & Maria Lemon. Joseph H. Bodine attests ages, bm.
    19 Feb. 1842. Shel.
Ellzey, William & Frances H. Westwood, ward of William Westwood,
    brother. Robert Armistead, bm. 4 March 1799. Cam.
Elwell, Aaron G. & Mary Marshall, dau. of Jacob Marshall. Nathan
    H. Janney, bm. 24 Oct. 1844. Shel.
Elwill, Eli & Catharine Milburne. m. 1807-1808. Mines.
Emberson, Thomas & Margaret Craven. m. 23 March 1820. Dunn. Shel.
Embrey, Richard H. & Margaret E. Caywood (Cawood). Francis M.
    Carter proves ages, wit. 2 Sep. 1850. MarReg. m. 19 Sep. 1850.
    Dashiell.
Emerson, John W. & Sarah E. Purcell. Fathers consent, wit. 9 Oct.
    1851. MarReg.
Emich, Frederick & Sarah Ann Wire, with Maryland license. m.
    2 Aug. 1842. ParReg A.
Emmick, Samuel & Molly Rodgers. m. 18 April 1808. Littlejohn.
Emrich, Adam, son of Jacob Emrich & Anna Maria Hackman, dau. of
    Peter Hackman; both single. By license. m. 4 April 1811.
    ParReg A.
Enders, Jacob & Catherine Luke. Wit: A. M. Moore. 5 June 1853.
    MarReg. m. 16 June 1853. Whittle.
Ervin, Levi & Sahra Davis; both single. By license. m. 12 Dec.
    1816. ParReg A.
Eskridge, Richard & Elizabeth Read, spinster. License: 12 June
    1764. FeeBk 1.
Etcher, Peter & Nancy Fowler. P. Saunders attests age. Alfred
    Dulin, bm. 21 June 1848. Cam.
Evans, Adam & Maria Allen; both single. By license. m. 6 April
    1820. ParReg A.
Evans, Daniel & Mary Evans, dau. of Jacob Hugeley, bm. 27 Aug.
    1796.
Evans, David & Jane Golden. m. 9 Jan. 1804. Littlejohn.
Evans, George & Sarah Thomas. m. 3 March 1796. Littlejohn.
Evans, Harvey & Nancy Grubb. John Grubb attests bride's age.
    John Earnest attests groom's age, bm. 23 Oct. 1833. Shel.
Evans, Jesse & Mary Gideon, dau. of Peter Gideon,bm. 9 Jan. 1809.
    Littlejohn.
Evans, John & Elizabeth Evans. 25 July 1821. T. Littleton.
Evans, John & Mary Jacobs. m. 13 Dec. 1796. Littlejohn.
Evans, John & Mary Loveless. m. 11 Jan. 1798. Littlejohn.
Evans, Jonathan & Louisa E. Locker. George Locker proves bride's
    age, wit. 5 Jan. 1852. MarReg.

LOUDOUN COUNTY MARRIAGES

Evans, Samuel, b. 2 March 1813 & Mary Ann Myers, ward of
Washington Myers, bm. Jonathan Painter, bm. Jesse Evans
signs, attests groom's age. 12 Dec. 1836. Shel.
Evans, Thomas A.H. & Mary Elizabeth Forrest, widow. Bushrod
Grigsby, bm. 2 Feb. 1837. Shel.
Evans, William & Elizabeth Bennett. m. 13 June 1813. McPherson.
Everhart, Christian & Elizabeth Fry. m. 1807-1808. Mines.
Everhart, Israel & Maria Ropp. m. 1 Dec. 1836. Hauer.
Everhart, John & Matilda A. Everhart. Solomon Everhart attests
ages, bm. 4 Jan. 1845. Shel.
Everhart, Joseph & Sarah Feitchter. Thomas Lambaugh attests
bride's age, bm. 21 Oct. 1846.
Everhart, Joshua & Elizabeth Wyatt, in Maryland. m. 13 April
1837. ParReg A.
Everhart, Michel & Christinia Wirtz. m. 6 Dec. 1800. Littlejohn.
Everhart, Nathaniel W. & Darcas Frits. m. 13 Sep. 1840. Larkin.
Everhart, Philip P. & Mary E. Crawford, dau. of Daniel T.
Crawford, bm. 19 Feb. 1849. m. 27 Feb. 1849. Dulin. Shel.
Everhart, Solomon & Sarah Ann Edwards, dau. of Joseph Edwards,
bm. Israel Everhart attests groom's age. 12 Oct. 1835. m.
15 Oct. 1835. Shel.
Everhart, Solomon, Sr. & Mary Ann Wenner, dau. of William Wenner,
bm. Solomon Everhart, Jr. attests ages. 1 June 1835. m.
4 June 1835. Hauer. Shel.
Everheart, Nathaniel W. & Darcas Frits. John Earnest attests
bride's age. Daniel Miller attests groom's age, bm. 10 Aug.
1840. Shel.
Everheart, William & Catharine Deakins. Oliver Edward attests
bride's age. Philip Everheart, bm. 13 Aug. 1838. Shel.
Evins, Adam & Sarah Geist (Geists). By license. m. 5 Oct. 1826.
ParReg A.
Ewell, Bertrand & Catherine B. Alexander. m. 7 Nov. 1798.
Littlejohn.
Ewell, John & Louisa S. Seeders (Seaders). Wit: John Seeders.
16 Nov. 1852. MarReg. m. 16 Nov. 1852. Gover.
Ewers, Ammon & Nancey Torbett. m. 6 Feb. 1821. Gilmore.
Ewers, Barton & Rachel Jurey. m. 12 Feb. 1798. Littlejohn.
Ewers, David & Mercy Baldwin. m. 24 Jan. 1795. Littlejohn.
Ewers, Franklin & Emily Jackson Gibson Baldwin, dau. of Ruth
Baldwin. Leonidas Peugh attests groom's age. Jonah Tavenner,
bm. 12 May 1845. Shel.
Ewers, Franklin & Virginia Furr. William G. Furr attests ages, bm.
8 April 1850. m. 10 April 1850. Eggleston. Shel.
Ewers, Jonathan & Mary Marks. m. 14 Dec. 1796. Littlejohn.
Ewers, Jonathan & Nancy McDaniel. Thomas Rogers, William Ewers,
bm. 13 March 1843. Shel.
Ewers, Jonathan & Phoebe Gregg. Abner Jury attests bride's age.
Townsend Jury, bm. 19 Oct. 1836. Shel.
Ewers, Jonathan & Sarah James. m. 21 Nov. 1804. Littlejohn.
Ewers, Richard & Lydia James m. 15 Feb. 1815. Littlejohn.
Ewers, Robert & Martha Gregg. m. 27 Dec. 1810. Dunn.
Ewers, William & Eliza E. Thatcher. William H. Poulton attests ages,
bm. 20 Feb. 1845. Shel.
Ewers, William & Nancy Blakely. m. 6 Nov. 1821. Dagg.

LOUDOUN COUNTY MARRIAGES

Eytcher, Christopher & Rachel Barshers. m. 9 Dec. 1806.
Littlejohn.
Fadely, Charles F. & Orra Moore Drish. William D. Drish, bm.
7 Sep. 1842. Shel.
Fadley, Jacob & Mary McNeledge. James McNedledge, bm. 5 Jan. 1799.
Littlejohn.
Fahly, Jacob, son of Johannes Fahly & Barbara Neisin, dau. of
Dewald Nies; both single. By license. m. 28 March 1792.
ParReg A.
Fainsworth (Farnsworth), Daniel & Sarah Hiskett. Stephen Mahaney
attests bride's age, bm. 11 Dec. 1788.
Fairfax, John W., ward of Joseph Janney & Mary Jane Rogers. M. M.
Lewis, bm. 26 Sep. 1848. Shel.
Falley, George & Mary Wolf. Thomas Shaffar attests bride's age,
bm. 18 Feb. 1791.
Falley, Jacob & Barbara Neise. John Fally attests bride's age,
bm. 26 March 1792.
Falton, Maky (Makey) & Plezy Hague, dau. of Amos Hague. Israel
Phillips attests groom's age, bm. 20 Feb. 1809.
Farlow, John & Mary Suddoth. Thomas Fouch, bm. 23 Oct. 1784.
Farmer, Philip & Sarah Wilkison. m. 17 Dec. 1820. Gilmore.
Farnsworth, Daniel & Elizabeth Johnson. m. 22 April 1810.
T. Littleton.
Farr, Elijah & Sarah Potts. m. 24 June 1824. T. Littleton.
Farr, Stephen D. & Mary Ann Bardon, dau. of James Barden. J.
Stanhope attests groom's age, bm. 15 May 1841. Cam.
Faucit, John & Hannah Bateman. m. 16 Aug. 1809. Littlejohn.
Fauntleroy, Charles M. & Janet P. Knox, dau. of Thomas P. Knox,
bm. 18 Jan. 1847. m. 19 Jan. 1847. Boyd. Shel.
Fawcett, Elisha & Rebecca Janney. m. 28 May 1829. Taylor, Clerk.
Fawley, Anthony & Catherine Snutts. m. 11 Jan. 1796. Littlejohn.
Fawley, Jacob & Elizabeth Magaha. John Magaha attests ages.
Thomas W. Edwards, bm. 20 Jan. 1846. m. 22 Jan. 1846.
ParReg A. Shel.
Fawley, John & Edith Titus. Tunis Titus attests bride's age, bm.
6 June 1837. m. June 1837. Campbell. Shel.
Fawley, John & Margaret Newlon. Adam Wolf attests bride's age, bm.
10 Aug. 1787.
Fawley, Joseph & Aryann Catherine Cordell, dau. of Adam Cordell,
bm. 2 Nov. 1846. m. 3 Nov. 1836. ParReg A. Shel.
Fawley, Peter & Susanna Spring. m. 20 Feb. 1800. Littlejohn.
Fawley, William & Elizabeth Compher, dau. of John Compher, bm.
25 Jan. 1836. m. 28 Jan. 1836. Hauer. Shel.
Feagan, James & Mary McCrae. m. 22 Dec. 1836. White.
Feagan, Nicholas & Nancy Stone. Bride states she's between 29 and
30 years of age. Stephen Hehir, bm. 22 Aug. 1796.
Feagans, Daniel & Jane Virts, dau. of William Virts, who attests
groom's age, bm. 26 Dec. 1832. Shel.
Feagans (Figgins), James & Mary Ann McCrae. Joseph Nichols attests
bride's age, bm. 17 Dec. 1836. Shel.
Feagans, Silas H. & Sarah J. Wilder. John W. Shipley attests
groom's age, bm. Henry Wilder, bm. 11 July 1842. Shel.

45

Feagins, William H. & Elizabeth Thompson. Lorenza Thompson
    attests bride's age. James Feagins attests groom's age, bm.
    26 Dec. 1838. Shel.
Fearce, Cline & Jane Wilson. m. 12 Feb. 1806. Littlejohn.
Fearst, John & Catharine Miller. m. 27 May 1805. Littlejohn.
Fearst, John & Michel (Micheal) Myers. William Harrison attests
    bride's age, bm. 1 Nov. 1796. m. 3 Nov. 1796. Littlejohn.
Feaster, George & Laura Jane Curry, dau. of Robert Curry, bm.
    Alexander Poland attests groom's age. 8 March 1849. m.
    8 March 1849. Gover. Shel.
Fegin (Feagins), Daniel & Violet Combes, dau. of Joseph Combes.
    Christopher Metcalfe, bm. 3 Feb. 1767.
Feitchter (Fichter), George & Sarah Thomas. James McManaman
    attests ages, bm. 11 March 1809.
Felingame, Benjamin F. & Elizabeth Jane Thyer. Catesby Jones
    attests bride's age, bm. 7 April 1831. Shel.
Fenton, Enoch & Ruth E. Nichols. Thomas Nichols, bm. 17 Aug.
    1847. Shel.
Fenton, John & Mary M. Steer. m. 28 Sep. 1825. FFMM.
Fenton, John W. & Frances C. Barton, dau. of Sarah Barton. John
    Weadon attests groom's age, bm. 22 May 1843. Shel.
Fergerson, Romulus & Catharine F. Ayres, dau. of Samuel Ayres.
    John F. Allen, bm. 21 May 1850. Cam.
Ferguson, Amos & Mary Curtis. m. 24 May 1814. Dunn.
Ferno, John & Sarah Antes. Samuel Orrison, Jr. attests ages, bm.
    6 Sep. 1838. Shel.
Fever, Benjamin & Pamela Stephens. Edward Stephens attests bride's
    age, bm. 1 March 1787.
Fichter, George & Sarah Thomas. m. 10 March 1809. Saunders.
Fidler, John & Rebeccah Lambert, widow. Stephen Rozell declares
    bride's age, bm. 15 July 1786.
Field, John & Margaret Pearle. William Pearle, bm. 3 Nov. 1767.
Field, Timothy & Rachel Walker. m. 22 Jan. 1818. Williamson.
Fields, James & Maria Richardson. Martha Fields consents. William
    Taylor attests bride's age, bm. 1 March 1836. m. 3 March 1836.
    Broaddus. Shel.
Fields, Luke & Catharine Shell. Alfred Jones attests ages, bm.
    James Wilson, bm. 11 May 1840. Shel.
Fields, William & Elizabeth Jones, dau. of John Jones, bm. 14 Sep.
    1773.
Filler, _____ & Margaret A. Filler. m. 6 March 1851. Startzman.
Filler, Armistead T. M. & Lydia M. Stuck, dau. of Mary M. Stuck.
    Samuel E. Washington, bm. 24 Dec. 1849. Shel.
Filler, Benjamin & Mary Hines. John Wine attests bride's age, bm.
    12 March 1832. Shel.
Filler, Frederick & Elizabeth Cordell, dau. of Adam Cordell who
    attests groom's age, bm. 22 March 1809.
Filler, Frederick & Catharine Cordell. m. 1806. Mines.
Filler, Jacob & Mary Ann Filler, dau. of Michael Filler, wit.
    Samuel Filler proves groom's age, wit. 1 March 1851. MarReg.
Filler, John & Catherine Crumbacker. Jacob Crumbacker attests
    bride's age, bm. 1 Feb. 1799. Shel.
Filler, John C. & Ann Riley. Jacob Shaffer attests bride's age, bm.
    4 Oct. 1836. m. 6 Oct. 1836. Hauer. Shel.

Filler, John M. & Emily Ann Divine, dau. of William Divine, who attests groom's age, bm. 24 July 1841. Shel.

Filler, Samuel & Mary Elizabeth Spring. m. 26 Nov. 1848. ParReg A.

Filler, Solomon & Juliet F. Divine, dau. of William Divine, who attests groom's age, bm. 16 Feb. 1846. m. 26 Feb. 1846. ParReg A. Shel.

Finch, Colvin & Sinah Simmonds. John Ritchie, bm. 3 Dec. 1782.

Firth, George & Elizabeth Turner. m. 10 Aug. 1807. Littlejohn.

Fisback, Wailliam & Anne Edwards. m. 7 June 1809. Littlejohn.

Fish, Henry & Mary Ann Burson, dau. of Laban Burson. Wit: Cyrus Burson, John Burson. John Burson, bm. 10 Sep. 1832. Shel.

Fish, Robert & Mary Ann Lumm, dau. of John Lumm, bm. Joshua Nichols affirms groom's age. 1 Oct. 1833. Shel.

Fishback, James N. & Sarah Hanson, widow. Archibald Wilson, bm. 17 March 1795.

Fisher, Michael & Catharine Ruse. Christian Ruse, bm. 11 Oct. 1802. Littlejohn.

Fisher, Nelson & Mahulda Brooks. Benjamin Brooks attests bride's age, bm. 17 Dec. 1834. Cam.

Fitsimmons, James & Mary Kelly. Conn O'Neale attests bride's age, bm. 5 Feb. 1793.

Fitzhugh, Nathaniel & Hannah Lane, dau. of William Lane. Joseph Kelley, bm. 1 Feb. 1796. Cam.

Fitzhugh, Thomas L. & Sally E. Powell. m. 7 Aug. 1820. Williamson.

Flagg, Thomas & Martha Ransom. Josiah White, Jr. attests bride's age, bm. 9 Oct. 1792.

Flanegan, John & Betsey Cunnard. Hopkins Rice attests ages, bm. 29 Aug. 1792.

Fleetwood, Isaac & Sarah Rider. Michael Kenselo attests bride's age, bm. 13 Feb. 1790.

Fleming, George & Ann Otley, dau. of James Otley. William Fleming attests groom's age, bm. 7 March 1833. Shel.

Fleming, Sanford & Sarah Blinco. m. 9 March 1845. Gover.

Fleming, William & Sarah Gibson. m. 23 March 1826. Williamson.

Fletcher, John G. & Alice J. Fletcher. Joshua Fletcher attests ages, bm. 23 April 1846. m. 24 April 1846. Hayes. Shel.

Fletcher, Joshua & Marcia Lanham. m. 27 Sep. 1824. Dagg.

Fling, George & Amelia Lattimore. Leven Knotts attests bride's age, bm. 12 April 1791.

Fling, George W. & Susan Tillett. Joseph Blincoe, Jr. attests ages, bm. 4 Jan. 1849. Cam.

Fling, James T. & Sarah E. Lyon. Wit: Alexander Lyon. 18 Dec. 1852. MarReg. m. 21 Dec. 1852. Helm.

Fling, Sandford & Sarah Blincoe. Richard H. Presgraves attests ages, bm. 3 March 1845. Cam.

Fling, William & Ann Lattimore. Samuel Jackson attests bride's age, bm. 13 Dec. 1787.

Flinn, George & Evelina Wilson, dau. of John Wilson. Levi G. Ewers, bm. 9 Feb. 1829. m. 19 Feb. 1829. Williamson.

Florance, George N. & Mariah E. Moors. Wit: James W. Mankins. 12 Dec. 1853. MarReg.

Florence, Albert B. & Catherine L. Skinner, dau. of Amos Skinner, who attests groom's age, bm. 14 Feb. 1833. Cam.

Florence, George N. & Mariah L. Moore, at Eagle Hotel, Leesburg.
m. 15 Dec. 1853. Cross.

Floriday, Patrick & Cassander Allison. Richard Allison, bm.
7 March 1792.

Flowerie, French & Sarah Darr. m. 20 Feb. 1803. Dunn.

Flowers, John & Catharine Monroe. m. 10 July 1828. Tippett.

Flowers, Thomas & Margaret Smith. John A. Binns, bm. 15 May 1833.
m. 28 May 1833. Dorsey. Shel.

Floyd, James & Permelia Anderson. m. 15 Aug. 1816. T. Littleton.

Floyd, Lewis & Jane Duval. m. 14 May 1818. Williamson.

Floyd, William & Hannah Vance, dau. of James and Margaret Watkins
(Wattkins). William Grimes, bm. 5 Oct. 1790.

Foley, Enoch & Martha Skinner. Nathaniel Skinner attests bride's
age, bm. 23 Nov. 1841. Cam.

Foley, William & Abigale James. David James attests ages, bm.
9 Feb. 1835. Cam.

Follen, Daniel & Hannah Ewers. m. 7 Jan. 1823. Dunn. Shel.

Folley, Aquila & Anna Babe. m. April 1811. Dunn.

Forbet, Thomas & Ruth Furguson. m. 28 Jan. 1795. Littlejohn.

Forbs, John & Ann Evelina. m. 26 Dec. 1797. Littlejohn.

Forbs, Martin & Rebekah Wilson. Robert Wilson, bm. 31 March 1797.
m. 4 April 1797. Littlejohn.

Ford, Elijah & Rosanna Randolph. "Freedom proved as well as ages
by certificates of Freedom." John W. Moore, bm. 24 Sep. 1849.
m. 25 Sep. 1849. Gover. Shel.

Ford, Richard & Martha Thomas. Levi White, bm. 3 Nov. 1849. m.
8 Nov. 1849. Gover. Shel.

Ford, William & Mellion Simson, dau. of Richard Simpson. Thomas
Cockerill attests bride's age, bm. 29 Oct. 1792.

Foreman, Lewis & Elizabeth Fox, dau. of Samuel Scott who says
she is 22 years old 1st June next. Wit: Robert Scott.
Benjamin Wiggenton, bm. 18 Feb. 1781.

Foreman, William & Sarah Dodd. m. 6 Aug. 1801. Littlejohn.

Forest, Luke S. & Mary Ann Middleton, widow. John M. Wilson, bm.
28 Nov. 1836. Shel.

Forrest, Luke S. & Mary Kendle. French Thompson attests bride's
age, bm. 10 May 1841. Shel.

Forsythe, William & Louisa Jane Steadman, dau. of John Stedman.
T. J. Steadman attests groom's age, bm. 19 Dec. 1843. m.
19 Dec. 1843. Gover. Shel.

Fortney, John & Mary Langley. John H. Riddle attests groom's age.
Alexander Langley, bm. 26 Feb. 1817. Shel.

Fossett, John & Hannah Batement. John Bartlett attests ages, bm.
16 Aug. 1809.

Foster, William & Phoebe Guilder. m. 3 March 1822. T. Littleton.

Foster, William H. & Rachel Hibbs, widow. Thomas A. Drean attests
groom's age, bm. 14 April 1829. m. 16 April 1829. Williamson.

Fouch, Abraham & Nancy Sedgwick, widow. John Curry (Corry), bm.
31 March 1787.

Fouch, Amos & Ann Combs. m. Jan. 1809. Dunn.

Fouch, Amos & Ellen Stephens. Gustavius Elgin attests bride's age.
Lewis Cross, bm. 7 Oct. 1837. Shel.

Fouch, Amos & Ellen Stephens. Isaac Torreyson attests bride's age.
bm. 17 Oct. 1837. Shel.

LOUDOUN COUNTY MARRIAGES

Fouch, Amos & Sarah McGuygan. William Rollings attests bride's
age, bm. 1 Jan. 1833. Cam.
Fouch, Daniel & Sarah Hawling. m. 22 Jan. 1801. Littlejohn.
Fouch, Daniel T. & Mary Margaret Hough, dau. of Mary Hough. Leven
W. S. Hough, bm. 21 Feb. 1846. Shel.
Fouch, Isaac & Mary Steadman. m. 12 Aug. 1816. Littlejohn.
Fouch, Isaac, Jr. & Nancy Coxen, alias Halling. Thomas Fouch
attests bride's age, bm. 23 Sep. 1792.
Fouch, Jacob & Perence (Peunce) McDaniel. William Williams
attests bride's age, bm. Wit: W. Bronaugh, Jr. 1 March 1786.
Fouch, Jonathan & Chloe McDaniel. Stephen Emrey attests bride's
age. Aaron Sanders, bm. 6 May 1795.
Fouch, Temple & Rebecca Torrison. William Torrison attests ages,
bm. 21 Jan. 1839. Shel.
Fouch, Thomas & Sarah Coombs, dau. of Jno. Coombes. Joseph Combs,
bm. 8 June 1779.
Fouch, Thompson & Nancy Davis. m. 29 Jan. 1811. Littlejohn.
Fouck (Fouch), Amos & Ellen Stephens, at house of Mr. Rollins,
overseer to Mrs. Blincoe, near Goose Creek. m. 17 Oct. 1837.
Adie.
Fout, George & Margaret Pickings, in Maryland. m. 5 April 1838.
ParReg A.
Fowke, William & Mary Mason Bronaugh. R. D. Fowke, bm. 2 Oct.
1792.
Fowke, William L. & Margret Saunders, widow. m. 20 July 1813.
Henkle.
Fowler, Aron & Sarah Rollins. m. 22 Nov. 1800. Littlejohn.
Fowler, Meoren & Susannah Moxley. Daniel Moxley attests bride's
age, bm. 25 Dec. 1788.
Fox, Alfred & Mary F. Carroll. Bride's father consents, wit.
27 Oct. 1851. MarReg.
Fox, Alfred & Sarah Ann Lucas. Henry Parker, bm. 28 April 1842.
Shel.
Fox, Ambrose & Hannah James. Jonathan Swindler, bm. 12 Jan. 1790.
Cam.
Fox, Ambrose & Sarah McManaman. James McManaman (McMamamy) attests
bride's age, bm. 27 June 1797.
Fox, Amos, Jr. & Mary Hutchison. Joseph Fox asks certificate for
groom. Jeremiah Hutchison, Jr. asks certificate for bride.
Sam. Riddle, bm. 6 Aug. 1795.
Fox, Asa & Mary Kenanck. Thornton Kinanck (Kendrick) attests
bride's age, bm. 2 Feb. 1795.
Fox, Bartletson (Barlettson) & Elizabeth Baden (Braden). William
Fox, bm. 11 Feb. 1793.
Fox, Ezra & Mary Schryock. Michael Schryock, bm. 27 July 1799.
Fox, George & Amanda Ferrill, sister of Nelson Ferrill who
attests bride's age, bm. Theodore N. Dawson certifies Fox
family mulattoes - free persons; also knows Ferrell family and
understands them to be free persons. Jonathan Petit and T. M.
McIlhany state Amanda is "now Free and that Her mother was a
white woman - (she) is the Daughter of Joseph Ferrill and
Dorcas Ferrill, Decd". 26 Dec. 1845. Shel.
Fox, George & Elizabeth Walker. Uriah Fox attests bride's age, bm.
30 March 1791.

49

Fox, George & Jane Hamilton. m. 28 Feb. 1816. Littlejohn.
Fox, George & Nancy Venander. m. 21 Aug. 1823. Dunn. Shel.
Fox, George K. & Francis Edwards. Tilghman Gore, bm. 11 July
    1831. Shel.
Fox, James & Rebeccah Jeans, widow. Francis Hereford, bm.
    9 June 1794.
Fox, James & Sarah Ann Pierce. Charles Binns, bm. 11 Nov. 1833.
    m. 30 Nov. 1833. Baker.
Fox, John & Nancy Mayer. m. 9 Sep. 1816. Dunn.
Fox, William & Hannah Pierce, dau. of William Pierce, who attests
    groom's age, bm. 27 Aug. 1831. Shel.
Fox, William & Mary Braden. William H. Harding, wit. James Fox
    attests bride's age, bm. 22 July 1790.
Fox, William & Mary Timms. m. 11 Nov. 1813. Littlejohn.
Fraizer, John & Elizabeth Hair. m. 30 Dec. 1814. Littlejohn.
Frame, James M. & Anna H. Brown. m. 20 May 1830. Taylor, Clerk.
Frame, James M. & Jane Roberts. Wit: Stephen Roberts. 18 March
    1853. MarReg. m. 22 March 1853. Gover.
Frances, Albert & Icey Blaker. William Shields attests ages, bm.
    3 Feb. 1840. Shel.
Francis, Bennett & Mary Ann Crupper, ward of Seth Smith, who
    affirms groom's age, bm. 15 July 1833. m. 18 July 1833.
    Furlong. Shel.
Francis, Edward & Ann E. B. Hamilton. m. 27 Nov. 1828. Tippett.
Francis, Richard & Maranda Lewis. James Hill attests ages, bm.
    5 Jan. 1839. Shel.
Francis, Thomas & Leannah Gulick. m. 9 Feb. 1826. Evans.
Francis, William & Mary Romine, dau. of John Romine. William
    Francis, Isaac Brown, bm. 6 Feb. 1787.
Francis, William H. & Mary E. Glasscock, dau. of Uriel Glasscock,
    bm. 10 Aug. 1837. Cam.
Frank, Samuel & Hannah Smith. m. 3 Jan. 1814. Littlejohn.
Franklin, Henry T. & Mary Ann Gear, widow. Joshua McDannah
    (McDonock) attests ages, bm. 17 July 1830. Shel.
Franklin, John W. & Martha A. Driscoll, dau. of Mary Driscoll.
    B. T. Franklin, bm. 8 July 1844. Shel.
Franklin, Joseph & Elizabeth Smyth. William Ferry (Farrey) attests
    bride's age, bm. 25 Feb. 1786.
Franklin, William & Mary Jane Lowe , dau. of Rector Lowe, bm.
    Benjamin Franklin attests groom's age. 13 Nov. 1839. Shel.
Franks, Benjamin & Nancy Ellen Gouchonouer. Jacob Gouchnauer, bm.
    30 April 1842. Shel.
Frasier, Herod T. & Nancy E. Littleton. Townsend Frazier proves
    J. K. Littleton's signature, wit. 28 May 1852. MarReg.
Frazer, Johannes, widower & Maria Wenner, widow. By license.
    m. 6 Dec. 1825. ParReg A.
Frazer, William & Mary Ann Thomson. m. 23 Oct. 1817. T. Littleton.
Frazier, Herod T. & Nancy E. Littleton. m. 1 June 1852. Hirst.
Frazier, James & Ann Dawson. m. 19 Sep. 1822. Gilmore.
Frazier, James L., son of John Frazier & Mary Grubb. William D.
    Grubb, bm. 26 Oct. 1841. m. 28 Oct. 1841. ParReg A. Shel.
Frazier, Moses & Phobe Race. Phillip Long chosen guardian by
    groom and bride, bm. 9 May 1809. m. 1808-1809. Mines.

LOUDOUN COUNTY MARRIAGES

Frazier, Townsend & Sarah Elizabeth Littleton, dau. of John T. L.
    Littleton. R. C. Littleton, bm. 10 Nov. 1845. Shel.
Freast, Conrad & Elizabeth Wilson. m. 21 Dec. 1802. Littlejohn.
Fred, Frank L. & Sallie J. Rogers. Thomas Rogers proves ages,
    wit. 29 Nov. 1851. MarReg. m. 3 Dec. 1851. Herndon.
Fred, John & Rachael Palmer. m. 25 July 1821. Dagg.
Fred, Joseph, son of Thomas Fred & Hannah Pierce. William
    Chambers attests bride's age, bm. 4 Dec. 1809.
Fred, Joseph, Sr. & Elizabeth Peyton. Joseph H. Fred attests
    bride's age, bm. 1 June 1837. Shel.
Fredd, Thomas & Elizabeth Torbart. James Torbart (Torbert)
    attests bride's age, bm. 2 Aug. 1788.
Freed, Henry & Catharine Clyce, dau. of John Clyce. Israel
    Phillips attests groom's age, bm. 21 Jan. 1809. m. 1808-1809.
    Mines.
Freed, Samuel, son of Henry D. Freed & Elizabeth Trammell.
    Thomas Templar, "this day chosen guardian" to bride, bm.
    Henry D. Freed, bm. 9 Aug. 1830. Shel.
Freeman, Howard C. & Courtney W. E. M. French. Daniel J. French
    attests ages, bm. 13 Oct. 1837. m. 15 Oct. 1837. Newman. Cam.
Freeman, Walter T. & Sallie A. Short. Bride's mother consents in
    writing. 1 March 1852. MarReg. m. 2 March 1852, at Mrs.
    Short's, Middleburg. ParReg B.
French, Daniel & Eunice Dunham, dau. of Amos Denham, who attests
    ages, bm. 14 Jan. 1800. Shel.
French, George & Susannah Moss, dau. of Thomas Moss, bm. 13 April
    1796.
French, James & Nancy Collins, orphan, neighbor of Joseph Lane,
    is between 23 and 24 years old. Lane lives at "Farmer's
    Delight". James Brady, bm. 18 Dec. 1793.
French, James & Nancy Triplett. m. 21 Aug. 1817. Williamson.
French, John & Catharine Carter, dau. of Richard Carter. Thomas
    Lewis, Jr., bm. 13 March 1794.
French, Lewis & Eliza Marshall. James Whitacre attests ages, bm.
    8 Feb. 1836. m. 15 Feb. 1836. Morgan. Shel.
French, Mason & Ann Lewis, dau. of Thomas Lewis, who signs
    consent, "myself & wife". Charles Binns, bm. 20 Jan. 1783.
French, Reuben & Catharine Watkins. Samuel Beavers attests bride's
    age, bm. 3 Jan. 1833. m. 3 Jan. 1833. Dorsey. Shel.
French, Thomas & Nancy Howell. John Howell, bm. 2 April 1795.
French, William & Martha L. Taylor. m. 22 Feb. 1814. Henkle.
French, William H. & Mary Ann Hanes, dau. of Mary Hanes. Hester
    Hurst attests groom's age. Thomas W. Hart, bm. 22 Jan. 1838.
    Shel.
French, William T. & Rachel A. Hough. William S. Wood attests
    ages, bm. 4 Feb. 1848. m. 8 Feb. 1848. Shuford. Shel.
Frey, Andreas, son of Peter Frey and wife & Elisabeth Schrey
    (Schreys). By license. m. 20 Jan. 1820. ParReg A.
Frey, Daniel & Christina Auchslein; both single. By license.
    m. 1 Dec. 1825. ParReg A.
Frey, Jacob, son of Peter Frey & Elisabeth Spring, dau. of
    Andreas Spring; both single. By license. m. 11 Feb. 1813.
    ParReg A.

51

Frey, Johannes, son of Phillip Frey and wife & Elisabetha
Auchslein, dau. of David Auchslein; both single. By
license. m. 17 May 1821. ParReg A.

Frey, Johannes, son of Peter Frey and wife & Maria Trittenbach;
both single. By license. m. 4 May 1820. ParReg A.

Frey, Johannes & Susanna Kehlerin. m. 8 May 1786. ParReg A.

Frey, Joseph & Margretha Phale; both single. By license. m.
22 April 1829. ParReg A.

Frey, Joseph Henrich, son of Widow Willemanin & Christina
Cooperin, stepdaughter of Engelbrecht. By proclamation.
m. 27 Oct. 1793. ParReg A.

Frey, Michael & Maria Heckman; both single. By license. m.
14 June 1827. ParReg A.

Frey, Noah & Susan Crim. m. 19 Dec. 1851. ParReg A. Shel.

Frey, Peter, elder of the congregation & Margretha Schwenckin,
dau. of late Michael Schwenck. By license. m. 19 May 1812.
ParReg A.

Frey, Peter, son of Peter Frey & Sarah Trittebach (Trittebachs).
By license. m. 4 Nov. 1824. ParReg A.

Fritts, Jefferson & Jane Day. Hector Osborne attests ages, bm.
15 Sep. 1832. Shel.

Fritts, William & Amy Ann Spates. John W. Hammerly attests ages.
John W. Hummer, bm. 12 Aug. 1844. Shel.

Fritz, George & Mary Hague. Stephen Donaldson attests ages, bm.
13 Aug. 1802. Littlejohn.

Fritz, John & Rebecca Chamblin. William M. Bollington appointed
bride's guardian this day and attests groom's age, bm.
11 April 1831. Shel.

Frizel, William Henry & Mary C. Hutchison (Hutcheson). James G.
Otley attests ages, bm. 11 March 1847. m. 18 March 1847.
Herndon. Shel.

Fry, Daniel & Susan Anderson, dau. of John Anderson. William
Galleher attests groom's age, bm. 24 Dec. 1838. Shel.

Fry, Isaack & Catharine Eggy; both single. By license. m. 11 May
1830. ParReg A.

Fry, John, son of Peter Fry, who says his son is more than 21
years & Sarah E. Baker, dau. of George Baker, bm. 1 Jan.
1849.

Fry, John H. & Mary Martha Cordell. m. 14 Jan. 1851. Startzman.

Fry, Joseph C. & Margaret Jane Ruse. m. 21 March 1850. ParReg A.

Fry, Nicholas & Margeret Ansell. m. 11 March 1794. Littlejohn.

Fry, Nonah & Susanna Crim. John H. Crim proves ages, wit.
16 Dec. 1851. MarReg.

Fry, Peter & Sarah Jacobs. m. 10 Dec. 1796. Littlejohn.

Fry, Samuel, son of Nicholas Frye & Christena Stoneburner.
10 May 1830. m. 8 June 1830. ParReg A.

Fry, Samuel & Genilla Beans. m. 22 Feb. 1813. Littlejohn.

Fry, William & Elizabeth Fawley (Phaley), dau. of Henry Fawley,
who attests groom's age, bm. 6 May 1831; both single.
m. 12 May 1831. ParReg A.

Frye, Isaac & Catherine Eakey, ward of John Fawley, bm. 10 May
1830. Shel.

Frye, John & Mary Dixon. m. 29 March 1811. Littlejohn.

Frye, John, who write German script & Susannah Keelin. Nicholas
Keedlar, bm. 6 May 1786.

Frye, John M. & Emily Crider. m. 11 Feb. 1819. Williamson.

Frye, Joseph & Margaret Fawley, dau. of John Fawley, who attests groom's age, bm. 16 April 1829.

Frye, Joseph C. & Mary Jane Ruse. John Ruse, bm. 18 March 1850. Shel.

Frye, Leonard & Susannah Spring, dau. of Jacob Spring. Henry Spring attests bride's age. Nicholas Frye, father of Mary Young, bm. 15 Dec. 1834. m. 18 Dec. 1834. ParReg A. Shel.

Frye, Martin & Susanna Davis. John Falley attests bride's age, bm. 10 Aug. 1835. Shel.

Frye, Nicholas & Margaret Ansell. John Erskins attests bride's age. Richard W. John, bm. 11 March 1794.

Frye, Peter & Sarah Jacobs. Thomas Jacobs, bm. 10 Dec. 1796.

Frye, Philip & Catharine Virtz. Conrad Virtz, bm. 1 April 1796. m. 5 April 1796. Littlejohn.

Fulkerson, Benjamin & Elizabeth Harper. m. 31 May 1810. Dunn.

Fulkerson, Josiah & Margaret Gheen. 13 Aug. 1804. Davis.

Fuller, John & Elizabeth Border. William Wenner, Jr. attests bride's age. William Wenner, bm. 23 Oct. 1790.

Fulton, David & Jane Carr. m. 1821-1822. Mines.

Fulton, David & Phebe Gibson. m. 6 Feb. 1826-9 Feb. 1826. Burch.

Fulton, George & Hannah Ball. m. 27 Feb. 1805. Littlejohn.

Fulton, Hugh & Susannah Lybough. Joseph Lybough attests bride's age, bm. 19 Jan. 1780.

Fulton, James & Sarah Stoneburner. m. 2 Jan. 1822-21 March 1822. Mines.

Fulton, John & Jane E. Taylor. m. 13 March 1827. Tuston.

Fulton, John E. & Massey Warner, dau. of Israel Warner, bm. William Butler, bm. 10 Aug. 1840. m. 10 Aug. 1840. Gover. Shel.

Fulton, Robert & Tacey Daniel, widow. Joseph D. Taylor, bm. 18 Sep. 1830. Shel.

Fulton, Robert, Jr. & Sarah Powell. Elisha Powell attests bride's age, bm. 11 Sep. 1792.

Fulton, Robert S. & Sarah E. Gore. m. 2 Jan. 1822-21 March 1822. Mines.

Fulton, William & Hanah Millan, dau. of William Millan. Daniel Howell, Thomas Millan, bm. 21 Sep. 1778.

Fulton, William & Martha Hawling, dau. of Isaac W. Hawling, wit. 24 Oct. 1852. MarReg. m. 26 Oct. 1852, at house of bride's father. Adie.

Fulton, William & Mary B. Elgin, dau. of Walter Elgin, bm. 2 April 1832. Shel.

Furginson, Samuel & Mary Bradfield. m. 27 June 1803. Littlejohn.

Furguson, Charles & Nancy Birchett. m. 14 July 1808. Saunders.

Furguson, Romulus & Catherine Ayres. John J. Hogeland attests groom's age, bm. 18 Feb. 1850. Cam.

Furguson (Forgizen), William & Phoebe Golden, ward of William Woodford, bm. 13 March 1809.

Furnace, John & Pircillia Patterson. m. 13 Aug. 1810. Littlejohn.

Furr, Ebin & Emily J. Moore, dau. of Peyton Moore, who attests groom's age, bm. 11 Nov. 1844. m. 14 Nov. 1844. Massey. Shel.

Furr, Enoch & Sarah Clawson. James Urton attests bride's age, bm. 5 March 1787.

Furr, Fenton & Susan E. Gill, dau. of John L. Gill. Leven P. Chamblin, bm. 2 Nov. 1839. Shel.

Furr, Henry & Mary Ann Chappell. m. 27 March 1849. Dodge.
Furr, Kemp & Mary Ann Chappell, dau. of James Chappell, "under
  age of Twenty one". Moses B. Furr attests groom's age, bm.
  21 March 1849. Shel.
Furr, Minor & Febe Roberts. m. 16 April 1813. Littlejohn.
Furr, Moses B., son of Moses and Margaret Furr, Clarke Co., Va.
  & Mary C. Anderson, dau. of Jeremiah and Mary J. Anderson.
  Bride's father proves groom's age, wit. 18 Nov. 1853. MarReg.
  m. 22 Nov. 1853. Ridgeway.
Furr, Richard E. & Octavio Franklin. Benjamin Franklin proves
  bride's age, wit. 15 Feb. 1851. MarReg. Wills.
Furr, William & Nancy Bates, dau. of Jesse Bates, bm. 23 July
  1799.
Furr, William G. & Mary Agnes Furr. Thomas G. Humphrey attests
  ages, bm. 14 Jan. 1839. Shel.
Gadsby, William & Jane K. Smith. Edmund Tyler, bm. 7 Dec. 1837.
  m. 7 Dec. 1837, in Aldie, in home of Edmund Tyler. Shel.
Gaines, William A. & Massey A. Osburn. Benjamin F. Stevens
  proves bride's age, wit. 1 Feb. 1851. MarReg. m. 6 Feb. 1851.
  Eggleston.
Galeher, John & Sarah Clark. m. 10 June 1813. Littlejohn.
Gallaher, Samuel N. & Phobey Owsley. m. 4 April 1805. Williamson.
Gallaher, William & Polly Clarke. John Donohoe attests bride's
  age. Alexander Waugh, bm. 28 Sep. 1799. Shel.
Galleher, David K., son of Sarah Galleher & Caroline Norton.
  Edmund R. Garrett attests bride's age, bm. 13 June 1837.
  Shel.
Galleher, Francis W. & Emily E. Stover, dau. of Edwin A. Stover,
  bm. 19 Jan. 1846. Cam.
Galleher, James W. & Elizabeth B. Rhodes. George Rhodes, bm.
  22 April 1844. Shel.
Galleher, Moses O. & Evelina Lovett. Daniel W. Lovett attests
  bride's age. William H. Galleher attests groom's age, bm.
  2 Dec. 1834. Shel.
Galleher, Thomas & Patsy Leith. m. 19 Dec. 1816. Watt.
Gallighar, George & Catherine McCuan. John Littlejohn attests
  bride's age. Joseph Longly, bm. 5 Nov. 1796.
Galliher, Thomas & Patsy Leith. m. 19 Dec. 1816. Watt.
Galloway, William & Patsy Bond. m. 13 June 1816. T. Littleton.
Galloway, Woodford & Harriet Andrews. Luther C. Cunard attests
  ages, bm. 5 Aug. 1832. m. 9 Aug. 1832. Baker. Shel.
Gant , Charles & Cornelia E. Aogans. Bride's father present and
  the man producing his free papers. 6 Dec. 1852. MarReg.
Gant, James W. & Ann Elizabeth McCarty, dau. of Florance
  McCarty, who proves groom's age, wit. 31 March 1851. MarReg.
  m. 3 April 1851. Gover.
Gant, Martin & Tacey Jane Hixson. Benjamin Hixson, bm. 30 Oct.
  1843. Shel.
Gardner, Andrew & Hannah Milner. Isaac Milner attests bride's age,
  bm. 5 Jan. 1799.
Gardner, Arthur & Ann Wagley. m. 24 June 1795. Littlejohn.
Gardner, James & Nancy Taylor. Bride's father consents in writing.
  Groom's age taken for granted. 10 Nov. 1852. MarReg.
Gardner, Leonard & Margaret Carnes. m. 11 May 1812. J. Littleton.

Gardner, William & Ann Gover. George Head, bm. 19 Sep. 1833. Shel.

Gardner, William & Sarah Harper. m. 1807-1808. Mines.

Garner (Gardner), Andrew & Hannah Milnor. Isaac Milner attests bride's age, bm. 5 Jan. 1799. Littlejohn.

Garner, Lewis & Nancy Dunkin. m. 18 March 1800. Littlejohn.

Garret, Stephen & Euphemia Beans. m. Dec. 1809. Dunn.

Garrett, Alfred & Eliza Beavers. m. 18 Dec. 1827. Chapman.

Garrett, Aren & Nancy Musgrove. m. 15 May 1812. J. Littleton.

Garrett, Barton & Mary McFaden. John McFaden attests bride's age, bm. Walter Woodyard, bm. 30 Oct. 1833. Shel.

Garrett, George L. & Elizabeth Rinker. Edward J. Rinker attests ages. Oscar F. Reed, bm. 10 Sep. 1849. m. 13 Sep. 1849. Eggleston.

Garrett, Israel & Mary Young, dau. of David Young, bm. 13 June 1836. m. 16 June 1836. Broaddus. Shel.

Garrett, John F. & Anna Bell Wilson, dau. of Charlotte Wilson. Thomas W. Edwards, bm. 20 Feb. 1844. Shel.

Garrett, Joseph & Elizabeth Harden, dau. of Elizabeth Harden. Levi Gulick attests groom's age, bm. 10 March 1834. Shel.

Garrett, Joseph & Margaret Garrett. Benjamin Garrett attests bride's age, bm. 11 Nov. 1791.

Garrett, Nicholas & Ann Furniss. m. 29 March 1816. Littlejohn.

Garrett, Richard Henry & Margaret McCarty. Giles Jackson, bm. 6 March 1849. Cam.

Garrett, Samuel & Abigail Cravans. m. 1807-1808. Mines.

Garrett, Samuel H. & Sarah E. Garrett. William H. Fitzhugh proves bride's age, wit. Thomas E. McCoole proves groom's age, wit. 12 Jan. 1852. MarReg.

Garrett, Stephen & Euphame Beans. James Beans attests groom's age, bm. 20 Nov. 1809.

Garrison, Lewis J. & Martha Alexander. Richard Alexander attests ages, bm. 1 Jan. 1846. m. 6 Jan. 1846. Benton. Shel.

Gassaway, Charles & Catherine Noland. m. 9 June 1825. Dunn. Shel.

Gaunt, George W. & Alice E. Rogers. Cuthbert Rogers, wit. 8 Aug. 1853. MarReg. m. 14 Aug. 1853. Marders.

Gaunt, John, son of Samuel Gant & Sarah Ann Watkins, dau. of Ann Brown. William Davis, bm. 5 Nov. 1832. Shel.

Gaver, John C. & Martha Ann Divine, dau. of William Divine, who proves groom's age, wit. 10 Feb. 1852. MarReg.

Geist, Johannes & Catharina Adams; both single. By license. m. 1 Jan. 1824. ParReg A.

Gellott, Coleman, of Baltimore, Md. & Mary Virginia Rust, dau. of General George Rust, Exeter. m. 2 April 1851. Adie.

Georg, Johannes, Jr. & Margretha Phahle; both single. By license. m. 17 Aug. 1828. ParReg A.

George, Isaiah H., of Jefferson Co. & Sarah F. Leach, ward of John Burket, Jr., who proves groom's age, wit. 13 Jan. 1851. MarReg. m. 16 Jan. 1851. Chenoweth.

George, John & Sarah Long. John Everheart attests ages, bm. 13 June 1840. Shel.

George, John, Jr. & Rosanna M. White. John H. White attests bride's age, bm. 27 Oct. 1834. m. 4 Nov. 1834. Frye. Shel.

George, Samuel & Eliza C. Grubb. Curtis Grubb attests groom's
   age, bm. 10 Nov. 1842. m. 15 Nov. 1842. Hauer. Shel.
George, Solomon & Mary Denges. Henry S. Wunder attests ages, bm.
   14 Sep. 1838. m. 13 Dec. 1838. Hauer.
George, Solomon & Sarah Ann Everheart, dau. of Philip Everheart.
   Solomon Everheart attests groom's age, bm. 22 Feb. 1834.
   m. 25 Feb. 1834. ParReg A.
George, Traverse & Esther Sinclair. m. 3 Jan. 1804. Williamson.
George, William & Phobe Carter. m. 15 Jan. 1807. Williamson.
German, Henry & Ruth Vanskiver. m. 28 Dec. 1826. Tuston.
Gest, Rector & Ann Shepherd. m. 26 Oct. 1812. Littlejohn.
Gest, Thomas, Jr. & Elizabeth Ashford. m. 30 Nov. 1808. Littlejohn.
Gheen, James & Winifred Bodine, dau. of John Bodine, bm. 28 March
   1836. Cam.
Gheen, Leroy & Rachel Young. Henry Young attests bride's age, bm.
   7 Jan. 1833. Shel.
Gheen, Thomas & Amey Gheen. Robert Power, guardian, bm. 9 Feb.
   1835. Cam.
Gheen, Thomas & Kathy Atwell. m. 21 March 1804. Dunn.
Gheen, Thomas & Nancy Harrop. James Harrop, bm. 13 Jan. 1809.
   m. 13 Jan. 1809. Davis.
Gibbins, Stephen & Catherine Swart. John Swart attests bride's
   age, bm. 14 Oct. 1799. Cam.
Gibbs, William & Catherine Harrop. m. 21 Aug. 1810. Davis.
Gibson, Abner & Margaret Smith. m. 11 Feb. 1808. Williamson.
Gibson, Abner & Susannah E. Powell. m. 27 Nov. 1828. Williamson.
Gibson, Allen & Mahalda Stillions, dau. of William Stillions.
   James Chappell attests groom's age, bm. 1 Nov. 1847. m.
   4 Nov. 1847. Dodge. Shel.
Gibson, Alpheus, son of Moses Gibson, Culpepper Co. & Harriet A.
   Aldridge, dau. of Doct. John Aldridge. Moses Gibson, bm.
   6 Oct. 1829.
Gibson, Israel & Alice Carter. m. 27 Nov. 1817. Williamson.
Gibson, James, son of Solomon Gibson & Mary Beans, dau. of
   Samuel Beans. Solomon Gibson, Samuel Beans, bm. 11 May 1829.
Gibson, John & Ruth Janney. m. 22 Feb. 1776. FFMM.
Gibson, Joseph & Maria Jenkins. m. 12 Jan. 1826. Evans.
Gibson, Joshua & Mary Ann McVeigh, dau. of Jesse McVeigh. James H.
   McVeigh, bm. 26 Dec. 1834. Shel.
Gibson, Moses & Lydia Leonard. m. 15 Feb. 1775. FFMM.
Gibson, Richard G. & Amanda Shumate. Bride's father consents, wit.
   William Fulton proves groom's age, wit. 12 Feb. 1853. MarReg.
   m. 15 Feb. 1853. Duncan.
Gibson, Samuel & Ruth Vickers. m. 13 Sep. 1827. Baker.
Gibson, Solomon & Jane W. Cooper. William Galleher attests bride's
   age, bm. 13 June 1836. Shel.
Gibson, Solomon & Reba. James. m. 27 April 1801. Littlejohn.
Gibson, Thomas E. & Mary Jane Tinsman, dau. of Nancy Tinsman,
   widow. James Chappell attests groom's age, bm. 24 Nov. 1845.
   m. Nov. 1845. Torrence. Shel.
Gibson, William & Sarah N. Smith. Lloyd Noland, bm. 23 May 1842.
   Shel.
Giddings, William, of Ohio & Ann Eliza Moffett. Robert Moffett
   attests groom's age, bm. 4 July 1846. m. 8 Sep. 1846, at home
   of her father near Waterford. Adie.

Gideon, George & Elizabeth Miller. m. 19 Aug. 1812. J. Littleton.
Gideon, William & Frances Booth. James Booth attests bride's age,
    bm. 17 Dec. 1836. m. Dec. 1836. Campbell. Shel.
Gilbert, Joseph H. & Ann E. Franklin. William Mercer proves
    bride's age. Robert Matthews proves groom's age, wit. 27 Jan.
    1851. MarReg. m. 4 Feb. 1851. Herndon.
Giles, John & Sarah Perfect. m. 13 Nov. 1811. Littlejohn.
Gilham, Thomas & Mary Triplett, dau. of Abel Triplett, bm. 14 Dec.
    1799. Shel.
Gill, Barnabas & Sarah Niel. m. 12 Dec. 1796. Littlejohn.
Gill, Daniel & Ann Vickers. m. Oct. 1802. Dunn.
Gill, Jerry & Tamer Dawson. m. 5 Dec. 1805. Littlejohn.
Gill, John L. & Catherine M. Furr, dau. of Minor Furr. John G.
    Humphrey, bm. 17 May 1836. m. 30 May 1836. Morgan. Shel.
Gill, John L. & Hannah Carter. m. 19 Feb. 1818. Dagg.
Gill, John L. & Mary Todd. William Beatty, bm. 16 June 1841. m.
    30 June 1841. Herndon. Shel.
Gillespey, Jacob T. (L.) & Susan W. Bennett. Nimrod Cummins
    attests ages, bm. Isaac B. Baldwin, bm. 9 March 1841. m.
    9 March 1841. Gover. Shel.
Gipson, Solomon & Jane W. Cooper. m. 25 June 1836. Morgan.
Glascock, Alfred & Margaret Carrington, widow. Roger Chew, bm.
    31 Oct. 1835. m. 3 Nov. 1835. Baker. Shel.
Glascock, Herod & Edith Chamblin. Mary Chamblin consents. Albert
    G. Chamblin, bm. 10 March 1834. m. 13 March 1834. Baker.
    Shel.
Glascock, Minor & Maria H. Keene. John Woolf attests ages, bm.
    11 Nov. 1844. Shel.
Glascock, Thomas P. & Catharine McIntyre. Benjamin Rust, Jr.
    attests ages, bm. 2 March 1830. m. 9 March 1830. Baker.
Glasscow, Henry & Cathrine Carnickel. m. 24 March 1803.Littlejohn.
Glosser & Sarah Tucker. Nicholas Tucker, bm. 9 Sep. 1799.
    Littlejohn.
Gochenour (Gochenauer), David & Elizabeth Blakely (Bleakley).
    William Blakely attests bride's age, bm. 5 Sep. 1840. m.
    8 Sep. 1840. Herndon. Shel.
Gochnauer, Jacob & Elizabeth Anderson. m. 16 Dec. 1819.
    Williamson.
Gochnauer, Joseph & Harriet Ann Davis, dau. of William Davis,
    who attests groom's age, bm. 3 Feb. 1832. m. 7 Feb. 1832.
    Green. Cam.
Godfrey, William & Mary E. Thomas, free colored people. Bride's
    father consents, wit. 28 Feb. 1853. MarReg. m. 8 March
    1853. Benton.
Goff, Adam & Leticia Daliham. C. Binns, Jr., guardian. Stacey
    Hains, Lettia Daliham, bm. 19 Feb. 1799. Littlejohn.
Gohr, Trueman & Lydia Georg, dau. of Johannes Georg and wife;
    both single. By license. m. 29 April 1819. ParReg A.
Goings, Peyton & Bitey Nighing. m. 12 Oct. 1808. Saunders.
Good, Alexander & Catharine Kyle. m. 10 June 1810. Williamson.
Goodhart, Henry & Mary E. Mason. Adam Mason, bm. 24 Oct. 1846.
    Shel.
Goodhart (Goodheart), Jacob & Polly Fawley, dau. of John Fawley
    who attests groom's age, bm. 27 March 1809. Littlejohn.

Goodhart, Washington & Sophia Emich. m. 11 March 1841. ParReg A.
Goodheart, Henry & Mary Elizabeth Mason. m. 25 Oct. 1846.
    ParReg A. Shel.
Goodheart, John & Lucinda Rhodes. Spence Minor attests bride's
    age, bm. 12 Sep. 1836. m. 13 Sep. 1836. ParReg A. Shel.
Goodheart, Washington & Sophia Emich. Frederick Eamick attests
    ages, bm. 8 March 1841. Shel.
Goodin, Robert F. & Lettice Vermillian. Joseph Shugars attests
    ages, bm. 6 Jan. 1837. Shel.
Gooding, David & Ann Birdsall. m. 27 Dec. 1806. Littlejohn.
Gooding, David & Susnh. Smallwood. Anthony Wright affirms
    bride's age. Charles Binns, Jr., bm. 5 Sep. 1799. Littlejohn.
Gooding, William & Lucretia Smallwood. m. 17 March 1802.
    Littlejohn.
Goodridge, Philip & Nancy Jacobs. John Rose attests bride's age.
    John Moore attests groom's age, bm. 31 Aug. 1829.
Goodwin, William & Sally Myres. m. 21 July 1806. Littlejohn.
Gooley, Jacob & Margaret Shively. Cornelius Morgan attests ages,
    bm. 6 Jan. 1809. Littlejohn.
Gorden, John & Elizabeth Randal. m. 26 Dec. 1826-28 Dec. 1826.
    Burch.
Gordon, Samuel G. & Martha Margaret Clarke. John H. T. Clark, bm.
    11 June 1838. m. 12 July 1838. Broadus. Shel.
Gordon, Wellington & Fars. A. Powell. William H. Gray, bm.
    5 June 1843. Shel.
Gore, Jacob & Mary Barruck. John Barruch, bm. 18 Aug. 1797.
Gore, Joseph & Catharine Lightfoot, widow. Thomas R. Saunders,
    bm. 30 June 1835. Shel.
Gore, Joshua & Frances Cockerill. 7 Aug. 1810. m. 12 Aug. 1810.
    T. Littleton.
Gore, Joshua & Susanna Clark. m. 14 Jan. 1793. Littlejohn.
Gore, Mark & Elizabeth Geddy. 12 Feb. 1810. m. 22 Feb. 1810.
    T. Littleton.
Gore, Solomon & Rachel March. m. 25 Oct. 1800. Littlejohn.
Gore, Thomas & Mary Ann Webb. Peter Gore attests ages, bm.
    28 July 1846. Shel.
Gore, Thomas & Permelia Osborn. m. 10 Dec. 1811. Littlejohn.
Gore, Tilghman & Ruana Elgin, widow. James Hamilton, bm. 11 July
    1831. Shel.
Gore, William & Sarah Ann Swann. James M.Swann attests ages, bm.
    1 March 1841. Shel.
Gossum, William & Elizabeth Buckley. m. 25 Dec. 1797. Hoskinson.
Gourley, Abraham & Elizabeth Richards. m. 25 Feb. 1816. T.
    Littleton.
Gover, Anthony P., Alexandria, D.C. & Sarah Janney. m. 8 Nov.
    1815. FFMM.
Gover, Carey C. & Susan Rincker. James Fritz, bm. 2 April 1844.
    Shel.
Gover, Edward R. & Elizabeth Rathie. Joseph L. Rathie attests
    bride's age, bm. 16 Sep. 1844. Shel.
Gover, Edwin R. & Ellen Hammerly. Edgar Jarvis attests bride's
    age, bm. 17 April 1849. m. 18 April 1849. Eggleston. Shel.
Gover, John W. & Sarah Jane Harding. Ages "Taken for granted both
    being known". 1 Sep. 1852. MarReg. m. 12 Sep. 1852. Benton.

Gover, Joseph & Miriam Taylor. m. 9 Nov. 1814. FFMM.

Gover, Robert R. & Catherine Cary. m. 17 Oct. 1816. Littlejohn.

Gover, Samuel & Sarah Janney. m. 16 Dec. 1784. FFMM.

Gower, Peter & Mary Fisher. m. 10 April 1800. Littlejohn.

Gowings, James & Catharine A. Jordon. John L. Jordon attests ages, bm. 2 Jan. 1832. Cam.

Grady, Edward B. & Sarah Taylor. Peter C. Rust attests ages, bm. 19 May 1809. m. 21 May 1809. Fristoe.

Grady, Francis T., Dr. & Jane Serena Powell, dau. of Cuthbert Powell. m. 17 June 1834, at Llangollen, residence of bride's father. Adie.

Graham, Robert & Ann Cumpton. 21 Aug. 1799. Littlejohn.

Graham, Thomas & Jemimah Cockerill. m. 1804. McPherson.

Graham, William & Nancy Stoner. Charles F. Wright, bm. 27 Dec. 1848. Shel.

Graham, William & Sarah Stone. Thompson Stone attests bride's age, bm. 21 May 1836. m. May 1836. Campbell. Shel.

Grant, Singleton & Sarah Cockrill. m. 4 Sep. 1806. Littlejohn.

Gras, Thomas & Barbara Rapp; both single. By license. m. 22 March 1812. ParReg A.

Graves, Benjamin & Mary Compher, dau. of Peter Compher, bm. Francis Thompson attests groom's age. 4 March 1836. m. 10 March 1836. G. Frye. Shel.

Graves, Joshua & Elizabeth McDonail. m. 27 Feb. 1820. T. Littleton.

Gray, Algemon S., Harrisonburg, Rockingham Co. & Annie Henderson, dau. of Richard H. Henderson, Leesburg. m. 26 May 1836, at house of bride's father. Adie.

Gray, Asher W. & Martha L. Luckett. Francis W. Luckett attests bride's age, bm. 28 May 1845. m. 28 May 1845, at house of bride's father. Adie. Shel.

Gray, Joseph G. & Mary Eliza Ellzey, dau. of Col. William Ellzey. John Gray, bm. 3 Dec. 1834. m. 3 Dec. 1834, at house of bride's father. Adie. Shel.

Gray, Nicholas & Mary Hall. David Martin, bm. 9 June 1796.

Gray, Ralph & Dolly Waggle. m. 6 May 1808. Littlejohn.

Gray, Robert W. & Mary Elizabeth Bentley, dau. of Robert Bentley, bm. 16 June 1840. m. 27 May 1840, at house of bride's father. Adie. Shel.

Gray, Samuel & Febe Smith. m. 18 April 1812. J. Littleton.

Gray, William H. & Ellen D. Powell, dau. of Cuthbert Powell. m. 8 Nov. 1836, at house of bride's father. Adie.

Gray, William H. & Frances W. Ellzey. John Gray, bm. 20 Jan. 1830. Cam.

Gray, William S. & Sarah Ann Orrison, dau. of Margaret Orrison. David Orrison, bm. 6 Dec. 1841. Shel.

Grayham, William & Tamer McGavock. m. 1820-1821. Mines.

Grayson, George W. & Juliett A. Murray, ward of Landon L. Carter, bm. 1 Sep. 1834. m. 3 Sep. 1834. Furlong. Shel.

Grayson, John B. & Mary Ann Tyler. William B. Tyler, bm. 12 Jan. 1846. m. 15 Jan. 1846, at house of bride's father. Adie. Shel.

Green, Edward & Malinda Darne, dau. of James Darne. James W. Darne, son of James Darne, attests ages, bm. 28 March 1838. Shel.

Green, George M. & Mary Miller. m. 10 Dec. 1833. Humphreys.

Green, Henry & Thodotia Simpson, ward of James Sinclair, bm. James McDonough attests groom's age. 6 Dec. 1830. Shel.

Green, John E. & Mary Jane Insor (Inson). A. S. Tebbs attests bride's age. C. Hunton (Hinton), bm. 18 Nov. 1843. m. 19 Nov. 1843. Gover. Shel.

Green, John L. & Mary Elizabeth Moore. Jesse W. Mobberley attests groom's age and that bride's widow of Abner Moore, bm. 7 May 1838. Shel.

Green, John P. H. & Alvinda Osburn, dau. of Richard Osburn. George Moore, bm. 11 Sep. 1848. m. 20 Sep. 1848. Nixon. Shel.

Green, Joseph & Elenor Popkins. m. 10 Dec. 1798. Littlejohn.

Green, Valentine & Helah Robinson, dau. of John Robinson, in Maryland. m. 17 March 1836. ParReg A.

Greenlease, John H. & Ruth Hannah Taylor, dau. of Charles Taylor, bm. 12 Jan. 1846. m. 15 Jan. 1846. Massey. Shel.

Greenlease, William S. & Mary Ann Hughes. Thomas P. Matthews attests bride's age, bm. 13 March 1837. m. 16 March 1837. Broaddus. Shel.

Greentree, Matthew & Elizabeth Henning. m. 28 Sep. 1807. Littlejohn.

Greenwall, Daniel & Arthemise Clark. m. 1809-1810. Mines.

Greenwood, Henry & Margaret Stoneburner. Henry Stoneburner attests ages, bm. 11 May 1829.

Gregg, Abner, son of John Gregg & Sarah Smith, dau. of William Smith. m. 30 Dec. 1779. FFMM.

Gregg, Aron & Mary Hixon. m. 7 Jan. 1804. Littlejohn.

Gregg, Caleb & Hannah Warford. m. 19 Nov. 1795. Littlejohn.

Gregg, Elisha, son of George and Elizabeth Gregg & Martha Lovett, dau. of Daniel Lovett. m. 1 March 1775. FFMM.

Gregg, George & Elizabeth Wilson. m. 8 Dec. 1800. Littlejohn.

Gregg, George & Margaret Todhunter. m. 27 Dec. 1780. FFMM.

Gregg, George & Percilla S. Clerk. m. 11 Feb. 1806. Littlejohn.

Gregg, George, Jr. & Mary Gregg. m. 14 Sep. 1780. FFMM.

Gregg, Gibson & Mary R. Cockran (Cochran). Tholemiah Cockran attests ages, bm. 14 Dec. 1835. m. 17 Dec. 1835. Monroe. Shel.

Gregg, Gilford G. & Jemina Gregg. Enos Nicholas attests ages, bm. 15 Feb. 1831. Shel.

Gregg, Henry H. & Jane J. Osburn, dau. of Richard Osburn, Sr., bm. 28 Nov. 1848. m. 1 Dec. 1848. Nixon. Shel.

Gregg, John & Hannah Steer. m. 7 Sep. 1775. FFMM.

Gregg, Joseph G. & Martha A. Shepherd. Alfred Megeath attests ages, bm. 3 April 1846. m. 9 April 1846. Herndon.

Gregg, Josiah & Margaret Hand. m. 22 Jan. 1795. Littlejohn.

Gregg, Nathan & Susan R. Gregg. Samuel Pursel (Purcell), Jr., bm. 16 May 1829. Shel.

Gregg, Samuel, son of Thomas and Rebekah Gregg & Ann Sinclear, dau. of James and Mary Sinclear. m. 15 June 1785. FFMM.

Gregg, Samuel & Sarah Rattican. m. 6 Dec. 1802. Littlejohn.

Gregg, Thomas & Amey Gregg. m. 3 Dec. 1766. FFMM.

Gregg, Thomas & Elizabeth Case. 19 Feb. 1851. MarReg.

Gregg, Thomas & Hannah Brown, dau. of John Brown, bm. 20 March 1799. Shel.

Gregg, Thomas & Naomia Whitacre. m. 26 Sep. 1803. Littlejohn.

LOUDOUN COUNTY MARRIAGES

Gregg, Thomas, Kennett, Chester County, Pa. & Rebekah Janney,
dau. of Jacob Janney. m. 7 Oct. 1762. FFMM.
Gregg, William & Elizabeth Brown, dau. of William Brown, bm.
5 Sep. 1831. m. 8 Sep. 1831. Green. Shel.
Gregg, William & Rebekah Gregg. m. 4 Nov. 1769. FFMM.
Gregg, Wilson & Margaret Lightfoot. Presley McDaniel attests ages,
bm. 27 June 1832. Shel.
Greggs, Thomas & Catherine Lacey. m. 3 Jan. 1811. Littlejohn.
Gregroy, Thomas & Sarah Hood. m. 10 Feb. 1801. Littlejohn.
Gregsby, Nathaniel & Susannah Keene. m. 29 March 1827.
Williamson.
Griffin, Charles & Martha M. Brabham, dau. of Mary Brabham.
Groom's authorization by Jesse Griffin, Prince William Co.,
his father. James Smitson, bm. 28 Dec. 1842.
Griffith, Abraham, son of Isaac Griffith, Baltimore County, Md.
& Rachel Taylor, dau. of Thomas Taylor. m. 30 Dec. 1788.
FFMM.
Griffith, Israel T. & Mary Eleanor Weatherill. William H. Hough
attests bride's age. C. W. Binns, bm. 6 April 1831. Shel.
Griffith, James & Elizabeth Hall. Joshua Roberts attests ages, bm.
26 Dec. 1835. m. 29 Dec. 1835. G. Frye. Shel.
Griffith, John, Jr. & Hannah Homan. Jenkin Oxley, bm. Hannah
Homan, otherwise called Hannah Stephens, bm. 7 Dec. 1799.
Littlejohn. Shel.
Griffith, John T. & Malinda Jane Yates. Wit: Franklin A. Yates.
21 Dec. 1852. MarReg. m. 23 Dec. 1852. Dodge.
Griffith, John W., Hopewell, Frederick County & Kezia T. Smith.
m. 24 Jan. 1844. Bond, Clerk.
Griffith, Thomas & Sarah Vanhorne. m. 23 May 1822. Gilmore.
Grigg, Peter & Emily Crain. m. 29 Dec. 1825. Evans.
Grimes, Andrew & Molley Goins. m. 11 April 1810.
Grimes, Henry & Ann Elizabeth Cridler, dau. of John Cridler, bm.
22 Oct. 1835. Shel.
Grimm, David & Elisabetha Mouerin, from Maryland; both single.
By license. m. 9 Dec. 1819. ParReg. A.
Grinwood, Henrich & Margretha Steinbrenner; both single. By
license. m. 21 May 1829. ParReg A.
Grobb, Benjamin & Catharina Schmidt; both single. By license.
m. 4 Dec. 1828. ParReg A.
Grof, Samuel & Sarah Stier; both single. By license. m. 12 Jan.
1815. ParReg A.
Gropp, Mr. & Elizabeth Jackson; both single. By license. m.
28 Nov. 1816. ParReg A.
Gross, John & Patience Ramsey, dau. of John Ramsey, bm. Daniel
Wine attests groom's age. 30 Nov. 1833. Shel.
Grov, Philip & Eva Demmerich; both single. By license. m. 11 Feb.
1819. ParReg A.
Grubb, Benjamin J. & Rebecca Grubb. Curtis Grubb attests ages,
bm. 18 Sep. 1839. m. 25 Sep. 1839. Hauer. Shel.
Grubb, Curtis & Rachel Ann Locker. Garrett Locker attests bride's
age, bm. 5 Dec. 1846.
Grubb, Ebenezer & Mary Smallwood. Bayn Smallwood, bm. 4 April
1801.

Grubb, Ebenezer & Leah Wertz, dau. of late Jacob Wertz and
wife; both single. By license. m. 22 July 1820. ParReg A.
Grubb, Hiram & Pleasant Hurdle. T. R. Williams attests ages, bm.
6 May 1850. Shel.
Grubb, Joseph & Mary Daniel. Eli Pierpoint attests bride's age,
bm. 31 Oct. 1831. Shel.
Grubb, Joseph & Susannah Coe. m. 1809-1810. Mines.
Grubb, Richard & Charity Morrison. m. 1807-1808. Mines.
Grubb, William & Susanna Tally, widow. John Miller, bm. 10 April
1799. Shel.
Grymes, Sylvester & Sarah Davis, widow. Nicholas Grymes, bm.
21 Jan. 1799. Cam.
Gulatt, Charles & Eleanor Sinclair. George Sinclair attests
bride's age, bm. 17 Nov. 1835. Trott. Shel.
Gulick, Amos & Sarah M. Bealle. m. 5 Dec. 1825-6 Dec. 1825.
Burch.
Gulick, David T. & Mary Simpson, dau. of French Simpson. Sanford
Gulick attests groom's age, bm. 13 Nov. 1843. m. 21 Nov.
1843. Herndon. Shel.
Gulick, Francis & Nancy Craig. David T. Gulick attests ages, bm.
18 March 1844. Shel.
Gulick, James H. & Ann V. Simpson, dau. of French Simpson, bm.
Sanford P. Rogers attests groom's age, bm. 11 Feb. 1839.
Shel.
Gulick, Sanford, son of George Gulick, aged about 40, never m.
before & Nancy R. Gulick, dau. of William Gulick, aged about
25, never m. before. Wit: William Gulick. 22 Nov. 1853.
MarReg. m. 24 Nov. 1853. Trott.
Gulicks, Francis & Elizabeth Spencer. m. 22 Jan. 1798. Littlejohn.
Gullatt, Charles & Rebecca B. Lewis. m. 25 Sep. 1820. Dagg.
Guthart, Henrich & Elisabetha Steinbrenner, dau. of Daniel
Steinbrenner; both single. By license. m. 11 April 1816.
ParReg A.
Hackmann, Johannes, son of Peter Hackmann & Catharina Phale,
dau. of Jacob Phale; both single. By license. m. 11 April
1811. ParReg A.
Hackney, Aaron, Frederick County, Va. & Hannah Gregg. m. 31
March 1768. FFMM.
Haffner, Friderich & Elisabetha Stautzenberger; both single.
By license. m. 9 Oct. 1814. ParReg A.
Hagan, Thomas & Rosanna Chilton. m. 28 May 1811. Littlejohn.
Hagerman, Barnett & Mary Cox. m. 27 June 1813. McPherson.
Hagerman, William & Elizabeth Jenkins. m. 28 Jan. 1817.
Williamson.
Hague, Frances & Mary Towner. m. 29 Jan. 1793. Littlejohn.
Hague, James & Elizabeth Huff. m. 18 Nov. 1805. Littlejohn.
Hague, Joshua & Mary Pool. m. 13 June 1801. Littlejohn.
Hague, Samuel & Elizabeth Holms. m. 12 April 1810. Littlejohn.
Hague, Samuel & Jane Shuard. m. 23 Dec. 1773. FFMM.
Haile, Henry & Sarah Luckett. m. 12 Oct. 1815. Dunn.
Hained, William & Roza. Shryoak. m. 3 Jan. 1796. Littlejohn.
Haines, Daniel & Mary Marsh. m. 12 Dec. 1808. Dunn.
Haines, Simeon & Elizabeth Randall. m. 27 Nov. 1783. FFMM.

Haines, Washington & Mary Elizabeth Sample. Armistead T. M.
Hough, bm. 25 Dec. 1840. Shel.
Hains, Amos & Jane Wrenn. m. 24 May 1805. Rozell.
Hains, Edward & Sarah Campbell. m. 1821-1822. Mines.
Hains, Frederick & Alice James. m. 5 Jan. 1824. C. Frye.
Hains, Joseph & Mariah Handy. m. 29 July 1807. Williamson.
Hains, Joseph A. & Mary Ann McGeath. Joseph D. Burke attests
ages, bm. 25 July 1843. Shel.
Haley, James & Emily Hunt. John Hunt attests ages, bm. 23 Feb.
1839. Shel.
Hall, David & Nancy Chew. Roger Chew attests ages, bm. 6 Dec.
1841. m. 22 Dec. 1842 (?), house of Roger Chew. Adie. Shel.
Hall, Henry & Sarah Harper. Thomas Harper, bm. 23 Jan. 1800.
Hall, Horatio W. & Sally Cox, dau. of Patty Cox, formerly
Newman, sister of Bazell Newman. Hezekiah Newman, bm. 18 Aug.
1845. Shel.
Hall, John Wesley & Sarah E. Rice, dau. of Thirza Rice, bm. and
Jesse Rice, deceased. 12 June 1833. Shel.
Hall, Jonathan & Francinia Francis. m. 19 Nov. 1795. Littlejohn.
Hall, Josias & Mary Nixon. m. 13 March 1793. Littlejohn.
Hall, Thomas S. & Angelina Boyle, ward of Edward Tyler, bm.
18 June 1834. m. 19 June 1834. Furlong. Shel.
Halley, Barton & Catherine Heath, dau. of Andrew Heath, Sr.
Joshua Hutchison, bm. 8 April 1799.
Halling, Isaac W. & Frances Best. m. 16 Oct. 1817. Dunn. Shel.
Ham, Matthias & Mary Popkins. m. 17 Feb. 1820. T. Littleton.
Hames, Peter & Mary Smith. m. 31 Aug. 1843. ParReg A.
Hamilton, Charles & Nancy Janney. m. 25 April 1822. Dunn. Shel.
Hamilton, David & Rebecca Reed. m. 2 Dec. 1816. Littlejohn.
Hamilton, Eli J. & Virginia Heaton. James Heaton, bm. 10 May
1847. m. 12 May 1847. Massey. Shel.
Hamilton, Eliphalet & Sarah Tracy. m. May 1825. Evans.
Hamilton, Henry H. & Maria S. Gibson, dau. of Abner Gibson, bm.
16 Jan. 1845. Shel.
Hamilton, James & Elizabeth Bennet. m. 8 April 1794. Littlejohn.
Hamilton, James & Sarah Gilasby. John Bishop, bm. 22 Feb. 1816.
Hamilton, Jams' H. & Margeret McCout. m. 30 March 1802.
Littlejohn.
Hamilton, James T. & Rebecca J. McAtee, dau. of Harrison McAtee.
John F. Poston attests groom's age, bm. 30 July 1844.
Hamilton, James W. & Caroline A. Householder, dau. of Gideon
Householder, bm. Amos Janney affirms groom's age. 6 Dec. 1843.
m. 12 Dec. 1843. ParReg A. Shel.
Hamilton, John & Permilia Graham. Elijah Peacock attests bride's
age. Charles G. Eskridge, bm. 2 March 1840. Shel.
Hamilton, Presly & Ruth H. Russell, dau. of Thomas Russell, who
attests groom's age, bm. 24 Jan. 1842. m. 27 Jan. 1842. Hauer.
Shel.
Hamilton, Robert & Ruth Harris. m. 21 July 1793. Littlejohn.
Hamilton, William & Betsy Griffeth. m. 4 Jan. 1802. Littlejohn.
Hamilton, William & Jane Darley. George W. Hunter attests groom's
age, bm. 8 Aug. 1833. Shel.
Hamintree, David & Mary Beach. m. 23 March 1793. Littlejohn.

Hamm, David & Sarah Hart, dau. of Jonathan Hart, who attests
groom's age, bm. 25 Nov. 1844. Shel.

Hamman, Georg & Maria McKimmin; both single. By license. m.
24 Sep. 1828. ParReg A.

Hammatt, Edward & Sarah Moss. m. 6 Aug. 1816. Littlejohn.

Hammatt, John W. & Mary R. Hammat, dau. of Edward Hammat, wit.
8 June 1852. MarReg. Duncan.

Hammatt, Samuel & Wineford Howel. m. 16 Feb. 1811. Littlejohn.

Hammatt, William & Sophia Water. William D. Drish attests bride's
age, bm. 9 July 1829.

Hammerly, John & Jane Drish. m. 23 Oct. 1804. Littlejohn.

Hammerley, John W. & Margaret Johnson. m. 23 Sep. 1845. Gover.

Hammerly, John & Catharine Ann Zillers (Zillus). Abraham Hewett,
bm. 26 Dec. 1842. m. 27 Dec. 1842. Gover. Shel.

Hammerly, John W. & Margaret Johnson. John W. Gover, bm. 23 Sep.
1845. Shel.

Hammerly, Mandley & Eliza A. Brown. Asa Brown, bm. 9 Dec. 1840.
Shel.

Hammet, Giles & Alice Barnett. m. 24 Nov. 1819. Griffith.

Hammet, John & Fanny Sanders. m. 22 March 1806. Littlejohn.

Hammondtree, Samuel & Sarah Brown. m. 8 June 1820. Dagg.

Hammontree, George H. & Margaret Miller. m. 28 Nov. 1825-1 Dec.
1825. Burch.

Hammontree, William & Dorcas Manley. John S. Manly, bm. 19 Jan.
1829.

Hamner, Thomas L. & Harriett H. Wilson. William H. Gray, bm.
24 Jan. 1844. Shel.

Hampton, Fenton & Sarah A. Cockerell, dau. of John Cockerell, who
attests groom's age, bm. 13 Feb. 1850. m. 19 Feb. 1850.
Herndon. Shel.

Hampton, George F. & Alcinda G. Bowles. Wit: David Bowles. 7 June
1853. MarReg. m. 7 June 1853. Herndon.

Hampton, Mandley & Emily J. Moore, dau. of Samuel Moore, who
attests groom's age, bm. 16 April 1844. Shel.

Hampton, William & Catharine Spence. m. 28 Dec. 1824. McDowell.

Hancock, Ebin T. & Emma F. Potts, dau. of William Potts, who
gives consent. William Potts, bm. 3 April 1830. m. "lic.
6 April 1830." G. Frye. Shel.

Hand, Hugh & Elizabeth Orrison. m. 13 Aug. 1804. Littlejohn.

Handless, Moses & Nancy King, free Negroes. m. 25 Aug. 1807.
McPherson.

Handy, William H. & Elenor McGeath. m. 28 Jan. 1808. Williamson.

Haney, John & Mary J. Boland. Wit: Thomas and A. Boland. Return
dated 2 Dec. 1850. Plunkett.

Hanks, Cephas & Phoebe Mock. m. 1821-1822. Mines.

Hann, David & Sarah Hart. m. 27 Nov. 1844. Massey.

Hann, William & Alcinda Richards. m. 30 Dec. 1824. T. Littleton.

Hannah, William & Vise Hampton. m. 22 Oct. 1822. Dagg.

Hansborough, Joseph & Sarah Myers. m. 12 March 1813. Littlejohn.

Hansbourgh, William & Elizabeth Miller. m. 11 Feb. 1804.
Littlejohn.

Hanvey, James D. & Emma Littleton, dau. of Thomas Littleton, bm.
24 Nov. 1845. Shel.

Harbert, John & Lettice Hutchison, dau. of Joseph Hutchison.
James Hutchison attests groom's age, bm. 23 Jan. 1809. Cam.

Hardacker, Mardochay & Barbara Crimm; both single. By license.
m. 1 June 1820. ParReg A.

Harden, John R. & Ann Amanda Wortman. Wit: Isaac Wortman. 16 Oct.
1852. MarReg. m. 19 Oct. 1852. Gover.

Harden, Joseph S. & Frances Jane Dennis. Henry Dennis attests
ages. Thomas Bell, bm. 29 Dec. 1841. Cam.

Harden, Lewis & Edy Thatcher. m. 18 March 1807. Littlejohn.

Harden, Lewis B. & Patsey Garrison. Wit: Albert Harden. 21 May
1853. MarReg. m. 29 May 1853. Gover.

Harden, Presley & Sarah Seers. m. 27 Sep. 1803. Littlejohn.

Harding, Albert & Ellen E. Fox. James Hutchison attests ages, bm.
25 Oct. 1838. Cam.

Harding, John H. & Darcus S. Davis. m. 23 May 1810. Littlejohn.

Harding, Thomas J. & Susan Latham, dau. of Nancy Latham. Wesley
White, bm. 16 Nov. 1839. Shel.

Hardy, Amos & Catherine Schry. m. 6 Nov. 1812. Littlejohn.

Hardy, Henson & Elizabeth Matthews. Warner Benjamin proves ages,
wit. 31 May 1852. MarReg. m. 1 June 1852. Gover.

Hardy, Hugh William & Louisa J. Hamilton. James Benjamin attests
ages, bm. 31 July 1848. Shel.

Hardy, Thomas & Sarah Bagly; both single. By license. m. 31 July
1825. ParReg A.

Harlan, Aaron & Edeth G. Burson. m. 10 Sep. 1828. Williamson.

Harper, Charles & Rachel Smither. m. 20 March 1797. Littlejohn.

Harper, Charles, Fairfax County & Sarah Janney. m. 28 Dec. 1791.
FFMM.

Harper, Ignatius & Francis Ann Thomas, free Negroes. Wit: Asa
Jackson, Elias Hughes, Samuel Smart. m.15 July 1847, in
Montgomery County, Md. Birkby.

Harper, James & Elvina Mahonny. Jacob Shriver attests bride's
age. 13 Oct. 1834. Shel.

Harper, James & Jane Jones. m. 30 Oct. 1817. Keyes.

Harper, Johannes & Catharina Stacks; both single. By license.
m. 4 May 1820. ParReg A.

Harper, John & Mary Evans. m. 1807-1808. Mines.

Harper, Jonathan & Jane Woodard, dau. of Jabez Woodard. His
mother attests groom's age. J. Woodard, bm. 1 Aug. 1839.
Shel.

Harper, Julius & Virginia Johnson. Groom's consent signed by
Margaret Harper, who says he's in his 22nd year. "license to
marry Catharine Harper" signed by Margret Harper; John
Johnson says groom's son of "Catharine Harper". John Johnson,
bm. 2 Sep. 1844.

Harper, Robert & Mary A. Newton. Charles B. Ball attests bride's
age, bm. 25 June 1850. m. 27 June 1850. Smith. Shel.

Harper, Sampson & Polly Cox, widow. Stasee Harper attests groom's
age. Augustine McDaniel, bm. 30 April 1835. Shel.

Harper, Sampson & Susannah Davis. Jeremiah Davis attests ages,
bm. 24 Aug. 1841. m. 26 Aug. 1841. ParReg A. Shel.

Harper, Thomas & Sarah Fulkerson. License date: 27 Dec. 1803.
Davis.

Harper, Washington & Debby Roberts. Jonathan Harper attests
   bride's age. William Harper attests groom's age, bm. 30 Oct.
   1837. Shel.
Harper, William & Ann Mondy. John Umbaugh attests bride's age,
   bm. 29 May 1837. Shel.
Harper, William & Maria Mollin. By license. m. 24 Dec. 1822.
   ParReg A.
Harper, William & Mary T. Newton. m. 1809-1810. Mines.
Harper, William & Nancy Parsons. m. 1807-1808. Mines.
Harper, William & Tamar Brooks, widow. Samuel Harper, bm. 17 Aug.
   1835. Shel.
Harr, William & Rachel Humphrey. m. 25 May 1820. Dagg.
Harris, Amos & Jane Wrenn. m. 23 May 1805. Roszell.
Harris, Enoch & Elizabeth Davis. John Davis attests ages, bm.
   28 Dec. 1829.
Harris, George, of Waterford, son of George and Susanna Harris,
   the latter deceased, of Baltimore, Md. & Sarah Ann Littler,
   dau. of John and Ann Littler, now Ann Moore, formerly of
   Wilmington, Dela. m. 26 May 1824. FFMM.
Harris, Isaac & Sarah Wren. m. 7 Nov. 1796. Littlejohn.
Harris, James Henry & Margaret Virginia Vauters. Philip Hamm
   proves bride's age. William Vauters proves groom's age.
   3 March 1851. MarReg.
Harris, James S. & Mary A. Sutherland. William P. Harris, bm.
   13 Sep. 1842. Shel.
Harris, Jeremiah & Isabella Ewers. Robert Ewers attests ages,
   bm. 9 Jan. 1809. m. 12 Jan. 1809. Hemphill. Shel.
Harris, Middleton & Prudy Thomas. m. 9 Aug. 1811. Littlejohn.
Harris, Richard L. & Sally Beales. John Johnson attests ages, bm.
   14 Dec. 1839. Shel.
Harris, Samuel & Elizabeth Wren. m. 13 Jan. 1803. Littlejohn.
Harris, William & Elizabeth Holmes. m. 22 Oct. 1772. FFMM.
Harris, William A. & Frances Murray, dau. of Elizabeth Murray.
   Edward C. Murray, bm. 16 Nov. 1840. Cadden. Shel.
Harrison, Burr W. & Sarah Powell. m. 3 Jan. 1822. Williamson.
Harrison, Daniel P. & Jane C. Harrison. m. 17 May 1821. Dagg.
Harrison, Edward Jacqueline & Sally Pendleton Powell. Bride's
   father consents in writing. B. P. Noland proves groom's
   age, wit. 6 June 1853. MarReg.
Harrison, Ephmn. & Nancy Murphy. m. 29 April 1794. Littlejohn.
Harrison, Francis L., about 25 years & Mary Mahala McKim, about
   25 years; both single. Wit: Jonathan J. Moore. 19 Sep. 1853.
   MarReg. m. 18 Sep. 1853. Duncan.
Harrison, Henry T., Leesburg & Jane Elizabeth Lee. m. 6 Feb. 1834,
   at Sully, Fairfax County, Adie.
Harrison, James & Sally Shepherd. m. 20 Jan. 1814. Littlejohn.
Harrison, James M. & Susan E. Bailey, dau. of Sydnor Bailey. James
   Rust attests bride's age, bm. 4 Aug. 1834. m. 7 Aug. 1834, at
   house of bride's father. Adie. Shel.
Harrison, Samuel S. & Sarah Rhodes, dau. of Randolph Rhodes.
   William J. Adams attests groom's age, bm. 24 Nov. 1841.Shel.
Harrison, Thomas H., son of James Harrison & Priscilla E. Cooke,
   dau. of Levi Cook. Stephen D. Beach, bm. 27 June 1844. Shel.

Harrison, William & Sarah Riley, dau. of Richard Riley, bm.
James Harrison attests groom's age. James Riley, bm.
28 April 1840. m. 30 April 1840. Larkin. Shel.
Harrison, William S. & Catharine Whitmore. Michael Whitmore, bm.
15 Feb. 1843. Shel.
Harrope, James & Mary Cohages (Cohagen). m. Nov. 1806. Dunn.
Harry, William & Margaret Griffith. m. 2 March 1845. Massey.
Hart, John R. & Mary Jane Palmer. Wit: Samuel E. Palmer. 15 Nov.
1852. MarReg. m. 18 Nov. 1852. Dodge.
Hart, Joseph & Sarah Rawlings. Enoch Glascock, bm. 15 Sep. 1837.
m. 21 Sep. 1837. Broaddus. Shel.
Hart, William & Eliza Sutherland. John Varnes attests bride's
age, bm. 28 May 1838. Shel.
Hart, William T. & Emiline Frances Thatcher, dau. of Mary Thatcher.
George Richardson, bm. 3 Dec. 1836. Shel.
Hartacker, Leonhard & Elisabetha Jones; both single. By license.
m. 26 July 1821. ParReg A.
Hartley, Benjamin & Dorothy Leslie. John Jones, Jr. attests ages,
bm. 5 March 1845. m. 3 March 1845. ParReg A. Shel.
Hartness, John & Barbara Darr. m. 9 Oct. 1796. Littlejohn.
Hatch, Jesse P. & Jane S. Hawling. m. 18 June 1827. Tuston.
Hatcher, George & Prudence Woodward. m. 28 May 1778. FFMM.
Hatcher, James & Susanna Nichols. m. 16 Aug. 1807. Dunn.
Hatcher, Jesse & Ann Miller. m. 9 Nov. 1811. Littlejohn.
Hatcher, John & Sarah Tavener. m. 25 April 1801. Littlejohn.
Hatcher, Jonah & Adeline S. Gregg. Enos Nichols attests bride's
age, bm. 12 Aug. 1833. Shel.
Hatcher, Jonah & Sarah Hough. m. 12 Nov. 1804. Littlejohn.
Hatcher, Joseph & Hannah Reeder. m. 21 Aug. 1802. Littlejohn.
Hatcher, Joshua & Sarah Ann Gregg. David Reece, bm. 26 Jan.
1835. Shel.
Hatcher, Thomas & Rebekah Nichols. m. 14 April 1773. FFMM.
Hatcher, Thomas & Sarah Lacey. m. 30 Jan. 1816. Littlejohn.
Hatcher, Thomas E. & Elizabeth P. Gregg. Samuel Purcell attests
ages, bm. 16 May 1829.
Hatcher, William, Jr. & Mary McCray. m. 27 May 1779. FFMM.
Hatton, Henry & Ruth A. Taylor. Isaac E. Steer attests ages, bm.
16 Dec. 1845. Shel.
Hauk, George & Mary Allen, dau. of James Allen, who attests
groom's age, bm. 24 Aug. 1842. Shel.
Haukins, Joseph & Ester Dewis. By license. m. 8 June 1812.
ParReg A.
Hauks, Steils & Ann Newhaus. By license. m. 18 Sep. 1817.
ParReg A.
Haushalter, Daniel, widower & Priscilla S. Gregg, widow. By
license. m. 12 Feb. 1824. ParReg A.
Haushalter, Gideon, son of late Adam Haushalter and his late
wife & Juliana Kerns, dau. of Jacob Kerns and wife; both
single. By license. m. 18 May 1820. ParReg A.
Haushalter, Johannes, son of Daniel Haushalter and wife & Nantzy
Strahm, dau. of Michael Strahm and wife; both single. By
license. m. 4 May 1820. ParReg A.
Haven, Edward & Reba. Rider. m. 9 June 1810. Littlejohn.

67

Havener, Armistead & Sarah A. Walter. John Walter attests
    groom's age, bm. 18 Oct. 1843. Cam.
Havener, Bazzell & Rachel Lafever. William Lafever, bm. 10 Jan.
    1831. Cam.
Havener, James William & Lucinda Muse. Thomas H. Muse proves
    bride's age, wit. Groom's father, wit. 15 Dec. 1851. MarReg.
    m. 16 Dec. 1851, at house of bride's mother. Adie.
Havener, John & Mary Bridges. m. 22 Feb. 1798. Littlejohn.
Havener, John A. & Rhoda Ann Lee. Bride's father, wit. 13 June
    1853. MarReg. m. 16 June 1853, residence of John Lee. Cushing.
Havener, Thomas A. & Mary Catharine Moran, dau. of Catharine
    Moran. Alexander Moran attests groom's age, bm. 10 Sep. 1845.
    m. 11 Sep. 1845. Gover. Cam.
Havener, William M. & Serepta (Sarepta) Tolston. Bazil Havener,
    Fielding Tolston, wit. 8 Nov. 1852. MarReg. m. 11 Nov. 1852.
    Gover.
Havenner, James B. & Hortensia Dawson, dau. of Sarah Ann Dawson.
    Walker J. Muse, bm. 27 March 1848. Cam.
Havenner, Michael & Charlotte Workman, dau. of Isaac Workman,
    who attests groom's age, bm. 17 Jan. 1845. m. 21 Jan. 1845.
    Gover. Cam.
Havenner, Philip F. & Lucretia (Lucetta) Milstead. Bride's
    father, wit. William A. Havenner attests groom's age, wit.
    9 Feb. 1853. MarReg. m. 10 Feb. 1853. Rodgers.
Havenner, Silas, son of Joseph Havenner & Julia Ann Rollinson,
    dau. of John Rolinson. Joseph Havenner, bm. 10 Jan. 1831.
    Cam.
Hawes, Samuel & Lydia Swick. m. 14 Aug. 1818. Williamson.
Hawk, George & Mary Allen. m. 25 Aug. 1842. Hauer.
Hawk, William & Rebecca Boss. m. 13 Feb. 1800. Littlejohn.
Hawke, Elijah & Eliza Water. Jacob Waters attests ages, bm.
    15 March 1843. m. 23 March 1843. ParReg A. Shel.
Hawkings, John W. & Mary Wiley. Isaac Brown attests ages, bm.
    18 Feb. 1847. Shel.
Hawkins, Joseph, Jr. & Mary Ann King, dau. of William King, bm.
    John Nixon attests groom's age. 29 July 1835. Shel.
Hawling, Sidney & Eliza Osburn. Richard Osburn, Jr., bm. 1 Jan.
    1849. m. 9 Jan. 1849. Dulin. Shel.
Haws, John & Elizabeth Haws, dau. of Asa Haws. William Alexander,
    bm. 10 Nov. 1845. m. 13 Nov. 1845. Benton. Shel.
Haws, William & Elizabeth Lanham. James Haws, bm. 9 Dec. 1846.
Haynes, Washington & Mary Elizabeth Sample. m. 29 Dec. 1840.
    Roszell.
Hays, Mathias & Rhoda Carter, dau. of William Carter, bm.
    16 Jan. 1809.
Head, Christopher C. & Emily J. Steadman. John A. McDonaugh
    attests ages, bm. 5 Sep. 1839. Shel.
Head, George & Hannah Gover. Robert Gover, bm. 21 July 1831. Shel.
Head, George & Polly Gover. Joseph Talbott attests bride's age,
    bm. 9 Jan. 1809.
Head, George, Jr. & Polly Gover. m. 9 Jan. 1809. Littlejohn.
Head, George R. & Sarah Virginia Gover. Edwin R. Gover attests
    bride's age, bm. 14 Nov. 1848. Shel.

Head, William & Mary Sophia Gover. George R. Head proves ages,
   wit. 5 Feb. 1851. MarReg. Gover.
Heart, William & Rebecca Cowgill. m. 26 Sep. 1813. McPherson.
Heater, Eli & Cornelia Ann Costs. Jonathan Costs attests ages,
   bm. 30 Dec. 1842. Shel.
Heater, George Henry, colored Man & Susan Sharper alias Duncan.
   "I issued both of their certificates of Freedom - that in
   said certificates their ages are proved to be upwards of 21
   years of age. Presly Saunders." Presly Saunders, bm.
   26 March 1849.
Heater, Solomon & Caroline H. Wunder, dau. of Hy. S. Wunder, bm.
   16 Dec. 1836. m. Dec. 1836. Campbell. Shel.
Heath, Gustavus J. & Ann M. Popkins. James H. Popkins attests
   ages, bm. 5 Aug. 1848. Shel.
Heath, Gustavius J. & Eliza J. Chappel, dau. of John C. Chappel.
   John Heath, bm. 7 Feb. 1844. Shel.
Heath, John & Sarah J. Goram. Samuel Goram attests ages, bm.
   "Mary Jane" on outside of bond. 4 Nov. 1844. Cam.
Heaton, James & Hannah Spencer. m. 1 Aug. 1803. Littlejohn.
Heaton, James, son of James Heaton and Deborah Richards and
   grandson of Thomas Drake & Leah Carter. William Carter, bm.
   18 Sep. 1809. Shel.
Heaton, Jonathan & Patience Osborne. m. 28 Sep. 1812. Littlejohn.
Heckman, Peter, son of Peter Heckman and wife & Maria Schlotzer,
   dau. of Johannes Schlotzer; both single. By license. m.
   17 Sep. 1812. ParReg A.
Heckman, Peter, son of Conrad Heckmann & Regina Bogerin, dau. of
   late Joseph Boger. m. 15 Dec. 1784. ParReg A.
Heckmann, Michael & Catharina Schumachern; both single. By
   license. m. 18 Nov. 1813. ParReg A.
Heeter, Eli & Cornelia Ann Cost. m. 3 Jan. 1843. ParReg A.
Heffner (Heffnar), George & Hannah Fawley, dau. of Henry Fawley.
   William Fry attests groom's age, bm. 4 Aug. 1840. m. 6 Aug.
   1840. Hauer. Shel.
Heffner, John & Sarah Swank (Schwenk), dau. of Philip Swank
   (Schwenk), bm. 22 April 1834. m. 24 April 1834. ParReg A.
   Shel.
Hefner, Adam & Hannah Edwards. Solomon Smith attests bride's age,
   bm. 13 June 1848. Shel.
Helm, Joseph & Mary E. Carr. William Carr, bm. 3 Sep. 1834. Shel.
Hemerly, William & Sally Woodey. m. 23 June 1810. Littlejohn.
Hempstone, Cephas, of Maryland & Mary Eleanor Belt, at house of
   Alfred Belt. Bond: 19 Nov. 1834. m. 28 Nov. 1834. Adie.
Hempstone, Yadock & Mary M. Harris, dau. of Samuel B. Harris, bm.
   21 May 1832. Shel.
Hemsley (Hamersley), Thomas S. & Emily A. Noland. A. G.
   Waterman, bm. 14 Oct. 1830. Shel.
Henderson, Andrew & Mahalah Reed, dau. of Jonathan Reed. Hector
   Pearce, bm. 17 Feb. 1830. Shel.
Henderson, Archibald & Henrietta Gray. Charles G. Eskridge, bm.
   20 Feb. 1834. m. 26 Feb. 1834, at house of John Gray,
   Leesburg. Adie. Shel.
Henderson, Charles W. & Delila Campbell. Thomas N. Dicky appears
   Fairfax County to attest groom's age. John Campbell, bm.
   22 July 1844. Shel.

Henderson, George W. & Lucinda Hunt. Norval Craig attests ages,
  bm. 22 June 1848. Shel.
Henderson, John & Mary Duncan. m. 7 Jan. 1815. Littlejohn.
Henderson, Robert A. & Elizabeth L. Hawkins. William H. Henderson,
  bm. 18 Nov. 1845. m. 19 Nov. 1845, at house of Dr. Thomas H.
  Claggett, Leesburg. Adie. Shel.
Henderson, Robert W. & Elizabeth Campbell. John Campbell attests
  groom's age, bm. 6 Feb. 1838. Shel.
Henderson, Samuel E. & Matilda Morgan. Ishmael Vanhorne attests
  bride's age, bm. 31 Jan. 1831. m. 3 Feb. 1831. ParReg A. Shel.
Henry, G. W. & Duannah Hamilton. m. 30 April 1827. Tuston.
Henry, Stephen & Nancy A. Willett. m. 5 Dec. 1803. Littlejohn.
Hensey, Thomas & Eliza Jane Harrison. James Harrison attests
  ages, bm. 14 Aug. 1841. Shel.
Hepburn, Thomas & Elizabeth Morris. m. 12 Sep. 1803. Littlejohn.
Herbert, William & Elizabeth Wood. m. 14 Dec. 1807. Littlejohn.
Hereford, Thomas P. & Matilda W. Lacy. B. B. Beard, bm. 9 Aug.
  1839. Shel.
Hereford, William T. & Julian Hutchison, dau. of Henry H. Hutchison,
  bm. Thomas A. Hereford, Sr. attests groom's age. 16 May 1836.
  m. 24 May 1836. Herndon. Shel.
Herrick, Walter & Deberoh Roach. m. 27 May 1805. Littlejohn.
Herrington, George C. & Sarah A. Milburn. George W. Miskell
  attests ages, bm. 13 Aug. 1844. Shel.
Herron, William & Malinda Combes. m. 5 Nov. 1815. Dunn.
Herschelmann, Georg & Elisabeth Landers. m. 3 Dec. 1789. ParReg A.
Herven, Edward & Abigal Hummer. m. 5 Aug. 1796. Littlejohn.
Heskett, James M. & Martha M. Barton. James A. Bloxham attests
  ages, bm. 21 Jan. 1833. m. 24 Jan. 1833. Baker. Shel.
Heskett, Norval V. & Emily Howell. Burr P. Chamblin attests ages,
  bm. 4 May 1846. m. 5 May 1846. Massey. Shel.
Heskett, William & Klarisa Tramell; both single. By license. m.
  5 Sep. 1819. ParReg A.
Hess, John & Elizabeth Connard. m. 7 Dec. 1807. Littlejohn.
Hesser, Andrew & Mary Bitzer. m. 27 Oct. 1825-1 Nov. 1825. Burch.
Hesser, David & Alcinda Thompson. m. 19 Feb. 1822. T. Littleton.
Hesser, John & Lyea Markes. m. 5 Oct. 1824. T. Littleton.
Heuton, Johannes & Anna Piecock, widow. By license. m. 20 Dec.
  1827. ParReg A.
Hewes, Matthew & Catherine Adams. m. 13 June 1810. Littlejohn.
Hewitt, Abraham & Isabel Wooddy, dau. of John Wooddy, who attests
  groom's age, bm. 1 Sep. 1847. Shel.
Hibbard, Job & Ruth Anne Janney. m. 27 March 1850. Taylor, Clerk.
Hibbs, Benjamin & Hannah Wilson. m. 27 Jan. 1813. Henkle.
Hibbs, Israel & Nancy Rhodes. John Wornal attests ages, bm.
  11 March 1844. Shel.
Hibbs, John R. & Catharine A. Gouchnauer. Jacob Gouchnauer
  attests groom's age, bm. 6 April 1842. Shel.
Hibbs, William & Mary Crates. m. 29 Nov. 1802. Littlejohn.
Hibbs, William & Sarah Cowgill. m. 20 June 1813. McPherson.
Hickman, George & Eleanora Kalb, dau. of Samuel Kalb, bm.
  Gideon Householder affirms groom's age. 14 Sep. 1840. m.
  17 Sep. 1840. Larkin. Shel.

70

LOUDOUN COUNTY MARRIAGES

Hickman, Peter & Mary E. Kalb. Samuel Kalb, bm. 20 Nov. 1846.
Hickman, Thomas H. & Louisa Virginia Vinsel. Bride's father, wit.
    3 June 1851. MarReg. m. 16 June 1851. ParReg A.
Hickman, William & Ann Eliza Everheart (Everhart). Elias Davis
    attests groom's age. Philip Everheart, bm. 18 Nov. 1839.
    m. 22 Nov. 1839. Hauer. Shel.
Hicks, George D. & Jane Morrison, dau. of Archibald Morrison.
    Horatio Slytes, bm. 4 May 1837. Shel.
Higdon, Charles H., son of James Higdon & Eliza Ann Beans. Aaron
    Beans attests bride's age, bm. 21 April 1849. Shel.
Higdon, James W. & Mary Jane Newton, dau. of John Newton. 28 Oct.
    1850. MarReg.
Higgins, Hugh, son of Thomas and Eliza Higgins, 23 years old, b.
    Ireland, farmer & Harriet E. Havener (Havenner), dau. of James
    and Lucindy Havenner, 23 years old, b. Loudoun. Thomas A.
    Havener, wit. 15 Nov. 1853. MarReg. m. 14 Nov. 1853, near
    Bell Mount.Gover.
Hill, James & Hannah Taylor. Charles Taylor attests bride's age,
    bm. 1 July 1809. m. 11 July 1809. Littlejohn.
Hill, James Washington & Mary Humphrey. Laban Lodge affirms
    bride's age, bm. 18 Oct. 1833. Shel.
Hillbert, Barnet & Cathrine Howard. m. 12 Nov. 1798. Littlejohn.
Hilliard, James & Mary Payne. m. 12 March 1826. Williamson.
Hilliard, Joseph & Ann Eliza Hough. m. 14 Sep. 1824. Littlejohn.
Hillman, Andreas & Maria Abel; both single. By license. m.
    13 Dec. 1821. ParReg A.
Hilton, Miles & Rebekah Mansfield. William Carnell attests bride's
    age, bm. 23 Sep. 1835. Shel.
Himble, Moses & Mary Acres. m. 9 Feb. 1807. Littlejohn.
Hinton, Miles & Rebecca Mansfield. m. 25 Sep. 1835. Broaddus.
Hipkins, Richard L. & Elizabeth Jacobs. James S. Sampson attests
    ages, bm. 13 March 1837. Shel.
Hirst, Aaron & Mary Cummings. m. 1806. Mines.
Hirst, Daniel & Martha Everheart. Nelson Everheart (Everhart)
    attests ages, bm. 29 July 1831. Shel.
Hirst, David, son of John and Mary Hirst & Ann Smith, dau. of
    Thomas and Rachel Smith. m. 6 April 1796. FFMM.
Hirst, Eli P. & Hannah Janny. m. 19 May 1831. Taylor, Clerk.
Hirst, Jesse & Mary Pierpoint, dau. of Obed Pierpoint. m.
    27 Dec. 1797. FFMM.
Hirst, William & Rebekah Kirk. Samuel M. Boss, guardian, affirms
    groom's age, bm. 23 June 1831. Shel.
Hisby, Richard & Elizabeth Shry. m. 22 Sep. 1810. Littlejohn.
Hitaffer, Henry & Milley Rennoe. m. 27 Feb. 1817. Williamson.
Hitaffer, James H., son of John and Sarah Hitaffer, 24 years, b.
    Loudoun, carpenter & Mary E. F. (J.) Rollins, dau. of
    William and Rebecca Rollins, 17 years, b. Loudoun. William
    Rollins proves groom's age, wit. 20 Sep. 1853. MarReg. m.
    22 Sep. 1853, near Leesburg. Gover.
Hitaffer, John & Sarah Dutro. m. 20 July 1817. Williamson.
Hixon, Abner H. & Harriet R. Reebleman (Rubleman). William M.
    Lynn attests bride's age, bm. 24 Dec. 1836. m. 23 Dec. 1836.
    Herndon. Shel.
Hixon, Benjamin & Mary Stone. m. 9 April 1796. Littlejohn.

71

Hixon, Benjamin & Tacey Humphrey. Abner Humphrey consents.
James Hixon, bm. 10 April 1809. m. 16 April 1809. Fristoe.
Hixon, David & Catharine Ruse. Daniel Rawlings, bm. 27 May 1809.
Littlejohn.
Hixon, David & Martha King. m. 13 June 1794. Littlejohn.
Hixson, John H. & Maria V. Lynn. William M. Lynn attests bride's
age, bm. 3 Dec. 1845. m. 4 Dec. 1845. Herndon. Cam.
Hixson, Thomas H. & Sarah E. Gulick. William Gulick attests
groom's age, bm. 15 Jan. 1847. m. 19 Jan. 1847. Trott.
Hoching, Richard & Lucinda Dewar. m. 16 May 1820. Williamson.
Hof, Georg, widower & Elisabeth Wein. By license. m. 13(?) Dec.
1811. ParReg A.
Hoff, John & Martha I. Blincoe. m. 30 Nov. 1843. Ward.
Hoffer, Jacob & Margretha Doman(?), from Maryland; both single.
By license. m. 11 Feb. 1821. ParReg A.
Hoffman, Enoch & Delila Conard, dau. of David Conard, who attests
groom's age, bm. 19 Oct. 1840. m. 22 Oct. 1840. Larkin. Shel.
Hoge, Elwood & Sarah Orrison. John Vansickler attests ages, bm.
9 March 1829.
Hoge, Francis, Leesburg, son of John and Anne Hogue, the former
deceased & Ruth Rattiken, dau. of James and Susannah Rattiken.
m. 4 Jan. 1786. FFMM.
Hoge, Isaac, son of Solomon and Ann Hoge & Elizabeth Nichols, dau.
of James and Elizabeth Nichols. m. 29 April 1784. FFMM.
Hoge, Joshua G. & Susan H. Plaster, dau. of Henry Plaster, Jr.
David H. Plaster, bm. 10 April 1845. Shel.
Hoge, Solomon & Mary Nickols. m. 1 Nov. 1773. FFMM.
Hoge, William & Mary McGeath. Stephen McGeath attests ages, bm.
11 Dec. 1809.
Hoge, William & Rachel E. Janney. James Hoge attests ages, bm.
22 Feb. 1850. Shel.
Hoge, William & Sarah Nixon. m. 23 Feb. 1801. Littlejohn.
Hogeland, Jackson & Amanda Malvina Hart, dau. of Jonathan Hart.
James Hogeland attests groom's age. Daniel Hart, bm.
30 March 1842. Shel.
Hogeland, William S. & Margaret M. Ayres, dau. of Samuel Ayres.
Jackson Hogeland attests groom's age, bm. 9 Nov. 1847. Cam.
Hoggins, John & Elenor Herbert. m. 1809-1810. Mines.
Hogue, James & Hannah Janney. m. 21 June 1827. Janney, Clerk.
Hogue (Hoge), James & Phila Holmes, dau. of William Holmes. John
Holmes, bm. 10 Oct. 1833. Shel.
Hogue, James & Rachel Farish. m. 15 April 1813. Dunn.
Hogue, Thomas & Mary Anne Simpson, dau. of John Simpson, bm.
23 Sep. 1833. Shel.
Hogue, Thomas, son of Francis Hogue & Sarah Wilkinson, dau. of
Joseph and Barbara Wilkinson. m. 2 May 1775. FFMM.
Hogue, William & Rachel Bowles. m. 23 Oct. 1826-26 Oct. 1826.
Burch.
Hollan, Sylvester & Sally Mathews. m. 28 April 1853. Duncan.
Holland, _____ & Mac Rollens (? sic); both single. By license.
m. 19 Aug. 1829. ParReg A.
Holland, John & Rachell Hibbs. m. 1 Oct. 1797. Littlejohn.
Holland, Sylvester & Sally Mathers. Mother's consent in writing;
his age taken for granted. 28 April 1853. MarReg.

Holland, Zachariah & Mary Pack, dau. of William Pack. Charles
Cushman, bm. 19 Nov. 1799. Littlejohn.
Holliday, Henry & Mary Ann Lewis. William Kent attests ages, bm.
7 Sep. 1840. m. 24 Sep. 1840. Herndon. Shel.
Holliday, William M. & Rebecca Louisa Powell, dau. of H. B.
Powell. William L. Powell proves groom's age, wit. 3 Jan.
1852. MarReg.
Hollingsworth, Charles L. & Nancy C. Weatherill (Wetherile).
Samuel S. Stone attests ages, bm. 19 March 1850. m. 26
March 1850. ParReg A. Shel.
Hollingsworth, Isaac, son of Isaac and Harriet Hollingsworth,
22 years old, b. and residing at Milldam, Frederick County,
Va., farmer & Alcinda M. Gibson, dau. of Dr. Alpheus and
Harriet Ann Gibson, b. and residing at Salubria, Loudoun.
Bride's father proves groom's age, wit. 7 Oct. 1853. MarReg.
m. 25 Oct. 1853. Adie.
Hollingsworth, Jehu (John?) & Senior McDaniel. m. 10 Dec. 1807.
Littlejohn.
Hollingsworth, John & Elizabeth Nicholls. m. 14 Sep. 1820. T.
Littleton.
Hollingsworth, Robert I., Frederick County, Va. & Rachel J.
Stone. m. 16 Sep. 1847. FFMM.
Holmes, Elisha & Hester Thomas. Mahlon Thomas attests bride's
age. Levi White attests groom's age, bm. 19 Jan. 1839. Shel.
Holmes, Fenton & Sarah E. Simpson. John G. Hoge attests groom's
age, bm. John Simpson, bm. 8 Feb. 1841. m. 19 Feb. 1841.
Herndon. Shel.
Holmes, Jacob & Catharina Neuschwager; both single. By license.
m. 9 May 1816. ParReg A.
Holmes, John & Lydia Vansickle. m. 17 Feb. 1825. Dunn. Shel.
Holmes, Lott & Sarah Nichols. m. 23 April 1829. Taylor, Clerk.
Holmes, Warner & Elizabeth Smith. William Smith attests groom's
age, bm. 26 March 1838. Shel.
Holmes, William, Gent. & Elizabeth T. Canby. m. 23 Dec. 1830.
Taylor, Clerk.
Holms, John & Alice Lewis. m. 21 Oct. 1802. Littlejohn.
Holtzclaw, James M. & Martha Virginia Hancock. Bride's father
consents in writing. Thomas Lewis proves groom's age, wit.
26 Nov. 1853. MarReg.
Homan, Reuben Stephens & Martha Griffith. John Griffith, bm.
25 Feb. 1799.
Hooe, Howson & Nancy Reed, dau. of John Reed, bm. 20 Nov. 1833.
m. 21 Nov. 1833. Dorsey. Shel.
Hooff, ·John & Martha J. Blincoe. Charles G. Eskridge, bm. 29 Nov.
1843. m. 30 Nov. 1843. Ward. Shel.
Hooff, Philip H. & Elizabeth Blincoe. Charles W. Blincoe, bm.
11 Feb. 1847. Shel.
Hook, John B. & Jane Clapham. m. 14 May 1816. Littlejohn.
Hooper, James & Catharine Adams. Henry Adams attests ages, bm.
8 Nov. 1830. m. 14 Nov. 1830. ParReg A. Shel.
Hope, Christian & Nancy Willson. m. 4 April 1797. Littlejohn.
Hope, James & Sarah Vanpelt. Jonathan Wright attests ages.
John H. McCabe, bm. 2 April 1833. Cam.

Hope, John A. & Lydia Catharine Reed. Richard Brown attests ages,
    bm. 9 April 1838. m. 12 April 1838. Tapler. Shel.
Hope, Joshua T. & Massa Gore. William Moss attests bride's age,
    bm. 9 March 1829.
Hope, Peyton & Mary Hope. James Wilson, guardian, bm. 14 Feb.
    1831. Cam.
Hope, William P. & Elenor Harrison. m. 12 July 1810. Williamson.
Hopkins, Harry & Elizabeth Binns. m. 24 Feb. 1811. Littlejohn.
Hopkins, Philip & Joannah H. Carter. John C. Murry attests
    bride's age,bm. 4 Oct. 1838. Shel.
Hopkins, Samuel, son of John and Elizabeth Hopkins, Ann Arundel
    County, Md. & Hannah Janney, dau. of Joseph and Hannah Janney.
    m. 29 Aug. 1792. FFMM.
Hopkins, Thomas S. & Sally L. Harris, dau. of Samuel Harris.
    James Hamilton, bm. 15 Oct. 1831. Shel.
Hopwood, Christopher & Martha Coombs.   14 Feb. 1764. FeeBk 1.
Horn, Abram & Elizabeth Ridenbaugh. m. 31 Oct. 1805. Littlejohn.
Horner, William & Ann Harper. m. 3 Feb. 1801. Littlejohn.
Horseman, Joseph & Hannah Whaley. William Whaley, bm. 19 Aug.
    1809.
Horseman, William & Sarah Johnson. Benjamin Johnson attests
    bride's age, bm. 3 Dec. 1832. Shel.
Horton, Malcolm & Margaret A. Denham. Oliver Denham attests
    bride's age, bm. 25 July 1832. m. 29 Feb. 1832. Green. Shel.
Hoskins, Caleb & Sally Davis. Note on front - "Father in the
    bond". John Davis, bm. 14 Jan. 1799.
Hoskins, Joseph & Ann Cooley. m. 2 Nov. 1811. Littlejohn.
Hoskins, William & Susanna Wilson, dau. of James Wilson, bm.
    15 March 1799. Cam.
Hoskinson, Andrew J. & Eleanor Wilson. Rd. Houser, bm. 11 Oct.
    1832. Cam.
Hoskinson, Charles & Sarah Sanders. m. 11 Oct. 1803. Littlejohn.
Hoskinson, Hillery & Elenor Spates. m. 27 July 1819. Littlejohn.
Hoskinson, John K. & Sarah Ann Benedum. Henry Benedum, bm. 2 Dec.
    1839. Shel.
Hoskinson, Robert J. (T.) & Elizabeth Tavenner. Thomas Rogers
    attests ages, bm. 24 Nov. 1847. m. 25 Nov. 1847. Dulin. Shel.
Hoskinson, Thomas & Ann Hoskinson. Henry Saunders, Jr. attests
    bride's age, bm. 10 March 1849. Shel.
Hoskinson, Thomas W. & Virginia McClanahan. Oscar Nesmith proves
    signatures, wit. 18 Sep. 1852. MarReg.
Hough, Amasa, son of William and Eleanor Hough & Ann E. Bond,
    dau. of Joseph and Elizabeth Bond. m. 8 Nov. 1820.
    Mendenhall, Clerk. FFMM.
Hough, Amos & Elizabeth Wilson. m. 10 April 1771. FFMM.
Hough, Armistead T.M. & Harriet Elizabeth Elliott. George N.
    Tracey attests ages, bm. 1 March 1842. m. 6 March 1842.
    Herndon. Shel.
Hough, Benjamin & Margaret Payne. m. 30 Jan. 1806. Littlejohn.
Hough, Benjamin & Rachel Umbaugh. William Worsley, bm. 2 Dec.
    1841. Shel.
Hough, Bernard & Sarah Ann Clendening. William Clendening, Jr.
    attests ages, bm. 27 July 1837. Shel.

Hough, Charles & Ary (Airy) Ann Slater, dau. of Samuel Slater,
    who attests ages, bm. 9 Nov. 1844. m. 12 Nov. 1844. ParReg A.
Hough, Charles & Mary Hougue. m. 9 Feb. 1814. Littlejohn.
Hough, Denzio Chaulette, son of William H. Hough & Eleanor H.
    Schooley, dau. of Jonas P. Schooley, bm. 24 Feb. 1849.
Hough, Garrett & Mary Moore. George Head attests bride's age, bm.
    5 July 1841. m. 5 July 1841. Gover. Shel.
Hough, George & Mary Mahonner. m. 15 Jan. 1807. Littlejohn.
Hough, George W. & Jane Hurdle (Hurdell), dau. of Nancy C. Hurdle,
    Waterford, Va. Richard H. Edwards, bm. 23 Oct. 1848. m.
    26 Oct. 1848. Eggleston. Shel.
Hough, George W. & Mary Catherine Shawen, dau. of Mary Shawen.
    J. A. Braden attests groom's age, bm. 25 March 1833. Shel.
Hough, Henry & Mary Stiffler, m. 23 April 1800. Littlejohn.
Hough, Howard & Phebe Ann Moore. Garrett Hough attests ages, bm.
    5 March 1842. Shel.
Hough, Isaac & Fanny Braden. m. 9 Nov. 1798. Littlejohn.
Hough, Isaac S. & Mary Jane Paxson, dau. of Samuel Paxson, bm.
    12 March 1832. Shel.
Hough, John & Cathrine Wildman. m. 20 Dec. 1804. Littlejohn.
Hough, John & Mary Ann Grubb, dau. of John Grubb, who attests
    groom's age, bm. 24 Dec. 1838. Shel.
Hough, John & Mary Shepherd. m. 16 Jan. 1810. Littlejohn.
Hough, John, Jr. & Lydia Hollingsworth. m. 29 April 1772. FFMM.
Hough, John Edward Stephen & Eguenia T. (S.) Dawson. James
    Sinclair attests bride's age, bm. 20 June 1849. m. 20 June
    1849, at Mrs. Samuel Dawson's. Adie. Shel.
Hough, John P. & Hannah A. Schooley. Samuel Hough, bm. 2 May
    1836. Shel.
Hough, Jonah & Pleasant Hogue, Culpepper County, Va. m. 30 Nov.
    1803. FFMM.
Hough, Joseph B. & Elizabeth Hough. Joseph Hough attests ages, bm.
    13 March 1846. m. 16 March 1846. Shuford. Shel.
Hough, Joseph S. & Mary M. Hough. Benjamin Hough attests ages, bm.
    29 April 1837. Shel.
Hough, Mahlon, son of John Hough & Mary Stabler, dau. of Edward
    Stabler, of Dinwiddie County, Va. m. 6 March 1782. FFMM.
Hough, Philip H. & Elizabeth Blincoe. m. 11 Feb. 1847, at house
    of bride's mother, Leesburg. Adie.
Hough, Robert R. & Sarah Donohoe. m. 16 April 1816. Littlejohn.
Hough, Samuel, son of John Hough & Ann Stabler, dau. of Edward
    Stabler, of Dinwiddie County, Va. m. 30 April 1783. FFMM.
Hough, Samuel & Elizabeth Skinner. m. 2 Jan. 1797. Littlejohn.
Hough, Thomas & Peggy Skinner. Samuel Hough attests bride's age,
    bm. 31 Jan. 1799. Littlejohn.
Hough, William & Jane Clendening. m. 21 May 1794. Littlejohn.
Hough, William & Sarah N. Love. E. A. Love attests ages, bm.
    21 Jan. 1843. Shel.
Hough, William H. & Ann Steer. m. 30 April 1806. FFMM.
Hough, William H. & Eliza N. Brown. m. 23 July 1845. FFMM.
Hough, William H., of B. & Hannah Ann Williams, dau. of Syddnah
    Williams, bm. 21 Feb. 1850. m. 26 Feb. 1850. Eggleston. Shel.
Hough, William H., of Benjamin & Phebe Ellen Hough. Joseph Hough
    attests ages, bm. 18 Oct. 1845. Shel.

Hough, William H., Jr. & Sarah E. Bond. m. 22 May 1850. FFMM.
Houser, Abram & Elizabeth Myres. m. 14 Sep. 1810. Littlejohn.
Houser, Christian & Hannah Lafeber. m. 14 Oct. 1809. Littlejohn.
Houser, Henry & Agnes Wildman. m. 6 May 1809. Littlejohn.
Houser, Jacob & Abigal Hanks. m. 21 Aug. 1806. Littlejohn.
Houser, Jacob & Sarah Catharine Fields. Samuel Orrison attests
    ages, bm. 19 Jan. 1846. Shel.
Houser, Philip & Betsey Vaughters, dau. of Richard Vaughters, bm.
    23 Jan. 1839. m. 24 Jan. 1839. Keppler. Shel.
Householder, Adam & Sarah Janney. m. 13 Nov. 1797. Littlejohn.
Householder, Adam & Sush. Ricketts. m. 15 Nov. 1796. Littlejohn.
Householder, Daniel & Catherine Smith. m. 7 April 1796. Littlejohn.
Householder, Hamilton & Caroline M. Axline. Joseph E. Axline
    attests ages, bm. 4 Dec. 1848. m. 12 Dec. 1848. Dulin. Shel.
Householder, Hamilton & Mary Virginia Stone, dau. of John Stone,
    who proves groom's age, wit. 31 Dec. 1851. MarReg.
Householder, Jacob & Catherine Compher, dau. of Peter Compher,
    bm. 14 Nov. 1836. m. 17 Nov. 1836. ParReg A. Shel.
Howard, Benjamin & Mary A. Mason. m. 14 Feb. 1811. Littlejohn.
Howard, Michael & Elizabeth Ullam, dau. of John Ullam, who
    attests groom's age, bm. 6 Feb. 1809. m. 1808-1809. Mines.
Howard, Thomas & Mary Trunnell. m. 28 May 1802. Littlejohn.
Howel, Daniel & Francis Sheckles. m. 14 March 1814. Littlejohn.
Howell, Daniel & Elizabeth Monday. Henry Read attests ages, bm.
    1 Jan. 1844. Shel.
Howell, James M. & Martha C. Huffman, dau. of John Huffman, bm.
    12 Jan. 1847. m. 19 Jan. 1847. Massey. Shel.
Howser, Christopher & Rosannah Lafaber. William Lafaber attests
    bride's age, bm. 14 Oct. 1809.
Howser, Henry & Agnes Wildman. Joseph Wildman consents. Simon A.
    Binns, bm. 6 May 1809.
Howser, Richard & Mary Ann Haig (Hague). James Haig attests
    groom's age, bm. 21 Dec. 1829. m. 22 Dec. 1829. Tippett.
Hudley, Benjamin & Martha Hall, free persons of colour; ages in
    free papers recorded in the office. 7 Aug. 1851. MarReg.
Hudspeth, Ahijah W. & Sarah W. Hurst. J. T. Massey attests
    bride's age, bm. 1 March 1847. m. 2 March 1847. Massey.Shel.
Huesket, Samuel & Elizabeth Thomas. m. 29 April 1824. Baker.
Huffman, Jacob & Catherine Koist. Cutlop Koist, bm. 22 June
    1799. Littlejohn.
Huffman, John & Mary Piott. m. 30 Dec. 1800. Littlejohn.
Hugeley, John & Elizabeth Harper. m. 17 Dec. 1796. Littlejohn.
Hughes, Constantine, son of Matthew and Elizabeth Hughes, of
    Bucks County, Pa. & Elizabeth Nickols, widow of Thomas
    Nickols, deceased, dau. of William and Elizabeth Janney.
    m. 10 Jan. 1782. FFMM.
Hughes, David L. & Margaret F. Simpson, dau. of French Simpson.
    George R. Jackson, bm. 22 Jan. 1849. m. 23 Jan. 1849. Herndon.
    Shel.
Hughes, Elias & Fanny Taylor. m. 6 Dec. 1816. Littlejohn.
Hughes, Hugh & Elizabeth Poulson. m. 26 Dec. 1804. Littlejohn.
Hughes, Isaac & Reba. Nixon. m. 5 March 1803. Littlejohn.
Hughes, Isaac & Sarah Hixon, dau. of James Hixon, bm. 3 April
    1809.

76

Hughes, Thomas, son of Matthew and Elizabeth Hughes, deceased &
   Sarah Schooley, dau. of John and Mary Schooley. m. 3 Jan.
   1779. FFMM.
Hughes, William H. & Emily Simpson. John Simpson, bm. 13 May
   1844. Shel.
Hughs, John H., son of J. Hughes & Martha Ann Rogers, dau. of
   Dinah Rogers. Samuel Rogers, bm. 25 March 1833. Shel.
Hughs, Samuel & Elizabeth Heyold. m. 26 Oct. 1807. Littlejohn.
Hugley, Charles & Elizabeth McIntosh. m. 17 Nov. 1812. Littlejohn.
Hugley, James & Mary Hummer. m. 25 Aug. 1807. Littlejohn.
Hummer, Benjamin & Dorothy R. Noble. John S. Noble attests ages,
   bm. 23 Feb. 1838. Shel.
Hummer, Benjamin & Emily Havener. Joseph Havener attests ages.
   Orlando K. Sheid, bm. 17 Feb. 1840. Cam.
Hummer, George W. & Emeline C. Miller. John L. Bascue attests
   ages, bm. 28 Sep. 1849. m. 4 Oct. 1849. Eggleston. Shel.
Hummer, George W. & Leah J. Tippett, dau. of John C. Tippett,
   who attests groom's age, bm. 17 Jan. 1849.
Hummer, James W. & Frances Rollison. Silas Havener, bm. 30 June
   1842. Cam.
Hummer, Levi & Martha Bridges. m. 15 March 1815. Littlejohn.
Hummer, Thomas & Joana Saunders. John E. Stewart attests ages,
   bm. 23 Dec. 1848. Shel.
Humphrey, Abner G. & Mary Lodge. m. 28 Nov. 1820. Dagg.
Humphrey, Abner G. & Mary C. Lodge, dau. of Joseph Lodge, who
   attests groom's age, bm. 26 May 1847. m. 1 June 1847.
   Massey. Shel.
Humphrey, Jacob & Sarah Lewis. Edward Connard, Jr. attests bride's
   age, bm. 28 Dec. 1799. Shel.
Humphrey, Jesse & Mary Cating. m. 22 June 1802. Dunn.
Humphrey, John & Elizabeth Vanpelt. m. 28 July 1808. Dunn.
Humphrey, Marcus & Margaret ("Peggy") Marks, dau. of Abel Marks.
   Bennet Marks attests ages, bm. 5 June 1809.
Humphrey, Solomon & Catharine J. Moss. Presley Saunders attests
   ages. Thomas Birkby, bm. 2 Sep. 1844. Shel.
Humphrey, Thomas G. & Phebe Ish. m. 23 Oct. 1827. Chapman.
Humphrey, Thomas L. & Dorcas Osburn. Harrison Osburn attests ages,
   bm. 20 Oct. 1847. m. 28 Oct. 1847. Dulin. Shel.
Humphrey, Thomas L. & Sarah Jenkins. m. 20 July 1820. Dagg.
Humphrey, Thomas M. & Lydia Whitacre. James Whitacre attests
   bride's age, bm. 17 April 1833. Shel.
Humphrey, William L. & Jane A. Pearson, dau. of Craven Pearson.
   Joseph Pearson attests groom's age. L___ Luckett, bm.
   14 Oct. 1844. Shel.
Humphreys, James & Rebecca McClosky, dau. of William McClosky,
   who attests groom's age, bm. 12 Feb. 1829.
Humphreys, Thomas K. & Helen A. Cordell, dau. of Presley Cordell,
   bm. 14 Jan. 1834. Shel.
Humphry, Joseph & Sarah Updike. m. 6 March 1815. Littlejohn.
Humphrys, James & Rebecca McClosky. m. 12 Feb. 1829. Tippett.
Hunbury, Daniel B. & Charlotte Chambers. In bond, Jacob
   Stoutsenberger attests Samuel Dixon's age. Daniel T.
   Crawford, bm. 13 April 1841. Shel.
Hunsey, Thomas & Eliza Jane Harrison. m. 19 Aug. 1841. Herndon.

Hunt, Amos & Ellen Wilson. m. 18 July 1828. Tippett.
Hunt, Eli & Isabella Tavener. m. 26 Sep. 1816. Littlejohn.
Hunt, George T. & Maria West. M. McIlhany, bm. 11 Feb. 1834.Shel.
Hunt, Gerard L. W. & Jane Johnston. m. 2 March 1820. Williamson.
Hunt, Joel & Elizabeth Wire. m. 3 June 1853. Grubb.
Hunt, John & Elizabeth Hurdle. m. 2 Jan. 1815. Littlejohn.
Hunt, Jonathan & Mary Eleanor Hunt. m. 25 Nov. 1810. T. Littleton.
Hunt, Joseph & Sally Hilliard. m. 24 June 1802. Littlejohn.
Hunt, Joseph E. & Elizabeth Talley. Smith Reed attests ages, bm.
    15 Oct. 1849. m. 19 Oct. 1849. Eggleston. Shel.
Hunt, Lewis & Mary Garner. W. W. Kitzmiller, bm. 8 Dec. 1834.Shel.
Hunt, Major & Mary Wilson. C. Binns attests bride's age. William
    Roberts, bm. 11 Nov. 1799. Littlejohn.
Hunt, William & Elizabeth Saunders. m. 20 Oct. 1812. Littlejohn.
Hunt, William & Mary Jane Bolon. Aquila Mead, Jr. attests ages,
    bm. 31 May 1843. Shel.
Hunt, William & Rebecca Romine. m. 30 March 1820. Dagg.
Hunter, Elijah & Elizabeth Sexton. Elijah Hunter, James Solomon,
    James Munroe, bm. 3 Feb. 1801. Littlejohn.
Hunter, George W., Jr. & Mary A. Conrad, dau. of David Conrad,
    bm. 8 Feb. 1836. Cam.
Hunter, John & Jane Rose, dau. of Richard Rose. Alfred Rose
    attests ages, bm. 18 Dec. 1829.
Hunter, John & Nancy Neer, dau. of Henry and Susanna Neer.
    John Neer, bm. 19 Feb. 1799. m. 28 Feb. 1799. Hutt.
Hunter, William & Sibila Wertz, dau. of Peter Wertz and wife.
    By license. m. 14 Nov. 1822. ParReg A.
Hunton, John H. & Amanda M. Butcher, dau. of John H. Butcher.
    Martin O. Butcher, bm. 10 Sep. 1839. Shel.
Hurst, James W. & Elizabeth J. Mount, dau. of S. R. Mount, wit.
    14 March 1853. MarReg. m. 15 March 1853. Greer.
Hutcheson, Beverly & Mary P. Hixson, dau. of Benjamin Hixson,
    who attests groom's age, bm. 23 April 1832. Shel.
Hutcheson, Melville B. & Lucinda Presgraves. Richard Hutcheson
    attests ages. George Rose attests bride's age, bm. 23 July
    1832. Cam.
Hutchingson, Joseph & Elizabeth Major. m. 10 Sep. 1798.
    Littlejohn.
Hutchison, George & Esther Edwards. m. 1807-1808. Mines.
Hutchison, George H. & Susan Beatty. John Beatty proves ages,
    wit. 11 Nov. 1850. MarReg. m. 12 Nov. 1850. Eggleston.
Hutchison, George W. & Courtney Ann Bradshaw. Mother consents in
    writing. John Akers proves groom's age, wit. 21 Feb. 1852.
    MarReg.
Hutchison, Henry & Susannah Plaster. m. 13 Nov. 1817. T. Littleton.
Hutchison, Lewellin & Julia Ambler. Fielding Littleton, bm.
    Vincent L. Ambler attests ages, bm. 8 Feb. 1841. Cam.
Hutchison, Pickering & Sarah E. Hatchison. William Ambler attests
    ages, bm. 25 Aug. 1847. Cam.
Hutchison, Redding & Catherine B. Hutcheson. William Ambler
    attests ages, bm. 10 April 1834. Cam.
Hutchison, Sampson & Rachel Harding, dau. of Thomas Harding.
    Edward Harding, bm. 8 May 1834. m. 20 May 1834. Baker. Shel.

Hutchison, Thomas & Mary Ellen Gist. Charles W. Gist attests
   bride's age, bm. 16 Jan. 1837.
Huter, Phillip, widower & Magdalena Schover (Schovers). By
   license. m. 9 March 1826. ParReg A.
Hutt, James & Alcinda Wynkoop. Thomas J. Morgan attests bride's
   age, bm. 17 May 1850. m. 19 May 1850. Burton.
Hutton, Joseph & Sarah Janney. m. 16 Sep. 1761. FFMM.
Hutton, Samuel & Sarah Cadwalader. m. 8 Sep. 1785. FFMM.
Hyat, James & Amy Pancoast. m. 19 Dec. 1800. Littlejohn.
Hyatt, Thomas & Henritta Jay, dau. of David Jay, bm. 12 April
   1799. Shel.
Iden, George & Matilda Brown. m. 28 Aug. 1812. J. Littleton.
Iden, John T. & Virginia Stover. Father's statement proves bride's
   age; "the other's age apparent". 17 Dec. 1851. MarReg.
   Dashiell.
Iden, Jonah & Mary Vernon. m. 3 Feb. 1806. Littlejohn.
Iden, Randolph & Matilda Howser. m. 8 March 1819. Griffith.
Iden, Samuel & Sarah Bishop. License: 10 Oct. 1803. Davis.
Iden, Thomas & Elizabeth Hill. m. 1820-1821. Mines.
Ingram, John & Margaret Magaha. Daniel Miller attests bride's age.
   George W. Wilt attests groom's age, bm. 14 Aug. 1843. Shel.
Ingram, John & Tamer Potts. m. 1815. Littlejohn.
Inoro, Joseph & Ann Pugh. m. 8 April 1846. Shuford.
Insor, John & Mary Jane Woodly (Woody), ward of John A. Binns.
   Creighton Sanders, bm. 15 April 1830. Shel.
Irwin, Thomas, Alexandria, son of Thomas and Abigail Irwin &
   Elizabeth Janney. m. 31 Aug. 1791. FFMM.
Ish, George H. & Elizabeth M. Adams. Francis T. Adams, bm.
   10 Nov. 1845. Cam.
Ish, Robert A. & Parmelia Hixson. Benjamin Hixon, bm. 1 Nov.
   1838. Broadus. Shel.
Jackson, Benjamin & Elizabeth Clapham. m. 11 Jan. 1807.
   Littlejohn.
Jackson, George & Margaret Megeath. Alfred Megeath attests
   bride's age, bm. 30 Oct. 1848. Shel.
Jackson, Giles T. & Sophronia Eveline Dennis, dau. of Matilda
   Carter. William A. Dennis, bm. 20 April 1847. Cam.
Jackson, Hezekiah & Phebe Gibert, colored. Registrars show them
   free and of age. Proved by Elijah Holmes. 11 Nov. 1850.
   MarReg.
Jackson, Isaiah & Lucy M. Young, dau. of John Young, bm. 2 Dec.
   1845. Shel.
Jackson, Lewis & Eleanor Carrico, dau. of James Carrico, bm.
   19 Dec. 1833. Shel.
Jackson, Lewis Caton & Ann Gilbert. G. W. Paxson attests ages, bm.
   29 Dec. 1843. Shel.
Jackson, Samuel & Susan Grimes. Jonathan West, bm. 9 Sep. 1831.
   Shel.
Jackson, Samuel C. & Margaret Ann Donohoe. George D. Smith
   attests groom's age. Edward Hammat attests bride's age, bm.
   25 Oct. 1834. m. 28 Oct. 1834. Dorsey. Shel.
Jackson, Thomas & Amelia Counard. m. 1821-1822. Mines.
Jackson, William & Julia Ann Woodard. William W. McDonough
   attests groom's age, bm. 8 Oct. 1840. Gover. Shel.

LOUDOUN COUNTY MARRIAGES

Jackson, William & Margaret Stoneburner. James Gilmore, bm.
    16 Dec. 1829.
Jackson, William B., son of Benjamin Jackson & Rebecca T. Dulen.
    Benjamin Jackson attests bride's age, bm. 6 April 1833. Shel.
Jacky, Peter & Milia Jams; both single. By license. m. 21 Sep.
    1820. ParReg A.
Jacob, alias Jacob Bonce & Mary Robison, free people of colour.
    Charles Binns, bm. 30 Sept. 1830. Shel.
Jacobs, ____ & Catharine Miller. m. 8 April 1853. ParReg A.
Jacobs, Adam & Rachel Edwards. m. 10 May 1827. Tuston.
Jacobs, Elgin & Eleanor Lyders. m. 13 Feb. 1827. Burch.
Jacobs, Roswell Posey & Susan R. Plaster, in Maryland. m. 13 Nov.
    1832. ParReg A.
Jacobs, Ryland & Catherine Wolf. Wit: Charles Speaks. 14 March
    1853. MarReg.
Jacobs, Ryland & Elizabeth Thomas. William Chamblin, bm.
    Acknowledged 29 Oct. 1832. Dorsey. Shel.
Jacobs, Thomas & Sarah Green. m. 23 Feb. 1797. Littlejohn.
Jacobs, William & Catharine Shaw. m. 3 Sep. 1819. Griffith.
Jacobs, William & Maria Chamblin. m. 9 April 1822. C. Frye.
James, Abel & Sarah Heath, dau. of Andrew and Hannah Heath.
    James McKim attests ages, bm. 22 March 1809. Littlejohn.
James, Charles E. & Sarah Warner, dau. of Israel Warner, who
    proves groom's age, wit. 5 Nov. 1850. MarReg. m. 12 Nov.
    1851 (?). Chenoweth.
James, Charles W. & Martha Brown, dau. of Daniel Brown. Joseph
    Richardson, bm. 29 Oct. 1832. Shel.
James, Craven & Catharine Louisa Morris. Mahlon J. Morris
    attests groom's age, bm. 9 March 1840. Shel.
James, Cravan & Emily A. Blakeley, Mrs. Wit: James H. Nichols.
    24 Jan. 1853. MarReg. m. 27 Jan. 1853. Greer.
James, Ellwood B. & Elizabeth Ann Richardson. Joseph Richardson,
    bm. 11 Sep. 1835. m. 15 Sep. 1835. Monroe. Shel.
James, Hannibal & Charloote P. Bradfield. Jefferson C. Thomas
    attests ages, bm. 4 Feb. 1841. Shel.
James, John & Sarah James. David James attests ages, bm. 13 May
    1829.
James, John & Sarah B. Mershon. Henry Mershon attests ages, bm.
    28 Feb. 1832. Shel.
James, Joseph & Rebecca Garrett. Samuel Garrett attests ages, bm.
    30 Oct. 1809.
James, Levi & Martha Ellen Paxson, dau. of Samuel Paxson, who
    attests groom's age, bm. 1 March 1850. m. 5 March 1850.
    Eggleston. Shel.
James, Mahlon, son of Elijah James & Rachel Ann Paxson, dau. of
    Samuel Paxson. Elijah James, Samuel Paxson, bm. 8 Oct. 1836.
    Shel.
James, Mason & Patience Nichols, ward of Nathaniel Nichols, bm.
    Dolphin Nichols, bm. 13 Nov. 1837. Shel.
James, Matson & Hannah Thomas. Mahlon Thomas attests ages, bm.
    13 March 1837. Shel.
James, Richard & Sarah Ann Waltman. Jacob Waltman, bm. 5 Nov.
    1842. Shel.

LOUDOUN COUNTY MARRIAGES

James, Robert & _____. John Simpson attests ages, bm. 13 Dec.
    1841. Shel.
Jameson, Malcom & Julia M. Thompson, dau. of John Thompson, who
    attests groom's age. David Weatherly, bm. 26 Jan. 1831. Cam.
Janney, Abel & Mary Janney. m. 3 April 1771. FFMM.
Janney, David & Elizabeth Moore. m. 1 Feb. 1809. FFMM.
Janney, Eli & Elizabeth White. Samuel Gregg, bm. 27 Feb. 1801.
    Littlejohn. Shel.
Janney, Eli & Sarah Vandeventer. Joseph Vandevanter attests
    bride's age, bm. 23 Jan. 1809. m. 1808-1809. Mines.
Janney, Isaiah B. & Hannah S. Hirst. m. 12 Sep. 1836. White.
Janney, Israel, son of Jacob and Hannah Janney & Pleasant
    Hague, dau. of Francis Hague. m. 5 May 1773. FFMM.
Janney, James & Susanna Reed. m. 9 March 1824. Dunn.
Janney, James C. & Rebecca Jane Walker. m. 20 June 1838. FFMM.
Janney, James M. & Sarah Ann Lupton, Frederick County, Va. m.
    21 April 1830. FFMM.
Janney, Jesse & Susan Bleakley. Wit: James H. Nichols. 24 Nov.
    1852. MarReg.
Janney, Johannes, widower & Elisabeth Wilkinson, single. By
    license. m. 16 Dec. 1829. ParReg A.
Janney, John & Elizabeth Wilkinson, dau. of Thomas Wilkinson, who
    states bride was born 1806. John A. Binns, bm. 14 Dec. 1829.
Janney, Joseph, Jr. & Elizabeth Russell. m. 7 March 1816.
    T. Littleton.
Janney, Joseph, Jr. & Mary Holmes. m. 4 June 1778. FFMM.
Janney, Mahlon & Rachel White. m. 11 Nov. 1805. Littlejohn.
Janney, Mahlon & Sarah Plummer, Frederick County, Maryland, dau.
    of Samuel and Sarah Plummer, Prince George's County, Maryland.
    m. 29 Aug. 1758. FFMM.
Janney, Mahlon, Jr. & Sarah Brown. James Brown, bm. 26 June
    1799. Littlejohn.
Janney, Moses, Waterford & Beulah Mendenahll, Waterford. m.
    18 Oct. 1826. FFMM.
Janney, Nathan H. & Lydia Jane Pursel, ward of Jas. M. McKay, who
    notes "I concur with the above Mary Purcel". James H.
    Pursel attests groom's age, bm. 31 May 1847. Shel.
Janney, Stacy & Hannah Brown. m. 10 April 1776. FFMM.
Janny, Isaiah B. & Hannah S. Hirst. William Brown attests
    bride's age, bm. 12 Sep. 1836. Shel.
Janny, Jesse & Susan Bleakley. m. 2 Dec. 1852. Greer.
Jeffers, Anderson & Harriot Perfect. m. 26 Aug. 1819. Littlejohn.
Jeffries, Braxton B. & Tacy (Lucy) H. Daniel. Sampson G.
    Dowdell attests ages, bm. 17 Dec. 1840. m. 22 Dec. 1840.
    Gover. Shel.
Jeffries, John William & Eliza Johnston, dau. of Baldwin Johnson.
    Braxton Jeffries, bm. 17 July 1837. Shel.
Jenkins, Amos, son of Silvester Jenkins & Catherine Jenkins.
    Silvester Jenkins attests bride's age, bm. 29 May 1829.
Jenkins, Edward & Martha L. Keene. Richard Keene attests ages,
    bm. 27 Jan. 1837. m. 2 Feb. 1837. Herndon. Cam.
Jenkins, Elijah & Rebecca Chilton. m. 8 Feb. 1806. Littlejohn.
Jenkins, Levi & Mary Hickman. m. 21 Sep. 1814. Littlejohn.
Jenkins, Levi & Nancy Hendrick. m. 1809-1810. Mines.

LOUDOUN COUNTY MARRIAGES

Jenkins, Matthias & Catharine Harper. m. 22 Aug. 1851. ParReg A.
Jenkins, Reuben & Eleann Ruter, ward of Herod Osburn, bm. 9 Aug.
    1833. Shel.
Jenkins, Sampson & Julia Burch, dau. of Barbary Birch. Lewis D.
    Burch, bm. 24 Aug. 1835. Cam.
Jenkins, Samuel & Frances C. Miskill. William Miskell, bm. 30 Dec.
    1844. Cam.
Jenkins, Samuel & Louisa Hough, dau. of Bernard Hough. Wm. G. (?)
    Jenkins attests groom's age. J. A. Binns, bm. 25 Feb. 1829.
    Shel.
Jenkins, Thomas & Ann Whaley. George W. Hunter attests ages, bm.
    John Minis, bm. 23 July 1840. Cam.
Jenkins, Thomas & Sarah E. Jenkins. Herod Jenkins attests ages,
    bm. 29 March 1842.
Jenkins, Washington & Edah Howell. Jesse Howell attests ages, bm.
    24 Sep. 1832. Shel.
Jenkins, William & Elizabeth Dove, dau. of William Dove, bm.
    Elijah Jenkins attests groom's age. 24 Dec. 1829.
Jenkins, William & Maria Moton. m. 2 Dec. 1823. Dagg.
Jenkins, William G. & Martha A. Smith. Wit: Stephen P. Smith.
    21 Nov. 1853. MarReg. m. 24 Nov. 1853. Herndon.
Jenney, Lot & Sophia Holmes. m. 26 May 1813. Littlejohn.
Jennings, Larkin D. & Mary Ann Margaret Rogers. Sanford Rogers,
    bm. 28 April 1838. Shel.
Jennings, William & Ann Moxley. Abigail Moxley attests ages, bm.
    9 Dec. 1841. Shel.
Jett, Peter & Nancy Lane, ward of Joseph Lane, bm. 26 Oct. 1809.
Jinkins, Elias & Dania Thomas. m. 27 Aug. 1803. Littlejohn.
Jinkins, Elias & Catherine Harper. Washington Harper proves ages,
    wit. 11 Aug. 1851. MarReg.
Jinkins, Henry & Margaret Offett. m. 14 Nov. 1809. Littlejohn.
Jinkins, Simon & Nancy Muse. m. 10 April 1810. Littlejohn.
Jinkins, Solomon & Sarah Jackson. m. 16 Dec. 1805. Littlejohn.
John, William & Frances Chitton. m. 19 Feb. 1798. Littlejohn.
Johnson, A. M. & Sarah C. Hoffman, dau. of John Hoffman, bm.
    22 Nov. 1848. Shel.
Johnson, Absalom, son of William Johnson & Louisa Jane Hough.
    Ann M. Whaley attests bride's age. James M. Carr, bm. 16 June
    1841. m. 10 June 1841. Gover. Cam.
Johnson, Alexander & Miranda Craven. m. 22 Sep. 1835. White.
Johnson, Alexander W. & Sarah Ann Fichter (Fechter), dau. of
    Mrs. Orange. James Orange attests groom's age, bm. 24 Aug.
    1840. m. 24 Aug. 1840, house of Mr. Orange, Leesburg.
    ◆Adie. Shel.
Johnson, Amos & Matilda Middleton. Lovell H. Middleton attests
    ages, bm. 7 March 1829. m. 15 March 1829. Baker.
Johnson, Amos W. & Susan Bell. Charles W. Lane proves bride's
    age, wit. 3 April 1852. MarReg. m. 13 April 1852. Trott.
Johnson, Arthur C. & Mary Jane Clowes. A. M. Vandevanter attests
    bride's age, bm. 23 Oct. 1843. m. 7 Nov. 1843, at house of
    bride's mother. Adie. Shel.
Johnson, Daniel & Britannia Lomax. m. 14 Feb. 1821. Dagg.
Johnson, David & Maria Snowden. By special permission. m. 14 Oct.
    1832. ParReg A.

Johnson, Fenton & Elizabeth Jane Stephenson. Thomas J. Brabham
    attests ages, bm. 17 Feb. 1840. Cam.
Johnson, George & Nancy Young. m. 25 Sep. 1817. T. Littleton.
Johnson, George W. & Nancy Wright, dau. of William Wright, who
    attests groom's age, bm. 2 March 1842. m. 3 March 1842. Phelps.
    Shel.
Johnson, James A. & Nancy Clowes. Charles B. Hamilton attests
    bride's age, bm. 16 May 1834. Shel.
Johnson, James H. & Alice Ann Dulin. Daniel Shreve proves ages,
    wit. 3 Sep. 1850. MarReg.
Johnson, John & Caroline Staley, dau. of Jacob Staley, who
    attests groom's age, bm. 31 March 1834. Shel.
Johnson, John & Mary Debell, widow. License: 13 Sep. 1762.
    FeeBk 3.
Johnson, Peter W. & Anna S. Drish, dau. of William D. Drish, bm.
    31 Oct. 1848. m. 1 Nov. 1848. Nixon. Shel.
Johnson, Richard & Nancy Marts, with Maryland license. m. 4 Oct.
    1836. ParReg A.
Johnson, Robert, from Maryland & Malinda Mills, widow. By
    license. m. 26 Feb. 1818. ParReg A.
Johnson, Sydnor B. & Rosanna R. Heskit. Joseph B. Gourley
    attests ages, bm. 16 April 1839. Shel.
Johnson, Thomas & Louisa Palmer. Otho Riggs attests ages, bm.
    4 Sep. 1832. Shel.
Johnson, Thomas & Thurza Gibson. m. 11 Jan. 1823. Dagg.
Johnson, William & Sally Bayless. m. 12 Oct. 1820. Dunn.
Johnson, Zopher & Elizabeth Romine. 13 Aug. 1810. m. 16 Aug.
    1810. T. Littleton.
Johnston, Alexander & Maranda Craven, dau. of James Craven, bm.
    22 Sep. 1835. Shel.
Johnston, Charles A. & Mary R. Boss. Samuel W. Boss, bm. 13 Sep.
    1838. Shel.
Johnston, Hanson & Jane White. Daniel Henley (Handley) attests
    ages, bm. 10 June 1799. Cam.
Johnston, John & Catherine Frey. m. 28 Oct. 1814. Littlejohn.
Johnston, John & Nancy McMullan. Archd. McMullan attests bride's
    age, bm. 22 March 1799. Shel.
Johnston, Nimrod & Alice A. Athey. James W. Athey attests ages,
    bm. 27 Oct. 1845 (1846). Shel.
Jolliffe, Joseph N. & Sarah E. Janney. m. 9 Feb. 1843. Bond,
    Clerk.
Jolly, Landon, son of Jacob Jolly & Margaret Linch (Lynch). John
    Smallwood, Jesse Richards, bm. 17 Aug. 1833. Shel.
Jones, Abel & Julian Vanpelt, ward of Cyrus Burson, bm. 14 Feb.
    1831. m. 15 Feb. 1831. Green. Shel.
Jones, Alfred & Rosetta Gibson. Thomas Poulton attests groom's
    age, bm. 12 Jan. 1829. m. 13 Jan. 1829. Tippett.
Jones, Catesby & Mary Tarperman. m. 25 June 1818. Williamson.
Jones, Catesby & Susannah Nicewanger. m. 30 Aug. 1826-7 Sep.
    1826. Burch.
Jones, James H. & Frances Ann Watson. m. 5 Jan. 1853. Smith.
Jones, John & Elizabeth Simpson. m. 21 Sep. 1808. Littlejohn.
Jones, John, Jr. & Lydia H. Potts. Samuel D. Leslie attests
    bride's age, bm. 8 Dec. 1845. Shel.

Jones, Jonas & Nancy Drury. m. 19 Aug. 1803. Littlejohn.
Jones, Landon & Sarah E. Wynkoop, dau. of Elizabeth Wynkoop.
  Garret Wynkoop, bm. 13 Dec. 1841. Shel.
Jones, Leven T. & Lydia C. Russell. Bride's father consents, wit.
  28 Jan. 1852. MarReg.
Jones, Notley & Margaret Summer. m. 11 April 1796. Littlejohn.
Jones, Thomas & Elizabeth Hunter. m. 1804. McPherson.
Jones, Thomas & Lucinda Baldwin. John L. Chamblin attests ages,
  bm. 1 Sep. 1834. m. 4 Sep. 1834. Furlong. Shel.
Jones, William & Margaret Smith. m. 9 Dec. 1811. Littlejohn.
Jones, William T. & Harriet J. Norris, dau. of Rachel Norris.
  George R. Donaldson attests groom's age, bm. 7 March 1850.
  Shel.
Jonston, Charles & Henniritta M. Owings. m. 13 Oct. 1800.
  Littlejohn.
Jonston, James & Elizabeth Mason. m. 8 March 1802. Littlejohn.
Jonston, William & Mary Beaton. m. 30 Oct. 1810. Littlejohn.
Jonstone, George & Mary Brooklante. m. 10 Oct. 1796. Littlejohn.
Jonstone, John & Sarah Gulick. m. 25 Jan. 1796. Littlejohn.
Jonstone, William & Margaret Ish. m. 13 Dec. 1804. Littlejohn.
Jordan, Joshua & Susanna Evans. m. 27 Aug. 1812. J. Littleton.
Jorden, Robert & Jane Craig. m. 11 March 1811. Littlejohn.
Jordon, John & Jane Randel. m. 13 Dec. 1802. Littlejohn.
Joyce, George & Jane Iden. m. 22 Dec. 1825. Dunn. Shel.
Jury, Abner & Mary Ewers. m. 22 Jan. 1795. Littlejohn.
Jury, Lewis & Mary Richards. John Richards, bm. 13 Nov. 1809.
Jury, Reese & Nancy Clewes. m. 4 June 1805. Littlejohn.
Jury, Silas & Ann Tharp. m. 1807-1808. Mines.
Jury, Townshend J. & Mary Ann Drake. John G. Humphrey, bm.
  m. 31 Oct. 1831. Shel.
Kabrich, Georg & Elisabetha Miller; both single. By license.
  m. 17 Jan. 1822. ParReg A.
Kabrich, George & Jane Morrison. Edward Morrison attests ages,
  bm. 27 Feb. 1835. m. 5 March 1835. Hauer. Shel.
Kabrick, Isaiah Randolph, son of George Kabrick & Amelia Morrison,
  dau. of John Morrison, bm. George Kabrick, bm. 26 Feb. 1848.
  Shel.
Kabrick, John M., son of George Kabrick & Eva M. Frye, dau. of
  John Frye, bm. 6 Nov. 1848. Shel.
Kaigh, John H. & Mary E. Triplett. William Mirshon attests bride's
  age, bm. 4 Aug. 1832. Cam.
Kalb, Andrew H., son of Absalom Kalb & Ann James. Elijah James,
  bm. 8 Oct. 1836. Shel.
Kalb, Jesse D. & Mary Eliza Virtz, dau. of Conrad Virtz, who
  attests groom's age, bm. 12 Dec. 1840. m. 17 Dec. 1840.
  Larkin. Shel.
Kalb, John G. R., son of Samuel Kalb, who states he was born 1824
  & Ellen H. Slater, dau. of William Slater, who attests
  groom's age, bm. 31 Dec. 1847. m. 4 Jan. 1848. Williard. Shel.
Kane, John & Polly Kirk. m. 18 Oct. 1797. Littlejohn.
Karnes, Peter & Sally Greenwell. Elias Jenkins attests ages, bm.
  20 Nov. 1847. Shel.
Kearnes, Peter & Mary Smith, dau. of Margaret McCarty, formerly
  Smith, bm. 26 Aug. 1843. Shel.

Kearsley, John & Margeret Steward. m. 4 Jan. 1803. Littlejohn.
Kebrick, Isaiah & Amelia Morrison. m. 27 Feb. 1848. Williard.
   Shel.
Kebrich, John M. & Eva Matilda Fry. m. 9 Nov. 1848. ParReg A.
Keeble, Edwin A. & Susan R. Cochran, dau. of Richard Cochran.
   A. G. Waterman, bm. 27 April 1830. m. 29 April 1830.
   Williamson. Shel.
Keen, Francis & Mary Marshall, dau. of Thomas Marshall, bm.
   7 Sep. 1796.
Keen, John & Amanda F. Broaddus, dau. of W. F. Broaddus. Lewis D.
   Means attests groom's age, bm. 31 Jan. 1840. Shel.
Keene, Thomas W. & Robertus E. A. Jacobs, dau. of Elam Jacobs who
   states bride's under 21 years. John W. Jacobs attests groom's
   age, bm. 28 Dec. 1849. m. 1 Jan. 1850. Dulin. Shel.
Kees , James F., son of Hannah Kees & Louisa A. Tavenner, dau.
   of Nancy Tavenner. Wit: Samuel T. Davis. 24 Nov. 1853.
   MarReg. m. 24 Nov. 1853. McGee.
Kees, Josiah G. & Mary E. O'Neal, dau. of Thomas O'Neal, bm.
   Thomas Rogers affirms groom's age. 4 Dec. 1848. m. 12 Dec.
   1848. Herndon. Shel.
Kelley, John & Elizabeth Robbin. m. 1 March 1809. Littlejohn.
Kelley, John & Louisa Dennis. George Briscoe affirms bride's
   ages, bm. 14 May 1833. Shel.
Kelly, Lawson & Amanda J. Clowe, dau. of William H. Clowe, bm.
   Landon Worthington attests groom's age, bm. 28 Dec. 1836.
   Shel.
Kelly, Michal & Charity Race. m. 28 Dec. 1796. Littlejohn.
Kelly, William & Rebecca Hawkins. m. 14 May 1811. Littlejohn.
Kemp, Henry & Sarah Hite. m. 25 Sep. 1797. Littlejohn.
Kendal, Adam & Peggy Smithey. m. 16 Jan. 1808. Littlejohn.
Kendel, William & Youlyanne Burnhouse. m. 10 June 1811.
   Littlejohn.
Kendrick, William L. H. & Louisa E. Swart. David Daniel attests
   ages, bm. 2 Aug. 1845. Shel.
Kenedy, Jonathan & Mary Gr____. m. 12 Dec. 1814. Littlejohn.
Kenedy, Matthew & Ann McVicker. m. 21 May 1794. Littlejohn.
Kennedy, Jonathan & Nelly Maberry, free Negroes; both over 21.
   Samuel Jackson, bm. 21 Nov. 1831. Shel.
Kennee, Matthew M. & Sarah Elizabeth Torbert. m. 24 Nov. 1835.
   Trott.
Kennerly, Samuel & Ann Alexander Lafferty, widow. m. 23 April
   1827. Kennerly.
Kent, Benjamin & Sarah Kent. m. 28 Feb. 1805. Williamson.
Kent, Harrison & Malinda Henry. Richard Tavenner, bm. 7 Jan.
   1830. m. 7 Jan. 1830. Tippett.
Kent, Richardson & Louisa A. Lowe, dau. of Henry Lowe, who
   attests groom's age, bm. 2 May 1842. Shel.
Kent, Thomas, Dr. & Susannah Amanda Carter, dau. of Eden Carter.
   Francis M. Carter, bm. 4 Feb. 1850. Shel.
Kercheval, Robert H. & Unity Kenne, dau. of George Keene. Willis
   A. Kercheval attests groom's age, bm. 9 March 1840. m.
   12 March 1840. Broaddus. Shel.
Kerns, Abrahm & Naomi Ish. m. 1820-1821. Mines.

Kerns, David & Elisabetha Schmidtin, dau. of Widow Schmidt; both
single. By license. m. 12 March 1812. ParReg A.
Kerns, Jacob & Charlotta Schlotzer, dau. of Jacob Schlotzer, Sr.
and wife. By license. m. 18 May 1820. ParReg A.
Kerns, Jacob, widower & Elisabeth Evins, widow. By license. m.
16 Aug. 1827. ParReg A.
Kerns, Samuel & Louisa Miller; both single. By license. m.
3 April 1814. ParReg A.
Kerns, William & Mrs. Margaret Schaeffer. m. 11 March 1845.
ParReg A.
Kessler, Philip & Mary Everhart. Philip Derry attests ages, bm.
2 Jan. 1847. Shel.
Keys, William & Mary A. Tavenner, dau. of Eli Tavenner, bm.
15 Feb. 1848.
Kidwell, Alexander & Amelia Gibson. Bride's father attests
groom's age. Aaron Gibson, bm. 22 Aug. 1842. m. 23 Aug. 1842.
Phelps. Shel.
Kidwell, Coleman, guardian of said Emeline & Emeline Sunnis.
George W. Thompson, bm. 10 Dec. 1832. Shel.
Kidwell, Gabriel & Sophia M. Welch, dau. of James Welch, bm.
Andrew Hesser affirms groom's age. 14 Jan. 1833. Shel.
Kidwell, Horatio & Sarah Burkett. m. 28 May 1821. Dunn. Shel.
Kidwell, James & Catherine Marony. m. 22 Dec. 1813. Littlejohn.
Kidwell, John & Susan Blundon. W. Blundon, bm. 19 June 1847. Shel.
Kidwell, Thomas & Elizabeth Freast. m. 18 March 1801. Littlejohn.
Kidwell, Thomas & Mary Jury Townsend J. Jury attests bride's age,
bm. 8 Jan. 1834. m. 16 Jan. 1834. Baker. Shel.
Kidwell, Zedikiah (Zaceriah) & Mary Ross (Ropp), dau. of Nicholas
Ross. Nelson Everheart attests ages, bm. 21 March 1831. m.
24 March 1831. G. Frye. Shel.
Kiefer, Fridrich, son of Michael Kiefer & Maria Kemper, dau. of
Johannes Kamper. By license. m. 11 Dec. 1791. ParReg A.
Kiefer, Georg, widower & Milia Spring, single. By license. m.
4 June 1829. ParReg A.
Kiefer, Georg & Sarah Mann; both single. By license. m. 21 May
1826. ParReg A.
Kiefer, Jacob, son of Friderich and Magdalena Kiefer & Magdalena
Wentzeln, dau. of Georg and Catharina Wentzel; both single.
By license. m. 30 Nov. 1820. ParReg A.
Kiefer, Johannes, son of Michael Kiefer & Eva Edelmanin, dau. of
Mr. Edelman; both single. By license. m. 13 Dec. 1810.
ParReg A.
Kiefer, Johannes (Sic.) & Magdalena Heckmannin, dau. of Peter
Hackmann and wife; both single. By license. 10 April 1820.
ParReg A.
Kieffer, William & Anna E. Jenkens; both single. By license. m.
17 May 1827. ParReg A.
Kilgour, Alexander & Margaret Ann Stribling, ward of M. McIlhany.
John Janney, bm. 1 Nov. 1832. G. Frye. Shel.
Kilgour, James M. & Louisa McIlhany, dau. of James McIlhany.
Robert J. T. White, bm. 24 Nov. 1843. m. 30 Nov. 1843, at
home of bride's father. Adie. Shel.
Killroy, Michael & Catharine Beatty. Thomas S. Dornell attests
bride's age, bm. 6 Jan. 1844. Shel.

LOUDOUN COUNTY MARRIAGES

Kimber, John & Jean Buchhanan. m. 27 July 1820. T. Littleton.
Kimmel, Joseph & Catherine Hoffman, in Maryland. m. 10 March
    1836. ParReg A.
Kinder, Azariah & Mary Jane Kidwell. Hezekiah Kidwell attests
    ages, bm. 21 July 1841. Shel.
King, Augustine & Elizabeth A. Starkey, dau. of Isaac Starkey.
    James Gibbs attests groom's age, bm. 8 Jan. 1845. m. 9 Jan.
    1845. Massey. Shel.
King, Bennet & Mary Hixon. m. 15 Nov. 1795. Littlejohn.
King, Francis F. & Hannah Jones, dau. of Thomas Jones. Abel
    Jones attests groom's age, bm. 15 Feb. 1830.
King (alias Lucas), Henry & Barshaba (alias Barshaba Proctor).
    m. 15 Oct. 1811. Littlejohn.
King, William & Tacy Daniel. William Gilmore, bm. 15 Sep. 1831.
    Shel.
Kins, William & Jane Merchants (?); both single. By license. m.
    14 Oct. 1828. ParReg A.
Kinsel, John & Sophena Daymude, ward of John Kinsel. James
    Daymude attests groom's age. John Hutchison, bm. 9 March
    1829.
Kipheart (Kiphart), Thomas & Mary Skinner. Mary Skinner. bm.
    4 March 1809. Littlejohn.
Kirk, William & Nancy Drish. m. 28 June 1810. Littlejohn.
Kirkpatrick, James L. & Jane E. Hooe. Norval Craig proves ages,
    wit. 25 Dec. 1850. MarReg. m. 26 Dec. 1850. Eggleston.
Kirst (Kest), Solomon & Elizabeth Evans. Adam Evans attests
    groom's age, bm. 27 Dec. 1831. Shel.
Kirvings, John S. & Frances Towner. m. 31 May 1852. Holland.
Kist, Solomon & Elizabeth Evence; both single. m. 12 Jan. 1832.
    ParReg A.
Kitchen, William & Eliza Shelby, widow, dau. of John Noggle, bm.
    30 Oct. 1848. Gover. Shel.
Kittle, James & Nancy Carr. James Carr attests bride's age. Amos
    Carr, bm. 7 Feb. 1832. Shel.
Kitzmiller, Archibald M. & Anne E. Hilliard, dau. of Joseph
    Hilliard, bm. 3 Oct. 1833. Dorsey. Shel.
Kizer, Martin & Barbara Razer. Benjamin Jackson attests ages, bm.
    9 Feb. 1829.
Klein, Julius N., son of Elizabeth Klein & Mary F. Mount, dau. of
    Stephen R. Mount. James Mount attests groom's age, wit.
    25 Oct. 1853. MarReg. m. 31 Oct. 1853. McGee.
Klein, Maddison C. & Hester B. Janney. John A. Klein attests
    groom's age. Jacob Janney attests bride's age, bm. 15 Nov.
    1831. Shel.
Knight, Benjamin & Priscilla Jackson. m. 1807-1808. Mines.
Knott, Ignatius M. & Mary Lee Seeders. Sarah S. Seeders consents.
    James Sinclair, bm. 20 Nov. 1848. Shel.
Knox, Joseph & Jane Patterson. m. 24 Dec. 1794. Littlejohn.
Kobland, Johannes, widower & Prissila Cohl, single. By license.
    m. 24 Aug. 1824. ParReg A.
Koist, Peter & Ann Butler. Jacob Huffman, bm. 12 Aug. 1799.
    Littlejohn.
Korner, Gottlieb & Catharina Frey; both single. By license.
    m. 9 April 1821. ParReg A.

Krantz, William H. & Julia Ann Beavers. Bride's mother consents
    in writing. S. B. T. Caldwell proves groom's age, wit. 6
    April 1853. MarReg. m. 7 April 1853, at Wheatland. McGee.
Kreps, Jacob & Catherine Speck. m. 16 Feb. 1815. Littlejohn.
Krumbach, Johannes & Catharina Hahn; both single. By license.
    m. 2 April 1820. ParReg A.
Kuffer, Georg & Anna Maria Edelmann. By license. m. 11 Oct. 1796.
    ParReg A.
Kuhlman, Daniel W. J. (S. M.) Justice & Caroline Diedericks.
    Daniel Dedericks, bm. 1 Jan. 1846. m. 15 Jan. 1846, at
    house of bride's father, Belmont, Loudoun. Adie. Cam.
Kuhlman, George J. D. & Catharine Ann Truslow. Daniel Dedricks
    attests ages, bm. 12 Nov. 1846. m. 17 Nov. 1846, in church
    at Belmont. Adie. Cam.
Kutz, Michael & Elenor Langten. m. 27 Nov. 1811. Littlejohn.
Kyle, John & Winefred Powell. m. 24 Feb. 1818. Williamson.
Lacey, Charles H. & Julia Ann Williams. m. 4 May 1852. Duncan.
Lacey, John & Abigail Garrett. m. 1821-1822. Mines.
Lacey, John & Betsey Ann Vanpelt. Josephus Powell attests bride's
    age. John H. McCabe, bm. 27 May 1833. Shel.
Lacey, Joseph B. & Mary Fannie Richards, dau. of Jesse Richards.
    John Wornall attests ages, bm. 16 May 1849. Shel.
Lacey, Thomas & Sarah Braden. m. 1807-1808. Mines.
Lacey, William & Sarah Richardson. m. 15 April 1803. Littlejohn.
Lacey, William & Susanna Watts. m. 3 Oct. 1812. Littlejohn.
Lacock, James & Mary Ann White. James Higdon attests ages, bm.
    14 Nov. 1842. Shel.
Lacy, Charles H. & Julia Ann Williams. David J. Rice proves ages,
    wit. 3 May 1852. MarReg.
Laes, Jacobus L. & Nantzy Jackson; both single. By license. m.
    13 Sep. 1821. ParReg A.
Lafaber (Lafeber), William & Mary Oatyer (Octher), dau. of Peter
    Oatyer, bm. 9 Aug. 1809. Littlejohn.
Lafever, Henry & Mary French. m. 29 Aug. 1822. Gilmore.
Lafever, Henry & Sally W. Hammerly. "The father of each party -
    requested the issue of the written license." William Lefever,
    bm. 20 April 1846. Shel.
Lalor, Jeremiah & Eliza Marmaduke. Samuel Marmaduke attests
    bride's age, bm. 12 Jan. 1832. Dorsey. Cam.
Lamb, Samuel & Anna E. Emerson. Judson Emerson, bm. 20 May 1850.
    Shel.
Lamb, Samuel & Lucy Orrison. Wit: James W. Stedman. 7 June 1853.
    MarReg.
Lamb, William, son of Nancy Lamb & Elizabeth Gregg, dau. of George
    Gregg. Charles F. Anderson, bm. 12 Sep. 1840. Shel.
Lambert, William Thomas & Harriett Whaley. Joseph Magaha proves
    ages, wit. 3 Feb. 1851. MarReg.
Lamborn, Parmenas, son of Thomas and Dinah Lamborn, of Chester
    County, Pa. & Hannah Williams, dau. of William Williams,
    deceased and Elizabeth Williams, since married to Benjamin
    Pardum. m. 2 May 1798. FFMM.
Lang, Phillipp & Christina Meile. m. 9 March 1786. ParReg A.
Lang, William & Lidia Jung; both single. By license. m. 23 Feb.
    1826. ParReg A.

LOUDOUN COUNTY MARRIAGES

Langley, Alexander & Nelly Shortness. m. 16 Jan. 1798.
Littlejohn.
Langley, Walter & Susanah Boyd. m. 25 Sep. 1806. Littlejohn.
Lanham, George & Rebecca Swich. m. 9 Dec. 1824. T. Littleton.
Lanham, John & Margaret F. Costello. John H. Costello proves ages,
wit. 27 Dec. 1851. MarReg. m. 30 Dec. 1851. Eggleston.
Lanham, William & Rebecca Gibbs, dau. of William Gibbs, who
attests groom's age. James Gibbs, bm. 25 Aug. 1834. Shel.
Lapintons, Abram & Johanah Yates. m. 9 Feb. 1797. Littlejohn.
Larew, James & Elizabeth Jane Webb. m. 22 June 1848. Monroe.
Larue, John D. & Maria Osburn. Joel Osburn, bm. 30 Nov. 1848.
m. 5 Dec. 1848. Eggleston. Shel.
Larue, Richard & Hannah Lewis, dau. of Jehu and Alice Lewis, late
of Loudoun. m. 8 April 1789. FFMM.
Lasly, Johannes & Rahel Morrison; both single. By license. m.
14 Aug. 1828. ParReg A.
Late, Jacob & Elizabeth Miller. Christian Miller attests ages,
bm. 5 Sep. 1809. m. 1808-1809. Mines.
Latham, Robert & Sarah Rust. m. 4 Sep. 1821. Dagg.
Latham, Thomas & Sarah R. Hixson. James S. Oden proves bride's
age, wit. 24 Sep. 1852. MarReg. m. 3 Oct. 1852. Marders.
Latimer, John & Lydia Ann Dulin. Newton Keene attests bride's
age, bm. 11 Jan. 1836. Cam.
Laughborough, Nathan & Ann H. Rose. Wit: James McSherry, Helen
Gallaher. Return dated 13 Nov. 1849. Plunkett.
Laurence, William & Philippa Jones. m. 12 June 1823. Dunn. Shel.
Laury, Friderich & Elisa Reidenbach; both single. By license.
m. 7 July 1825. ParReg A.
Law, Samuel & Margaret McPherson. m. 22 Aug. 1816. J. Frye.
Lawrence, Alexander & Emily McCormick. m. 16 April 1825. Tuston.
Lawrence, Thomas L. & Ann Louisa Binns. m. 24 Nov. 1814.
Littlejohn.
Lawson, James W. & Evelina Frye, dau. of Philip Frey. Philip
Frye, body of bond, bm. Joseph Frey signs and attests groom's
age. 28 Nov. 1840. Shel.
Lawson, James M. & Evalina Frye. m. 1 Dec. 1840. Herndon.
Lay, Edward & Susan Wolf. Peter Crim attests ages, bm. 16 Oct.
1844. Shel.
Laycock, Samuel & Matilda Blaker. William Shields attests bride's
age, bm. 12 Dec. 1836. Shel.
Laypold, Daniel & Barbara Adams; both single. m. 2 May 1831.
ParReg A.
Leach, Harrison & Margaret McGennis. m. 18 March 1815. Littlejohn.
Leachman, William & Nancy Adams. m. 1 July 1803. Dunn.
Leaming, George & Nancy Farris. m. 1807-1808. Mines.
Lee, Alfred & Margaret M. Peyton. Squire Lee attests ages, bm.
10 Aug. 1840. Cadden. Shel.
Lee, Doddridge C. & Catharine E. Hickman, with Maryland license.
m. 30 March 1845. ParReg A.
Lee, George & Sally M. Henderson. m. 18 Aug. 1827. McCan.
Lee, John & Elenor Wade, dau. of Hezekiah Wade, bm. 23 Dec. 1809.
Littlejohn.
Lee, John F. & Sarah E. Jones. Wit: bride's father. 3 Oct. 1853.
MarReg. m. 6 Oct. 1853. Herndon.

89

Lee, Joshua & Theodosia Warford. Abraham Warford, bm. 27 Sep.
    1799. Cam.
Lee, Matthew P. & Ann Berkley. Nathaniel S. Oden, bm. 13 May
    1833. m. 23 May 1833. Newman. Cam.
Lee, Richard E. & Ann C. McDonald. Tilghman Gore, bm. 30 Dec.
    1844. Shel.
Lee, William & Susanna T. Peyton (Payton), dau. of William
    Peyton, bm. 7 Nov. 1831. m. 10 Nov. 1831. Baker. Shel.
Leech, Thorton & Mary Turner. m. 11 Feb. 1816. Littlejohn.
Leeman, Jacob & Elizabeth Lewis, dau. of Daniel Lewis, who
    attests groom's age, bm. 12 Oct. 1848. Shel.
Lefeber, Henry & Elizabeth Reed. m. 14 Nov. 1808. Littlejohn.
Lefever, Henry & Salley W. Hammerley. m. 21 April 1846. Gover.
Lefever, William & Mary Francis Rose, dau. of Kitty S. Rose.
    James W. Wiley, bm. 9 Dec. 1845. m. 10 Dec. 1845. Gover.Cam.
Leffol, Henrich & Juliana Reitenbach; both single. By license.
    m. 31 March 1829. ParReg A.
Legg, Harrison & Ann Beckham. m. 3 Feb. 1814. McPherson.
Legg, Jacobus & Elenor Stein; both single. By license. m. 29 Oct.
    1823. ParReg A.
Legg, Lewis & Elizabeth Beavers. m. 11 Feb. 1806. Littlejohn.
Legg, Lewis & Malvina F. Finch. James Whitacre, bm. Marshall
    Finch signs bottom of bond. 11 Sep. 1844. Cam.
Legg, Lewis & Susan Cummings, dau. of Delilah Cummings. Thomas
    Cummings attests groom's age, bm. 7 Feb. 1842. Shel.
Leith, James & Virginia Ann Cox, dau. of Samuel Cox. Joshua G.
    Hogue attests ages, bm. 15 Nov. 1844. Shel.
Leith, Randolph H. & Martha C. Gregg. Wit: Peter Gregg. 9 June
    1853. MarReg. m. 16 June 1853. Hirst.
Leith, Theodore & Veturia Ann Plaster, dau. of Henry Plaster, Jr.
    L. L. Carter, bm. 1 Nov. 1837. Shel.
Lemm, Thomas & Mariah Bodine. Joseph H. Bodine attests ages, bm.
    31 Dec. 1836. Shel.
Lemmon (Lemon), Jacob & Mary Jane Bodine (Badine). Andrew M.
    Cridler attests ages, bm. 13 April 1840. Gover. Shel.
Lenhart, John Henry & Elizabeth Short. m. 30 July 1840. Hauer.
Lewelling, John & Mary Burson. m. 9 March 1807. Littlejohn.
Lewis, Charles & Mary Ann Linch (Linck). Washington Lewis attests
    ages, bm. 5 June 1843. m. 8 June 1843. ParReg A. Shel.
Lewis, Charles T. & Ann Sophia Rust, dau. of Benjamin Rust. Henry
    M. Rust attests bride's age, bm. 4 May 1847.
Lewis, Henry & E. J. Chattin. Robert C. Leachman proves bride's
    age, wit. Henry Lewis, guardian, proves groom's age, wit.
    7 Oct. 1850. MarReg.
Lewis, James & Louisa Risby, free Negroes. Nathan Minor, bm.
    4 Sep. 1832. Shel.
Lewis, Jesse & Elizabeth Triplett. m. 1 April 1824. Williamson.
Lewis, John & Rachel Bezella. m. 25 April 1810. Littlejohn.
Lewis, Joseph & Elizabeth O. Grayson. m. 10 Nov. 1825. Dunn.Shel.
Lewis, Robert & Caroline Amanda Lynnd (Lynd). Nicholas Lynnd
    attests ages, bm. 4 Oct. 1848. m. 5 Nov. 1848. ParRegA. Shel.
Lewis, William & Emily Johnson, in Maryland. m. 23 April 1839.
    ParReg A.
Lewis, William & Sarah Ritecar. m. 5 Oct. 1811. Littlejohn.

LOUDOUN COUNTY MARRIAGES

Lickey, John W., son of William Lickey & Euphama (Uphamia) Fred.
    John Vansickler attests bride's age. William Lickey, bm.
    31 March 1835. m. 2 April 1835. Baker. Shel.
Lickey, Sampson (Samson) & Mary Carson. James A. Reid attests
    ages, bm. 1 Jan. 1838. Tapler. Shel.
Licky, John & Elizabeth Saddler. m. 18 Dec. 1813. Littlejohn.
Liggett, Samuel W. & Catharine Wright. Edward Rinker, bm. 1 Jan.
    1846. Gover. Shel.
Lilley, Joseph & Eve Coist. m. 8 Dec. 1803. Littlejohn.
Lindsey, Samuel & Ann Murphey. m. 1807-1808. Mines.
Linguin, Joseph & Mary McMekin. m. 3 Feb. 1802. Littlejohn.
Linn, Nickolaus & Elisabetha Kieffer; both single. m. 11 Dec.
    1828. ParReg A.
Linsay, Thomas & Nancy Hammett. m. 18 Feb. 1808. Littlejohn.
Lionhard, John Henry, who signs in German & Elizabeth Short.
    Charles G. Eskeridge says "it appears he will be 22 years old
    the 10th Sept 1840". Frederick Miller, bm. 29 July 1840.Shel.
Little, M. L. & Julia Ann Davis. m. 29 March 1849. Herndon.
Littleton, Eli & Emily Ward. Marcus D. Littleton proves bride's
    age, wit; "the other party taken for granted". 20 Nov. 1851.
    MarReg. m. 27 Nov. 1851. Eggleston.
Littleton, Franklin & Margaret Littleton. Bride's father consents
    in writing. Oscar Littleton proves groom's age, wit. 27 Dec.
    1853. MarReg.
Littleton, John & Margaret Carter. m. 27 Jan. 1852. Dodge.
Littleton, John & Rebecca Elgin. John A. Binns, bm. 11 Sep. 1835.
    Shel.
Littleton, John R. & Margaret Carter, dau. of Richard Carter, wit.
    22 Jan. 1852. MarReg.
Littleton, John W. & Elizabeth A. Tavener, dau. of James Tavener.
    William Tavener attests groom's age, bm. 21 March 1829.
Littleton, John W. & Emily Carter, dau. of Samuel Carter. William
    Horseman attests groom's age, bm. 2 March 1844. Shel.
Littleton, Richard C. & Catharine Mildred Thompson, dau. of
    Mildred T. Thompson. John M. Orr attests groom's age, bm.
    29 April 1844. m. 1 May 1844, at house of Samuel Campbell,
    Middleburg. Adie. Shel.
Littleton, Richard K. & Keturah R. Carter, dau. of Edward Carter.
    Fielding Littleton attests groom's age, bm. 28 March 1829.
Littleton, Sampson & Kitty (Kelly) Cockrill. Joseph Marmaduke
    Cockrill, bm. 18 Dec. 1799. Littlejohn.
Littleton, Thomas & Francis Harriman. m. 13 Oct. 1800. Littlejohn.
Livingston, John, Waterford & Elizabeth Pierpoint, dau. of Obed
    and Esther Pierpoint. m. 7 Feb. 1821. Mendenhall, Clerk.FFMM.
Livingston, Lewis & Amey Powell, dau. of Leven H. Powell, bm.
    3 Nov. 1835. m. 5 Nov. 1835. Baker. Shel.
Lloyd, Frederick, of Henry, Illinois & Lucy Lee Powell. Bride's
    father consents in writing. John D. Powell attests groom's
    age, wit. 13 Oct. 1852. MarReg. m. 13 Oct. 1852. Adie.
Lloyd, Joseph A. & Margaret Gheen. Charles Thomas Denham attests
    bride's age, bm. 12 Jan. 1833. Shel.
Lloyd, William & Emily J. Milbourn. Gideon Milbourn attests ages,
    bm. 22 May 1848. Shel.

91

Lobe, Henry N. & Elizabeth E. Roberts, in Maryland. m. 24 May
    1843. ParReg A.
Locker, Leven & Sarah Darr. m. 12 Aug. 1805. Littlejohn.
Lockhart, Jefferson & Margaret Waltman. m. 27 Oct. 1836. Hauer.
Lockhart, Leven & Margeret White. m. 12 Jan. 1801. Littlejohn.
Lockheart, Jefferson & Margaret Waltman. Joseph Miller, son of
    William Lockheart, of Hampshire County, attests bride's age,
    bm. 26 Oct. 1836. Shel.
Lockhert, John & Sally Ann Bradfield. Bride's father consents, wit.
    2 June 1851. MarReg.
Lodge, Abner & Tamzen Nicholls. m. 21 May 1822. T. Littleton.
Lodge, Herman & Marsha A. Lodge, dau. of Joseph Lodge, wit.
    27 Sep. 1850. MarReg. m. 2 Oct. 1850. Smith.
Lodge, Samuel & Rebecca Russell. m. 27 Feb. 1817. T. Littleton.
Logan, John & Mary Ann Walker, dau. of Ben Walker, bm. Samuel
    Logan attests groom's age. 20 Feb. 1840. Shel.
Logan, Samuel & Sarah D. Davis. Thomas S. Davis proves ages, wit.
    30 Sep. 1850. MarReg. m. 8 Oct. 1850. Herndon.
Long, Clairborn & Elizabeth A. Richards. m. 14 Nov. 1834. Trott.
Long, Henry & Rebecca Braden. m. 26 March 1803. Littlejohn.
Long, James & Malinda Davis. James Boothe attests ages, bm. 4 Aug.
    1837. m. 6 Aug. 1837. Hauer. Shel.
Long, James & Sarah C. Carrin, dau. of Eden Carnine, bm. 10 Jan.
    1848. Shel.
Long, John & Mary Clarke, of Fauquier County, Va. m. 30 Oct.
    1782. FFMM.
Long, William & Lucinda Crooks. William Divine, chosen bride's
    guardian and attests groom's age, bm. 9 Sep. 1833. Shel.
Long, William & Mary Hurdle. Amos Neer attests ages, bm. 13 Nov.
    1837. Shel.
Longshear, Thomas & Letitia Bradfield. m. 28 Dec. 1797.
    Littlejohn.
Longshore, Vincent & Sarah Hart. m. 1 Nov. 1821. T. Littleton.
Lott, Parkinson L. & Mary Smale, dau. of Simon Smale, bm. Miss
    Francis Lott attests groom's age. 20 March 1832. Shel.
Loughborough, Nathan & Aunice H. Rose. William A. Stephenson, bm.
    13 Nov. 1849. Shel.
Love, Charles & Jane Noland. m. 23 Oct. 1810. Littlejohn.
Love, Eli N. & Caroline A. Moore. T. M. Moore proves ages, wit.
    31 Aug. 1850. MarReg. m. 3 Sep. 1850. Herndon.
Love, Fenton M. & Elizabeth Morris, dau. of Mahlon Morris. Jonah
    Nichols, bm. 13 March 1837. Shel.
Love, James & Susannah Nichols. m. 26 Dec. 1801. Littlejohn.
Love, James D. & Susan A. Shipman. Burr Brown attests ages. James
    Sinclair, bm. 7 Nov. 1844. Shel.
Love, James J. & Sarah Amelia Hurst. M. C. Klein, guardian, bm.
    12 March 1849. m. 15 March 1849. Gover. Shel.
Love, Richard H. & Elizabeth Mat. Lee. m. 20 Feb. 1812. Dunn.
Love, Samuel & Rebeccah Nichols. m. 1808-1809. Mines.
Love, Thomas & Sarah Pierpoint. m. 3 Feb. 1802. FFMM.
Love, Thomas B. & Eliza H. Gibson. John D. Baldwin attests ages,
    bm. 15 Jan. 1847. m. 16 Jan. 1847. Hayes. Shel.
Lovelass, Aquila & Elizabeth Acton. m. 14 Dec. 1793. Littlejohn.
Lovelass, Benjamin and Chloe Collins. m. 19 March 1796. Littlejohn.

Loveless, George W. & Eliza Hamilton, ward of Christopher Houser,
   bm. John Loveless attests groom's age. 18 Sep. 1848. m.
   24 Sep. 1848. Herndon. Shel.
Lovett, Daniel & Rachell Cruthers. George McManomy (McMannama)
   attests bride's age, bm. 8 Feb. 1799. Littlejohn. Shel.
Lovett, Edmond & Christian Carruthers. m. 30 April 1806.
   Littlejohn.
Lovett, James P. & Lucinda Dowdel. m. 4 June 1827. Tuston.
Lovett, John & Naomi Dunken. m. 7 Feb. 1813. McPherson.
Lovett, Jonathan & Matilda Norton. m. 17 Dec. 1818. Williamson.
Lovett, Thomas A. & Harriet Atwell. Manly Atwell attests bride's
   age. James P. Lovett attests groom's age, bm. 18 Feb. 1835.
   m. 19 Feb. 1835. Baker. Shel.
Low, Samuel & Margaret McPherson. m. 22 Aug. 1816. J. Frye.
Lowdes, James & Mary Gibbons. m. 27 Dec. 1826. Tuston.
Lowe, Charles James & Mary Noggle. Both fathers consent, wit.
   1 Jan. 1851. MarReg. Wills.
Lowe, Edward Thomas, ward of A. S. Anderson & Amelia Smallwood,
   ward of Joshua Pusey. C. W. D. Binns, bm. 13 Feb. 1832.Cam.
Lowe, Henry & Mary Siddler. m. 12 Jan. 1805. Littlejohn.
Lowe, Hiram T. & Eliza Vincel, with Maryland license. m. 15 Oct.
   1846. ParReg A.
Lowe, James & Margaret Owens. m. 30 May 1824. Dunn. Shel.
Lowe, John & Ann Dawson. William Franklin attests groom's age.
   Richard Dawson, bm. 14 Aug. 1843. Shel.
Lowe, Joseph & Emily Garret. m. 17 June 1845. Herndon.
Lowe, Moses & Margaret V. Beales, ward of Richard White. William
   Lowe attests groom's age, bm. 4 Jan. 1848. Shel.
Lowe, Thomas & Cathrine Rinker. m. 3 Nov. 1808. Littlejohn.
Lowe, William, son of Jane Lowe & Jane Pomeroy. John H. Thomas
   attests bride's age, bm. 14 Sep. 1846. Shel.
Lowe, William & Matilda Lawson. m. 1 March 1818. Dunn. Shel.
Lowe, William & Sufronia (Safronia) Figgins. Wit: James Fields.
   28 Nov. 1853. MarReg. m. 29 Nov. 1853. Nixon.
Lownes, Hyatt & Elizabeth Emery. m. 7 March 1793. Littlejohn.
Lowry, Jacob & Mary Smith. m. 1807-1808. Mines.
Loy, Adam, made ward of John Fawley "this day" & Sarah Frye,
   dau. of John Frye, bm. John Fawley, bm. 14 Dec. 1830. Shel.
Loy, Edward & Susan Wolf. m. 24 Oct. 1844. ParReg A.
Loyd, Edward & Ruth Buttler. m. 24 Dec. 1801. Littlejohn.
Loyd, James & Mary L. Harrison. Bride's mother authorizes
   marriage. 26 Oct. 1850. MarReg.
Loyd, William & Emily Iden Milbourn. m. 25 May 1848. Eggleston.
Loyde, John & Rebecca Janny. m. 29 Nov. 1798. Littlejohn.
Lucas, Barton & Elizabeth Craven. m. 11 Dec. 1813. Littlejohn.
Lucas, James & Juda Grimes. m. 12 Sep. 1814. Littlejohn.
Luckett, Francis W. & Sarah Bronaugh. m. 20 Dec. 1810. Dunn.
Luckett, Josias (Josiah) C. & Mary Ann Graham. James Graham, bm.
   20 Jan. 1844. m. 23 Jan. 1844. ParReg A. Shel.
Luckett, Ludwell & Ann C. Bronough. m. 3 Dec. 1822. Williamson.
Luckett, Roger C. & Margaret H. White. Joshua White attests ages,
   bm. 24 Oct. 1844. m. 24 Oct. 1844, St. James Church, Leesburg.
   Adie. Shel.
Luckett, Samuel & Sarah Clapham. m. 14 Dec. 1801. Littlejohn.

Luckett, Samuel C. & Mary B. Hamilton. Charles B. Hamilton, Jr. attests ages, bm. 13 May 1833. m. 21 May 1833. ParReg A.Shel.

Luckett, William C. & Mary Virtz. John Virtz attests bride's age, bm. 12 March 1838. Shel.

Luckett, William C. & Matilda Jacobs, dau. of Elizabeth Jacobs, who says bride was 21 years on 4 Jan. 1830. William B. Jackson attests groom's age, bm. 11 Jan. 1830.

Ludwick, Christian Goodlip (Gottlieb) & Susanna Derry. Matthias Prince attests bride's age, bm. 30 Dec. 1833. m. 9 Jan. 1834. Hauer.

Luis, Washington & Elisabeth Bagert (?); both single. By license. m. 18 Sep. 1815. ParReg A.

Lumm, Samuel & Almedia Gibson. Solomon Gibson, bm. 11 Oct. 1830. Shel.

Luntz, Lorenzo & Jane Fred. William Luntz attests bride's age. William Greenway, bm. 8 Jan. 1845. Shel.

Lupton, Amos & Hannah Janney. m. 19 May 1826. Janney, Clerk.

Luter, Hugh & Elizabeth Stephens. m. 30 Dec. 1796. Littlejohn.

Lyles, Archibald M. & Harriet F. Fitchter. m. 28 Aug. 1828. Tippett.

Lynch, William P. (B.) & Laura R. Chamblin. Bride's father, wit. Gentleman's age taken for granted.19 March 1853. MarReg. m. 29 March 1853. Herndon.

Lyne, William & Sush. Settle. m. 26 Dec. 1807. Littlejohn.

Lynn, Ezekiel & Elizabeth Potts, widow. Michael Lynn, bm. 8 Aug. 1831. m. 26 Aug. 1831. Green. Shel.

Lynn, James F. & Violinda Ann Skillman, dau. of Abraham Skillman, bm. Benjamin F. Thomas attests groom's age. 29 Oct. 1831. Shel.

Lynn, John T., son of Joseph R. Lynn & Nancy H. D. Currell. William M. Lynn, bm. 25 Nov. 1843. Shel.

Lynn, Joseph R. & Parmelia Currell. John H. Hixon attests bride's age, bm. 22 Dec. 1834. m. 23 Dec. 1834. Furlong. Shel.

Lyon, Henry M. & Eliza J. Walters. Joseph Edwards attests ages, bm. 24 Feb. 1844. Shel.

Lyons, Alfred, son of John Lyons, 23 years "May last" & Mary E. Perry, dau. of Hezekiah Perry. Manly R. Perry, bm. 8 July 1843. Shel.

Lyons, John & Nancy B. Hieronymous. m. 17 Nov. 1822. Dunn.

Macra, James & Jane Chaffinch. m. 15 Aug. 1804. Littlejohn.

Madden, John & Margaret Chamber. m. 16 Nov. 1805. Littlejohn.

Maddison, Ambrose & Rachel Fulten. m. 11 May 1812. J. Littleton.

Maffett, Henry H., 25 years, born Loudoun, farmer & Alice A. Jenkins, dau. of Wesley and Nancy Jenkins, 25 years, born Loudoun. m. 17 Nov. 1853, in Leesburg. Gover.

Magaha, Armisted & Margaret Wenner. John W. Wenner proves ages, wit. 31 Jan. 1852. MarReg.

Magaha, John & Civilla Cooper, dau. of Sarah Macpherson. Henry Adams proves groom's age. William Magaha, bm. 29 Oct. 1847. m. 31 Oct. 1847. Williard. Shel.

Magaha, John & Margaret Magaha. Daniel Miller attests bride's age, bm. 2 Oct. 1830. m. 3 Oct. 1830.Hutchinson. Shel.

Magaha, Joseph & Ann M. Jinkins. John T. Tuttle attests ages, bm. 19 Jan. 1847. Shel.

94

Magaha, Samuel & Priscilla Cloud, dau. of Sidney Cloud, mother,
    of Lovettsville. Joel Hunt attests bride's age, bm. 22 March
    1841. m. 25 March 1841. ParReg A. Shel.
Magill, Charles T. & Mary D. Bronough. m. 26 Sep. 1816.
    Williamson.
Magill, Henry R., Dr., Frederick County, Va. & Ann Elizabeth
    Mason, dau. of William T. T. Mason, bm. 21 Nov. 1833. m.
    21 Nov. 1833, at house of bride's father, Leesburg. Adie.
    Shel.
Mahoney, John & Catharine Miller. Jonathan Cunard attests bride's
    age, bm. 5 Sep. 1835. Shel.
Mahony, Thacker & Emily Ann Merchant. William Merchant attests
    bride's age, bm. 20 Sep. 1844. Shel.
Mails, Benjamin & Rahel Heckman; both single. By license. m.
    29 May 1828. ParReg A.
Major, James T. & Hannah Ann Harris. m. 31 Jan. 1832. C. Frye.
Major, Jacob & Sarah Snoots. John Snoots attests ages, bm.
    19 Dec. 1846. Shel.
Major, James J. & Hannah Ann Harris. James Major attests groom's
    age. John A. Binns, bm. 13 Jan. 1832. Shel.
Manfield, John & Margaret Stewart. m. 13 Jan. 1795. Littlejohn.
Mankins, James & Sarah Ann Havener. William D. Havener attests
    ages, bm. 12 Jan. 1846. m. 13 Jan. 1846. Gover.
Mann, George William & Leanna Conard, dau. of John Conard, bm.
    9 May 1845. Shel.
Mann, Jacob & Anna Ruse. George Whitmore attests bride's age, bm.
    29 March 1847. m. 1 April 1847. Shuford. Shel.
Mann, Johannes, son of Johannes and Magdalena Mann, Sr. & Leha
    Eberhard, dau. of Philip and Carlotha Eberhard; both single.
    By license. m. 11 March 1824. ParReg A.
Mann, Johannes, Jr., widower & Sarah Campher, single. By license.
    m. 3 Aug. 1826. ParReg A.
Mann, Joseph & Elisabeth Philler; both single. By license. m.
    28 Dec. 1826. ParReg A.
Mann, Samuel & Charity Morrison, dau. of Edward Morrison, wit.
    5 Jan. 1852. MarReg.
Manning, Nathaniel & Euphamia Lacey. m. 26 April 1803. Littlejohn.
Mantony, Joseph & Mary Hilburn. 17 Dec. 1803. Davis.
Marchant (Merchant), Philip & Mary White. m. 5 Aug. 1796.
    Littlejohn.
Marders (Mardirs), Lovell & Catharine J. Rogers, dau. of S.
    Rogers. 6 Oct. 1851. MarReg. m. 14 Oct. 1851. Herndon.
Markes, George & Mahaley O'Neale. m. Sep. 1806. Dunn.
Marks, Abel & Nancy Littleton. m. 24 June 1824. T. Littleton.
Marks, George Smith & Mary (Nancy) Carolina Conard, ward of
    L. C. Cunard, bm. Albert Chamblin attests groom's age.
    9 March 1829. m. 12 March 1829. Baker.
Marks, John & Sarah Powell, dau. of William Powell. John
    Overfield attests ages, bm. 9 Dec. 1809.
Marks, Law & Rachel Boyce. m. 20 Oct. 1796. Littlejohn.
Marks, Samuel & Susanna Overfield. 5 May 1810. m. 7 June 1810.
    T. Littleton.
Marlow, William & Elisabeth Bozwel; both single. By license.
    m. 6 Aug. 1818. ParReg A.

Marmaduke, Andrew J., parents deceased, of Fauquier County,
    tailor & Henrietta M. Cox, dau. of Samuel Cox. Wit: John W.
    Cox. 4 Nov. 1853. MarReg. m. 8 Nov. 1853. Hirst.
Marquis, Fielden & Rebeckah Kitchen. m. 30 June 1804. Jefferson.
    Shel.
Marr, John & Catharine J. Horner. m. 10 July 1816. Williamson.
Marshal, Robert A. M. & Sarah Ann Hessner. m. 4 March 1852.
    Massey.
Marshall, Joseph & Sarah Hague. m. 4 April 1804. Littlejohn.
Marshall, Revell & Eleanor Orr. m. 30 March 1820. Dagg.
Marshall, Robert A. M. & Sarah Ann Hesser. Wit: James E. Hesser.
    28 Feb. 1852. MarReg.
Martin, David & Ann E. Carr. m. 26 June 1804. Littlejohn.
Martin, James & Margart Taylor. Payton Taylor attests ages, bm.
    2 Sep. 1833. Shel.
Marts, John & Christena Miley. Vincent Miley attests ages, bm.
    27 April 1841. Shel.
Martin, John & Rachel Dowling. m. 21 April 1800. Littlejohn.
Martin, John W. & Mary E. Dulaney. James H. Vandevanter, bm.
    22 Dec. 1848. m. 23 Dec. 1848, at Mrs. Wildman's, Leesburg.
    Adie. Shel.
Marvin, William & Ann R. Wampler. m. 20 Dec. 1846, in schoolroom
    at Belmont, Major Mercer's. Adie.
Mason, Daniel & Elizabeth Waller, dau. of George Waller. Peter
    Mason attests groom's age, bm. 23 Oct. 1837. Shel.
Mason, James & Olivia Hill, dau. of James Hill, bm. 23 March
    1835. m. 25 March 1835. Baker. Shel.
Mason, John William, son of Adam Mason & Adalade Vertz, dau. of
    John Verts, wit. 15 Oct. 1851. MarReg.
Mason, Westward T. & Ann Noland. m. 20 Jan. 1806. Littlejohn.
Massie, James & Ann Brown. m. 23 Dec. 1819. Williamson.
Mateer, James & Eliza Ann Tynan. m. 1821-1822. Mines.
Maters, William & Margarett Brooks. John W. Haines attests ages,
    bm. 21 May 1846. Shel.
Mathews, Edward J., son of Mordecai and Ruth Mathews, Baltimore
    County, Md., both deceased & Sarah H. Gover, dau. of Jesse
    and Miriam Gover. m. 14 Oct. 1841. FFMM.
Mathews, James & Rebecca C. Copeland. m. 10 May 1838. Hauer.
Mathews, John & Lynda Moreland. Philip Moreland, bm. 14 Nov.
    1809. m. 1808-1809. Mines.
Mathias, Daniel T. & Martha Oswald. John H. McCabe, bm. 15 Sep.
    1829. Birkby.
Matthew, Simon & Susanna Frits, dau. of George Frits (Fritch), bm.
    10 March 1834. Shel.
Matthews, James & Rebecca C. Copeland. m. 10 May 1838. ParReg A.
Matthews, John & Mary Orrison. m. 14 Dec. 1796. Littlejohn.
Matthews, Jonathan & Rebecca C. Copeland. David Copeland attests
    groom's age, bm. 7 May 1838. Shel.
Matthews, Thomas P. & Jane P. Hughes. John A. Hughs attests bride's
    age. Samuel P. Canby attests groom's age, bm. 25 March 1833.
    Shel.
Matthias, Daniel T. & Martha Oswald. John H. McCabe, bm. 15 Sep.
    1829.
Maurer, Adam & Nanzy Mack; both single. By license. 18 Jan. 1827.
    ParReg A.

Mavin, William & Ann B. Wampler, Mrs. George Adie attests
bride's age. Presley Saunders, bm. 19 Dec. 1846. Cam.
Maxtey, alias Lee, Peter & Ann Mariah Gant. m. 11 Oct. 1849.
Gover.
May, James H. & Sarah Jane Barnhouse, dau. of Jane M. Barnhouse.
Joseph Barnhouse attests groom's age, bm. 19 Nov. 1849.
Shel.
May, William H. & Sarah S. Benton, dau. of William Benton, wit.
9 May 1853. MarReg. m. 31 May 1853. Herndon.
McAfrey, Iram & Sarah Martin. m. 7 Nov. 1822. Williamson.
McArtor, James & Mary Ball. m. 21 July 1804. Littlejohn.
McArtor, Moses & Mary Wilson. m. 7 Dec. 1800. Littlejohn.
McAtee, Harrison & Reba. Ashford. m. 24 Feb. 1807. Littlejohn.
McAtee, John F. & Julia A. Horsman. Levi G. Ewers attests ages,
bm. 31 Aug. 1833. Shel.
McAtee, Richard & Permelia Kidwell, dau. of Sarah Kidwell.
Daniel Hart, bm. 3 Feb. 1845. Shel.
McBee, Townshend & Sarah Blaker. William Templer attests ages,
bm. 20 Sep. 1830. Shel.
McBride, John & Sarah Watkins. Daniel Fuhrs, bm. 25 Dec. 1799.
Cam.
McCabe, James E. & Amanda Littleton. Erasmus H. Fox attests ages,
bm. 22 Nov. 1848. m. 23 Nov. 1848. Nixon.
McCabe, John H. & Margaret H. D. Tebbs, widow. Charles Binns, bm.
4 Aug. 1831. Shel.
McCabe, Patrick C. & Maria C. Lee. 18 Aug. 1827 Return. McCan.
McCaffery, John & Nancy Pettit. m. 13 Dec. 1802. Littlejohn.
McCallester, Daniel & Reba. Wright. m. 2 June 1807. Littlejohn.
McCartor, Henry & Martha Curry. m. 18 Jan. 1826. Tuston.
McCartor, Jonathan & Minerva Beans. m. 29 March 1826. Tuston.
McCarty, Albert G. & Lucinda B. Peyton. m. 20 Oct. 1823. Roszell.
McCarty, Dennis & Ann Eliza Skinner, dau. of Gabriel Skinner, bm.
22 April 1833. Shel.
McCarty, John & Emily Jane Coe. Rueben Cockerill, Mary Coe, bm.
14 Sep. 1837. Shel.
McCarty, John M. & Ann Lucinda Lee. m. 14 Dec. 1820. Dunn. Cam.
McCarty, Mahlon & Eliza Thomas. m. 23 Aug. 1826. Tuston.
McCarty, William & Emily Mason. m. 24 Oct. 1816. Dunn.
McCathy, Patrick & Margeret Hardey. m. 19 April 1803. Littlejohn.
McCaves, John & Sarah Kipdike. m. 24 April 1797. Littlejohn.
McClelland, William B. & Sarah A. Janney. m. 14 July 1852. Smith.
McClenan, John & Elizabeth Ropp, with Maryland license. m.
19 May 1842. ParReg A.
McClenen, John & Mary Nancy McDaniel, orphan of James McDaniel
and ward of Thomas Rogers. John H. Crim attests groom's age.
John Tavenner, bm. 14 Dec. 1840. Shel.
McClenland, William B. & Sarah A. Janney. William Smith proves
ages, wit. 12 July 1852. MarReg.
McClun, John, son of Thomas and Hannah McClun, of Frederick
County, Va. & Elizabeth Beal, dau. of Joseph & Hannah Beal.
m. 1 June 1797. FFMM.
McCluskey, Daniel & Rebekah Myers, widow. Jonathan Conrad, bm.
13 May 1799. Shel.
McConahey, Samuel & Anne Batson. m. 5 April 1804. Williamson.

McCormick, Francis & Rosannah Ellzey, dau. of Lewis Ellzey. R.
    Mortimer Ellzey states bride was 21 years on the 18th or 19th
    of "last month". James Sinclair, bm. 20 Nov. 1839. Shel.
McCormick, John & Polly Curtis. m. 16 March 1796. Littlejohn.
McCormick, John A. & Ann Fadely, dau. of Jacob Fadly. John B.
    Patterson attests groom's age. Thomas H. Clagett, bm. 15 Jan.
    1829.
McCoy, George M. & Ann Rebecca Stream. John Snoots, Jr. attests
    ages, bm. 30 May 1849. m. 30 May 1849. Eggleston. Shel.
McCrady, James & Lindney Russell. m. 9 Dec. 1813. McPherson.
McCray, William & Elizabeth Hatcher. Mahlon Gore attests ages,
    bm. 9 Feb. 1846. Shel.
McCrum, Robert & Ann Dailey. m. 14 March 1816. Littlejohn.
McCullough, William & Clarissa P. Dagg. Frances T. Grady attests
    ages, bm. 6 Sep. 1834. m. 9 Sep. 1834. Baker. Shel.
McDade, John & Sarah Hile. m. 11 Feb. 1794. Littlejohn.
McDaniel, Archibald & Pricilla Thompson. John Thompson attests
    bride's age, bm. 30 July 1830. Shel.
McDaniel, Augustine & Elizabeth Lamb. William S. Harrison attests
    ages, bm. 30 Dec. 1840. Gover. Shel.
McDaniel, James & Rosana Osburn. Joel Osburn, bm. 15 April 1843.
    Shel.
McDaniel, John & Nancy Churchwell. m. 30 Dec. 1816. Davis.
McDaniel, Presley & Mary Lightfoot. Robert Moffett attests
    groom's age and consents for bride "his being her guardian",
    bm. 26 Nov. 1829. Tippett.
McDonald, Presley & May Noble. m. 9 Nov. 1824. T. Littleton.
McDonaugh, James & Elizabeth E. Gardner. David D. Merchant
    attests ages, bm. 10 April 1831. Shel.
McDonnaugh, William W. & Harriet H. Donaldson. m. 9 Aug. 1843.
    Gover.
McDonough, John A. & Elizabeth King. Washington Jarvis, bm.
    2 Feb. 1842. Shel.
McDonough, Joshua & Mary Akers. m. 19 Sep. 1824. T. Littleton.
McDonough, William W. & Harriet H. Donaldson, dau. of Elizabeth
    C. Donaldson. James McDonough, bm. 7 Aug. 1843. Shel.
McDowell, James & Sarah Ann Prince. Mathias Prince attests
    groom's age, bm. 14 Feb. 1838. m. 15 Feb. 1838. Hauer. Shel.
McFadon, Patrick & Margeret Anderson. m. 14 Oct. 1800. Littlejohn.
McFarland, Alexander & Bethany A. Lanham, dau. of William A.
    Lanham, who attests groom's age, bm. 1 Jan. 1845. Cam.
McFarland, Charles & Catharine Hughes. Thomas Hensey attests ages,
    bm. 26 July 1839. m. 1 Aug. 1839. Herndon. Shel.
McFarland, Joseph & Mary E. Caylor. Wit: Thomas L. Hoskinson.
    9 May 1853. Duncan.
McFarlin, James & Hannah Riley. m. 8 Sep. 1806. Littlejohn.
McFarlin, John & Margaret Marcus. m. 15 Sep. 1796. Littlejohn.
McFarlin, John & Martha Burgoine. m. 5 Oct. 1803. Littlejohn.
McFarling, James Landon & Mary Ann Tarleton. John E. Fulton
    attests ages, bm. 2 March 1840. Shel.
McFarling, William & Rachel Lewis, ward of Samuel Moore, bm.
    18 Aug. 1809.
McFee, John & Sarah Scrivner. m. 6 Aug. 1814. Littlejohn.

McGache, William & Catherine Bagent; both single. By license.
    m. 11 April 1830. ParReg A.
McGaha, Samuel & Julian Sanbower. Michael Sanbower attests
    groom's age, bm. John Bontz, bm. George Hefner signs.
    30 March 1839. Shel.
McGaha, William & Catherine Bagent. Henry Miller attests ages,
    bm. 5 April 1830. Shel.
McGarvock, Henry & Mary Wright. m. 30 Dec. 1813. Littlejohn.
McGavack, Henry & Mary Ann Elwell (Ebwell). Wit: Jonah Sands.
    2 March 1853. MarReg. m. 8 March 1853. Gover.
McGavack, John & Sarah Ann Wine. George H. Wine attests ages, bm.
    30 Jan. 1849. Shel.
McGavick, Patrick & Sarah Garner. David Orrison attests ages, bm.
    3 March 1829.
McGeath, Gabrill & Patty Adams. John Adams attests bride's age.
    Joseph Vandivender (Vandevanter), bm. 28 Oct. 1799.
    Littlejohn.
McGeath, James & Margaret Drake, ward of John G. Humphrey, bm.
    Lot Tavener attests groom's age. 25 Oct. 1830. Shel.
McGeath, Samuel & Mary Ann Handy. James Hogue (Hoge) attests
    ages, bm. 9 Sep. 1833. Shel.
McGeath, Thomas & Elizabeth Perfect. m. 28 Feb. 1805. Littlejohn.
McGee, Patrick & Mary Dailey. m. 12 Aug. 1828. Tippett.
McGurgan, William & Rebecca Millan, dau. of Joseph Mellon.John
    Blaker, bm. 30 March 1799. Littlejohn.
McHardy, Hugh & Louise Jane Hamilton. m. 1 Aug. 1848. Gover.
McIlhany, James & Margaret Henderson. m. 5 May 1825. Dunn.
McIlhany, Taliaferro M. & Ann Rogers. m. 30 Nov. 1827. Baker.
McIntosh, John & Mary (Clary) Ann Jones. Catesby Jones attests
    groom's age, bm. 30 Dec. 1844. m. 2 Jan. 1845. Shepherd. Shel.
McIntosh, Loyd & Cathrine Harper. m. 10 April 1805. Littlejohn.
McIntosh, Thomas & Elizabeth Silcott. m. 2 Jan. 1822-21 March
    1822. Mines.
McIntosh, William & Frances Osburn. Bride's father consents, wit.;
    "the other taken for granted". 6 May 1852. MarReg. m. 11 May
    1852. Holland.
McIntyre, Michal & Mary Edins. m. 3 April 1806. Littlejohn.
McKenna, Hiram & Amanda Fitcher (Fichter), dau. of George Fitcher,
    who attests groom's age, bm. 10 Oct. 1837. Cam.
McKenna, James L. & Ann Cecilia Lee. m. 24 Oct. 1816. Dunn.
McKennay, George & Elizabeth Thomas. Nancy Thomas attests bride's
    age. Eli Offutt, bm. 4 March 1809.
McKenney, Thomas & Susan Ann Clarke. James Clarke, bm. 5 Oct.
    1844. Shel.
McKennie, Matthew & Sarah E. Torbert. William Settle, bm. 19 Nov.
    1835. Shel.
McKenny, Thomas & Leah Gallaher, dau. of William Gallaher, bm.
    4 May 1799. Shel.
McKenzey, Enoch & Elizabeth West, spinster. License: 30 May 1765.
    FeeBk 2.
McKim, George W. & Martina Merchant, dau. of John Merchant, who
    attests groom's age, bm. 15 April 1840. Shel.
McKim, James & Martha Wright. m. 1807-1808. Mines.
McKim, James & Ruhannah Heath. m. 25 March 1800. Hoskinson.

McKimmy, John & Sarah Walters, alias Thornton. Alfred Belt, bm.
    22 Sep. 1837. Shel.
McKinley, John & Nancy Reed. m. 4 Jan. 1804. Littlejohn.
McKinney, George & Elizabeth Thomas. m. 4 March 1809. Littlejohn.
McKinney, James W. & Cornelia Brown. Asa Brown attests groom's
    age, bm. 6 Oct. 1849. m. 9 Oct. 1849. Eggleston. Shel.
McKinney, Thomas & Catharine Hooff. m. 28 July 1816. Williamson.
McKinny, Francis & Mary Jackson. m. 11 Nov. 1800. Littlejohn.
McKnight, James F. & Harriet E. Hough, dau. of Joseph Hough.
    Enos Nichols attests groom's age, bm. 27 Nov. 1833. Shel.
McKnight, Josiah & Hannah Thomas, dau. of John Thomas. Uriah
    McKnight, bm. 10 April 1809.
McKnight, Mason & Thurza (Thirza) Romine, dau. of Isaiah Romine,
    who attests groom's age, bm. 3 Nov. 1834. m. 6 Nov. 1834.
    Baker. Shel.
McLan, James & Mary Brown. m. 9 May 1808. Littlejohn.
McLongry, James & Rebecca Brook. m. 4 Jan. 1824. T. Littleton.
McMannamy, James & Mary Carr. m. 19 Feb. 1798. Littlejohn.
McMekin, William & Tilphia Pullin. m. 6 Feb. 1795. Littlejohn.
McMullen, Daniel & Barbara Stoneburner. Bride's father consents.
    William McMullen attests groom's age, bm. 13 March 1809. m.
    April 1809. Dunn.
McMullen, George & Sarah E. Craven, dau. of James Craven, wit.
    13 Jan. 1851. MarReg.
McMullen, William & Ann Wildman. Daniel McMullen attests groom's
    age. Jacob Wildman, bm. 30 March 1835. Shel.
McMullen, William & Elizabeth Beerley. m. 26 Dec. 1819. Dagg.
McMullin, George & Edith Craven. Samuel Rogers attests ages, bm.
    11 Jan. 1830. Shel.
McMullon, Archibald & Elizabeth Johnson. m. 23 Dec. 1804. Dunn.
McNealy, James & Mary Lowe, dau. of Henry Lowe, bm. William
    Reece (Rice) attests groom's age. 21 April 1836.
McNealy, John & Mary C. (E.) Everhart, dau. of David Everhart,
    bm. " - this is said McNealeys second marriage." 23 Jan.
    1847. m. 28 Jan. 1847. Shuford. Shel.
McNealy, John & Susan C. Miller. Gideon Householder attests ages,
    bm. 6 Feb. 1843. Mercer. Shel.
McNeeley, Sandford & Sarah Moran. Richard Howser attests bride's
    age, bm. 31 Dec. 1832. Cam.
McNulty, Hugh & Mary E. (C.) Davis (Lawes). William Carroll
    attests bride's age, bm. 9 Dec. 1847. m. 14 Dec. 1847.
    Shuford. Shel.
McPherson, Armistead & Agnes E. Ridout, dau. of Juby and Sally
    Ridout. Richard Tavenner attests groom's age, bm. 5 May
    1846. Shel.
McPherson, Benjamin & Eleanor Criss alias Guides, persons of
    color. Edward Hammat, bm. 25 Oct. 1838. Shel.
McPherson, Job & Mary Beatty. Isaac Frye attests ages, bm.
    1 June 1809.
McPherson, Maddison & Mary Barton. m. 7 Feb. 1822. T. Littleton.
McPherson, Matthew E. & Lucy E. Elgin. Wit: Gustavus A. Elgin.
    21 Dec. 1853. MarReg. m. 22 Dec. 1853, at house of Gustavus
    Elgin; both born and raised in Loudoun. Neither married
    before. Cross.

McPherson, Sebastian & Sally <u>Felby</u>, widow. Edward Thompson, bm.
   25 May 1836. Shel.
McPherson, William & Dianna Finnacom, dau. of Dianna Finnacom,
   "no father living". Silas Garrett, bm. 19 Jan. 1841. Shel.
McPherson, William & Nancy Ann Brown, sister of George Brown, bm.
   6 Dec. 1836. m. 15 Dec. 1836. Herndon. Shel.
McPherson, William E. & Mary Ann Davis. Wit: Charles E. Keene.
   7 July 1853. MarReg. m. 7 July 1853. Duncan.
McQueen, Patrick & Margaret Moore. License: 18 Oct. 1851.
   Dashiell.
McReady, Alexander & Nancy Summers. m. 10 April 1815. Littlejohn.
McVeigh, Hiram & Jane Elgin. m. 1821-1822. Mines.
McVeigh, Hiram & Mary E. White, dau. of John White. Theodore N.
   Davison, bm. 22 Dec. 1834. Shel.
McVeigh, James A. (H.) & Cynthia Ariel Guest, dau. of Job Guest.
   George Cuthbert Powell, bm. 19 May 1830. m. 25 May 1830.
   Davis. Shel.
McVeigh, William H., Dr., son of Townsend and Karen McVeigh,
   about 25 years, born in Middleburg & Hattie E. Rogers, dau.
   of Thomas and Elmina Rogers, about 20 years, born in Leesburg.
   Bride's father, wit. 22 Nov. 1853. MarReg. m. 23 Nov. 1853,
   at home of bride's father, near Harmony. Herndon.
McVey, Jesse & Ann Rodgers. m. 21 June 1795. Littlejohn.
Mead, Aquila & Lavina Bolen. m. 25 May 1811. Littlejohn.
Mead, Benjamin & Ann Patteson. m. 31 March 1785. FFMM.
Mead, Jonathan & Mary Jane Beatty. Thomas Mead, bm. 1 Jan. 1849.
   Shel.
Mead, Joseph & Elizabeth Fry. m. 22 Feb. 1813. Littlejohn.
Mead, Manly & Mary Ann Nichols, dau. of Jacob Nichols. Jacob
   Nichols, Jr., bm. 17 Dec. 1836. m. 27 Dec. 1836. White. Shel.
Mead, Samuel & Sarah Whitacre. m. 6 Sep. 1807. Littlejohn.
Mead, Thomas & Mary Ann Worsley, sister of William Worseley.
   Joseph Mead, bm. 10 Aug. 1844. m. 13 Aug. 1844, at house of
   bride's brother. Adie. Shel.
Means, Lewis D. & Alcinda A. Paxson. G. W. Paxson attests ages,
   bm. 23 Nov. 1841. Shel.
Meathrel, Richard & Julia E. Leedom, dau. of Isaac Leedom, who
   attests groom's age and that he's a widower, bm. 22 June
   1846. Cam.
Megeath, Alfred & Mary P. Humphrey, dau. of Thomas G. Humphrey,
   bm. 18 June 1850. m. 25 June 1850. Eggleston.
Meginnis, Daniel & Maria McClure; both single. By license. m.
   13 Dec. 1821. ParReg A.
Meisley (Meisler), William & Sophia Winn. 3 Sep. 1811. Littleton.
Mellon, Eli & Elizabeth Combs. m. 3 Aug. 1806. Dunn.
Mellon, Joseph & Nancy Evans. m. 20 July 1804. Littlejohn.
Melvin, Benjamin & Isabella Cockrel, dau. of Joseph Cockrel, bm.
   10 Jan. 1834. Shel.
Menroe, James & Lydia Campbell. m. 9 Nov. 1812. Littlejohn.
Mercer, Henry & Tacey Melton. m. 8 Feb. 1807. Littlejohn.
Mercer, William F. & Harriet J. Carr. David Carr, bm. 18 Nov.
   1845. Shel.
Merchant, David D. & Mary Ellen McDonaugh, dau. of James
   McDonaugh, bm. 10 Nov. 1831. Shel.

Merchant, James & Mary Ann Baker. George Shumaker attests ages, bm. 27 Aug. 1844. Shel.

Merchant, James & Rebekah Romine, dau. of Isaiah Romine, bm. 7 Nov. 1831. Shel.

Merchant, William & Nancy McClow. m. 9 Dec. 1811. Littlejohn.

Mershon, Benjamin & Mahalda Cunningham. William T. Saffer attests ages, bm. Bond not signed. 29 Dec. 1845. Cam.

Meyers, Peter & Catherine Spring, dau. of Casper Spring. m. 1 Oct. 1835. ParReg A. Shel.

Michael, Amos & Nancy Watts. m. 3 Oct. 1812. Littlejohn.

Mickie (Michie), Newton, of Augusta & Lalla (Salla) Gray, dau. of John Gray, bm. 21 Nov. 1842. m. 22 Nov. 1842, at house of bride's father, Leesburg. Adie. Shel.

Midcalf, Aaron & Elizabeth Keyes, dau. of Alexander Keyes, bm. Julia Ann Rulky attests groom's age. 30 Dec. 1845. m. 8 Jan. 1846, at house of bride's father, Leesburg. Adie. Shel.

Middleton, Smallwood & Cascy Lucas. Thomas Lucas attests bride's age. Joseph Gore, bm. 12 June 1799. Cam.

Milbourn, Aaron J. & Mary E. Loman. Charles H. Tavener proves bride's age, wit. 15 March 1853. MarReg.

Milbourn (Milbourne), Oliver & Mary Jane Jones. Jonathan Milbourn attests ages, bm. William Milbourne, bm. 6 Jan. 1840. Shel.

Milburn, David & Mary Saunders. m. 10 Aug. 1814. Littlejohn.

Milburn, John F. & Joanna Carruthers. Calvin F. Beales, bm. 11 Sep. 1843. Shel.

Milburne, Jonathan & Massey Oram. m. 20 April 1841. ParReg A. Shel.

Miley, Vincent & Rachel Marts. John Marts attests ages, bm. 17 Nov. 1838. Shel.

Millar, William H., Alexandria & Amy Ann Phillips, Waterford. m. 6 Dec. 1820. FFMM.

Millbourne, Jonathan & Sarah Sanders. m. 8 Sep. 1810. Littlejohn.

Miller, Abram.& Rachel Martin, dau. of John Martin. John Jackson, bm. 21 Dec. 1799. Littlejohn.

Miller, Andrew & Martha Hurst. m. 23 Oct. 1796. Littlejohn.

Miller, Armistead M. & Mary Ann Edwards. Solomon Everhart attests ages, bm. 2 Feb. 1846. m. 3 March 1846. ParReg A. Shel.

Miller, Christian & Sarah Near, dau. of Conrad Near, bm. 7 Jan. 1809. m. 1808-1809. Mines.

Miller, Daniel & Mary (Margt.) A. Klein (Kline). John A. Klein attests ages, bm. 20 May 1836. m. May 1836. Campbell. Shel.

Miller, Daniel & Nanzy Calir; both widowed. By license. m. 4 Sep. 1828. ParReg A.

Miller, David & Nansy Darry, dau. of Jacob Darry; both single. By license. m. 16 Nov. 1815. ParReg A.

Miller, Frederick & Edney Fitchter. George Fitchter, bm. 10 Oct. 1848.

Miller, Frederick & Elizabeth Stream. Henry Ruse attests bride's age, bm. 23 March 1835. m. 26 March 1835. Hauer. Shel.

Miller, Georg & Elisabetha Waldtman; both single. By license. m. 2 Dec. 1824. ParReg A.

Miller, Henrich & Elisa M. Gahn; both single. By license. m. 22 Jan. 1824. ParReg A.

Miller, Jacob, son of Peter Miller & Elisabetha Ernst; both
single. By license. m. 23 Dec. 1813. ParReg A.
Miller, Jacob & Mary Unkerfear. m. 9 Dec. 1797. Littlejohn.
Miller, Jeremiah T. & Mary Thompson. Mahlon Thompson attests
bride's age, bm. 6 Sep. 1830. Shel.
Miller, Job & Caroline Vincel. Jacob Shafer attests ages, bm.
25 Nov. 1843. Shel.
Miller, Johannes, son of Peter Miller & Catharina Rickert, dau.
of Widow Haushalter; both single. By license. m. 12 Sep.
1811. ParReg A.
Miller, Johannes & Margretha Philler; both single. By license.
m. 14 Feb. 1828. ParReg A.
Miller, John & Mary Langten. m. 26 Sep. 1812. J. Littleton.
Miller, John G. & Amanda Russell, ward of John Miller. 12 Nov.
1833. m. 12 Nov. 1833. Humphreys. Shel.
Miller, John J. (P.) & Margaret Donaldson. George R. Donaldson
attests ages. William McDonough, bm. 10 April 1845. Gover.
Shel.
Miller, Joseph & Mary (Maria) Anna Waltman, ward of Jonathan
Wenner, bm. 8 Feb. 1830. m. 12 Feb. 1830. ParReg A. Shel.
Miller, Moses & Christina Shoemaker, dau. of George Shoemaker.
Daniel Shoemaker, bm. 17 Oct. 1799. Littlejohn.
Miller, Robert H., Alexandria & Anna Janney, Hillsboro. m.
23 April 1823. FFMM.
Miller, Samuel & Hannah Potter. m. 1809-1810. Mines.
Miller, Thomas & Sarah Ellen Steel. Marcus L. Kendrick proves
ages, wit. 15 March 1852. MarReg. m. 28 March 1852. Duncan.
Miller, William & Anne Miller. m. 10 Nov. 1807. Littlejohn.
Miller, William & Elisabetha Edwart; both single. By license.
m. 26 Dec. 1827. ParReg A.
Miller, William & Maria Thomas, ward of John Ross, bm. 10 Jan.
1831. m. 16 Jan. 1831. Green. Shel.
Miller, William C. & Elizabeth Carpenter. John Thomas proves
bride's age, wit. 21 Feb. 1852. Dashiell.
Miller, William H., son of Mordicai Miller & Amy Ann Phillips,
dau. of Thomas and Rachel Phillips. m. 6 Dec. 1820.
Mendenhall, Clerk.
Milholland, Patrick & Melinda Sanford. m. 27 May 1806. Littlejohn.
Million, Lee & Nancy Handley, free people of color. Binns attests
ages. James Hamilton, bm. 23 March 1829.
Mills, Harrison & Frances R. Muse, ward of Thomas H. Muse, who
attests groom's age, bm. 27 Jan. 1844. Cam.
Mills, James & Nancy Page. m. 8 Feb. 1820. Griffith.
Mills, William & Mary Frost. m. 19 March 1818. Dunn. Shel.
Milner, Edward & Jane Updyke (Updike). Matthew Orrison attests
bride's age, bm. 3 Nov. 1799. Littlejohn.
Milner, George & Elizabeth Rinker. m. 27 May 1801. Littlejohn.
Milner, Jehu & Elenor Rhodes. m. 4 July 1798. Littlejohn.
Milner, John & Ester Hough. m. 6 Dec. 1796. Littlejohn.
Milstead, Townsend, son of Noah Milstead & Catherine Havener,
dau. of William Havener, wit. 17 Dec. 1850. MarReg.
Milstead, William H. & Mary Jane Davis. Wit: Philip F. Havenner.
29 Dec. 1852. MarReg. m. 4 Jan. 1853. Hirst.

Milton, Alexander R., Jr., of Frederick County & Ann Cecelia
White, dau. of Henry White. Frederick A. Davidson attests
groom's age, bm. 10 May 1837. Shel.

Minegar, John & Elizabeth Collett. m. 8 March 1813. Littlejohn.

Minick, John & Elizabeth Brookes. m. 15 Nov. 1797. Littlejohn.

Mink, Adam, son of Lorentz Mink and wife & Sarah Hackmanin, dau.
of Peter Hackman, Sr.; both single. By license. m. 17 Feb.
1820. ParReg A.

Minor, Daniel J. & Pleasant Nixon. George Nixon, bm. 30 March
1809. Littlejohn.

Minor, Franklin & Eleanor Anderson. "Minor age proved - by
certificate etc. duly authenticated under the hand of the
Court of Frederick County, Md." Francis W. Elgin attests
bride's age, bm. 28 June 1847. m. 29 June 1847. Adie.

Minor, Jackson M. & Mary E. Williams, dau. of Lyddnah Williams,
who attests groom's age, wit. 29 Jan. 1853. MarReg.

Minor, James & Nancy Shreve, dau. of Benjamin Shreve. Francis
Shreve attests ages, bm. 13 Sep. 1841. m. 14 Sep. 1841, at
house of bride's father. Adie. Shel.

Minor, John W. & Louisa A. Catlett, dau. of Charles J. Catlett.
W. C. Selden, bm. 20 June 1839. Shel.

Miskell, William C. & Catherine Peacock, dau. of William Peacock,
who attests groom's age, bm. 1 Jan. 1847. Shel.

Mitchal, Walter & Elizabeth Hoskins. m. 16 Feb. 1797. Littlejohn.

Mitchell, Benjamin & Nancy Hampton. m. 29 May 1821. Dagg.

Mitchell, Matthew & Elizabeth Schooley. m. 5 Sep. 1808. Saunders.

Mitchell, William H. & Sarah F. Perry. John S. Smith attests ages,
bm. 6 Feb. 1849. Cam.

Mobberley, Jesse W. & Catharine T. Moore. John Hough attests ages,
bm. 7 Jan. 1836. Shel.

Moberley, John J. & Mariah Underwood. George Lay, bm. 11 Nov.
1840. Shel.

Mock, Daniel & Maria Prill, dau. of Samuel Prill and wife; both
single. By license. m. 2 July 1818. ParReg A.

Mock, George W. & Mary Jane Jones. Adam Mason proves ages, wit.
6 Jan. 1852. MarReg.

Mock, George W. & Mary Ann Russell, dau. of William Russell, bm.
15 March 1834. Shel.

Mock, Isaac L. & Lydia Ann Ogden, dau. of Benjamin Ogden, bm.
"this is said Mocks second marriage." 6 March 1847. Shel.

Mock, John & Julia Beagle. m. 13 Oct. 1795. Littlejohn.

Mock, Joseph C. & Mary James. George W. Wock attests groom's age.
Elijah James, bm. 16 Nov. 1841. Shel.

Mock, Thomas J. & Rebecca Filler. m. 16 Jan. 1845. ParReg A.

Moffatt, David & Lettice Moss. m. 9 March 1808. Littlejohn.

Moffett, Huoh & Maria Beltz; both single. By license. m. 10 Nov.
1816. ParReg A.

Moffett, William & Susanna Lodge. m. 1807-1808. Mines.

Moffett, William B. & Louisa Klein, dau. of Lewis Klein, bm.
Robert A. Gover affirms groom's age. 14 Sep. 1833. Shel.

Moffett, William H. & Alice A. Jenkins. Bride's father consents
and proves groom's age, wit. 17 Nov. 1853. MarReg.

Mohr, Benjamin & Elisabeth Printz, dau. of Levi Printz. By
license. m. 14 Feb. 1811. ParReg A.

LOUDOUN COUNTY MARRIAGES

Mohrland, Daniel & Sarah Schember, dau. of Widow Schember. By
   license. m. 5 Feb. 1811. ParReg A.
Moll, Georg & Elisabeth Ruff; both single. By license. m. 21 Feb.
   1814. ParReg A.
Monday (Munday), Daniel & Mary Ann Taylor. George W. Johnston
   attests ages, bm. 9 March 1841. m. 16 March 1841. Gover. Shel.
Monday, John & Margaret Phillips. m. 10 Dec. 1822. Chapman.
Money, John Francis & Harriet Ellen Hough, dau. of William Hough.
   24 Feb. 1852. MarReg. m. 26 Feb. 1852. Gover.
Monroe, Charles W. & Caroline D. McPherson, dau. of Mary McPherson.
   Benjamin Barton attests Mary McPherson's widow of Madison
   McPherson and attests groom's age, bm. 1 July 1842. Shel.
Monroe, Harrison S. & Julia Ann Jenkins, dau. of William Jenkins,
   bm. 27 May 1843. Shel.
Monroe, Henson & Elizabeth Cammee. m. 8 Aug. 1819. Dunn. Shel.
Monroe, John & Mary Fadley. m. 28 Nov. 1816. Littlejohn.
Monroe, John H. & Catherine Eugenia Solomon. John A. Binns, bm.
   17 Feb. 1831. Shel.
Monroe, Stephen F. & Sarah E. McPherson, dau. of Mary McPherson,
   who's widow of Madison McPherson. Benjamin C. Barton attests
   groom's age, bm. 2 Feb. 1846. Shel.
Monroe, William & Catherine Lowe. m. 7 Nov. 1816. Littlejohn.
Moon, Isaac Wilberforce, son of Henry Moon, who says groom was
   born Sep. 1806 & Elizabeth Sullivan. Samuel Sullivan attests
   bride's age, bm. Alfred I. Dorsey attests groom's age, bm.
   19 Oct. 1833. Shel.
Moor, Johannes & Catharina Mann, dau. of Johannes Mann and wife;
   both single. m. 20 May 1815. ParReg A.
Moore, Abner & Catherine Detro. m. 29 Jan. 1824. Williamson.
Moore, Abram & Margeret Hartman. m. 3 Oct. 1801. Littlejohn.
Moore, George L. & Ann Amanda Russell, dau. of Henry Russell, bm.
   6 Oct. 1834. m. 14 Oct. 1834. Trott. Shel.
Moore, Isaac & Catharine Ann Kent, ward of John Beavers, bm.
   8 March 1841. Shel.
Moore, Isaac & Frances Morriss. m. 8 Feb. 1816. T. Littleton.
Moore, Isaac & Sarah Campble. m. 26 July 1802. Littlejohn.
Moore, Jacob & Rachel Wildman. m. 17 Sep. 1793. Littlejohn.
Moore, James, son of Thomas and Elizabeth Moore & Phebe Myers,
   dau. of Joseph and Phebe Myers. m. 9 Jan. 1782. FFMM.
Moore, James & Rebekah Talbott. m. 8 July 1818. FFMM.
Moore, James W. & Matilda Dulin. William B. Jackson attests
   bride's age, bm. 25 Oct. 1849. Dulin. Shel.
Moore, John & Elizabeth Ritacre. William Smith attests bride's
   age, bm. 10 Feb. 1832. Cam.
Moore, John & Martha Ann Lathrum, ward of John Fulton, bm.
   14 Feb. 1832. Shel.
Moore, John & Sarah Weeden. m. 12 June 1817. Williamson.
Moore, John W. & Amanda Tribby, ward of John B. Dutton, bm.
   24 Sep. 1849. m. 27 Sep. 1829. Eggleston. Shel.
Moore, Jonathan J. & Margaret Campbell, dau. of Margaret McKim.
   Charles William Schooley attests groom's age. James McKim,
   bm. 13 May 1844. Shel.
Moore, Josiah F. & Julia Ann Knott, who will "be 21 on the fourth
   of Nov 1840". William F. Moore attests groom's age. John
   Connor, bm. 17 Aug. 1840. m. 20 Aug. 1840. Herndon. Shel.

Moore, Mason & Margaret Ann Thomas. m. 2 Dec. 1823. Dagg.
Moore, Peter & Hannah Ewers. m. 19 July 1798. Littlejohn.
Moore, Peter & Susan Soloman. Elias Pool, bm. 14 July 1845. Cam.
Moore, Thomas & Ann Ewers. m. 19 Dec. 1796. Littlejohn.
Moran, Alexander & Vilinda C. Brabham, dau. of Mary Brabham.
    Frederick Brabham, bm in body of bond, but signed Francis M.
    Brabham. 10 June 1848. Shel.
Moran, John M. & Drusilla Ann Luck, dau. of Jordan B. Luck. Jesse
    Timms, bm. 6 Oct. 1835. m. 7 Oct. 1835. White. Shel.
Moran, Samuel & Anne Conner. m. 26 Feb. 1802. Littlejohn.
Moran, William & Mary Lyne, dau. of William Lyne. James E.
    Edwards attests groom's age, bm. 15 Sep. 1829. Cam.
More, Peter & Araminta Nisbet. m. 26 Oct. 1820. T. Littleton.
More, William & Helen Waters. m. 24 March 1797. Littlejohn.
Moreland, Dorsett & Elizabeth Spunogle. m. 1821-1822. Mines.
Moreland, James & Nancy Jones. m. 28 Aug. 1828. Tippett.
Moreland, Thomas & Sarah Rinker, dau. of Edward Rinker, who
    attests groom's age, bm. 11 March 1833. Shel.
Morgan, Charles & Mary Radcliff. Published 16 Sep. 1798.
    Littlejohn.
Morgan, Jesse & Nancy Wright. m. 11 Aug. 1801. Littlejohn.
Morgan, Job & Susan Shrigley. Enoch Shrigley attests bride's age,
    bm. 16 May 1831. Shel.
Morgan, Johannes & Margretha Diewer; both single. By license.
    m. 7 Jan. 1830. ParReg A.
Morgan, John, Waterford & Eliza McCormick, dau. of James and
    Ann McCormick, deceased. m. 4 Nov. 1812. FFMM.
Morgan, John & Sarah McLanahan. " - settlement before." Wit:
    P. Saunders. 8 Jan. 1853. MarReg. Duncan.
Morgan, John W. & Nancy E. Wynkoop. John H. Hughes proves ages,
    wit. 25 Feb. 1851. MarReg.
Morgan, Philip & Mary Winegardner, dau. of Adam Winegardner, bm.
    21 Oct. 1831. Shel.
Morgin, Phillip & Elisa Schumacher; both single. By license.
    m. 18 March 1824. ParReg A.
Moriarty, Michael & Jane Elizabeth Kidwell. John F. Kidwell
    proves ages, wit. 31 Dec. 1850. MarReg. m. 2 Jan. 1851.
    Dodge.
Morison, Andreas & Maria Russ; both single. By license. m.
    3 Oct. 1812. ParReg A.
Morlan, Stephin, son of William Morlan & Mary Rhodes, dau. of
    Mary Rhodes. m. 20 Oct. 1773. FFMM.
Morland, Samuel & Sarah Fredd. George Moreland, Frederick County,
    consents. Joseph H. Fredd attests bride's age, bm. 11 Aug.
    1834. Shel.
Morrallee, Michael & Emely Patience Osborn, dau. of Nicholas
    Osborne, bm. 20 Oct. 1830. Shel.
Morris, Frederick & Susannah Pool. m. 6 June 1826-8 June 1826.
    Burch.
Morris, Isaac & Mary Thompson. m. 13 June 1803. Littlejohn.
Morris, James & Elizabeth Fowler. Baldwin Johnson attests bride's
    age, bm. 30 July 1830. m. 1 Aug. 1830. Shel.
Morris, James D. & Ann Davis. Hugh S. Thompson, bm. 12 Feb. 1849.
    m. 13 Feb. 1849. Eggleston. Shel.

Morris, Mahlon & Ann Ogden. Andrew Ogden attests bride's age, bm. 18 Oct. 1837. Shel.

Morris, Mahlon & Catherine Giddion. m. 28 April 1802. Littlejohn.

Morris, Thomas & Catherine Fouch. m. 1815. Littlejohn.

Morris, William & Edy Canter, widow. Edward Morris, bm. 15 June 1799. Littlejohn.

Morrison, Archibald & Mary M. Kabrick, dau. of George Kabrick, who proves groom's age, wit. 31 May 1852. MarReg. m. 8 June 1852. Holland.

Morrison, Archibald & Nancy Roper. John H. Canby, bm. 26 Jan. 1799. Littlejohn.

Morrison, Archibald (of Edward) & Rachel Morrison. Edward Morrison attests bride's age, bm. 19 Nov. 1840. m. 24 Nov. 1840. ParReg A. Shel.

Morrison, Henry & Mary Ann Reed, dau. of Thomas Reed, who attests groom's age, bm. 6 April 1833. Shel.

Morrison, John & Elizabeth Brashears. m. 1 March 1810. Littlejohn.

Morrison, John & Sarah Grubb. m. 1807-1808. Mines.

Morrison, Robert & Elizabeth Morrison. m. 14 Feb. 1797. Littlejohn.

Morrison, William & Minta Bebbely. m. 1809-1810. Mines.

Moss, Carter & Susan Beveridge, sister of Andrew Beveridge, bm. William Fulton attests groom's age. 13 April 1829.

Moss, John & Effee Wright. m. 10 May 1813. Littlejohn.

Moss, John C. & Frances Wildman, dau. of William Wildman, who attests groom's age, bm. 20 Aug. 1846. Gover. Shel.

Moss, Stephen & Margaret McGue. m. 1 Nov. 1804. Williamson.

Moss, Thomas & Mary E. M. Rollings, dau. of Lewis Rollings, wit. 18 Jan. 1851. MarReg. Wills.

Moss, William & Mary Fields. James Fields proves bride's age, wit. 15 April 1851. MarReg.

Mossburgh, Peter K. & Margaret L. Phillips, dau. of Philip L. Phillips, bm. 24 May 1849.

Mott, Armistead R. & Virginia L. Bentley, dau. of Robert Bentley. Robert W. Gray attests ages, bm. 15 Dec. 1846. m. 16 Dec. 1846, at home of bride's father, Leesburg. Adie. Shel.

Mott, Isaac & Sarah Little, widow. License: 13 Aug. 1810. m. 28 Aug. 1810. T. Littleton.

Moul, George & Betheny Sanders. m. 22 April 1801. Littlejohn.

Mount, John E. & Mary J. Fitzhugh. Samuel K. Jackson, bm. 13 Nov. 1848. Krebbs. Shel.

Moxley, alias Lee, Peter & Ann Maria Gant, free persons of color. James Thomas, bm. 9 Oct. 1849. Shel.

Moxley, William & Jane Lush. m. 23 Dec. 1811. Littlejohn.

Moyer, Philip & Carey Peirce (Pierce). C. Binns, bm. 5 Dec. 1834. m. 6 Dec. 1834. Baker. Shel.

Muck, George & Sarah McArtor. m. 8 June 1811. Littlejohn.

Mudd, John & Patty Gibbs, dau. of James Lewin Gibbs. John Dowdell, bm. 9 March 1799. Cam.

Muirhead, John & Martha Myers, dau. of John Myres. Dl. Barecraft, bm. 28 Sep. 1799. Littlejohn.

Mull, George & Mary Filler. William A. Hamilton attests bride's age, bm. 21 Jan. 1842. m. 23 Jan. 1842. Hauer. Shel.

Mullen, Samuel & Barbara Oden. Charles B. Tebbs, bm. 30 Dec. 1844. Shel.

Mullen, Samuel & Lydia Ann Zeller, dau. of John Zeller. Abraham
    Hewitt, bm. 5 July 1847.
Mullen, Samuel & Mary A. Stoneburner. 31 July 1850. MarReg.
Mulligan, William B. & Ann M. Chilton. m. 3 June 1809.
    Littlejohn.
Mullin, Samuel & Lydia Ann Zeller. m. 6 July 1847. Gover.
Munday, Robert & Rosanna Frye, dau. of Nicholas Frye, bm.
    11 Feb. 1833. Shel.
Murphey, James & Ann H. Alder. m. 18 Oct. 1821. T. Littleton.
Murphey, Newton & Mahala Jones, dau. of Thomas Jones. Newton
    Hesser, bm. 3 Nov. 1831. Shel.
Murphey, Thomas & Jemima Davis, dau. of Thomas and Betty Davis.
    Tinley Murphey, bm. 9 Jan. 1799. Shel.
Murphy, Charles & Ann Elliott. m. 10 April 1793. Littlejohn.
Murphy, Hiram & Huldah F. Monroe. Wit: Thomas Monroe. 18 Oct.
    1852. MarReg. m. 20 Oct. 1852. Hirst.
Murphy, Newton & Mahala Jones. m. 8 Nov. 1831. Green.
Murray, Samuel Patrick & Elizabeth Carrol. Abraham Sinkfield, bm.
    29 Nov. 1836. m. 8 Dec. 1836. Morgan. Shel.
Murrey, John & Hannah Banacraft. m. 24 Jan. 1804. Littlejohn.
Murrey, Samuel & Elizabeth Carter. m. 14 Feb. 1813. McPherson.
Murrey, Samuel & Elizabeth Donohoe. m. 18 June 1800. Littlejohn.
Muschler, Adam & Catharina Derri, dau. of Baltaser Derri. m.
    12 Oct. 1784. ParReg A.
Muse, Edward & Nancy James. William Thrift attests bride's age.
    Bond - "taken off with the licence by Mistake". April 1799.
Muse, James H. & Ann Eliza Seeders, dau. of William Seeders,
    who attests groom's age, bm. 18 March 1841. Gover. Shel.
Muse, Thomas & Sydney Jane Havener. Michael H. Havener attests
    ages, bm. 26 Dec. 1836. Shel.
Muse, Thomas H. & Mary Neale. m. 21 May 1822. Gilmore.
Muse, Thomas M. & Nancy E. Peacock. m. 31 July 1851, on Seldon's
    Island, Maryland. Adie.
Musgrove, Samuel & Mary Dillon. m. 19 Sep. 1811. Littlejohn.
Musten, William & Sophiah Winn. m. 3 Sep. 1810. T. Littleton.
Myers, Charles F. (L.) & Susan H. Donaldson, dau. of Elizabeth C.
    Donaldson. Richard H. Edwards attests groom's age, bm.
    13 Aug. 1849. m. 28 Aug. 1849. Gover. Shel.
Myers, Elijah, son of Jonathan and Mary Myers & Mary Ball, dau.
    of William Ball. m. 16 Dec. 1778. FFMM.
Myers, Elijah P. & Margaret C. Monroe, dau. of Catherine Flowers.
    Columbus Jones attests groom's age, bm. 28 Nov. 1843. Shel.
Myers, Isaiah & Alice Yates, Junr. m. 15 Oct. 1777. FFMM.
Myers, Israel & Mary Titus. Mahlon Myers attests ages, bm.
    19 Dec. 1837. Shel.
Myers, Jacob & Mary Bailey. m. 24 March 1825. Dunn. Shel.
Myers, John, "widower between 35 and 40 years of age" & Mary A.
    Campbell, dau. of John Campbell, bm. 13 April 1847. m.
    15 April 1847. Gover. Shel.
Myers, John & Mary Perry. Wadsworth Shepherd attests ages, bm.
    4 Feb. 1829.
Myers, Joseph & Mary Wylie. m. Jan. 1804. Dunn.
Myers, Lambert & Rachel Eveland. Sydnor Bennett attests bride's
    age, bm. 20 Oct. 1841. Shel.

108

LOUDOUN COUNTY MARRIAGES

Myers, Mahlon & Amy Wright. m. 1807-1808. Mines.
Myers, Peter & Catherine Spring, dau. of Casper Spring, bm.
  28 Sep. 1835. m. 1 Oct. 1835. ParReg A. Shel.
Myers, Peter & Judith Chinn. m. 1 Jan. 1805. Williamson.
Myers, Samuel W. & Leva Jane Wynkoop. Peter Myers proves ages,
  wit. Nov. 1851. m. 6 Nov. 1851. Gover.
Myers, William & Mary Hannah Donaldson, dau. of Elizabeth C.
  Donaldson. Mahlon Myers, bm. 29 Feb. 1840. m. 29 Feb. 1840.
  Gover. Shel.
Myres, Isaac & Rachel Davis. m. 21 June 1800. Littlejohn.
Myres, Jonathan & Elizabeth Parker. m. 30 May 1796. Littlejohn.
Myres, Jonathan & Malinda Reed. William Graham, bm. 10 Feb. 1831.
  Shel.
Myres, Lambert & Mary Eveland. m. 17 Nov. 1800. Littlejohn.
Myres, Mahlon & Elizabeth Davis. John Coist attests ages, bm.
  29 Jan. 1838. Shel.
Myres, Mahlon, Jr. & Margaret Cooper. Presley K. Dorsey attests
  ages, bm. 10 Dec. 1833. Shel.
Myres, Washington & Margaret McIntosh. Lambert Myres attests
  bride's age, bm. 7 Dec. 1833. Shel.
Myres, William & Cornelia Myres. m. 17 Aug. 1793. Littlejohn.
Nalls, James & Lucretia Dowell. m. 21 Feb. 1822. Gilmore.
Nat, Peter & Elizabeth Philips. m. 23 May 1802. Littlejohn.
Neale, Daniel & Nancy Vanhorne. m. 28 Dec. 1803. Williamson.
Neale, John & Masey Whittacre. m. 21 Feb. 1805. Dunn.
Neale, Lewis, Frederick County, Va., son of Lewis Neale &
  Rachel Janney, dau. of Abel Janney. m. 15 June 1774. FFMM.
Neale, Robert & Margaret Wren. m. 22 Aug. 1805. Dunn.
Near, Amos & Sarah Connard, ward of William Paxson, bm. Samuel
  Near attests groom's age. 21 Sep. 1809. m. 1808-1809. Mines.
Near, David & Sally Ross. m. 14 Dec. 1807. Littlejohn.
Near, Henry & Lidia A. Derry. m. 5 Oct. 1837. Larkin.
Near, Jesse & Matilda Kalb. License: 9 May 1826. m. "same month".
  Dorsey.
Near, Thomas & Ellen K. Johnson. Wit: Charles W. Johnson. 21 Jan.
  1852. MarReg.
Needham, Thomas & Ann Catharine Evans. Harvey Evans attests ages,
  bm. 9 Aug. 1842. m. 11 Aug. 1842. Hauer. Shel.
Neer, G. Potts & Elizabeth Clendening. m. 1 July 1852. Holland.
Neer, Henry & Lydia Ann Derry. Michael Derry, bm. 2 Oct. 1837.
  Shel.
Neer, J. Potts & Elizabeth Clendening, dau. of William Clendening.
  Thomas R. Clendening proves groom's age, wit. 30 June 1852.
  MarReg.
Neer, Nathan & Jane Cunnard. m. 7 Jan. 1806. Littlejohn.
Neicwarner, Jacob & Ann Jenkins. m. 7 Dec. 1820. Dagg.
Neldon, John & Sebella Smith. Jacob Jacobs attests bride's age,
  bm. 13 April 1799. Shel.
Nelson, William & Verlenda (Virlinda) Ann Anderson. John P.
  Smart attests bride's age, bm. 21 July 1833. m. 21 Feb.
  1833 (?). Dorsey. Shel.
Nesmith, Oscar, son of Joseph and Sarah Nesmith, 32 years, b.
  Frederick County, Va., wheelwright & Susan Moore, dau. of
  Edwin and Louisa Moore, 17 years, b. Loudoun County. Charles
  W. Schooley proves groom's age, wit. 12 Dec. 1853. MarReg.

Neuhaus, Amos & Maria Trittenbach; both single. By license.
m. 1 March 1821. ParReg A.
Newhouse, David & Hannah Beans. m. 2 Feb. 1803. Littlejohn.
Newlan, George, son of Sarah and George Newland, the latter
deceased "not less than 18 or 19 years" & Amanda F.
Cockerill, dau. of Sanford W. Cockerille. John H. Cockerill,
bm. 11 Jan. 1838. Shel.
Newland, Samuel R. & Elizabeth Jane Kile, dau. of George Kile,
who attests groom's age, bm. 21 Nov. 1839. Shel.
Newlon, Charles A. & Lauretta C. Skinner. Thomas Skinner attests
ages, bm. 26 May 1847. m. 1 June 1847. Hayes. Shel.
Newlon, David & Rachel Richards. William Richards, bm. 15 March
1813.
Newlon, George & Winifred Urton, dau. of John Urton, bm. 5 Oct.
1799. Shel.
Newlon, John & Ruth Carter. Eden Carter, bm. 17 Dec. 1799. Shel.
Newlon, Nimrod & Mary Richards. Isaac Richards attests bride's
age, bm. 23 May 1831. Cam.
Newman, Benjamin & Eliza Newman. Samuel Core, guardian, bm.
9 Feb. 1835. Shel.
Newman, James T. & Amelia E. Lanham. Wit: William A. Lanham.
23 Feb. 1852. MarReg.
Newman, Thomas & Catherine Gardner. m. 22 April 1793. Littlejohn.
Newman, William & Mary Biscoe. Edward M. Baker attests ages, bm.
10 April 1837. Cam.
Newport, Jonah C. & Rachel Smith. m. 19 Feb. 1827. Taylor, Clerk.
Newton, Alexander & Elizabeth Henton, widow. John C. Newton, bm.
19 Jan. 1836. Shel.
Newton, Charles C. & Magdin (Magden) Hammerly, dau. of Jane
Hamerly. Parkerson L. Lott, bm. 24 Oct. 1832. Shel.
Newton, John & Harriot McCabe. m. 21 Jan. 1808. Littlejohn.
Newton, Nimrod & Mary Richards. m. 26 May 1831. Green.
Newton, Robert C. & Nancy Perfect. m. 25 July 1798. Littlejohn.
Nicewanger, Christian & Mary Waters. m. 15 Feb. 1820.
T. Littleton.
Nicewanger, John & Mary A. Nicewanger. m. 17 June 1809. Littlejohn.
Nicewarner, Stephen & Cineth Bats. m. 30 Oct. 1822. T. Littleton.
Nicholds, David & Leah Vickers. m. 11 March 1810. T. Littleton.
Nicholds, Enos & Eddna Gregg. m. 15 Feb. 1821. T. Littleton.
Nicholls, Nathaniel & Rachel Chamblin. m. 17 Nov. 1820.
T. Littleton.
Nicholls, William & Elizabeth Batson. m. 14 Feb. 1820. Dagg.
Nichols, Abraham E. & Sarah Miller, dau. of George Miller, bm.
22 Nov. 1836. m. 1 Dec. 1836. Hauer. m. 24 Nov. 1836.
ParReg A. Shel.
Nichols, Burr P. & Susannah Wilkison (Wilkinson). Evan Wilkison,
wit. 31 Jan. 1853. MarReg. m. 3 Feb. 1853. Greer.
Nichols, Dolphin & Anna Tracy. Bride's father consents, wit.
Enos Nichols attests groom's age, wit. 18 Nov. 1830. Shel.
Nichols, Eli & Elizabeth White, dau. of Thomas White, who
attests groom's age, bm. 9 Dec. 1809. m. 1808-1809. Mines.
Nichols, Eli H., son of Thomas Nichols & Elizabeth White. Bride's
father consents. Thomas Nichols, bm. 13 March 1848. Shel.
Nichols, Henry H. & Maria White. Levi White, bm. 14 March 1842.
Shel.

Nichols, Isaac & Olivia alias Olivi James. James P. Bradfield, bm. 22 Dec. 1830. Shel.

Nichols, Isaac & Rebekah Gibson. m. 10 Dec. 1767. FFMM.

Nichols, Isaac G. & Louisa White. Both fathers consent. Thomas Nichols, bm. 22 Jan. 1838. Shel.

Nichols, Isaac H., son of Thomas and Emily Nichols & Rebecca K. Brown, dau. of J. H. and S. Brown. Bride's father, wit. 11 Nov. 1853. MarReg. m. 15 Nov. 1853. Ridgeway.

Nichols, Jacob & Edith Nichols. James Sinclair, bm. 14 June 1848. Gover. Shel.

Nichols, Jacob & Janthy Smith. Samuel Nichols attests bride's age, bm. George McMullin attests groom's age, bm. 13 March 1837. Shel.

Nichols, James H. & Mary Jane Taylor. Wit: Timothy Taylor. 15 Dec. 1852. MarReg.

Nichols, Jonah & Fanny McDaniel. m. 1821-1822. Mines.

Nichols, Nathan B., son of Amos and Mariah Nichols, James County, lawyer of Bellmont County, Ohio & Sarah E. Hoge, dau. of W. and Mary Hoge, former deceased. Wit: William Hoge. 12 Nov. 1853. MarReg. m. 15 Nov. 1853. Ridgeway.

Nichols, Richards & Mary Jonestone. m. 20 June 1805. Littlejohn.

Nichols, Samuel & Harriett Handley, dau. of David Hanley, who attests groom's age, bm. 31 Jan. 1840. Shel.

Nichols, Thomas & Barbara Akers. m. 9 Jan. 1826-10 Jan. 1826. Burch.

Nichols, Thomas & Emily Holmes. m. 19 Oct. ____. Janney, Clerk.

Nichols, Thomas & Letitia Jenney. m. 8 June 1813. Littlejohn.

Nichols, William & Catherine Tavener. m. 20 Dec. 1827. Baker.

Nickols, John & Margaret Spencer. m. 18 Feb. 1779. FFMM.

Nieswanger, John & Mary Ann Nieswanger, dau. of Catharine Niswanger, who says bride was b. 3 Feb. 1766. Christian Nieswanger, bm. 17 June 1809.

Nisswaner (Niswaner), William A. & Barbara A. Conard. John M. Conrad attests ages, bm. 1 April 1850. m. 9 May 1850. Chenoweth.

Nixon, Asbury M. & Hannah Brown. Benjamin Brown, bm. 16 Nov. 1840. Shel.

Nixon, David & Rachel Carr. m. 26 June 1815. Littlejohn.

Nixon, James & Susan Ann Potts, dau. of Jonas Potts, bm. 23 May 1831. Shel.

Nixon, James W. & Martha Thomas, ward of Mahlon Thomas, bm. Thomas White attests groom's age. 12 Nov. 1832. Shel.

Nixon, Joel L. & Mary J. Turner. James D. McPherson attests ages, bm. 25 July 1845. Shel.

Nixon, John & Cassandra Tillett. Samuel Tillett, Sr., bm. 23 May 1831. Cam.

Nixon, John E. & Jane Elgin. m. 21 Jan. 1845, in Montgomery County, Maryland. Adie.

Nixon, Joil & Hanh. Millbourne. m. 26 Jan. 1807. Littlejohn.

Nixon, Jonah & Mary White, dau. of Levi White, who attests groom's age, bm. 4 Nov. 1844. Shel.

Nixon, Levi W. & Margaret Major. James D. McPherson, bm. 29 Dec. 1848. Shel.

Nixon, Lorenzo D. & Eliza A. Shaw, dau. of Rebecca Shaw. John
Barrett attests groom's age. Samuel M. Boss, bm. 10 Sep.
1833. Shel.
Nixon, William & Ann Myres. m. 17 Sep. 1807. Littlejohn.
Nixon, William & Sarah Clendening. m. 22 Jan. 1805. Littlejohn.
Noble, Thomas & Marian Reed, dau. of Catharine Reed. Elijah
Barnes, bm. 21 June 1833. m. 27 June 1833. Baker. Shel.
Noland, Charles & Elizabeth Shipman. William Lodge attests
bride's age, bm. 5 Sep. 1831. m. 13 Sep. 1831. Green. Shel.
Noland, George W. & Ruth H. Taylor, dau. of Ruth Taylor. Mahlon K.
Taylor signs. Barney Taylor, bm. 19 Dec. 1837. Shel.
Noland, Lloyd & Ann W. Powell. m. 5 Jan. 1814. Williamson.
Noland, Lloyd & Elizabeth W. Smith. Benjamin Smith attests bride's
age, bm. 18 Jan. 1829. m. 22 Jan. 1829. Williamson.
Noland, William & Harriet M. Armistead. Robert Armistead attests
ages, bm. 21 Sep. 1831.
Noland, William B. & Lucy T. Chinn. R. S. Chinn proves ages, wit.
9 Sep. 1850. MarReg. m. 10 Sep. 1850. Eggleston.
Noland, William H. & Harriet M. Armistead. Robert Armstead
attests ages, bm. 26 Sep. 1831. Cam.
Nollner, John & Mary Elizabeth Taylor, dau. of William Taylor.
William A. Harris attests bride's age. Charles G. Eskridge,
bm. 24 Nov. 1843. Shel.
Norred, William & Elizabeth E. Dowdell. Charles Williams,
guardian, bm. 13 June 1835. Shel.
Norred, William & Mary Ann Daniel. Lemuel Daniel attests ages,
bm. 15 May 1845. m. 27 May 1845. ParReg A. Shel.
Norris, Benjamin E., Frederick County, Maryland & Sarah Ann
Stone, dau. of Daniel and Sarah Stone. m. 18 Nov. 1835.
FFMM.
Norris, Ignatious & Mary Wade. m. 5 Sep. 1805. Littlejohn.
Norris, John & Hannah Sophia Birkby. Thomas Birkby, bm. 17 May
1832. Shel.
Norris, Thomas B. & Ann C. Dowell. Bride's father consents, wit.
Groom's age "taken for granted". 2 Oct. 1852. MarReg.
Norwood, Richard & Betsey Farris. m. 9 July 1797. Littlejohn.
Norwood, William & Elizabeth Dowdell. m. 18 June 1835. Jones.
Nott, Wilfred & Milly Tucker. m. 11 Aug. 1798. Littlejohn.
Nutt, Jonathan & Elizabeth Trebbe. m. 28 Nov. 1770. FFMM.
Obanfield, R. D. & Mary E. Elgin. m. 17 Nov. 1852. Rodgers.
O'bannon, Enoch W. & Sarah Jane Smallwood, dau. of Wesley
Smallwood. William Person attests ages, bm. 17 Dec. 1844.
Shel.
Obrien, Peter & Mary Donohoe. Arthur Orrison attests bride's age,
bm. 13 June 1836. White. Shel.
O'Bryan, Michael & Elizabeth Spinks. John Conner attests bride's
age, bm. 14 April 1846. Shel.
O'Connell, William & Elizabeth Jinkins. John Wornal attests ages,
bm. 8 Jan. 1844. Shel.
Oden, Solomon & Milley Ann Athey. Hezekiah Athey, bm. 5 July 1809.
Oden, Thomas & Barbara Drish. Samuel M. Edwards, bm. 31 May
1832. Shel.
Oeckslein, Heinrich & Catharina Beck, first dau. of Philip Beck.
m. 19 June 1785. ParReg A.

Offutt, Alfred D. & Elizabeth C. Washington. Eli Offutt attests
  ages. Edward S. Washington, Fairfax County, bm. 21 April
  1829. Shel.
Offutt, Thornton F. & Eliza Clayton. Joseph Conner attests
  bride's age. John B. Young, bm. 22 Sep. 1832. Shel.
Ogdon, Andrew & Elizabeth Shawen. m. 24 Dec. 1810. Littlejohn.
Ogdon, Charles & Margaret Mettinger. m. 5 Oct. 1805. Littlejohn.
Oldom, William & Magdalena Ziegenfussin. By license. m. 29 April
  1792. ParReg A.
Onal, Joseph & Lydia Eaton. m. 26 July 1798. Littlejohn.
O'Neil, Joseph & Mary Dwyer. Andrew Carroll attests bride's age,
  bm. 21 Jan. 1846. Shel.
Oniel, Ferdinando & Jane Orrison. m. 29 Dec. 1802. Littlejohn.
Oram, Henry & Jane Wise. William Wise attests bride's age, bm.
  23 Sep. 1833. Shel.
Orange, James & Susan Fichter, widow. Charles Binns, bm. 26 Nov.
  1834. m. 27 Nov. 1834. Dorsey. Shel.
Orem, Aaron Edward & Mary Ann Prince. John L. Prince, bm. 27 May
  1848. m. 30 May 1848. Monroe.
Orem, Armistead & Mary J. Clip. m. 14 Oct. 1841. Herndon.
Orison, Arthur & Elizabeth Hickman. m. 20 Jan. 1842. Hauer.
Orme, Thomas T. & Margaret M. Burson. John Armistead proves
  bride's age, wit.; "his taken for granted". 6 May 1852.
  MarReg. m. 30 June 1852. Hirst.
Orr, John Moore & Orra Lee, dau. of Dr. George Lee. Charles
  Miller, William Hawling Rogers, John Dalrymple Powell, bm.
  8 Nov. 1849. m. at house of bride's father, Leesburg. Adie.
  Shel.
Orr, Robert & Elizabeth Turley. m. 11 Aug. 1812. J. Littleton.
Orrison, Able & Nancy Hamilton. m. 15 June 1815. Littlejohn.
Orrison, Annanias & Catherine Cooper. m. 31 May 1826-25 June
  1826. Burch.
Orrison, Arthur & Elizabeth Harris. Thomas G. Dowdle (Dowdell)
  attests bride's age, bm. 13 June 1832. Shel.
Orrison, Arthur & Elizabeth Hickman. William Hickman attests
  ages, bm. 18 Jan. 1842. Shel.
Orrison, David L. & Margaret Elizabeth Fry, dau. of Isaac Fry,
  wit. 13 Jan. 1851. MarReg. m. 16 Jan. 1851. Startzman.
Orrison, John & Sarah Sherb, widow. Minor Bartlett, bm. 9 Dec.
  1834. Shel.
Orrison, Joseph & Jane E. Whaley, dau. of James Whaley. John G.
  Whaley attests groom's age, bm. 13 Dec. 1836. Newman. Cam.
Orrison, Presley & Mary Grayham. Andrew Grayham attests groom's
  age, bm. 2 Feb. 1832. Shel.
Orrison, Samuel W. & Margaret Field. Thomas I. Hanes attests
  ages, bm. 11 Feb. 1834. Shel.
Orrison, William P. & Parmelia A. McGarvick. Jonah Orrison
  attests ages, bm. 3 Jan. 1844. Shel.
Orum, Armistead & Mary Jane Clip, dau. of John Clip. George
  William Fairfax, bm. 13 Oct. 1841. Shel.
Osborn, Abner & Mary Weldon. m. 20 Nov. 1812. Littlejohn.
Osborn, Balem & Mary Chew. m. Oct. 1815. Littlejohn.
Osborne, Addison & Lydia Ann Osborne, dau. of Joel Osborne, bm.
  14 March 1836. Shel.

LOUDOUN COUNTY MARRIAGES

Osborne, James & Nancy Bartlett. George W. Bartlett attests
bride's age, bm. 18 July 1831. Shel.

Osborne, Joel & Massee Osborne. m. 30 March 1809. Littlejohn.

Osburn, Bushrod & Elizabeth V. Clowes. Thomas J. Clowes attests
ages, bm. 2 Dec. 1839. Shel.

Osburn, Herod & Priscilla Osburn. John Janny attests bride's age,
bm. 25 Aug. 1835. m. 27 Aug. 1835. Monroe. Shel.

Osburn, James & Nancy Bartlett. m. 19 July 1831. Baker.

Osburn, Joab & Emily J. Gibson, dau. of Israel Gibson. Leven P.
Chamblin, bm. 2 Nov. 1839. Shel.

Osburn, Jonah & Caroline N. (M.) Chew. m. 17 March 1840, at
house of bride's mother, Snickersville. Adie.

Osburn, Joshua & Alcinda Osburn, dau. of Richard Osburn, Jr.
Mortimer Osburn, bm. 13 May 1849. m. 17 May 1849. Eggleston.
Shel.

Osburn, Landon & Emily Worthington, dau. of Joseph Worthington,
who attests groom's age, wit. 8 Feb. 1853. MarReg. m. 10 Feb.
1853. Gover.

Osburn, Logan & Hannah Osburn, dau. of Herod Osburn, who attests
groom's age, bm. 9 Aug. 1833. Shel.

Osburn, Logan & Margaret C. Osburn, dau. of Balaam Osburn, bm.
10 May 1841. Shel.

Osburn, Mortimer & Mary Summers. William Summers attests groom's
age, bm. 12 Jan. 1841. Shel.

Osburn, Phineas & Elizabeth Ann Hope, dau. of John Hope, wit.
3 March 1852. MarReg. m. 8 March 1852. Massey.

Osburn, Phineas & Margaret Osburn. Morris Osburn attests groom's
age, bm. 30 Aug. 1830. Shel.

Osburn, Rolin (Rowland) & Charlotte Miley, dau. of John Miley.
David Osburn, bm. 20 Oct. 1830. Shel.

Osburn, Thompson & Sarah Osburn, dau. of Herod Osburn, who attests
groom's age, bm. 22 Jan. 1844. Shel.

Osburn, T. V. B. & Harriet Osburn, dau. of Joel Osburn, Sr., bm.
9 Oct. 1846. m. 11 Oct. 1846. Massey.

Osburne, Joel & Massey Osburne, ward of James Heaton, bm. 30
March 1809.

Overfield, John E. R. & Mary Vanskiver. m. 3 Feb. 1825. McDowell.

Overfield, Joshua & Ann Bitzer. m. 7 March 1816. Williamson.

Overfield, Manuel & Mary P. Osburn. Richard Osburn, bm. 5 Sep.
1842. Shel.

Owen, Robert & Elenor Craven. m. 1 April 1805. Littlejohn.

Owens, Edward & Eliza Jeffries. William Lewis attests bride's age,
bm. 1 Jan. 1841. Shel.

Oxley, Jesse & Sarah Hesser. Thomas Morris attests bride's age,
bm. 23 April 1831. Shel.

Pack, Thomas & Christiana Tucker. Jesse Philips, bm. 13 Feb. 1799.
Littlejohn.

Page, Gyion & Elizabeth Hereford. m. 15 Oct. 1795. Littlejohn.

Pain, William & Margret Mary Ann Furr. m. 19 July 1849. Gover.

Painter, Edward & Guely Connard. m. 11 April 1796. Littlejohn.

Painter, Robert & Julian Donaldson. m. 30 Jan. 1823. Moore.

Painter, Samuel & Martha Martin. Luke Green, bm. 12 Aug. 1799.
Shel.

Painter, William W. & Ann Eliza Long, dau. of Conrad Long, bm.
27 May 1850. m. 30 May 1850. Chenoweth. Shel.

Palmer, David & Sarah Osburn. m. 16 April 1822. T. Littleton.
Palmer, James & Sally Pain. License: 20 March 1810. m. 26 March
   1810. T. Littleton.
Palmer, James & Catherin Green. m. 5 Sep. 1810. T. Littleton.
Palmer, Johnson E. & Ann E. Taylor, dau. of Charles B. Taylor.
   Armistead M. Taylor attests bride's age, wit. 20 Jan. 1851.
   MarReg. m. 24 Jan. 1851, at house of bride's father. Adie.
Palmer, Richard & Mary Brockley. Wit: George Smallwood. 28 Feb.
   1853. MarReg. m. 24 March 1853. Nixon.
Palmer, Samuel & Mary Porter. Samuel Palmer, Jr. attests bride's
   age, bm. 18 Sep. 1835. Shel.
Palmer, Samuel L. & Nancy Thrift. James H. Chamblin attests
   bride's age, bm. 7 March 1842. Shel.
Palmer, Thomas & Elizabeth G. Tippett, dau. of John C. Tippett,
   bm. 19 April 1843.
Palmer, William & Rachel Cogill. Richard Carter attests bride's
   age, bm. 1 Feb. 1830. Shel.
Pancoast, John, Frederick County, Maryland & Mary Talbott. m.
   1 May 1799. FFMM.
Pancoast, John, Montgomery County Maryland & Ruth Nickols. m.
   26 Oct. 1779. FFMM.
Pancoast, John S. & Louisa Smith, ward of Samuel Pursell, who
   attests groom's age, bm. 12 Nov. 1838. Shel.
Pancoast, Joseph & Jane Ann Dowell, dau. of Conrad Dowell, wit.
   14 March 1851. MarReg. m. 18 March 1851, at house of bride's
   father. Adie.
Pancoast, Joseph & Sarah Philips. m. 3 March 1798. Littlejohn.
Parce, Ben & Sarah Pauling. m. 7 July 1795. Littlejohn.
Park, Amos & Hannah Bannermin. m. 30 June 1803. Dunn.
Parker, Chelton & Sarah Sears, ward of John Vandevanter, who
   attests groom's age, bm. 13 Oct. 1829.
Parker, Joseph, son of Nicholas and Martha Parker, the former
   deceased & Eliza Eblen, dau. of John and Mary Eblen. m.
   23 April 1765. FFMM.
Parker, Joseph & Mary Jolon (Idon). m. 22 March 1803. Littlejohn.
Parker, Presley & Lucy Ellen Perry, dau. of John D. Perry, bm.
   20 Oct. 1836. Shel.
Parker, Thornton & Hannah Brown. m. 26 Feb. 1824. Dagg.
Parker, William & Hannah McIlhany. m. 16 June 1812. J. Littleton.
Parmelion, Greenberry Garrison & Jane Venander. m. 1809-1810.
   Mines.
Parmer, Milburn & Rebecca Roberson. m. 25 Dec. 1824. T. Littleton.
Parsons, John L. & Jane Timms, dau. of Jesse Timms, bm. 12 Dec.
   1836. m. 20 Dec. 1836. White. Shel.
Patsch, Alexander & Ehry Pordom, single. By license. m. 12 March
   1826. ParReg A.
Patterson, John B. & Mahala S. Norton. m. 11 Jan. 1827. Tuston.
Patton, James & Jane Perry. m. 14 April 1804. Littlejohn.
Patton, John W. & Mary Ann Alexander. Richard Alexander attests
   ages, bm. 24 Dec. 1845. m. 25 Dec. 1845. Massey. Shel.
Paxon, Samuel & Martha Wright. m. 12 March 1814. Littlejohn.
Paxson, Charles E. & Eleanor Hough. Benjamin Hough attests
   groom's age, bm. 15 Jan. 1842. Shel.

Paxson, Griffith W. & Duanna C. Rickard (Rickert). George Rickard attests groom's age, bm. 21 March 1839. m. 26 March 1839. ParReg A.

Paxson, John C. & Louisa R. Nichols. James H. Nichols proves ages, wit. 28 July 1851. MarReg. m. 4 Aug. 1851. Herndon.

Paxson, William B. & Henrietta C. Hough. Benjamin Hough attests ages, bm. 12 Feb. 1840. Shel.

Paxton, Arthur, son of Jacob Paxton, deceased, of Hunderton County, New Jersey & Mary Parmelia Myers, dau. of Elijah and Mary Myers. m. 29 Oct. 1800. FFMM.

Payne, Isaiah & Judah Bonham. m. 2 Jan. 1810. T. Littleton.

Payne, James S. & Margaret Starkey. Edward Brooks, bm. 5 June 1845. Shel.

Payne, John & Rosah. Coutzman. m. 5 May 1804. Littlejohn.

Payne, John W. & Jarusa Jinkins. Travis Payne attests ages, bm. 31 Aug. 1846. Shel.

Payne, Jonathan & Martha Bonaham. m. 28 May 1807. Littlejohn.

Payne, Sanford & Abigail Lay. License: 6 Aug. 1765. FeeBk. 2.

Peach, Samuel & Rebecca Ann Gibson. m. 1822. Dorsey.

Peacock, Charles William & Deniza J. Reeves. Bride's father consents, wit. 19 March 1851. MarReg. m. 20 March 1851. Gover.

Peacock, Elijah & Mary Jane Wright. Jacob Crusin attests bride's age, bm. 28 Dec. 1841. m. 4 Jan. 1842. Hauer. Shel.

Peacock, Hezekiah & Mary Perice. m. 23 March 1800. Littlejohn.

Peacock, Lewis & Harriet A. Dawson. Bride's mother consents in writing. Fenton Slack proves groom's age, wit. 3 Jan. 1853. MarReg. m. 4 Jan. 1853. Rodgers.

Peacock, Noble B. & Lucinda Beans, ward of David Reece, who is guardian of other orphans of Aaron Beans, dec'd. Wesley J. Saunders attests groom's age. Henry Virts, bm. 17 Jan. 1843. Mercer. Shel.

Peacock, Samuel & Ruth Tongue. m. 30 Nov. 1796. Littlejohn.

Peacocks, John & Rapha Craig. m. 13 Aug. 1796. Littlejohn.

Pearce, Abijah & Sarah Brown. m. 23 Sep. 1802. Littlejohn.

Pearce, Manderville & Ann E. Pearce, dau. of Hector Pearce. David T. Pearce attests groom's age, bm. 19 Jan. 1846. Shel.

Pearce, Wesley (LS) & Jane Fox, alias Jane Pearce, widow of Edward Pearce. Jas. Leslie, bm. 4 Jan. 1840.

Pearson, Simon & Elizabeth Ellis. m. 26 July 1806. Littlejohn.

Pearson, William F. & Ann Elizabeth Vanhorne. Joseph F. Brown attests ages, bm. 12 Feb. 1846. Benton. Shel.

Peck, Asa & Ann Eliza. Hough. m. 18 July 1819. Littlejohn.

Peck, Clement A. & Mary Jane Saunders. Presly Saunders attests ages, bm. 15 Dec. 1849. m. 18 Dec. 1849. Eggleston. Shel.

Peck, Julius J. & Amanda C. Templar. Wit: Mortimer Thompson. 31 Jan. 1853. MarReg. m. 1 Feb. 1853. Rodgers.

Peck, Peter, widower & Catharina Hoffman, widow. By license. m. 10 Nov. 1818. ParReg A.

Peinler, Robert & Elisabeth Stier; both single. By license. m. 29 Nov. 1818. ParReg A.

Pendleton, Philip & Virginia M. Tutt. N. C. Mason attests bride's age, bm. 6 June 1838. Shel.

Penn, William & Mary Ann Copeland, dau. of John Copeland. George Hammer, bm. 21 Dec. 1831. Shel.

Perice, Aron & Susanna Poulson. 14 March 1799. Littlejohn.
Permer, Johannes, widower & Amilia Schmidt, single. By license.
    m. 7 Dec. 1824. ParReg A.
Perry, Erasmus & Adeline M. Sheid. Washington Hummer attests ages,
    bm. 14 Dec. 1840. Shel.
Perry, James & Jane Williams. m. 8 June 1810. Littlejohn.
Perry, Rowland & Sarah Collins. m. 4 April 1797. Littlejohn.
Perry, William & Martha Hamilton. m. 27 Aug. 1806. Littlejohn.
Perry, William & Susanna Turley, dau. of Giles Turley. John H.
    Gibbs, bm. 24 Dec. 1799. Cam.
Petit, George W. & Jemima Reed. Benjamin Stringfellow attests
    bride's age, bm. 1 Dec. 1831. Shel.
Pettebone, Elihu & Lydia Leach. Return published 1796.
    Littlejohn.
Pettett, Jonathan & Charlotte Clark. m. 26 Dec. 1814. Littlejohn.
Pettit, George W. & Jemima Reed. m. 6 Dec. 1831. Baker.
Peugh, Leonidas & Elizabeth McDaniel. Franklin Ewers attests
    groom's age. Thomas Rogers, bm. 8 Dec. 1845. Shel.
Peugh, Samuel & Mary Humphrey. m. 4 Jan. 1821. Dagg.
Pew, Spencer & Mary Hopewell. m. 11 April 1803. Littlejohn.
Peyton, Frances & Francis Ball. m. 7 April 1802. Littlejohn.
Peyton, Henry & Susan Jett, dau. of Burkett Jett, who attests
    groom's age, bm. 8 Sep. 1843. Shel.
Peyton, Lacey, son of Elizabeth Peyton who says he's a minor &
    Eliza Jones, dau. of Thomas Jones. Abel Jones, bm. 13 March
    1837. m. 30 March 1837. Brooke. Shel.
Peyton, Richard & Verlinda Yoates. m. 1 Aug. 1825-4 Aug. 1825.
    Burch.
Phahle, Georg & Mahala Strahm; both single. By license. m.
    24 Dec. 1828. ParReg A.
Phale, Jacob, son of Johannes Phale and wife & Elisabetha Mack;
    both single. By license. m. 13 March 1821. ParReg A.
Phelps, Elisha P. & Mary W. Bennett. Sydnor Bennett, bm. 27 Oct.
    1840. Shel.
Philips, Benjamin & Jemimah Grayham. John Grayham attests bride's
    age. Israel Phillips, bm. 26 July 1809. m. 1808-1809. Mines.
Philips, David & Elizabeth Canter. m. 4 July 1808. Littlejohn.
Philips, Israel & Sarah Folley. License: 9 April 1810. m. 3 May
    1810. T. Littleton.
Philips, John & Margaret Clark. m. 9 Aug. 1813. Littlejohn.
Philips, John & Percilla Pancoast. m. 27 Feb. 1806. Littlejohn.
Philips, John P. & Mary C. Warner. Charles Fenton Phillips
    attests ages, bm. 10 Feb. 1847. Shel.
Philler, Henrich & Elisabetha Schneider; both single. By license.
    m. 22 Dec. 1815. ParReg A.
Philler, Henrich & Sarah Wentzel; both single. By license. m.
    17 Jan. 1828. ParReg A.
Philler, Johannes & Marian Laury; both single. By license. m.
    21 Dec. 1817. ParReg A.
Philler, Michael & Margreth Lentz; both single. By license. m.
    7 March 1822. ParReg A.
Phillips, John G. & Elizabeth J. Oxley, dau. of Thomas Oxley,
    who attests groom's age, bm. 28 March 1846. Shel.
Phillips, John P. & Mary Catharine Warner. m. 14 Jan. 1847. Gover.

Phillips, Levi & Rebecca Nutt, dau. of Joseph Nutt, Sen. Thomas
Nutt, bm. 10 April 1809.
Phillips, Samuel & Anna Hill. m. 13 Dec. 1822. C. Frye.
Phillips, William & Anney Oxley. David Phillips, bm. 18 March
1809. m. 1808-1809. Mines.
Phred, Joseph & Elizabeth Boxham. m. 29 Dec. 1802. Littlejohn.
Pickins, George & Catherine Marks. m. 4 May 1813. Littlejohn.
Pidgion, William, son of Charles Pidgion, of Menallen Twnshp.,
York County, Pa. & Rachel Everett, dau. of John Everett, of
Hamiltons bans, York County, Pa. m. 9 Oct. 1760. FFMM.
Pierce, David T. & Orpha A. Bradfield. Joseph Bradfield attests
ages, bm. 4 Oct. 1845. m. 9 Oct. 1845. Wilmer. Shel.
Pierce, Edward, coloured & Jane Fox, colored. C. Binns, bm.
13 Jan. 1834. Dorsey. Shel.
Pierce, Gainer & Sinah McGeith. m. 1 Aug. 1822. Gilmore.
Pierpoint, Eli & Hannah Love. m. 1821-1822. Mines.
Pierpoint, Joseph & Rue Ann Hague, dau. of James Hague, who
attests groom's age, bm. 27 April 1831. Shel.
Pierpoint, Obed, Frederick County, Maryland & Esther Myres. m.
7 April 1773. FFMM.
Pierpoint, Samuel & Betsy Brown, dau. of Richard and Sarah Brown.
m. _____ April 1829. FFMM.
Piggott, Burr & Hannah J. Nichols, dau. of Thomas Nichols, bm.
13 April 1835.
Piggott, Jesse & Mary E. Florida. William Silcott attests bride's
age, bm. 3 Oct. 1849. Shel.
Piggott, Samuel & Sarah Verts, dau. of William Virts, who attests
groom's age, bm. 9 April 1830. Shel.
Piles, Francis, Jr. & Catharine Gordon. Francis Piles attests
ages, bm. 11 Jan. 1830.
Piles, Leonard & Rachel Weaver. m. 16 Aug. 1815. Littlejohn.
Pinkstaff, Leonard & Delila Glascock, widow. Samuel Turner, bm.
7 March 1809. Littlejohn.
Pinn, William & Margaret M. A. Furr. "Freedom of William Pinn
proved by producing his papers and proved to be the same by
William McIntosh. Margaret Mary Ann Furr registered in clerks
office as free papers is sealed and delivered to her - ."
William McIntosh, bm. 17 July 1849. Shel.
Pittman, John & Catherine A. Robinson. m. 1 Nov. 1797. Littlejohn.
Plaster, George & Mary Tracy, ward of Colonel Mitchell, bm. Henry
Hutchison attests groom's age. 12 May 1829. Shel.
Plies, Johannes & Elisabetha Wilkinson; both single. By license.
m. 6 April 1820. ParReg A.
Plummer, Thomas, Frederick County, Maryland & Elenor Poultney.
m. 29 April 1761. FFMM.
Poland, Robert, son of John Polen & Julia Frances Ann Cross, dau.
of Harrison Cross. S. L. Hodgson, bm. 12 Jan. 1848.
Polen, Benjamin & Elizabeth Wolford. m. 26 Feb. 1832. Hauer.
Polen, Nathaniel & Rachel Palmer. m. 10 Sep. 1822. Chapman.
Polen, Robert, of Prince William & Julia Frances Ann Cross, dau.
of Harrison Cross. Request for license: 11 Jan. 1848, by
Harrison Cross.
Poling, Benjamin & Elizabeth Woolford. Edward Poling attests
groom's age. William O. Stocks attests bride's age, bm. 21 Feb.
1833. m. 26 Feb. 1833. Shel.

LOUDOUN COUNTY MARRIAGES

Polston, John & Hanh. Buffington. m. 8 Jan. 1807. Littlejohn.
Pomphrey, Gabrell & Ann Hamilton. m. 26 May 1798. Littlejohn.
Poole, Elias & Margaret Tillett. m. 24 June 1827. Tuston.
Popkins, Craven & Catharine Colbert. John Mead attests ages, bm.
    29 Aug. 1839. Shel.
Popkins, William & Elizabeth Russell. Henson Squires attests ages,
    bm. 23 Dec. 1845. Cam.
Porter, C. (D.) W., Maryland & Mary E. Catlett. Charles Gassaway
    attests bride's age, bm. 23 April 1839. m. at house of
    Charles Gasaway. Adie. Shel.
Porter, Jesse & Mary Jacobs. George Jacobs attests ages, bm.
    27 March 1830. Shel.
Porter, John & Levicy Coats. m. 1807-1808. Mines.
Poston, Benjamin & Charlotte Miley. Benjamin Miley proves ages,
    wit. 24 April 1852. MarReg. m. 27 April 1852, at house of
    Benjamin Miley. Dodge.
Poston, Dawson & Roberta Ann Skinner. Isaac Starkey attests ages,
    bm. 22 April 1848. Krebbs. Shel.
Poston, John G. & Mary Catharine McAtee. Harrison McAtee consents.
    William W. Poston attests groom's age, bm. 30 May 1843. Shel.
Poston, Joseph & Elizabeth France. m. 9 June 1800. Littlejohn.
Poston, Joseph W. & Sarah Elizabeth Reed, dau. of Sarah Reed,
    sen. Presley C. Reed attests groom's age. Charles M.
    Littleton, bm. 1 Dec. 1846. m. 8 Dec. 1846. Benton. Shel.
Poston, William Washington & Susan Hamilton. Martha Thomas
    attests bride's age and states bride resides with John
    Beavers, bm. 9 Sep. 1839. Shel.
Pottenfeld, Samuel & (sic) Catharina Eberhard; both single.
    By license. m. 20 Sep. 1827. ParReg A.
Pottenfelt, Joseph & Elizabeth Alter; both single. By license.
    m. 22 Dec. 1829. ParReg A.
Pottenfield, Adam & Maria Strahm; both single. By license. m.
    20 April 1827. ParReg A.
Potterfield, Daniel & Eliza Garrett (Grant), dau. of Enos
    Garrett, bm. 23 Sep. 1835. m. Sep. 1835. Campbell. Shel.
Potterfield, Hay & Elizabeth Shoemaker. m. 18 April 1796.
    Littlejohn.
Potterfield, Israel & Elizabeth Lyons. Elam Jacobs attests ages,
    bm. 23 March 1833. m. 28 March 1833. ParReg A.
Potterfield, Jacob & Sarah Ann Rebecca Johnson. Robert Johnson
    attests groom's age, bm. 26 March 1838. Shel.
Potterfield, Jonah & Clarissa Amanda Thrasher, dau. of Sarah
    Thrasher. Archibald Thrasher attests groom's age, bm.
    14 March 1834. m. 18 March 1834. Hauer. Shel.
Potterfield, Jonathan, widower & Sarah Sackman, dau. of S.
    Martin Sackman. Jacob Sackman, bm. 27 July 1830. m. 29 July
    1830. Hutchinson. Shel.
Potterfield, Joseph & Elizabeth Ann Alder. John Allder attests
    groom's age, bm. 19 Dec. 1829.
Potts, Edward & Mary Backhouse, dau. of John and Mary Backhouse,
    of New Castle County, Dela. m. 2 Dec. 1792. FFMM.
Potts, Edwin H. & Jane E. Clendening. John Clendening attests
    ages, bm. 22 March 1844. Shel.

Potts, Enos & Martha Tavener. Solomon Ruse attests bride's age,
bm. Jonas Potts attests groom's age. 25 June 1832. Shel.
Potts, Frederick M. & Martha J. Osburn. Wit: Harrison Osburn.
27 Nov. 1852. MarReg. m. 30 Nov. 1852. Coombs.
Potts, Isaiah & Elizabeth Brown. m. 6 March 1804. Littlejohn.
Potts, John & Ruth Talley. Jacob Schriver attests bride's age,
bm. 12 Aug. 1833. m. 22 Aug. 1833. Hauer.
Potts, Jonas & Amanda Silcott. William Silcott attests ages, bm.
17 Jan. 1838. Shel.
Potts, Jonas & Mary Dowling, widow. John Potts, bm. 8 Aug. 1836.
m. 11 Aug. 1836. ParReg A. Shel.
Potts, Nathan & Eunus Walter. m. 3 April 1804. Littlejohn.
Potts, Thomas & Mary Ann White. Nathan White attests ages, bm.
22 May 1839. Shel.
Poulson, Mortimer & Olivia McFaden. John McFaden attests groom's
age. Richard Brown affirms bride's age, bm. 7 Aug. 1833. Shel.
Poulton, Alfred & Lydia Snyder. m. 15 July 1825-26 July 1825.
Burch.
Poulton, Franklin & Rachel Dowlan, dau. of Sarah McDaniel. Reed
Poulton attests groom's age. Alfred A. Eskridge, bm. 21 Dec.
1829.
Poulton, John & Hannah Marshall, dau. of John Marshall. Charles
Poulton attests groom's age, bm. 14 Aug. 1809.
Poulton, Thomas & Lucinda Hesser. m. 20 Jan. 1822. T. Littleton.
Poulton, William & Ann Jared. Joshua Nichols attests ages, bm.
14 June 1841. Shel.
Powell, Alfred B. & Hannah Smith. Charles F. Anderson attests
ages, bm. 31 March 1843. Shel.
Powell, Cuthbert, Gent. & Mary E. Powell. m. 1 May 1825.
Williamson.
Powell, Dade & Mary Leith. m. 10 Feb. 1808. Williamson.
Powell, Elisha & Ann Guy. m. 14 Feb. 1804. Williamson.
Powell, Evan W. & Elizabeth Everitt. Benjamin Davis attests ages,
bm. 15 Sep. 1849. Shel.
Powell, Francis W., Dr. & Harriet Harding, dau. of John J.
Harding, bm. 6 May 1835. m. 7 May 1835, at house of bride's
father, Leesburg. Adie. Shel.
Powell, John L. & Maria (Mariah) Louisa Grady, dau. of E. B.
Grady. William Chilton attests groom's age, bm. 12 Oct.
1829. March 1830 Return. Moore.
Powell, Leven H. & Elizabeth Cohagen. m. 13 July 1807. Dunn.
Powell, Thomas & Hester Ann Lum, dau. of John Lum, bm. Peyton
Powell attests groom's age. 8 Sep. 1834. Shel.
Powell, William & Hannah H. Galleher. Moses O. Galleher attests
ages, bm. 11 Feb. 1835. Shel.
Powell, William L. & Ann Maria Powell. m. 12 Oct. 1820.
Williamson.
Power, Richard W. A. & Susanna E. Davis. Ananias Orrison attests
ages, bm. 30 Sep. 1835. Cam.
Power, Robert & Arminda Gheen, ward of Walter Power, bm. 10 May
1830. Cam.
Power, Walter & Mary Orrison. m. 1 Sep. 1802. Littlejohn.
Prescott, Nathan & Mahala Lucas. Mary Lucas attests groom's age.
James Lucas, bm. 20 March 1813.

LOUDOUN COUNTY MARRIAGES

Presgraves, William & Mary Ann Presgraves. Lewellen Hutcheson
attests ages, bm. 2 Sep. 1830. Cam.
Preston, Charles W. & Lydia Ann Bolon. John F. Smith proves ages,
wit. 21 Sep. 1850. MarReg.
Preston, Francis, Washington County, Va. & Martha Virginia Moffett,
dau. of Robert Moffitt. John Aldridge proves ages, wit.
31 March 1851. MarReg. m. 3 April 1851. Adie.
Preston, George W. & Mary Beaty. Mother's consent in writing;
J. R. Copeland proves groom's age, wit. 26 Sep. 1851.
MarReg. Wills.
Price, Eli M., son of John and Susan M. Price, Baltimore County,
Maryland & Eliza Ann Schooley, dau. of Mahlon and Elizabeth
Schooley, the latter deceased. Bride's father consents, wit.
16 April 1851. MarReg. m. 16 April 1851. FFMM.
Price, George & Elizabeth Clapham. Samuel Dawson, bm. 30 Jan.
1832. Shel.
Price, John & Ruth Russell, in Maryland. m. 20 April 1834.
ParReg A.
Price, William B. & Sarah P. S. Martin, ward of John Lauphier.
Fielding Littleton, bm. 9 Jan. 1832. Cam.
Prill, Samuel & Amanda Davis Smith. Kitty Burchett attests
bride's in her "22nd year since Oct last passed". William
Burchitt, bm. 1 Jan. 1834. m. 7 Jan. 1834. Wicks. Shel.
Prince, John & Matilda Cole, dau. of Priscilla Cole. Jacob
Bontz, bm. 11 Aug. 1840. m. 13 Aug. 1840. Hauer. Shel.
Prince, John L. & Elizabeth Everhart, dau. of Daniel and Martha
Hirst (mother of Elizabeth). Nelson Everhart, bm. 31 Aug.
1846. m. 3 Sep. 1846. ParReg A. Shel.
Prince, Levi & Elizabeth Goodhart. m. 21 Jan. 1801. Littlejohn.
Prince, Mathias & Mary Merchant. John Merchant attests bride's
age, bm. 8 Sep. 1842. Shel.
Prince, Nathan & Mary Ann Ross, dau. of Simon Ross, who attests
groom's age, bm. 22 March 1809. m. 1808-1809. Mines.
Prince, Nathaniel & Mary Tavenner. William N. Everhart attests
bride's age, bm. 17 June 1850. Shel.
Prince, Nathaniel & Sarah W. Dakins (Dickens). George Jay attests
groom's age, bm. 8 April 1839. m. 11 April 1839. ParReg A.
Hauer. Shel.
Printz, Matheaus, son of Levi Printz & Magthalena Derry, dau. of
Jacob Derry; both single. By license. m. 14 May 1812. ParReg A.
Probasco, Samuel, widower & Sarah Baal, widow. By license. m.
17 Feb. 1828. ParReg A.
Prosser, William M. & Mary Ish. Robert A. Ish attests bride's
age, bm. 12 Aug. 1839. m. 20 Aug. 1839. Herndon. Cam.
Protsman (Protzman), Francis & Mary Connor. Ann Baker attests
bride's age. Hugh Connor, bm. 23 Dec. 1833. Shel.
Pugh, Joh, Hopewell, Frederick County, Va. & Ruth Janney, Goose
Creek. m. 16 Nov. 1843. Bond, Clerk.
Pugh, Jonah & Susannah Pugh. m. 1 June 1820. Dagg.
Puller, Joseph & Mary Sanders. m. 22 Dec. 1806. Littlejohn.
Pumphrey, James & Elizabeth Hamilton. m. 1808-1809. Mines.
Purcell, James Heaton & Patience Osburn. Joel Osburn attests
groom's age, bm. 25 Sep. 1845. Shel.

Purcell, Lott & Hannah Taylor, dau. of Joseph Taylor, bm.
    Manly Atwell attests groom's age. 28 Jan. 1833. Shel.
Purcells, Joseph & Sush. Myres. m. 29 Dec. 1807. Littlejohn.
Purdum, Benjamin & Elizabeth Williams. m. 9 Dec. 1789. FFMM.
Pursell, George & Martha Potts. m. 1821-1822. Mines.
Pursell, Valentine V. & Mary Ann Paxson. m. 1821-1822. Mines.
Pusey, Joshua & Mary Nixon. m. 25 Jan. 1811. Littlejohn.
Pyott, John & Ann Nixon. James Vermillion attests bride's age, bm.
    28 March 1837. Shel.
Pyott, John & Sarah Eblin. m. 31 Dec. 1809. Littlejohn.
Qeke, Richard, Baltimore County, Maryland & Hannah M. Lupton,
    dau. of Isaac and Tamson Lupton, deceased. m. 17 March 1836.
    FFMM.
Quail, William & Susan Shipman. Landon Shipman attests ages, bm.
    11 Oct. 1842. Cam.
Queen, Patrick & Margaret Moore. John F. Kidwell proves bride's
    age, wit. 18 Oct. 1851. MarReg.
Quick, Armistead & Margaret Powell. Catesby Jones attests ages,
    bm. 28 Aug. 1837. Shel.
Quick, John C. & Maria Benedum. m. 1815. Littlejohn.
Raab, Simon & Barbara Derry (?); both single. By license. m.
    18 Nov. 1815. ParReg A.
Racener, Lenard & Sussanah Hixon. m. 18 Oct. 1806. Littlejohn.
Rady, Richard & Maria Haffner; both single. By license. m. 4 Oct.
    1818. ParReg A.
Ralph, John & Sarah Millan. m. 9 Aug. 1802. Littlejohn.
Ramsay, John & Clarissa Coutsman. m. 18 Jan. 1794. Littlejohn.
Randal, Charles & Eliza Ann Middleton. m. 27 Sep. 1827. Baker.
Randall, James, a minor, son of Joseph Randall & Sarah Petit.
    Jonathan J. Petit attests bride's age, bm. 8 Oct. 1833. m.
    18 Oct. 1833. Furlong. Shel.
Randall, William & Rachel Johnson. m. 24 Dec. 1816. Williamson.
Randell, Joseph & Susanna Hampton. m. 18 Jan. 1821. Williamson.
Rataie, John & Elizabeth Rust. m. 3 Nov. 1827. Baker.
Rathie, Benjamin D. & Sarah D. Fadely, dau. of Jacob Fadely.
    C. W. G. Eskridge, bm. 24 Nov. 1841. Shel.
Rathie, Joseph T. (L.) & Mary Ellen Garner. Benjamin D. Rathie
    attests bride's age, bm. 4 Jan. 1848. m. 6 Jan. 1848. Gover.
    Shel.
Ratliffe, Richard & Casandra Hains. m. 8 Aug. 1812. J. Littleton.
Rattle, John B. & Elizabeth Dawson. m. 10 June 1808. Littlejohn.
Rawling, James & Betsey Mock. m. 19 Dec. 1801. Littlejohn.
Rawlings, Lewis & Margaret Donahoe. m. 17 Feb. 1825. Dunn. Shel.
Rawlings, Richard & Hannah Edwards. m. 5 May 1810. Littlejohn.
Rawlins, Thomas & Elizabeth Ball. m. 14 Dec. 1816. Littlejohn.
Razor, Jacob & Daveus Harper, widow. By license. m. 3 Jan. 1822.
    ParReg A.
Read, Charles W. & Isabella V. Green. m. 11 Feb. 1846. Gover.
Read, Joseph & Jane Thompson. m. 30 Nov. 1812. Dunn.
Reader, William A. & Mary Ewers, dau. of William Ewers. Franklin
    Ewers attests groom's age, bm. 16 Nov. 1846. Shel.
Rector, Daniel W. & Sarah Keene. Thomas Keene attests ages, bm.
    2 June 1845. Shel.

Rector, George H. & Elizabeth A. P. Backhouse, dau. of George
    Backhouse. David Lovett proves groom's age. D. M. Divine, bm.
    11 Oct. 1847. m. 12 Oct. 1847. Dulin. Shel.
Rector, Joseph & Elizabeth Little. m. 1 Jan. 1810. Littlejohn.
Rector, Samuel M. H. & Catharine Ann Goodin. Norval Craig
    attests ages, bm. 27 Dec. 1845. Massey. Shel.
Redman, Andrew & Nancy Kelley. m. 7 June 1806. Littlejohn.
Redman, Benjamin & Nancy James. m. 13 Dec. 1813. Littlejohn.
Reece, Edward & Sarah Smith. m. 18 Jan. 1786. FFMM.
Reed, Charles W. & Isabella V. Green, dau. of Henry Green, who
    attests groom's age, bm. 9 Feb. 1846.
Reed, Harmon & Rosanah Burkett. John Bikit (Burkett) attests
    groom's age, bm. 8 Aug. 1842. Shel.
Reed, Henry & Lydia Dillehay. Hyram Reid attests ages, bm.
    19 March 1838. m. 20 March 1838. Hauer. Shel.
Reed, James A. & Mary E. War, dau. of John War, bm. 7 Jan. 1835.
    Shel.
Reed, James & Rebecca Copeland, widow. Henson Vermillion, bm.
    7 March 1809.
Reed, John & Elizabeth Roades. m. 1 (9) Jan. 1795. Littlejohn.
Reed, John & Maranda Winecoop. John M. Kabrick attests ages, bm.
    12 Oct. 1848. Shel.
Reed, Jonathan & Ann Brown. m. 18 Dec. 1823. Roszell.
Reed, Jonathan & Elizabeth Walker. m. 5 Oct. 1814. Littlejohn.
Reed, Joseph & Sarah Triplett. m. 12 Aug. 1824. Dunn. Shel.
Reed, Landon O. & Rebecca J. (G.) Fleming, dau. of Dinah Fleming.
    George Fleming, bm. 1 Dec. 1834. m. 18 Dec. 1834. Furlong.
    Shel.
Reed, Oscar F. & Eveline Fleming. m. 13 Feb. 1834. Furlong.
Reed, Oscar F. & Nancy Catherine Russell, dau. of Jemima
    Russell. 4 Nov. 1851. MarReg.
Reed, Philip & Amanda Smallwood. John A. Moore attests groom's
    age. John Thomas attests bride's age, bm. 14 Oct. 1830. Shel.
Reed, Presley Combs & Lucy Catharine Lewis. Bride's mother
    consents in writing. Joseph W. Poston proves groom's age, wit.
    6 June 1853. MarReg.
Reed, Smith & Caroline Elizabeth Roach, dau. of James Roach.
    Oliver G. Butts attests ages, bm. 15 Jan. 1849. m. 18 Jan.
    1849. Dulin. Shel.
Reed, Walter B. & Mary Ann Reid. m. 10 Oct. 1812. Littlejohn.
Reeder, Gourley & Catherine Powell. m. 18 Feb. 1823. Dunn.
Reichart, Johannes & Margretha Cadel; both single. By license.
    m. 30 July 1815. ParReg A.
Reichenback, Jacob & Everline Bell; both single. m. 8 June 1830.
    ParReg A.
Reid, John & Sarah Harrison. m. 29 Feb. 1816. T. Littleton.
Reid, Minor & Betsey B. Marshall. m. 1809-1810. Mines.
Reid, Oscar Fitzallan & Eveline Fleming. Elam C. Veale attests
    ages, bm. 3 Feb. 1834. Shel.
Reid, Samuel & Ann Brown. m. 14 March 1808. Littlejohn.
Reimer, Jacob & Susanna Jeds; both single. By license. m. 31 Dec.
    1812. ParReg A.
Renekan, Edward & Sarah Carroll. William Carroll attests ages,
    bm. 25 Feb. 1843. Shel.

Renoe, Thomas & Sarah Beavers. James Beavers attests ages, bm.
    18 Jan. 1809.
Reparke, John & Elizabeth Pancoast. m. 10 March 1796. Littlejohn.
Repold, Christian, son of Georg Repold & Maria Margreta Rohrbach,
    dau. of Adam Rohrbach; both single. By license. m. 12 Nov.
    1793. ParReg A.
Rhine, Edward & Nancy Cole. Peter Cole attests bride's age, bm.
    27 Feb. 1837. Shel.
Rhodes, Edward & Reba. Fraizer. m. 14 April 1804. Littlejohn.
Rhodes, George, widower & Catherine Dyer. Samuel M. Boss attests
    bride's age, bm. 31 Oct. 1829. m. 3 Nov. 1829. Tippett.
Rhodes, George & Mary Milner. m. 21 Nov. 1798. Littlejohn.
Rhodes, Joseph & Mary Ann Brown. Joseph Brown, bm. 27 March 1838.
    Shel.
Rian, William & Elizabeth Yabower, dau. of John Yabower, who
    signs in German, bm. 9 March 1841. Shel.
Rice, David James & Elizabeth Bolan, dau. of Ezra Bolan, who
    attests groom's age, bm. 5 Sep. 1844. Shel.
Rice, Isaac M., son of Thursa Rice & Eliza Ann Boland, dau. of
    Ezra Boland. David J. Rice, bm. 18 Jan. 1845. Shel.
Rice, Jesse & Thurza Lacey. m. 28 Oct. 1812. Littlejohn.
Rice, Jesse L. & Lucinda War. William W. McDonough attests ages,
    bm. 9 Nov. 1846. Shel.
Rice, John & Janet Cockrille. m. 3 April 1797. Littlejohn.
Rice, Samuel D. & Mary Rhodes. dau. of Randolph Rhodes. Lewis H.
    Saunders, bm. 14 March 1837. m. 15 March 1837. Alomory. Shel.
Rice, Thomas S. & Lucelia C. Gibson, dau. of A. Gibson. A. M.
    Gibson, bm. 2 April 1841. Shel.
Rice, William H. & Jane Rhodes. George Rhodes, bm. 29 May 1838.
Richard, Henry & Elizabeth Faraught. m. 2 Jan. 1834. Hauer.
Richard, John P. & Anna Smarr. m. 12 Oct. 1795. Littlejohn.
Richards, Humphrey & Hannah Milburne. William Milburn attests
    ages, bm. 3 Feb. 1835. Shel.
Richards, Isaac & Hannah Triplett. Thompson Richards attests ages.
    Humphrey Richards, bm. 30 Dec. 1833. Shel.
Richards, Jesse & Eleanor Jenkins. m. 14 Feb. 1821. Dagg.
Richards, John & Anna B. Saunders. m. 10 Oct. 1816. Littlejohn.
Richards, John & Jane Palmer. m. 25 Oct. 1827. Baker.
Richards, John R. & Mary E. Gantt. Thomas W. Edwards, bm. 20 Feb.
    1844. Shel.
Richards, Josiah & Hanah Gourley. m. 3 Feb. 1821. T. Littleton.
Richards, Leven & Evaline Jenkins, dau. of John Jenkins. John P.
    Jenkins, bm. 21 March 1838. m. 27 March 1838. Trott. Shel.
Richards, Richard & Margaret Vickers. m. 12 Nov. 1818. Dagg.
Richards, Sampson & Betsy Taylor. m. 14 Sep. 1808. Littlejohn.
Richards, Samuel & Elizabeth Barton. m. 3 Oct. 1796. Littlejohn.
Richards, Samuel & Mary B. Livingston. m. 28 Feb. 1822.
    T. Littleton.
Richards, Thomas & Jane Lynch. Isaac Richards attests ages, bm.
    23 May 1831. m. 26 May 1831. Green. Cam.
Richards, Thomas & Margaret Orrison. David Orrison attests ages,
    bm. 23 Feb. 1830.
Richardson, William & Richardetta Sims, dau. of William Sims, bm.
    "free papers proving him self to be more than 24 years - ."
    21 Nov. 1846. m. Nov. 1846. Gover. Shel.

Richarts, Wesly & Maria Henrich; both single. By license. m.
28 Sep. 1815. ParReg A.

Richets, Thomas & Ann Downs. m. 25 Sep. 1817. Williamson.

Richey, Philip & Margeret Mender. m. 12 Jan. 1801. Littlejohn.

Rickard, Henry & Elizabeth Faraught. Jacob Beil attests bride's
age, bm. 21 Dec. 1833. Shel.

Rickard, Peter & Elizabeth Everhart. m. 2 Dec. 1805. Littlejohn.

Rickard, William H. & Catharine A. Wine. George Henry Wine, bm.
9 March 1844. m. 12 March 1844. ParReg A. Shel.

Rickert, Georg & Catharina Kiefer, dau. of Frederich Kiefer; both
single. By license. m. 2 Sep. 1813. ParReg A.

Rickert, Georg, widower & Sibilla Frey, single. By license. m.
29 March 1825. ParReg A.

Ridgeway, Benjamin D. & Ann Elizabeth Kent. William G. Kent
attests ages, bm. 24 Aug. 1840. m. 25 Aug. 1840. Herndon.
Shel.

Ridgeway, George W. & Martha Bussey. John T. Bussey, bm.
29 May 1846. Shel.

Ridgeway, Romulus R. & Elizabeth Stillious (Stillions). Wit:
Samuel Stillious. 22 March 1852. MarReg. m. 23 March 1852.
Dodge.

Riebsaamen, Henrich & Catharina Prill; both single. By license.
m. 17 Oct. 1816. ParReg A.

Riebsaamer, Henrich, widower & Emilein Ritsherdson, single. By
license. m. 5 Feb. 1824. ParReg A.

Ried, Joseph & Evelein Remain; both single. By license. m.
14 Aug. 1827. ParReg A.

Riggs, Azariah & Jane Thomas. m. 17 Sep. 1796. Littlejohn.

Riley, Joshua & Polly Barker. m. 25 April 1811. Littlejohn.

Riley, Michael & Elizabeth Conden, widow. Thomas Jacobs, bm.
25 Nov. 1809.

Riley, Richard & Elizabeth McCartor. Moses McCartor attests ages,
bm. 9 Nov. 1809.

Ringgold, Tench & Mary A. Lee. m. 31 Oct. 1815. Dunn.

Rinker, Charles W. & Jane Ann Breward (Brewer). John H. Breward
proves bride's age, wit. 2 Feb. 1852. MarReg. m. 10 Feb.
1852. Gover.

Rinker, Edward & Nelly Sly. m. 3 Feb. 1806. Littlejohn.

Rinker, Edward J. & Sarah Jane Brown. Charles J. Brown proves
ages, wit. 15 Dec. 1851. MarReg.

Rinker, John L. & Susannah Johnson. Simon Smale attests groom's
age. William Johnson, bm. 4 April 1833. Shel.

Rinker, Thomas Schley, son of Edward Rinker & Ann Fectehler,
ward of John A. Binns. Edward Rinker, bm. 25 Oct. 1830. Shel.

Rion, William, Jr. & Elizabeth Yabower. m. 11 March 1841. Gover.

Ritchie, Daniel & Louisa Axline (Auchslein), dau. of David
Axline, who attests groom's age, bm. 11 May 1829; both
single. By license. m. 13 May 1829. ParReg A.

Ritchie, George M. & Catharine E. Heffner. Abraham H. Hanes
attests ages, bm. 6 Oct. 1846. Shuford. Shel.

Ritchie, Philip & Nancy McGaha, dau. of David McGaha. William
McGaha, bm. 29 June 1833. m. 30 June 1833. Hauer. Shel.

Ritchie, Solomon & Eliza Ann Ross, dau. of Nicholas Ross. Nelson
Everheart attests groom's age, bm. 10 Sep. 1839. m. 12 Sep.
1839. Hauer. Shel.

Riticor, Amasa & Catherine Pullin. m. 28 March 1795. Littlejohn.
Riticor, Charles & Susanna Moss. John Moss, bm. 13 Dec. 1842.
Riticor (Riticre), John & Elizabeth Jane Lee. Joshua Lee, bm.
    13 March 1839. m. 19 March 1839. Herndon. Cam.
Ritter, Jacob B., Clark County & Margaret Jenkins, dau. of
    William Jenkins, who attests groom's age, bm. 12 Sep. 1842.
    m. 15 Sep. 1842. Trott. Shel.
River, Joshua & Minto Cross. m. 27 Dec. 1801. Littlejohn.
Rivers, Jacob & Martha Ridout, colored persons. Registered free
    and ages and freedom proved by J. B. Beans. MarReg. m.
    18 Nov. 1850. Gover.
Rivers, John & Harriet Beavers. John Allison attests ages, bm.
    19 May 1838. m. 20 May 1838. Raymond. Shel.
Roach, George & Sarah Cummings, dau. of John Cummings, who
    attests groom's age, bm. 14 Nov. 1809. Littlejohn.
Roach, James & Elizabeth Gregg. m. 2 June 1779. FFMM.
Roach, Joseph & Francis Brown. m. 29 June 1803. Littlejohn.
Roach, Mahlon & Polly Currell. m. 9 Jan. 1804. Littlejohn.
Robbins, Isaac H. & Euselia (Eusebia) M. Turner. Wit: William F.
    Simpson. 31 May 1852. MarReg. m. 1 June 1852. Duncan.
Roberson, Arthur & Mahala Lyder. m. 9 Feb. 1832. Green.
Roberts, Isaac & Lucinda E. Wince. Alfred Shields attests ages,
    bm. 16 Oct. 1846. Shel.
Roberts, John & Lydia Boothe. Simon Matthew attests ages, bm.
    23 Aug. 1841. m. 26 Aug. 1841. Shel.
Roberts, John, son of Mary and Richard Roberts of Frederick
    County, Maryland & Rebekah Scott, dau. of Jacob and Elizabeth
    Scott, the former deceased. m. 2 Jan. 1788. FFMM.
Roberts, Robert & Nancy Thompkins. m. 3 Dec. 1804. Littlejohn.
Roberts, Samuel & Betsey Barrington Lewis. m. 1807-1808. Mines.
Roberts, Thomas & Mary S. A. Heskett. Stephen Roberts attests
    bride's age, bm. 26 Nov. 1849. m. 29 Nov. 1849. Eggleston.
    Shel.
Roberts, William & Ruth Tribbee. m. 19 Nov. 1813. Littlejohn.
Robertson, John & Elizabeth Pursley. m. 1806. Mines.
Robertson, Seth D. & Christiana Mason. Adam Mason attests bride's
    age, bm. 15 Dec. 1834. Shel.
Robertson, William & Sarah Fernandis. Jesse Timms attests ages,
    bm. 8 March 1809.
Robey, Alexander F. & Mary Jane Ross. William Ross attests ages,
    bm. 27 Feb. 1847. m. 11 March 1847. Dodge. Shel.
Robey, Thompson B. & Mildred A. Nalls. m. 29 Jan. 1848. Hayes.
Robey, William, colored & Rachel Ann Watson, colored. Bride's
    parents consent. 22 April 1851. MarReg. m. 23 April 1851.
    Smith.
Robey, William T. & Mary Hibbs. Lary Claiborne attests ages, bm.
    3 Sep. 1838. Shel.
Robinson, Arthur S. & Mahala Lyder. William D. Robinson attests
    ages, bm. 2 Feb. 1832. Shel.
Robinson, Goldsborough, Kentucky & Frances A. Lee. m. 6 Sep.
    1842, at house of Calvert Stewart, Fairfax County, Va. Adie.
Robinson, John & Elizabeth Sands. m. 28 March 1798. Littlejohn.
Robinson, Joseph H. & Elizabeth F. Blackwell, dau. of Benjamin
    Blackwell. William Robinson says groom born 26 May 1811.
    Hugh Campbell, bm. 15 July 1833.

Robinson, Lewis & Eleanor Morgan, "upwards of 22 years old", dau. of Nancy Morgan; free people of colour. James Grimes, bm. 29 Nov. 1831. Shel.

Robinson, Peyton & Elizabeth Carter, dau. of Samuel Carter, bm. 2 Sep. 1833. Shel.

Robinson, Seth D. & Christiana (Christena) Mason. m. 16 Dec. 1834. ParReg A. Hauer. Shel.

Robinson, William & Sarah Fenandis. m. 8 March 1809. Littlejohn.

Roby, Colbert & Nancy Ross. m. 9 Jan. 1845. Dodge.

Roby, William T. & Mary Hibbs. m. 5 Sep. 1838. Broadus.

Rockwell, Samuel & Elisabeth Jacobs; both single. By license. m. 6 May 1813. ParReg A.

Roderick, Joshua & Mary Hamilton. m. 6 Aug. 1835. Monroe.

Rodgers, John & Huma Philips. m. 28 Feb. 1797. Littlejohn.

Rodrick, Joshua & Mary Hamilton. Solomon Derry attests bride's age, bm. 30 July 1835. Shel.

Rogers, Arthur & Hannah Nichols. Isaac Nichols attests bride's age, bm. 26 April 1830. Shel.

Rogers, Asa & Ellen L. Orr. William A. Powell attests bride's age, bm. 2 May 1829.

Rogers, Edwin & Alice Ann Cross, dau. of Harrison Cross, who attests groom's age, bm. 10 April 1837. m. April 1837. Newman. Cam.

Rogers, Edwin & Ann Elgin. John Elgin attests bride's age, bm. 15 Sep. 1832. Shel.

Rogers, Hamilton & Mary Hawling. m. 23 Oct. 1823. Williamson.

Rogers, Hugh, of Clifton & Rosalie D. Powell. John D. Rogers proves consent of bride's father; William H. Rogers, Jr. proves groom's age, wit. 23 Sep. 1851. MarReg. m. 24 Sep. 1851. Dodge.

Rogers, James & Martha Hawling, ward of Hamilton Rogers, bm. 20 Nov. 1830. Shel.

Rogers, John & Nancy Skinner. m. 1806. Mines.

Rogers, John D., of Middleburg & Parke F. Wellford, of Culpeper. m. 26 Oct. 1853, at "Farley", Culpeper County, Va. ParReg B.

Rogers, Lloyd N., of Maryland & Hortensia M. Hay, dau. of George Hay, groom's attorney in fact, bm. 24 June 1829.

Rogers (Rodgers), Owen, Hampshire County, Va. & Mary Roach, dau. of Richard and Hannah Roach. m. 29 Nov. 1780. FFMM.

Rogers, Richard L. & Nancy H. McVeigh, dau. of Jesse McVeigh. James H. Gulick attests groom's age, bm. 26 Nov. 1836. m. 20 Nov. 1836. Broaddus.

Rogers, Samuel & Jane E. Adams, dau. of Richard Adams, bm. 14 Nov. 1836. m. 15 Nov. 1836. Broaddus. Shel.

Rogers, Sanford P. & Susan E. Simpson. Sanford Gulick attests groom's age. French Simpson, bm. 4 April 1842. Shel.

Rogers, Thomas & Elmina S. Chamblin, dau. of Charles Chamblin. Fielding Littleton, bm. 13 Sep. 1830. m. 21 Sep. 1830. Baker. Shel.

Rogers, William & Elizabeth Hixon. m. 7 Nov. 1822. Dagg.

Rogers, William & Ruth White. T. M. McIlhany, bm. 13 March 1843. Shel.

Rogers, William H. & Mary Jane Rogers. Hamilton Rogers attests ages, bm. 22 Sep. 1834. m. 23 Sep. 1834. Broaddus. Shel.

Rogue, Robert & Jane Burson. m. 27 Oct. 1815. Littlejohn.

Rohrer, Christian & Elisabetha Hoffer; both single, from Maryland.
By license. m. 11 April 1821. ParReg A.

Rohrer, Jacob & Maria Funkin; both single. By license. m. 18 May
1820. ParReg A.

Roland, George & Francis Timms. m. 19 Aug. 1809. Littlejohn.

Roller, Aaron & Eliza Jane Cole. Thomas J. Marlow, bm. No date.
Shel.

Roller, Aaron & Eliza Jane Cole. Oliver Edward attests bride's
age. Levi David Roller, bm. 4 Dec. 1837. m. 7 Dec. 1837.
Hauer. Shel.

Roller, Conrad & Mariana Frederick. Leonard Frederick, bm.
29 Dec. 1845. m. 7 Jan. 1846. Shuford. Shel.

Roller, Daniel & Margretha Weynt; both single. By license. m.
18 Nov. 1824. ParReg A.

Roller, Frederick & Rachel Wyard. Michael Wyard (Wierd) attests
bride's age, bm. 26 Feb. 1829.

Roller, Friderich, widower & Rahel Weiert. By license. m. 26 Feb.
1829. ParReg A.

Roller, Friderich, widower & Rahel Wildt, single. By license.
m. 1 Aug. 1822. ParReg A.

Roller, Friderich, son of Conrad Roller and wife & Magdalena
Zenbauern, single. By license. m. 13 Aug. 1818. ParReg A.

Rollins, John R. & Lydia Virginia Hope. Bride's father consents,
wit. 19 Oct. 1852. MarReg.

Rollison, John & Elizabeth Cullison. m. 15 Jan. 1810. Littlejohn.

Rollison, William & Henrietta D. Solomon. Sandford Fling attests
ages, bm. 30 Aug. 1834. m. 31 Aug. 1834, at house on
Broadrun. Adie. Cam.

Ropp, Jacob & Isabella Crowen (Crowell). William Derry attests
ages, bm. 15 Jan. 1837. m. 19 Jan. 1837. Monroe. Shel.

Roop, Nicholas & Elizabeth Wattman. m. 9 Dec. 1809. Littlejohn.

Ropp, Samuel & Rachel Beamer. George Beamer attests groom's age,
bm. 7 Nov. 1842. Shel.

Rose, Christopher & Cathrine Evans. m. 23 Dec. 1805. Littlejohn.

Rose, George & Jane Boyd. m. 20 Jan. 1802. Littlejohn.

Rose, James & Rachel Saunders. m. 19 July 1807. C. Frye.

Rose, John & Elizabeth McCoy. m. 30 Dec. 1807. Littlejohn.

Rose, John C. & Mary F. Stover. William K. Ish attests groom's
age. Edwin Stover, bm. 8 Sep. 1845. Cam.

Rose, Robert T. & Harriet M. Swart. John M. Spencer, bm. 16 Sep.
1847. Shel.

Ross, David, Frederick County, Va. & Mary Janney. m. 7 Dec. 1808.
FFMM.

Ross, Davis & Ann Houser. m. 1807-1808. Mines.

Ross, James F. & Mary J. Gochnauer (Gochenauer). Mothers consent
in writing. 31 Oct. 1851. MarReg. m. 5 Nov. 1851. Herndon.

Ross, John N., son of John Ross, who says groom's under 21 years
& Susan M. Poston, dau. of Leonard R. Poston, who says
bride's 21 years. Benajmin J. Poston, bm. 8 May 1848. m.
8 May 1828. Krebbs. Shel.

Ross, John Thomas & Amanda Thomas, dau. of Herod Thomas, who
proves groom's age, wit. 28 Oct. 1851. MarReg. m. 4 Nov.
1851. Eggleston.

Ruff, Johannes & Elisabeth Lang; both single. By license. m.
4 Oct. 1825. ParReg A.
Rupp, George W. & Sarah Birkly. James H. Barnhart attests groom's
age. Richard B. Birkby attests bride's age, bm. 14 Nov. 1842.
Shel.
Ruse, David & Catharine Wynkoop. George W. Wynkoop attests ages,
bm. 25 July 1842. Shel.
Ruse, David & Sarah Vermillion, dau. of Garrison Vermillion, bm.
12 Jan. 1835. Shel.
Ruse, Jacob & Polly Sanders. m. 8 Oct. 1802. Littlejohn.
Ruse, John & Sarah Sands. m. 14 April 1812. J. Littleton.
Ruse, Lewis & Jemima Stone. Edward Stone attests groom's age, bm.
23 March 1830. Shel.
Ruse, Michael & Rachel Bellard. John Bellard, bm. 13 March 1809.
m. 1808-1809. Mines.
Rusk, Mandley Washington & Rozilla Gibson. Alfred Jones chosen
bride's guardian, bm. James Rusk attests groom's age. "This
bond & the license was executed on the 13th but entered in
a hurry as of the 12th. Jn. A. Binns." 13 Dec. 1830. Shel.
Russ, Henrich & Sarah Eberhart; both single. By license. m.
20 Jan. 1825. ParReg A.
Russell, Aaron & Tamson Underwood. Mortimer McIlhany attests
ages. Taliferro M. McIlhany, bm. 2 June 1829. Tippett.
Russell, Benjamin C. & Ethele Shipman. m. 28 Nov. 1822. Dagg.
Russell, Charles & Margaret Ewers. m. 16 March 1820. Dagg.
Russell, David & Esther Ann Coe. Elijah Coe attests ages, bm.
28 Feb. 1842. Shel.
Russell, George W. & Elizabeth J. James, dau. of Elijah James,
who attests groom's age, bm. 6 Nov. 1848. m. 7 Nov. 1848.
Dulin. Shel.
Russell, Harrison & Jemima Neile, ward of Nancy Neale. Samuel
Wright, bm. 14 Feb. 1831. Shel.
Russell, Henry & Matilda McDaniel. m. 20 June 1814. Littlejohn.
Russell, James, son of John and Hannah Russell, of Frederick
County, Maryland & Susannah Janney, dau. of Joseph and
Hannah Janney, the former deceased. m. 20 Nov. 1804. FFMM.
Russell, John & Ellen Amanda Hartman. Nelson Everhart attests
ages, bm. 23 June 1843. m. 27 June 1843. ParReg A. Shel.
Russell, John William & Vivian Russell, in Maryland. m. 2 Aug.
1838. ParReg A.
Russell, Jonathan & Elizabeth Edwards, dau. of Joseph Edwards,
who attests groom's age, bm. 29 Nov. 1847. m. 3 Dec. 1847.
Dulin. Shel.
Russell, Joshua, Frederick County, Maryland & Rachel Steer. m.
21 April 1824. FFMM.
Russell, Mahlon & Mary Ann Moone. m. 23 Oct. 1827. Baker.
Russell, Neale & Betsey Lanham. m. 25 April 1822. T. Littleton.
Russell, R. S. T. & Mary Ann Elgin. John Nixon proves ages, wit.
6 July 1850. MarReg.
Russell, Robert & Amelia A. G. Printz. Samuel J. Chamblin
attests ages, bm. 22 March 1847. m. 23 March 1847. Massey.
Shel.
Russell, Robert & Elizabeth Wolf. m. 10 Feb. 1806. Littlejohn.
Russell, Samuel & Ephamy McGeth. m. 15 Oct. 1812. Littlejohn.

Russell, Thadeus & Catharine Garrett. John Hurdle attests
bride's age, bm. 20 May 1830. Shel.
Russell, Thomas & Eleanor Tillett. m. 1821-1822. Mines.
Russell, Thomas & Mary Yearnest. m. 9 Sep.1811. Littlejohn.
Russell, William H. & Catharine Fairfax. Simpson Cooksey attests
ages, bm. 12 Sep. 1844. Shel.
Russell, William H. & Sarah E. R. Orrison, dau. of Jonah Orrison,
who attests groom's age, bm. 3 Dec. 1849. m. 4 Dec. 1849.
Eggleston. Shel.
Russer, Samuel & Nancy Turner, dau. of Robert Turner. Thomas
Wright attests groom's age. George W. Sagar, bm. 17 March
1834. Shel.
Rust, Bushrod & Margaret Carr. m. 14 Sep. 1815. Williamson.
Rust, James W. & Margaret Hickman. John Hickman attests ages,
bm. 27 Jan. 1845. Shel.
Rust, Manly T. & Sarah Chilton. m. 12 Sep. 1816. Littlejohn.
Rust, Peter C. & Elizabeth Taylor, dau. of Mandley Taylor, who
attests ages. William Elgin, bm. 1 Dec. 1799. Shel.
Rutter, Hugh & Elizabeth River. David Galleher attests ages, bm.
13 March 1837. Shel.
Rutter, James W. & Jane E. Handy. Alfred McGeath attests ages,
bm. 2 Nov. 1843. Shel.
Ryan, Albert & Emeline Solomon, dau. of Elizabeth Garrissen late
Solomon and ward of Rachel Garner late Solomon. William
McDonaugh attests groom's age, bm. 14 March 1839. Shel.
Ryan, William P. & Margaret B. McFarland. James A. McFarland, bm.
6 May 1843. Cam.
Ryley, Michael & Elizabeth Condon. m. 25 Nov. 1809. Littlejohn.
Ryne, Robert & Margaret B. Newton. Wit: John C. Newton. 19 Jan.
1852. MarReg. m. 20 Jan. 1852. Smith.
Ryon, George W. & Catharine Dorrell. Alfred Spates attests ages,
bm. 6 Dec. 1841. Shel.
Ryon, Henry & Margaret Thompson. m. 11 Dec. 1797. Littlejohn.
Ryon, Philip & Marsha Bridges. m. 1798. Notation: "March 5,
1797 omitted before ___."
Sackman, Carolus & Sarah Schaffer, dau. of Michael Schaffer and
wife. By license. 1824. ParReg A.
Sackman, Jacob & Sarah Winegardner, dau. of Adam Winegardner, bm.
J. Martin Sackman gives groom permission. 31 Aug. 1830. Shel.
Sackman, Samuel & Susan Mary Hixson, dau. of Stephenson Hixson,
bm. John Shafer attests groom's age. 20 Sep. 1831. Shel.
Saddler, Samuel & Elizabeth Thompkins. m. 13 Aug. 1808.
Littlejohn.
Saffer, Thomas A. & Mary Jane Tavenner, dau. of Fielding
Tavenner, who proves groom's age, wit. 25 Sep. 1850. MarReg.
m. 9 Oct. 1850. Eggleston.
Saffron, Samuel & Mary Ann Carr. m. 12 April 1826. Tuston.
Sagel, Johannes & Maria Watson; both single. By license. m.
22 Oct. 1822. ParReg A.
Sagle, George & Susan Tomer. John Near attests groom's age, bm.
24 Feb. 1829.
Sagle, Michael & Elizabeth Jacobs. Adam Jacobs attests bride's
age, bm. 4 Aug. 1834. m. 5 Aug. 1834. ParReg A. Shel.
Sahrbach, Michael & Elisabetha Adams; both single. By license.
m. 30 Dec. 1824. ParReg A.

Saintclair, James & Ruth Sopher. m. 29 Aug. 1808. Littlejohn.
Sample, Johannes, widower & Maria Hechus (?). By license. m.
1 March 1827. ParReg A.
Sample, John & Lucy Smith. Israel Philips attests groom's age,
bm. 12 June 1809.
Sampson, James L. & Sarah Jacobs, ward of James Stidman (Stedman),
bm. 25 March 1830.
Sanbower, John & Emma Stoutsenburger. Jacob Stoutsenburger
attests groom's age, bm. 29 Sep. 1847. m. 30 Sep. 1847.
Shuford.
Sandburry, Benjamin & Sarah Guilders. m. 17 April 1817.
T. Littleton.
Sandeford, James & Mary Herbert. m. 7 June 1808. Littlejohn.
Sanders, Aaron & Mary Sanders. Benja. Sanders, bm. 31 Dec. 1796.
Sanders, Aron & Nancy Rose. m. 14 Feb. 1805. Littlejohn.
Sanders, Benjamin & Mary Catherine Blaker. Amos Beale attests
bride's age, bm. 24 Nov. 1834. Shel.
Sanders, Isaac & Mary Morris. m. 15 Jan. 1796. Littlejohn.
Sanders, John & Ann B. Rose. m. 16 May 1810. Littlejohn.
Sanders, Perry H. & Sarah A. Russell. Charles W. Russell attests
ages, bm. 4 Nov. 1844. Shel.
Sanders, Peter & Ann Jackson. m. 5 Feb. 1803. Littlejohn.
Sanders, Philip & Amanda Clarissa Bayles, dau. of Amos Bayles
(Beale), bm. 18 June 1831. Shel.
Sanders, Presley & Mary Sanders. m. 29 Sep. 1804. Littlejohn.
Sanders, Thomas & Jane Turner. License: 26 Oct. 1810. Littleton.
Sanders, Thomas & Sarah Hough. m. 11 May 1808. Littlejohn.
Sanders, Wilson C. & Sarah Ann Gregg. James Sinclair attests ages,
bm. 14 Sep. 1839. Shel.
Sandford, Augustinus M. & Lidia Strahm; both single. By license.
m. 7 Oct. 1824. ParReg A.
Sands, Jacob & Esther Brown. m. 8 Jan. 1794. FFMM.
Sands, Jonah & Sarah Janney. m. 18 June 1829. Taylor, Clerk.
Sands, Jonas & Ester Janney. m. 7 March 1803. Littlejohn.
Sands, Jonas & Tamer Tucker. m. 6 June 1803. Littlejohn.
Sands, Thomas & Ruth Birdshal. m. 1 March 1802. Littlejohn.
Sanford, Henry & Sarah Dulin. m. 16 July 1795. Littlejohn.
Sapp, John & Sarah Fitzgerald. m. 10 June 1811. Littlejohn.
Sappington, Charles W. & Amelia Rincher, in Maryland. m. 21 March
1845. ParReg A.
Sappington, John & Polly Taylor. m. 20 Dec. 1804. Littlejohn.
Sarbaugh, Jacob & Elizabeth Prince, dau. of Mathias Prince, bm.
6 Sep. 1834. Shel.
Sargant, George & Mary Fillinggim. Hanson Derry attests ages, bm.
30 Dec. 1846. Shel.
Sargent, John & Nomia Mitchal. m. 15 Oct. 1794. Littlejohn.
Sargent, William & Mary McNiel. m. 6 Sep. 1793. Littlejohn.
Sauder, Jacob & Sarah Schlotzer, dau. of Jacob Schlotzer, Jr.
By license. m. 4 Dec. 1814. ParReg A.
Sauder, Michael & Sussana Schlotzer; both single. By license.
m. 28 March 1822. ParReg A.
Sauder, Peter & Barbara Stautzenberger; both single. By license.
m. 3 March 1812. ParReg A.

Saunders, Curtis R. & Edith Saunders. E. Hammat, bm. 8 April 1834.
Shel.

Saunders, George & Elizabeth Boothe. m. 27 Nov. 1816. Littlejohn.

Saunders, Gunnell & Rachel Ann Saunders. Thomas Saunders attests
ages, bm. 17 Dec. 1829.

Saunders, Henry, son of Everet Saunders & Sarah Francis Hawling,
dau. of Isaac Hawling. Wit: Isaac Hawling, Jr. 13 Dec. 1852.
MarReg. m. 16 Dec. 1852. Adie.

Saunders, James, Jr. & Roena Eleanor Bale. Amos Bale (Beale), bm.
19 March 1831. Shel.

Saunders, Joseph & Margarett Triplett. m. 19 Sep. 1813. McPherson.

Saunders, Lee A. & Penelope M. Havenner. "Lee A. Saunders is
evidently upwards of 21 years." Thomas A. Havenner attests
bride's age, bm. 30 Jan. 1847. m. 2 Jan. 1847. Gover. Cam.

Saunders, Robert S. & Elizabeth Myers. John Veal attests ages, bm.
24 March 1830. Cam.

Saunders, Thomas & Mary Mead. Charles Shreves, bm. 3 Dec. 1832.
Shel.

Saunders, Wesley J. & Elizabeth Crim, dau. of John Crim, who
attests groom's age, bm. 14 Aug. 1843. m. 24 Aug. 1843.
ParReg A. Shel.

Scanland, Daniel J. P. & Sarah Vansickler. Wit: Philip Vansickler.
4 May 1853. MarReg. m. 10 May 1853. Herndon.

Scantland, John & Sophronia Thomas. m. 12 Jan. 1820. Williamson.

Scatterday, John & Reba. Ewers. m. 13 Oct. 1794. Littlejohn.

Schaefer, Michael & Maria Elisabetha Eberylin, dau. of Fried.
Eberly. m. 11 Aug. 1790. ParReg A.

Schaeffer, Johann Georg & Anna Catharina Marckertin. By license.
m. 4 May 1787. ParReg A.

Schaffer, Georg, son of Michael Schaffer and wife & Catharina
Frey, dau. of Peter Frey and wife; both single. By license.
m. 28 Oct. 1819. ParReg A.

Schaffer, Jacob & Malinda Selwuck; both single. By license. m.
15 Jan. 1830. ParReg A.

Schaffer, Johannes, son of Johannes Schaffer & Margretha Campher;
both single. m. 25 March 1830. ParReg A.

Schaffer, Johannes & Sussana Tall; both single. By license. m.
7 Nov. 1824. ParReg A.

Scharbach, Johannes & Elisabeth Schower; both single. By license.
m. 22 Dec. 1818. ParReg A.

Schart, Henrich, widower & Catharina Ullem, single. By license.
m. 12 March 1812. ParReg A.

Schart, Hesekia & Elisabeth Wittman. By license. m. 8 April 1830.
ParReg A.

Schart, Johannes, widower & Catharine Baumherner, single. By
license. m. 1 Jan. 1824. ParReg A.

Schart, Johannes & Charlotta Schower; both single. By license.
m. 15 Sep. 1825. ParReg A.

Schatt, Thomas E. & Maria Spring, single. By license. m. 8 Aug.
1826. ParReg A.

Scheaffer, Jacob & Carlotta Wenner; both single. m. 24 March 1831.
ParReg A.

Schembers, Jacobus & Sarah Berg; both single. By license. m.
17 Oct. 1811. ParReg A.

Schick, Johannes, widower & Catharina Schlotz, single. By license.
  m. 22 Aug. 1811. ParReg A.
Schirly, Isaac & Elana Rady; both single. By license. m. 7 Nov.
  1819. ParReg A.
Schlotzer, Anthony, son of Johan Schlotzer & Susana Wenzel, dau.
  of Johannes Wenzel. By license. m. 23 April 1812. ParReg A.
Schlotzer, Georg & Sarah Schuhmacher; both single. By license.
  m. 14 Dec. 1828. ParReg A.
Schlotzer, Jacob, son of Johannes Schlotzer & Christina Schlotzer,
  dau. of Jacob Schlotzer, Sr. By license. m. 27 Jan. 1818.
  ParReg A.
Schlotzer, Michael & Maria Aument; both single. By license. m.
  30 Nov. 1824. ParReg A.
Schlotzer, Samuel & Barbara Mayers; both single. By license. m.
  2 Aug. 1827. ParReg A.
Schmidt, Johan & Maria Ana Davis; both single. By license. m.
  9 Aug. 1829. ParReg A.
Schober, Simon & Charlotta Eberhardtin. m. 8 Nov. 1785. ParReg A.
Schofeild, John & Jane Moore. m. 12 Nov. 1807. McPherson.
Scholdfield, William & Hannah Redman. m. 10 Nov. 1806. Littlejohn.
Schooley, Charles William & Mary Hough, dau. of Garrett Hough,
  who attests groom's age, bm. 3 Aug. 1841. m. 13 Aug. 1841.
  Gover. Shel.
Schooley, Daniel & Sarah Myers. m. 7 Nov. 1821. Mendenhall, Clerk.
  FFMM.
Schooley, Elisha, son of John and Mary Schooley & Rachel Holmes,
  dau. of William and Mary Holmes. m. 16 Dec. 1779. FFMM.
Schooley, Ephraim, son of Reuben and Esther Schooley & Tacey
  Myers, dau. of Elijah and Mary Myers. m. 10 June 1812. FFMM.
Schooley, John, Jr. & Elizabeth Hough. m. 1 June 1796. FFMM.
Schooley, John, Jr. & Sarah Roberts, widow. Addison H. Clarke, bm.
  12 Nov. 1831. Shel.
Schooley, John Henry & Maria P. Norris. Presley Saunders attests
  ages. Charles W.Schooley, bm. 3 March 1846. Shel.
Schooley, Reuben E. & Rachel L. Steer. Lewis D. Waley proves ages,
  wit. 21 April 1851. MarReg. m. 23 April 1851. FFMM.
Schooley, Thomas A. & Hannah Hough. Garrett Hough attests ages,
  bm. 16 Nov. 1846. m. 19 Nov. 1846. Gover. Shel.
Schooley, William & Hannah Brown. m. 15 Nov. 1780. FFMM.
Schooley, William H. & Hannah Stocks, dau. of William Stocks.
  Stephen S. Stocks attests groom's age, bm. 11 Jan. 1841. Shel.
Schort, Johannes & Elisabetha Stockin, dau. of Peter Stock; both
  single. By license. m. 3 (?) Dec. 1812. ParReg A.
Schover, Adam E. & Catharina Pottenfeld; both single. By license.
  m. 2 Aug. 1827. ParReg A.
Schover, Georg & Sussana Sandbauer; both single. By license. m.
  16 June 1820. ParReg A.
Schower, Johannes, widower & Elisabeth Bauer, widow. By license.
  m. 18 Feb. 1830. ParReg A.
Schray, Paul & Catharina Lay; both single. By license. m. 13 March
  1823. ParReg A.
Schriekly, Samuel & Louisa Ehmig; both single. By license.
  m. 31 Jan. 1828. ParReg A.
Schumacher, Georg & Christina Prill; both single. By license. m.
  2 Dec. 1824. ParReg A.

Schumacher, George, son of Daniel Schumacher & Magdalena
    Frantzin, dau. of Nicolaus Frantzen. m. 7 June 1789. ParReg A.
Schumacher, Jacob & Elisabeth Cloninger. By license. m. 2 April
    1788. ParReg A.
Schumacher, Jacob & Sarah Philler, single. By license. m. 18 Aug.
    1825. ParReg A.
Schutz (?), Henrich & Nanzy Philler; both single. By license. m.
    8 Sep. 1825. ParReg A.
Schwenk, Phillip, widower & Anna Maria Henrich, widow. By license.
    m. 20 May 1815. ParReg A.
Scott, Benjamin & Sarah Randall, dau. of Joseph and Rachel
    Randall. m. 6 Sep. 1786. FFMM.
Scott, Carles, single & Elisabeth Richart (?), widow. By license.
    m. 17 Dec. 1817. ParReg A.
Scott, Charles & Cynthia Comstock. Noble S. Braden, bm. 28 Jan.
    1837. m. 4 July 1837. Campbell. Shel.
Scott, George & Margaret Newlan. License: 12 Feb. 1810.
    T. Littleton.
Scott, Gilbert & Mary (Maria) Ann (Anna) Wolford (Wollford).
    William Wolford, bm. 30 Jan. 1830. m. 2 Feb. 1830. ParReg. A.
    Shel.
Scott, James M. & Mary Hough. m. 1821-1822. Mines.
Scott, Moses & Rebecca J. Peugh. Charles Taylor, bm. 10 Dec. 1844.
    Shel.
Scott, Samuel & Ann E. Wright. John E. Wright attests ages, bm.
    22 June 1850. Shel.
Scott, Stephen & Sarah Talbott. m. 30 Jan. 1799. FFMM.
Scott, Thompson M. & Sarah Ann Ramsay, with Maryland license. m.
    25 Aug. 1848. ParReg A.
Scott, William & Eliza Hart. Benson Cornwell attests ages, bm.
    7 July 1845. m. 8 July 1845. Gover. Shel.
Scrivener, John & Sarah Seers. m. 3 Oct. 1807. Littlejohn.
Scrivner, William & Jane Wills. m. 22 May 1817. Williamson.
Scroggins, Benjamin & Jane C. McCaen, ward of Garrett Walker, bm.
    12 Feb. 1849. Shel.
Sealock, Samuel & Polly Powell. m. 10 Sep. 1808. Dunn.
Sears, Robert & Catherine Taylor. m. 11 April 1808. Littlejohn.
Sears, Thomas & Mary Daniel. m. 26 Sep. 1816. Williamson.
Sears, Thomas & Sarah Keyser. m. 14 April 1812. J. Littleton.
Seaton, James & Elizabeth Race, dau. of William Race, bm. 20 Oct.
    1799. Littlejohn. Shel.
Seaton, John W., son of Hiram Seaton & Frances A. Eaches, dau. of
    Thomas Eaches. John F. Newlon, bm. m. 1 Dec. 1840. Herndon.
    Shel.
Seaton, John W. & Nancy Lewis. Stephen Lewis attests ages, bm.
    11 July 1833. Shel.
Seeders, William & Sarah S. Drean. m. 15 July 1819. Littlejohn.
Seers, Hezh. & Cath. Hobbs. m. 27 Dec. 1802. Littlejohn.
Segel, Henrich & Tercky Gammelin. m. 3 Aug. 1785. ParReg A.
Seitz, Andrew & Amanda Yeaky, Mrs. John W. Shipley attests ages,
    bm. 7 Oct. 1848. m. 8 Oct. 1848. ParReg A. Shel.
Selby, William & Eliza Noggle. George Whitmore attests ages, bm.
    17 Feb. 1842. Shel.
Selcot, William & Elizabeth Darr. m. 7 Feb. 1797. Littlejohn.

Selden, Wilson C. & Mary B. Alexander, widow. m. 17 July 1817.
    Dunn.
Selden, Wilson C., Jr. & Eliza A. Lee. C. W. C. Eskridge, bm.
    10 June 1828.
Seldon, Wilson C., Jr. & Louisa T. Alexander. m. 20 June 1822.
    Dunn. Shel.
Selhman (Silmon),John J. M. & Ann E. Belt, dau. of Alfred Belt,
    bm. Thomas Dorrell attests groom's age. 28 Nov. 1842. m.
    29 Nov. 1842, at home of bride's father. Adie. Shel.
Senate, William & Eliza Whitter (Winters), free coloured. Wit:
    John Torreyson, Sydnor Bennett. Presly Saunders, bm. 11 Aug.
    1847. m. 17 Aug. 1847. Herndon. Shel.
Sentman, Jacob & Sarah Phinety. m. 11 Nov. 1811. Littlejohn.
Sergener, James & Harriet Harrison. m. 25 Nov. 1808. Williamson.
Serivener, John & M___ Scriener. m. 21 Dec. 1802. Littlejohn.
Settle, Abner H. & Isabella L. Hixon, dau. of Benjamin Hixon, bm.
    13 April 1835. m. 14 April 1835. Baker. Shel.
Settle, Abner H. & Mary Ann Kile, dau. of George Kile. Alexander
    Edmonds, bm. 3 Dec. 1839. Shel.
Settle, M.L. & Julia Ann Davis, dau. of H.M. Davis, of Middleburg.
    James W. Moxley attests ages, bm. 29 March 1849. Shel.
Settle, Martin & Ann Horseman. m. 23 Feb. 1811. Littlejohn.
Setzer, Philip & Emily Beach, dau. of John Beach. Martin Felckner
    attests groom's age. John Brack, bm. 22 March 1830. Shel.
Seward, Nicholas & Ann Sorrell. License: 25 May 1762. FeeBk 3.
Sexton, George & Martha Tribby. Thomas Gregg attests groom's age.
    David Reece attests bride's age, bm. 9 March 1846. Shel.
Sexton, James & Mary Ann Riley, dau. of Richard Riley, bm. 2 May
    1838. m. 3 May 1838. Hauer. Shel.
Sexton, John & Alcinda Parker. Chilton Parker attests bride's age,
    bm. 21 Dec. 1836. Shel.
Seybold, John, son of Jasper Seybold & Hannah Cranmer, dau. of
    Andres Cranmer. m. 30 June 1784. FFMM.
Seyferd, Henrich & Sara Schart; both single. By license. m. 31 Jan.
    1828. ParReg A.
Seygar, George & Christianna Firestone. Reynolds Kellison (Callason)
    attests bride's age, bm. 7 Oct. 1799. Shel.
Seygar, John & Eve Crombacker, widow. C. Binns, Jr., bm. 14 Oct.
    1799. Littlejohn. Shel.
Schackleford, Arthur & Susannah Fulton, dau. of Margaret Fulton.
    Bride "is an illegitimate child". Benjamin Boles attests
    groom's age, bm. 16 Nov. 1841. m. 17 Nov. 1841. Phelps. Shel.
Shacklet, Henry & Elizabeth Berkeley. m. 2 Oct. 1827. Williamson.
Shafer, Joseph Henry & Susan Spring. Parents consent. 25 Aug.
    1851. MarReg. m. 2 Sep. 1851. ParReg A.
Shaffer, Jacob & Charlotte Wenner, ward of Maurey Frayser. Jona.
    Winner, John Winner witness Martha Frazier, late Mary Winner,
    bride's guardian, sign certificate. Jona. Wenner, bm.
    14 March 1831. Shel.
Shaffer, Jacob & Malinda Clark. Abraham Smith attests ages, bm.
    9 Jan. 1830. Shel.
Shank, Andrew & Emily R. Smith. Josiah J. Janney attests ages, bm.
    18 May 1835. Monroe. Shel.

Shaver, Conrad & Mary Magdalene Razer. George Razor, bm. 10 June
    1799.
Shaver, John & Margaret Compher, dau. of John Compher, who attests
    groom's age, bm. 23 March 1830. Shel.
Shaver, William & Elizabeth Gossett. m. 10 Oct. 1796. Littlejohn.
Shaw, Hesekiah & Catherine Smith. m. 31 Dec. 1811. Littlejohn.
Shaw, Hezekiah & Elizabeth Whitmore. Jacob Smith, bm. 5 April
    1830. Shel.
Shaw, James & Anna Mumphred. John Bontz attests ages, bm. 24 Oct.
    1837. m. 26 Oct. 1837. ParReg A. Shel.
Shaw, James & Ann Humphrey. m. 26 Oct. 1837. Hauer.
Shaw, John & Cynthia Corwin. m. 6 May 1826. Tuston.
Shaw, John & Rebeckah Broomhall. John Schooley, Jr. consents.
    John Canby, bm. 26 Nov. 1799. Littlejohn.
Shawen, William C., son of D. Shawn & Ann C. Taylor, dau. of Col.
    T. Taylor. Timothy Taylor, bm. 14 Nov. 1844. m. 19 Nov. 1844.
    Massey. Shel.
Sheaffer, Charles & Eve Julian Sackman, dau. of J. Martin Sackman.
    Samuel Sackman attests groom's age, bm. 18 July 1829. Shel.
Shearman, Joseph, of Lancaster County & Susannah Chinn, dau. of
    Thomas Chinn. Noble Beveridge, bm. 28 Nov. 1799. Shel.
Shearwood, Hezekiah & Mary Ann Loveless. John Loveless proves
    bride's age, wit. 25 Nov. 1850. MarReg. m. 26 Nov. 1850. Gover.
Sheckels, Lewis & Amey Millon. m. 20 March 1817. T. Littleton.
Sheckles, Edward & Nancy Hensen. m. 8 Feb. 1812. J. Littleton.
Shedaker, John & Sally Willis, widow. C. Binns, Jr., bm. 12 Aug.
    1799. Shel.
Sheed, George & Rebecca Fox, widow. Charles Gulatt attests ages,
    bm. 20 April 1809.
Sheid, Orlando K. & Amanda M. F. Geaslin (Guslin). Charles A.
    Johnson, bm. 31 Oct. 1843. m. 2 Nov. 1843. Gover. Shel.
Sheilds, Joseph & Sarah Carnes. m. 17 March 1812. J. Littleton.
Shell, Mount Joy & Bitha Ann Fields. Luke Fields proves bride's
    ages, wit. 13 Feb. 1852. MarReg. m. 17 Feb. 1852. Nixon.
Shepherd, Charles & Milly Rhodes. m. 24 Feb. 1819. Griffith.
Shepherd, Jacob R. & Nancy Roszel. Gunnell Saunders, bm. 29 Oct.
    1841. Shel.
Shepherd, Nelson & Caroline Glascock. m. 29 Oct. 1825-1 Nov. 1825.
    Burch.
Shepherd, Parkerson (Parkinson) D. & Mary Ann Margaret Jennings.
    Sanford Rogers, bm. 11 May 1841. m. 25 May 1841. Herndon. Shel.
Sherb, Jacob & Maria West. m. 1 May 1817. T. Littleton.
Sherly, William & Elizabeth Legg. m. 9 Nov. 1813. Littlejohn.
Sherman, George M. & Harriet P. Surghnor. m. Dec. 1835. Campbell.
Sherzeo (Sherzer), John M. & Emza A. M. Figgins (Figgans). Wit:
    Lorenzo D. Thompson. 2 June 1852. MarReg. m. 10 June 1852.
    Holland.
Shets, Jacob & Elizabeth Koonts. m. 1809-1810. Mines.
Shields, Joseph & Latitia Young. m. 19 Jan. 1819. Griffith.
Shields, Joseph & Pamelia Scatterday. Thomas Davis, bm. 11 March
    1799. Littlejohn. Shel.
Shields, William R. & Susan Blaker. Benjamin Saunders attests
    bride's age, bm. 6 March 1832. Shel.

Shipley, John W. & Rebecca Elizabeth Helbringle (Hellnigle).
Henry M. Hardy attests bride's age, bm. 24 Dec. 1845. m.
29 Dec. 1845. Gover. Shel.

Shipley, John W. & Susan M. Cranwell, dau. of Susan Cranwell.
Carey C. Gover attests groom's age, bm. 18 April 1843. Shel.

Shipman, Landon & Catherine Tillett. Jas. Goram attests bride's
age, bm. William Kent attests groom's age, bm. 28 Jan. 1839.
Cam.

Shipman, Mason & Deborah Ann Wiley, dau. of Thomas H. Wiley, who
proves groom's age, wit. 28 Aug. 1850. MarReg. m. 29 Aug.
1850. Herndon.

Shipman, Samuel & Susan Fry. Martin Fry proves bride's age, wit.;
"his taken for granted". 6 Sep. 1852. MarReg. m. 7 Sep. 1852.
Gover.

Shipman, Stephen R., dau. of Elenor Shipman & Mary J. Stevens,
dau. of Enos Stevens. Wit: Enos Stevens, Elenor Shipman.
11 Dec. 1851. MarReg.

Shober, John & Elizabeth Gower. John Sarbaugh attests bride's age,
bm. 17 Feb. 1830. Shel.

Shoemaker, Daniel & Priscilla Purdum. m. 27 Feb. 1802. Littlejohn.

Shoemaker, George & Margaret Miller. m. 30 April 1796. Littlejohn.

Shoemaker, George & Sarah Grubb, dau. of John Grubb, who attests
groom's age, bm. 21 Jan. 1847. Shel.

Shoemaker, George W. & Mary Shriyley. Enoch Shryley attests ages,
bm. 26 Sep. 1831. Shel.

Shoemaker, Jacob & Priscilla Potterfield. m. 2 Jan. 1822-21 March
1822. Mines.

Shoemaker, Naylor & Sarah Tate. m. 18 Nov. 1830. Taylor, Clerk.

Shoemaker, Samuel & Mary C. E. Beall, dau. of David F. Beall.
David L. Beall attests groom's age, bm. 28 Sep. 1838. m.
2 Oct. 1838. Herndon. Shel.

Shoemaker, Simon & Catherine Emery. m. 13 Oct. 1810. Littlejohn.

Shoite, Jacob & Elizabeth M. Smith. m. Jan. 1837. Campbell.

Shorb, William & Sarah Carter. John S. Pancoast affirms ages, wit.
30 April 1851. MarReg.

Shore, James & Sarah Busson, dau. of Benjamin Busson, deceased.
Aaron Busson, son of James Busson, affirms bride's age.
Alexander Waugh, bm. 10 Oct. 1799.

Shores, James E. & Mary Jeffers. m. 21 Dec. 1820. Dagg.

Short, John & Mary Ann Smith, with Maryland license. m. 13 Feb.
1834. ParReg A.

Short, John P. H. & Elizabeth J. Atwell, dau. of Thomas Atwell,
deceased, and ward of Jesse McVeigh. James H. McVeigh, bm.
14 Dec. 1829.

Shorts, Jacob & Elizabeth M. Smith, ward of George Vincell, bm.
15 Jan. 1837. Shel.

Showers, Charles & Eliza F. Simpson. Wit: French Simpson. 10 Nov.
1853. MarReg. Herndon.

Shreve, Joshua & Darcus Wilson. m. 18 Nov. 1795. Littlejohn.

Shrift, Sanderson & Mary B. Shreve, dau. of Benjamin Shreve, Sr.
m. 29 Oct. 1844, at home of bride's father. Adie.

Shrigley, Samuel & Mary Shively. m. 1809-1810. Mines.

Shriver, David & Amelia Ropp. Samuel Ropp attests ages, bm. 26
Feb. 1838. m. 1 March 1838. Hauer. Shel.

137

LOUDOUN COUNTY MARRIAGES

Shriver, Jacob & Maria Kidwell. m. 8 April 1819. Keyes.
Shry, Jacob & Catherine Warford. Abraham Warford, bm. 31 Oct. 1799.
Shry, Paul & Mary Houser. m. 11 Aug. 1810. T. Littleton.
Shry, Powell & Nancy Heater. Solomon Heater, bm. 11 Sep. 1832. m. 13 Sep. 1832. Hauer. Shel.
Shry, William & Christina (Christena) Fawley. Jacob Fawley attests ages. Thomas W. Edwards, bm. 2 Jan. 1845. m. 9 Jan. 1845. ParReg A. Shel.
Shrye, Joseph & Monecai Dawson. m. 13 April 1811. Littlejohn.
Shryock (Shryoak), Rubin, son of George and Mary Shryoak, 24 years, b. Loudoun & Martha A. Gardner, dau. of Charles and Elizabeth Gardner, 24 years, b. Loudoun. Wit: Abner D. Lee. 12 Dec. 1853. MarReg. m. 15 Dec. 1853. Gover.
Shryock, George & Rebecca Howser. m. 15 Jan. 1849. Gover.
Shumaker, Joseph & Mary Catharine Miles, dau. of Benjamin Miles, who proves groom's age, wit. 16 May 1853. MarReg.
Shumaker, Samuel & Agnes Rebecca Merchant. Wit: Bride's father. Haml. Housholder proves groom's age, wit. 26 May 1851. MarReg.
Shuman, George W. & Harriet P. Surghnor, dau. of James Surghnor. William L. Bogue, bm. 14 Dec. 1835. Shel.
Shumate (Shoemate), Murphey C. & Diadama Elgin. Francis Shreve attests bride's age, bm. 7 Dec. 1837. m. 12 Dec. 1837. Keppler. Shel.
Shumate, Murphey C. & Margaret Elgin. Francis Elgin attests bride's age, bm. 22 Oct. 1831. Shel.
Shunk, Isaac & Bethany Oxley, dau. of Everitt Oxley, bm. 23 Dec. 1809. Shel.
Shyrock, George E. & Rebecca J. Howser, dau. of Richard Houser, who attests groom's age, bm. 12 Feb. 1849.
Shyrock, John & Mary J. Ellmore, dau. of John Ellmore. Richard H. Rose attests ages, bm. 12 Nov. 1844. Cam.
Sibbett, Jesse & Rachel Hummings, ward of David Carlisle, bm. 14 Aug. 1833. Shel.
Siddal, William & Sarah Paxton, Jr. m. 31 March 1802. FFMM.
Siddle, James & Nancy Hollam. m. 24 June 1795. Littlejohn.
Siddle, John & Ninia Whitacre. m. 14 Feb. 1804. Littlejohn.
Sidle, Francis & Catherine Moffett. m. 27 Dec. 1813. Littlejohn.
Siebert, Johannes & Maria Magdalena Schwenckin. m. 27 June 1786. ParReg A.
Silcott, Albert & Elizabeth Hutchison (Hutchinson). John W. Hanking, bm. 21 April 1845. m. 24 April 1845. Herndon. Shel.
Silcott, Jacob & Tamer Cowgill. m. 21 Feb. 1813. McPherson.
Silcott, James & Eleanor J. Hough. Samuel P. Thompson attests ages, bm. 25 Sep. 1843. Shel.
Silcott, James & Virginia C. Paxson, dau. of Samuel Paxson, wit. 12 Dec. 1851. MarReg. m. 16 Dec. 1851. Eggleston.
Silcott, Jesse & Sally McDaniel. m. 13 Jan. 1812. J. Littleton.
Silcott, Meshack & Emily Lodge. William Lodge attests ages, bm. 6 March 1846. m. 10 March 1846. Massey. Shel.
Silcott, Mortimer & Elizabeth W. Milburne. Wit: Gideon W. Milburne. 10 Oct. 1853. MarReg. m. 11 Oct. 1853. Duncan.

138

Silcott, William & Francis Eliza Downs. James H. Silcott attests
    ages, bm. 30 Aug. 1841. Shel.
Silcott, William & Sarah Violet. m. 20 Sep. 1821. Dagg.
Silket (Silcott), Abraham & Barsheba Tavener. m. 28 June 1800.
    Littlejohn.
Simmerman, Henry & Elizabeth Fairhurst. m. 9 Feb. 1803.
    Littlejohn.
Simmons, Benjamin & Catharine Legg. William Harrison attests ages,
    bm. 14 Aug. 1839. m. 22 Aug. 1839. Herndon. Shel.
Simmons, James T. & Eliza. Ann Money. Jonas Money attests ages,
    bm. 15 March 1845. m. 6 April 1845. Gover. Shel.
Simms, Isaiah & Elizabeth Darne. Gunnell Darne attests ages, bm.
    20 June 1835. Cam.
Simons, Edward & Ann Magaha (Magahy), dau. of Nancy Miller. Hiram
    Hardy, bm. 13 Sep. 1843. m. 21 Sep. 1843. ParReg A.
Simpson, Bernard & Ann M. Perry. Alfred Spates attests ages, bm.
    P. L. Lott, bm. 14 May 1838. Shel.
Simpson, Bernard & Dewanner Wildman. Charles Binns, bm. 10 Dec.
    1833. Shel.
Simpson, Charles William & Emily M. Luck. Jordon B. Luck attests
    groom's age, bm. 3 Dec. 1839. Shel.
Simpson, David & Elizabeth Gregg. m. 1 Jan. 1822. Gilmore.
Simpson, Francis R. & Deborah Merchant, dau. of James Merchant,
    bm. George Simpson attests groom's age. 24 Jan. 1829.
Simpson, Henson & Mary Baty. m. 10 Dec. 1807. McPherson.
Simpson, James L. & Sarah Jacobs. m. 25 March 1830. Tippett.
Simpson, John & Nancy Smith. m. 17 Dec. 1811. Littlejohn.
Simpson, John W., son of French Simpson & Mary Ann Adams, dau. of
    Richard Adams. French Simpson, Richard Adams, bm. 14 Feb.
    1848. m. 15 Feb. 1848. Herndon. Shel.
Simpson, Richard F. & Maria Louisa Noland. William Noland attests
    ages, bm. 31 May 1839. m. 13 June 1849, at Mrs. Lewis
    Barkley's, Aldie. Adie. Cam.
Simpson, Samuel & Rebecca M. Shreve, dau. of Benjamin Schreve, Sr.
    Benjamin Shreve, bm. 18 March 1844. m. 28 March 1844, at home
    of bride's father. Adie. Shel.
Simpson, Silas M. & Susan Ann Haines, dau. of Edward Haines, wit.
    John McCabe proves groom's age, wit. 5 April 1852. m.
    6 April 1852. Gover.
Simpson, William F. & Mary A. Newton, dau. of John C. Newton, bm.
    24 May 1832. Shel.
Simson, Francis R. & Deborah Marschent; both single. By license.
    m. 12 Feb. 1829. ParReg A.
Sinclair, George & Margaret Craven. m. 28 Dec. 1798. Littlejohn.
Sinclair, George & Ratha Ann Belt, dau. of Alfred Belt, bm.
    27 Nov. 1830. Shel.
Sinclair, George B. & Elizabeth Puller. m. 23 Dec. 1819.
    Williamson.
Sinclair, Isaac, of Harrison County & Eliza. Ann Moxley. Francis
    Moxley attests ages, bm. Lucian Fitzhugh, bm. 10 Oct. 1837.
    m. 2 Oct. 1837. Trott. Cam.
Sinclair, James & Cathrine Hibbs. m. 2 April 1800. Littlejohn.
Sinclair, James & Leannah Vandevender. m. 14 June 1827. Tuston.
Sinclair, John & Rachell Daniel. m. 24 April 1795. Littlejohn.

Sinclair, John & Susanna Dishman. m. 23 March 1817. Williamson.
Sinclair, John W., son of John Sinclair & Catharine Wynkoop,
    dau. of Elizabeth Wynkoop; "her father is dead". Thomas
    Wynkoop, bm. 19 Jan. 1848. Shel.
Sinclair, William & Alice Smith. m. 17 Nov. 1803. Williamson.
Singers, Charles & Elizabeth Cross. m. 1806. Mines.
Singleton, Robert & Jane S. Carr. m. 15 Jan. 1824. Dagg.
Sinquefield, Abram, alias Abraham & Joanna King. m. 24 Feb. 1822.
    T. Littleton.
Skillman, Bushrod W. & Sarah E. Gochnauer, dau. of Elizabeth
    Gochnauer. John Jones, Jr. attests groom's age, bm. 23 Sep.
    1844. Shel.
Skillman, Isaac & Nancy Whiteley. m. 10 Jan. 1798. Littlejohn.
Skillman, James & Elizabeth Carter. William Wilkison attests
    bride's age. Abraham Skillman, bm. 24 Sep. 1833. Shel.
Skilman, John & Lucinda Swartz. m. 29 Dec. 1825. Dunn. Cam.
Skinner, Alexander & Sarah Ann Cockran. W. B. Cochran, bm.
    25 Nov. 1837. Shel.
Skinner, Cornelius & Jane Carr, dau. of Peter Carr, bm. 20 Sep.
    1796.
Skinner, Cornelius & Sarah Smarr, widow. Charles Roberts attests
    bride's age, bm. 17 Aug. 1799. Cam.
Skinner, H. W. & Mary V. Nixon. Wit: Dennis McCarty. 26 March
    1853. MarReg. m. 29 March 1853. Herndon.
Skinner, James, son of Peter Skinner & Catherine Reid, ward of
    Peter Skinner, bm. 13 Dec. 1830. m. 21 Dec. 1830.
    Williamson.
Skinner, James & Elizabeth Beatty. John Beatty attests ages, bm.
    26 May 1849. m. 29 May 1849. Dulin. Cam.
Skinner, James & Jane Elizabeth Turner, dau. of C. Turner.
    Gabriel Skinner states groom was 21 years "6 Feb. last".
    James Priest, bm. 10 Jan. 1838. Shel.
Skinner, John R. & Nancy E. Robey. Bride's father consents in
    writing. George F. Byrne proves groom's age, wit. 31 July
    1852. m. 1 Aug. 1852. Hirst.
Skinner, John Richard & Sarah Burrill Stover, dau. of Edwin A.
    Stover, of Aldie. Lorenzo D. Walker, bm. 24 Feb. 1840. Shel.
Skinner, John T. & Susannah Tinsman. Bride's father consents in
    writing. Thomas E. Gibson attests groom's age, wit. 22 Jan.
    1853. MarReg. m. 27 Jan. 1853. Hirst.
Skinner, Phinealeas & Margaret Palmer. m. 27 Dec. 1806. McPherson.
Skinner, Usher & Rebecca Bronaugh. m. 28 Oct. 1819. Dagg.
Skinner, Usher & Scotty Spinks. George Hatton attests bride's
    age, bm. 31 Dec. 1844. Cam.
Skirving, John, Jr. & Frances E. Towner. Thomas B. Towner proves
    certificate, wit. 29 May 1852. MarReg.
Slack, Fenelon & Catherine S. Snyder. Henry Lefever proves
    bride's age, wit. 2 Sep. 1850. MarReg.
Slack, Fenelon & Margaret E. Tucker, dau. of Margaret Tucker, bm.
    6 Oct. 1836. Shel.
Slack, James & Ann Maria Triplett. James Chappell attests ages,
    bm. 17 Jan. 1843. Shel.
Slack, John & Juliet Lickey, dau. of William Lickey, bm. 20 Feb.
    1832. Shel.

Slack, John P. & Sigga Chapell. m. 23 Nov. 1820. T. Littleton.
Slack, Manly & Mahala Jane Saunders, dau. of Mahala Saunders.
  James W. Saunders attests groom's age, bm. 16 April 1844. Shel.
Slacks, Jeremiah & Reba. Riddle. m. 11 Dec. 1804. Littlejohn.
Slagle, Michael & Elizabeth Jacobs. m. 5 Aug. 1834. Hauer.
Slater, Jacob & Elizabeth Dorstimer. m. 1807-1808. Mines.
Slater, John G. & Annie E. Ruse, dau. of John Ruse, wit. 7 Dec.
  1852. MarReg.
Slaughter, Arthur & Sarah Fowke (Foukes). m. 28 May 1811.
  Jefferson.
Slocks, Georg & Christina Phaly, dau. of Johannes Phaly and wife;
  both single. By license. m. 29 April 1819. ParReg A.
Slocombs, Samuel & Mary Marchant. m. 18 Aug. 1796. Littlejohn.
Smale, Simon & Elizabeth Lott. Presley Saunders, bm. 30 June 1846.
  Shel.
Smallwood, Dennis & Jane Reed. m. 22 Dec. 1810. Littlejohn.
Smallwood, Henry & Reba. Rigney. m. 2 April 1803. Littlejohn.
Smallwood, Leven D., son of Mary Smallwood & Juliet Ann Perry.
  Presley Parker attests bride's age. Abner Carter, bm.
  30 Oct. 1837. Shel.
Smallwood, William, son of Polly Smallwood, surviving parent &
  Elizabeth Harden (Harding), dau. of Thomas Harden. Joseph
  Harden, bm. 8 Sep. 1832. m. 13 Sep. 1832. Baker. Shel.
Smart, John P. & Charlotte A. Oram. m. 7 Sep. 1848, at home of
  Mrs. M. Edwards. Adie.
Smart, John P. & Emely (Emily) Hilliard. Joseph Hilliard, bm.
  25 Nov. 1829. m. 26 Nov. 1829. Tippett.
Smart, John P. & Mary E. Wherry. Robert G. Bowie, bm. 12 Oct.
  1841. m. 13 Oct. 1841, at house of Mrs. Lucy Ball, Leesburg.
  Adie. Shel.
Smith, Aron & Jane Sinclair. m. 16 Aug. 1795. Littlejohn.
Smith, Augustus G. & Anna Maria Johnston. Charles A. Johnston
  attests bride's age, bm. 25 March 1835. m. 27 March 1834.
  Dorsey. Shel.
Smith, Benjamin & Sarah A. E. Blemar. Charles G. Eskridge, bm.
  18 Feb. 1830. Shel.
Smith, Charles & Emley Coe. m. 29 Sep. 1808. Dunn.
Smith, Charles & Mary Leach. m. 1806. Mines.
Smith, Daniel & Mary Palmer. m. 8 Dec. 1796. Littlejohn.
Smith, Daniel G. & Eleanor E. Hamilton. Charles G. Eskridge, bm.
  28 April 1845. Shel.
Smith, Ephraim & Julian M. Wissinger. Bernard Goslin attests ages,
  bm. 25 April 1843. ParReg A. Shel.
Smith, George & Mary Lamb. m. 1807-1808. Mines.
Smith, George D. & Martha L. Gregg, ward of Ann Sanders.
  Britton Saunders, bm. 9 Aug. 1831. Shel.
Smith, George W. H. & Mary Esther Rice, dau. of Thizza Rice, her
  mother, bm. 13 Sep. 1836. Shel.
Smith, Henry & Elizabeth O'Brien. George B. McCarty proves
  bride's age, wit. 30 Dec. 1850. MarReg. m. 2 Jan. 1851.
  Wilmer. ParReg B.
Smith, Henry & Sarah Vickers. m. 3 April 1802. Littlejohn.
Smith, Henry G., son of Hugh and Elizabeth Smith, formerly Jones,
  & Tingey Anna Dulany, dau. of Daniel F. Dulaney and Margaret
  Ann, his wife. 5 Dec. 1853. MarReg. m. 6 Dec. 1853. Villiger.

Smith, Hugh & Elizabeth Jones. m. 18 June 1819. Dagg.
Smith, Jacob & Mary Amick. George Vincell attests bride's age.
    Solomon Smith attests groom's age. Abraham Smith, bm. 26 March
    1838. m. 29 March 1838. Hauer. Shel.
Smith, Jacob & Sarah Spencer. m. 1 Dec. 1802. Littlejohn.
Smith, James & Mary Ann Eliza Price. George Price, bm. 29 Jan.
    1838. Shel.
Smith, James William & Permillia Osburn, dau. of Joel Osburn, bm.
    28 April 1834. Shel.
Smith, Jesse & Mary Tobin. m. 2 Sep. 1807. Littlejohn.
Smith, Job & Lydia Fry. Michael Frey attests ages, bm. 11 Aug.
    1845. m. 14 Aug. 1845. ParReg A. Shel.
Smith, John & Cornelia Ann Morris, dau. of Mahlon Morris. 11 Nov.
    1850. MarReg.
Smith, John & Mary Ann Davis. Anthony Davis attests ages, bm.
    8 Sep. 1829.
Smith, John & Mary Grubb. m. 1830. Moor.
Smith, John & Mary West, widow. License: Feb. 1765. FeeBk 2.
Smith, John & Sarah Grubb, dau. of Ebenezer Grubb. William Grubb
    attests groom's age, bm. 4 March 1829.
Smith, John & Sarah Hirst. m. 6 May 1784. FFMM.
Smith, John & Sarah Myers. m. 14 May 1766. FFMM.
Smith, John A. W. & Sally Odell Hall. Rev. John A. Collins attests
    bride's age. William F. Phillips, bm. 7 Feb. 1832. m. 8 Feb.
    1832. Green.
Smith, Livingston & Margaret H. Carnes. m. 9 Oct. 1817. Dunn.
    Shel.
Smith, Mahlon & Sarah Taylor. m. 1 March 1806. Littlejohn.
Smith, Middleton & Clarrisa Towner. Henry Newton, bm. 24 Oct.
    1833. Shel.
Smith, Nathaniel & Mary Craven. m. 27 June 1803. Littlejohn.
Smith, P. A. L. & Amanda Hunton. John Butcher attests ages, bm.
    8 Feb. 1844. Shel.
Smith, Patrick H. F. & Edmonia Hanock, dau. of George Hancock.
    C. F. Hancock attests groom's age, bm. 30 Jan. 1844. Shel.
Smith, Ralph & Amelia Hobbs. m. 13 May 1805. Littlejohn.
Smith, Samuel & Hannah L. Daniel. Joseph Grubb attests ages.
    Alfred H. Shields, bm. 8 April 1834. Shel.
Smith, Samuel & Mary Daniel. m. 11 April 1776. FFMM.
Smith, Solomon & Isabella Denges, with Maryland license. m.
    13 April 1835. ParReg A.
Smith, William & Caroline M. Wenner. John W. Wenner attests
    bride's age. George Whitmore attests groom's age, bm.
    18 March 1844. Shel.
Smith, William & Hannah Dulen. m. 20 Sep. 1803. Littlejohn.
Smith, William & Margaret Whiteley. License: 17 April 1765.
    FeeBk 2.
Smith, William & Mary Weeden. m. 8 March 1813. Littlejohn.
Smith, William H. & Elizabeth Bett, both of Maryland. m.
    19 March 1833. ParReg A.
Smith, William H. & Emily Grimes. Ryland P. Jacobs attests bride's
    age. John Butler, groom's guardian, bm. m. 11 Jan. 1841.
    Herndon. Shel.
Smith, William P. & Ann Virginia Burke. Bride's father consents.
    28 April 1852. MarReg. Duncan.

Smithey (Smithley), Elijah Martin & Catherine Davis. m. 31 Jan.
   1837. ParReg A. Hauer.
Smitley, Adam & Jane James. William Kendle attests ages, bm.
   8 June 1809. Saunders.
Smitley, Elijah Martin & Catherine Davis. John Spring attests
   ages, bm. 30 Jan. 1837. Shel.
Smitley, Soloman (Solomon) & Mary Bumcrotz, dau. of John Bumcrotz,
   bm. 9 May 1834. m. 15 May 1834. Hauer. Shel.
Smitson, Thomas & Eliza Ann Campbell, dau. of Sarah Campbell.
   Samuel C. Wynkoop attests groom's age, bm. 15 Oct. 1839. Shel.
Smittley, Solomon & Mary Baumkratz, dau. of John Baumkratz.
   m. 15 May 1834. ParReg A.
Smoot, Barton & Phebe Wilson. m. 17 Sep. 1807. McPherson.
Smoot, James & Nancy Triplett. m. 15 Feb. 1813. McPherson.
Smoot, Lewis & Mary Weedon. m. 22 May 1817. T. Littleton.
Smoots, James & Ann Mariah Fry. m. 26 April 1853. Gover.
Snoke, Solomon & Elizabeth Everhart. m. 18 April 1801. Littlejohn.
Smoots, Henry & Leannah Smith. Daniel Adams attests ages, bm.
   22 Dec. 1845. Shel.
Snoots, Henry & Mary Maker. m. 1809-1810. Mines.
Snoots, Jacob & Catherine Bontz. John Bontz attests bride's age,
   bm. 25 Aug. 1834. m. 28 Aug. 1834. Hauer. Shel.
Snoots, Jonas & Ann Maria Frye. Bride's mother consents in
   writing. Samuel Shipman proves groom's age, wit. 25 April
   1853. MarReg.
Snoots, Presley & Sarah Fry. Benjamin Miles attests ages, bm.
   18 March 1844. m. 21 March 1844. ParReg A. Shel.
Snoots, Samuel & Sarah Ellen Williams, dau. of Amelia A. Williams.
   Henry S. Williams attests groom's age, bm. 5 Nov. 1849. m.
   6 Nov. 1849. ParReg A. Shel.
Snootz (Snoots), John & Susan Cordell. William McCoy attests
   ages, bm. 3 Feb. 1840. m. 6 Feb. 1840. Hauer. Shel.
Snow, John & Scivilla (Sevilla) Slates, widow. Emanuel Waltman,
   bm. 20 April 1833. m. 21 April 1832. Hauer. Shel.
Snow, Joseph & Louisa Ann Wiard. Michael Wiard attests ages, bm.
   31 March 1846. Shel.
Snyder, Conrad & Mary Jane Kinder. John Kidwell proves ages, wit.
   17 July 1850. MarReg.
Soloman, William & Heneritia Cullison. m. 19 Aug. 1809.
   Littlejohn.
Solomon, James W. & Caroline Dove. William Dove attests ages, bm.
   14 Jan. 1847. Cam.
Solomon, William & Henrietta Calleson. Jeremiah Callison attests
   groom's age, bm. 19 Sep. 1809.
Sopher, James & Sarah Daniel. m. 13 March 1817. T. Littleton.
Souder, George P. & Rebecca Fry. Joseph A. Fry proves ages, wit.
   21 March 1853. MarReg.
Souder, John & Mary M. Filler. Jacob Housholder attests bride's
   age, bm. 23 March 1838. m. 29 March 1838. Hauer. Shel.
Souder, Philip & Rebecca Frey. m. 8 April 1852 (1853). ParReg A.
Soumy, Michael, Ireland & Sally E. Handy, Maryland. m. 2 Oct.
   1838, at Belmont, Miss Mercer's. Adie.
Sowders, Michael & Elizabeth Adams. m. 30 July 1796. Littlejohn.

LOUDOUN COUNTY MARRIAGES

Sowers, Daniel A. & Martha Rogers. William Rogers attests ages,
bm. 27 May 1839. m. 11 June 1839. Herndon. Shel.
Sowers, Daniel H. (G.) & Frances Ann Oden (Owden), dau. of
Nathaniel S. Oden. William Sowers, bm. 9 Feb. 1841. Herndon.
Cam.
Spangler, Thornton & Elizabeth Stewart. Charles B. Wildman, bm.
27 Dec. 1849.
Sparrow, James & Elizabeth C. Virts, dau. of Conrad Virts, who
attests groom's age, bm. 8 Oct. 1849. Shel.
Spates, Benjamin & Betsy McCabe. m. 10 June 1808. Littlejohn.
Spates, Samuel & Nelly Hoggins. m. 3 Dec. 1805. Littlejohn.
Spates, Thomas & Mary E. Money. Nicholas Money attests bride's
age, bm. 15 Sep. 1842. Shel.
Spates, Thomas & Mary C. Massey. m. 22 Sep. 1842. Gover.
Speakes, Charles E. & Sarah Ann Crim. George W. McKim attests
ages, bm. 6 May 1840. m. 28 May 1840. Hauer. Shel.
Speaks, James & Sally Gheen. Henry Hatton attests bride's age,
bm. 19 May 1838. Cam.
Speaks, Thomas J. & Rachel A. Darr. William A. Grubb proves ages,
wit. 12 April 1852. MarReg.
Spenca, William & Margeret Hutchinson. m. 27 Feb. 1800. Littlejohn.
Spence, John & Anne Brookes. m. 8 Dec. 1806. Littlejohn.
Spence, William & Elizabeth Kirk, sister of Malcolm Kirk. Thomas
W. Dorman attests groom's age. Malcolm Kirk, bm. 26 Aug. 1830.
Hutchinson. Shel.
Spencer (?), Jacobus B. & Anna Booth; both single. By license.
m. 19 June 1821. ParReg A.
Spencer, James & Louisa Young. m. 10 Nov. 1825. Dunn. Shel.
Spencer, Joseph & Ann Harvin. m. 23 Sep. 1819. Dunn. Shel.
Spillman, John A. & Susan Rogers. William Rogers attests ages, bm.
16 Nov. 1842. Shel.
Spinks, Charles W. & Martha V. Farr. Wit: Samuel Shryock. 8 Dec.
1852. MarReg. m. 9 Dec. 1852. Gover.
Spinks, James M. & Sarah Ann Lovelace. Wit: John T. Lovelace.
4 July 1853. MarReg. m. 14 July 1853. Duncan.
Spoonogle, Jacob & Jane Buffington. m. 10 Aug. 1801. Littlejohn.
Spring, Andreas, son of Andreas Spring and wife & Maria Bletscher,
dau. of Henrich Bletscher and wife; both single. By license.
m. 21 Nov. 1816. ParReg A.
Spring, Casper & Elizabeth Slater, dau. of Jacob Slater, who
attests groom's age, bm. 4 Dec. 1809.
Spring, David & Mathey Glade; both single. By license. m. 11 May
1826. ParReg A.
Spring, Elias & Lydia Shaffer (Schaeffer), ward of John O.
Schooley, bm. Peter Myers attests groom's age. 1 Nov. 1847.
m. 14 Nov. 1847. Williard. Shel.
Spring, Elias & Mary Ann Elizabeth Stoneburner. Bride's father
consents, wit. Groom's age "taken for granted". 24 May 1852.
MarReg. m. 27 May 1852. Startzman.
Spring, Henrich & Maria Roff; both single. By license. m.
17 April 1828. ParReg A.
Spring, Henry & Charlotte Carnes (Carne). John Williams attests
ages, bm. 18 May 1838. m. 24 May 1838. Hauer. ParReg A. Shel.
Spring, Jacob & Elizabeth Folly, dau. of John Folly, bm.
29 Oct. 1799. Shel.

144

Spring, Jefferson & Sophia F. Etcher, dau. of Peter Etcher, wit.
9 May 1853. MarReg. m. 10 May 1853. Gover.

Spring, Johannes, son of Andreas Spring and wife & Maria Davis;
both single. By license. m. 14 March 1822. ParReg A.

Spring, Joseph, son of Andreas Spring and wife & Elisabetha
Blashill; both single. By license. m. 28 Nov. 1822. ParReg A.

Spring, Joseph I. & Mary Ann Stream, in Maryland. m. 3 Nov.
1842. ParReg A.

Spring, Michael, son of Andreas Spring and wife & Rahel Alt, dau.
of the late Wilhelm Alt and wife; both single. By license.
m. 23 June 1822. ParReg A.

Spring, Samuel A. & Mary (Milly) A. Streams. Peter Myers attests
ages, bm. 8 March 1842. m. 10 March 1842. Hauer. Shel.

Spring, William & Lydia Ann Compher, dau. of John Compher, who
attests groom's age, bm. 18 March 1844. m. 19 March 1844.
ParReg A. Shel.

Squires, John & Elizabeth Taylor. License: 3 Sep. 1762. FeeBk 3.

Squires, John & Sarah Jane Carter. William H. Squires attests
ages, bm. 6 Nov. 1849. Shel.

Sry, John Henry, brother of William Sry & Mary Martha Cordell,
dau. of Adam Cordell, wit. William Sry, wit. 8 Jan. 1851.
MarReg.

Stallings, John W. & Mary Ann Dickey. William Hixson attests
ages, bm. 10 March 1841. Shel.

Standley, Micajah, Rennand, N. C. & Barbara Walker. m. 10 Oct.
1765, Bush Creek, Maryland. FFMM.

Standley, William, Hanover County, Va. & Elizabeth Walker, dau.
of William and Sarah Walker, the former deceased, his widow
married. m. 28 Nov. 1758. FFMM.

Starkey, Isaac & Libbe Waters. m. 8 Aug. 1814. Littlejohn.

Starkey, Isaac, Jr., son of Isaac Starkey & Eliza McAtee, dau.
of Harrison McAtee. James Gibbs, bm. 8 Jan. 1845. m. 16 Jan.
1845. Massey. Shel.

Statcups, William & Reba. Dillon. m. 16 Jan. 1796. Littlejohn.

Staurtenberger, Samuel, single & Maria Schlotzer, widow. By
license. m. 24 Jan. 1828. ParReg A.

Stautzenberger, Jacob, son of Johannes Stautzenberger and wife &
Maria Kern, dau. of Widow Kern; both single. By license.
m. 2 Nov. 1820. ParReg A.

Steadman, David & Elizabeth Dawson. John B. Ratthee attests ages,
bm. 18 Feb. 1833. Shel.

Steadman, Thomas Jefferson & Amy Phillips. James Steadman attests
groom's age. Edmund Phillips attests bride's age, bm. 25 July
1835. Shel.

Steadman, Uriah & Louisa Carpenter. ___ Glascock attests groom's
age. B. R. Simpson attests bride's age, bm. 15 Sep. 1840.
Gover. Shel.

Stedman, James W. & Cassandra Orrison. Bride's mother consents in
writing. Groom's age taken for granted. 12 Jan. 1853. MarReg.
Duncan.

Steel, Lendonis (Lendorus) & Mary Moreland, dau. of William
Moreland, bm. 30 Aug. 1809. Cam.

Steele, John Thomas & Martina McKim. William Merchant, bm.
5 April 1848. Shel.

Steele, Lewis & Leah Hazard. James D. McPherson attests bride's
    age, bm. 18 May 1847.
Steele, Lewis & Matilda Workman, dau. of Isaac Workman, bm.
    13 May 1829.
Steer, Benjamin & Ann Everitt. m. 7 Sep. 1774. FFMM.
Steer, Isaac, Waterford & Elizabeth Bond. m. 25 Aug. 1824. FFMM.
Steer, John & Elenor Boothe, dau. of James Boothe, bm. 13 Dec.
    1809. m. 1808-1809. Mines.
Steer, John & Jane Beatey. m. 14 Oct. 1793. Littlejohn.
Steer, Jonah & Mary E. Brown, dau. of Ephraim Schooley and widow
    of John H. Brown, in 22nd year. Charles Binns, bm. 15 Dec.
    1836. Shel.
Steer, Joseph & Sarah Moore. m. 29 Feb. 1804. FFMM.
Steer, Samuel L. & Harriot A. Taylor. m. 21 Nov. 1832. FFMM.
Steinbrenner, Adam & Elisabeth Mannin; both single. By license.
    m. 19 Sep. 1816. ParReg A.
Steinbrenner, Henrich, son of Daniel Steinbrenner & Maria
    Magalena Lang, dau. of Johannes Lang and wife; both single.
    By license. m. 28 Aug. 1817. ParReg A.
Steinbrenner, Michael, son of Peter Steinbrenner & Elisabetha
    Blatscher; both single. By license. m. 6 May 1813. ParReg A.
Stephens, Banister P. & Elizabeth Carns. Warner W. Shackelford
    attests ages, bm. 2 Dec. 1837. Shel.
Stephens, Giles & Mary Binley. m. 11 Feb. 1793. Littlejohn.
Stephens, Leven & Harriot Read. m. 1807-1808. Mines.
Stephens, William & Catharine Dennis. Enos Farnsworth attests
    ages, bm. Bond not signed. 13 March 1845. Cam.
Stephens, William & Monica Claggett. m. 23 April 1793. Littlejohn.
Stephenson, Hiram & Ruth Sarah Walker. Lorenzo D. Walker attests
    ages, bm. 23 June 1840. m. 25 June 1840. Herndon. Shel.
Stephenson, Richard & Elizabeth Summers, spinster. License:
    9 May 1764. FeeBk 1.
Stephenson, Thomas & Nancy Green. John Green, bm. 25 Feb. 1799.
    Shel.
Stephenson, William Andrew & Mary D. Grayson. George Mason
    Grayson, bm. 30 May 1833. Shel.
Steum, Michal & Mary Doughstiner. m. 18 Oct. 1796. Littlejohn.
Stevens, Alexander John & Roxanna Burgess, dau. of Margaret
    Burgess. William Burgess, Warner W. Shackelford, bm.
    7 Oct. 1839. Shel.
Stevens, Jas. & Reba. Webb. m. 5 Nov. 1806. Littlejohn.
Stevens, John & Mary Steel. Warner W. Shackelford attests ages,
    bm. 9 April 1834. Cam.
Stevens, John B. & Sally Ogdon. m. 25 March 1800. Littlejohn.
Stevens, Joseph M., son of Edward and Elizabeth Stevens, the
    former deceased, latter of Harrisonburg, Va. & Susan J. Brown,
    dau. of Edwin C. and Betsey Brown, late of Middleburg. Wit:
    J. T. Johnson. 25 Oct. 1853. MarReg. m. 26 Oct. 1853.
    Ridgeway.
Stevens, Thomas & Ann Pursel (Purcel). Joseph Pursel attests
    bride's age, bm. 6 March 1809. m. 1808-1809. Mines.
Stevenson, Hiram & Ruth Sarah Walker. m. 25 June 1840. Herndon.
Stewart (Steward), David & Ann Cooper. m. 16 Aug. 1806. Littlejohn.
Stewart, David & Margaret Gardner. m. 7 Nov. 1816. Littlejohn.

Stewart, David & Rebecca Wright. m. 12 Aug. 1808. Littlejohn.
Stewart, J. E. & Sarah M. Calvert. Jesse Calvert proves ages, wit.
    13 Sep. 1852. MarReg.
Stewart, James & Mierlinday Rutter. m. 20 Dec. 1804. Williamson.
Stewart, James W. & Mary Jane Cornine (Carnine), dau. of Eden
    Cornine, who attests groom's age, bm. 8 May 1848. m. 11 May
    1848. Eggleston. Shel.
Stichler, Georg & Saloma Stautzenberger; both single. By license.
    m. 4 March 1817. ParReg A.
Stickle, George & Sarah Downs. m. 23 Dec. 1819. Williamson.
Stier, Enos & Catharina Demery; both single. By license. m. 8 Jan.
    1818. ParReg A.
Stier, Georg & Maria Demery; both single. By license. m. 23 March
    1815. ParReg A.
Stier, Johannes & Eva Iwens (?); both single. By license. m.
    14 April 1814. ParReg A.
Stier, Samuel & Sarah Russel (?); both single. By license. m.
    18 June 1812. ParReg A.
Stigler, Christoper & Barba. Brewer. m. May 1797. Littlejohn.
Stocks, Joshua & Elizabeth Ellen McCutchen, dau. of Samuel
    McCutchen, "disabled from a severe attack of rhumatism".
    Thomas Davis attests groom's age, bm. 27 April 1846. Shel.
Stocks, Mahlon & Matilda J. Daniel, dau. of David Daniel, who
    attests groom's age. George Townshend, bm. 11 Dec. 1847.
    Shel.
Stocks, Mahlon & Matilda T. Farrel. m. 16 Dec. 1847. Shuford.
Stokely, Nehemiah & Elizabeth Carnacle. m. 13 June 1807.
    Littlejohn.
Stone, Daniel & Sarah Hough. m. 30 May 1798. FFMM.
Stone, John & Rebecca Wolford. John Wolford, bm. 15 May 1848.
    m. 16 May 1848. Dulin.
Stone, Joseph & Ruth Tribby, dau. of Tamar Tribby. Reed Poulton,
    bm. 21 Jan. 1833. Shel.
Stone, Peter & Mary Hurst. m. 2 April 1802. Littlejohn.
Stone, Samuel S. & Elizabeth A. Frank. Josiah J. Janney attests
    groom's age. Thomas J. Marlow, bm. 10 March 1834. Shel.
Stone, Washington & Mary Houser (Howser), dau. of Abraham Houser.
    Jacob Houser, Thompson Stone, bm. 23 Jan. 1836. m. 26 Jan.
    1836. Monroe. Shel.
Stone, William & Jemima Roach. m. 14 April 1812. J. Littleton.
Stoneburner, Fredk. & Elizb. Razor (Rasor), dau. of George Rasor,
    bm. 26 March 1799. Littlejohn.
Stoneburner, Godfrey & Margaret Barr. m. 6 Aug. 1805. Williamson.
Stoneburner, J. C. & Charlotte E. Conard. Abner A. Conard proves
    ages, wit. 12 May 1851. MarReg.
Stoneburner, Jacob & Jane Campbell. Alexander Poland attests
    bride's age, bm. 5 July 1848. m. 6 July 1848. Gover. Shel.
Stoneburner, Jacob & Rebecca Lefever. m. 27 July 1815.
    Littlejohn.
Stoneburner, Peter & Cathrine Compher. John Compher, bm. 20 June
    1831. m. 24 July 1831. ParReg A. Shel.
Stonestreet, James E. & Amelia Tillett, ward of Thomas Moss, bm.
    11 Jan. 1830. Cam.

Stoutsenberger, Samuel & Mary Catherine Tooley, in Maryland.
   m. 6 July 1843. ParReg A.
Strahm, Johannes & Christina Willd; both single. By license.
   m. 2 Dec. 1817. ParReg A.
Stream (Streem), Elias & Mary Ann Waters, dau. of Jacob Waters,
   who attests groom's age, bm. 24 Sep. 1831. Shel.
Stream, William, widower & Pleasant M. Garvick, widow. By license.
   m. 6 March 1828. ParReg A.
Street, Bazil (Bazell) & Hannah Calor, widow. Harman Bilzer, bm.
   11 Dec. 1799. Littlejohn. Cam.
Strehm, Henrich & Catharina Meyern; both single. By license. m.
   18 Sep. 1817. ParReg A.
Strehm, Jacob & Sussana Phale, dau. of Jacob Phale and wife; both
   single. By license. m. 28 March 1824. ParReg A.
Stribling, Francis J. & Amanda Mary Ann Heaton, dau. of Jonathan
   Heaton, bm. Thomas W. Edward attests groom's age. 23 Oct.
   1838. Shel.
Stringfellow, Benjamin & Susannah Hamilton. Wit: Joseph H. Fred.
   15 June 1853. MarReg. m. 19 June 1853. Trott.
Strother, Robert & Caroline Howard. Hiram McVeigh, guardian, bm.
   9 Jan. 1837. m. 10 Jan. 1837. Morgan. Shel.
Strother, William & Catherine Florence, both colored. Simon
   Smale proves bride's age, wit. 5 Jan. 1852. MarReg.
Strother, William & Catherine Flowers. m. 11 Jan. 1852. Gover.
Stuart, J. E. & Sarah M. Calvert. m. 21 Sep. 1852. Gover.
Stuart, James & Mary Whistleman. John Francis attests bride's age,
   bm. 25 Feb. 1799. Shel.
Stub, John Thomas & Martena McKim. m. 5 April 1848. Gover.
Suddeath, John & Eliza Kelley. George W. Dorrell, bm. 11 Dec.
   1848. Shel.
Suddith, Brown & Ann Sophia Harris. Howard Freeman attests ages,
   bm. 20 Feb. 1850. Cam.
Sullivan, Arthur & Emily A. Simpson. George Turner attests bride's
   age, bm. 11 May 1844. Shel.
Sullivan, George & Elizabeth James. James Keene attests ages, bm.
   25 Feb. 1848. Cam.
Sullivan, George & Winney Bussell (Basset). Sampson J. Hutchison
   attests bride's age, bm. 20 Aug. 1817. m. 21 Aug. 1817.
   Williamson. Cam.
Sullivan, Murto & Elizabeth Elliot. m. 27 Jan. 1800. Littlejohn.
Sullivan, Patk. & Nancy Wilson. m. 20 April 1793. Littlejohn.
Sullivan, William B. & Susan King. William King attests groom's
   age, bm. 19 Feb. 1838. Shel.
Sumer, Jacob & Eliza Lewis. m. 12 Oct. 1848. Gover.
Sumer, John & Ann Dillon. m. 21 March 1807. Littlejohn.
Summers, Henry & Mary Wade. m. 19 April 1811. Littlejohn.
Summers, Jacob & Betsy Elmore. m. 27 Feb. 1816. Littlejohn.
Summers, Samuel & Sally Dailey. m. 21 Aug. 1813. Littlejohn.
Summers, William & Albinah Janney, dau. of Elisha Janney. m.
   9 Mary 1821. FFMM.
Sutherland, William & Eliza Beatty. William H. Beatty attests
   bride's age. John H. Beatty, bm. 21 June 1832. Shel.
Sutherland, William, Jr., son of William Sutherland & Elizabeth
   Lowe. William McNabb attests bride's age, bm. 10 Aug. 1829.

Swan, William & Reba Douglass. m. 1796. Littlejohn.

Swank, Phillip H. & Mary Catherine Williams. Henry S. Williams proves ages, wit. 20 Jan. 1851. MarReg. m. 23 Jan. 1851. ParReg A.

Swank, William & Mary C. Williams. m. 23 Jan. 1851. Startzman.

Swart, Henry S. & Elizabeth J. Jinkins. William Foley attests ages, bm. 21 May 1846. Cam.

Swart, Lafayette W. & Huldah Gulick. John Iden attests bride's age. James W. Taylor, bm. 1 Jan. 1846. Cam.

Swartz, Thornton & Margaret Venander. m. 9 May 1822. Dunn. Shel.

Swayne, John & Sarah H. Parkins. m. 5 Oct. 1814. FFMM.

Sweeney, Albert & Mary Lett. m. 1 May 1811. Littlejohn.

Sweeney, Hugh J. & Eliza Frits. Nathaniel W. Everhart attests ages, bm. 13 April 1846. Shel.

Syphert, Georg, widower & Sarah Senbauer, single. By license. m. 27 Jan. 1825. ParReg A.

Tabler, Elijah & Caroline A. Johnson, dau. of Robert Johnson, who attests groom's age, bm. 1 Nov. 1843. m. 3 Nov. 1843. ParReg A. Shel.

Tabler, Jacob & Nancy McMekin. m. 24 May 1805. Littlejohn.

Tabler, William J., son of John Tabler, of Washington City, D. C. & Catharine King. R. B. Jeffries attests bride's age, bm. 20 July 1844. m. 8 Aug. 1844. Massey. Shel.

Talbert, Henry & Ann Moxley. m. 12 Feb. 1810. Littlejohn.

Talbert (Talbot), John & Eliza Perry, dau. of Hezekiah Perry. Marshall B. Perry attests bride's age, bm. 21 March 1835. m. 24 March 1835. Herndon. Shel.

Talley, John & Jane Wheatley. m. 6 May 1819. Keyes.

Tally, Ebenezer & Lavinia Gregory. Samuel Buffington attests bride's age, bm. 1 Nov. 1833. Shel.

Tally, Isaac & Rachel Harper. m. 1809-1810. Mines.

Tally, John & Barbara Wolf (Wolff). James Sexton attests ages, bm. 26 Aug. 1839. m. 29 Sep. 1839. Hauer. Shel.

Tally, Jonah & Ann Gore. m. 11 Nov. 1833. Humphreys.

Tally, Josiah & Ann Gore, dau. of Mark Gore, bm. 11 Nov. 1833. Shel.

Tally, William & Catharine Harper. m. 1809-1810. Mines.

Talton, Maky & Plezy (Plesy) Hague, dau. of Amos Hague (Hage). Israel Phillips, bm. 20 Feb. 1809. Shel.

Tamer, George & Mary Simpson. m. 21 Aug. 1817. Williamson.

Tandy, Moses & Mary Herod. m. 18 Sep. 1815. Littlejohn.

Tarbut, James & Maria Umphys. m. 1 Feb. 1835. Baker.

Tarleton, James & Elizabeth Johnston. m. 9 Nov. 1820. Williamson.

Tarleton, William, son of Mack Tarleten & Catherine Reed, dau. of Sarah Ritzer. William Bitzer, bm. 11 Oct. 1832. Shel.

Tarlton, Marpa & Amelia Vermillion. m. 12 Sep. 1825. Tuston.

Tauperman, John & Sarah Wilson. m. 15 July 1821. Harvey.

Tavender, George & Martha Nixon. m. 9 Nov. 1796. Littlejohn.

Tavener, George H. & Mary Ewers. Samuel A. Jackson attests bride's age, bm. 22 Aug. 1836. Shel.

Tavener, Isaac & Cathrine Silcot. m. 2 Aug. 1800. Littlejohn.

Tavener, Jesse & Cecilia Morris. m. 25 March 1830. Baker.

Tavener, Jonah & Sarah Jane Baldwin. m. 21 Aug. 1838. Broadus.

Tavener, Joseph & Nancy White. m. 5 Feb. 1798. Littlejohn.

Tavener, Loudon & Christinea Jackson. m. 21 Aug. 1823. Dagg.
Tavener, Mahlon & Susan Ann Nichols. William Tavener attests
    groom's age. Jonah Nichols, bm. 2 April 1842. Shel.
Tavenner, David P. (J.) & Martha A. Kile. George W. Bowman
    proves bride's age, wit. 22 May 1851. MarReg. m. 28 May 1851.
    Eggleston.
Tavenner, George N. & Elizabeth Hann, dau. of Matthias Hann, bm.
    Eli Tavenner attests groom's age. 20 Jan. 1836. m. 26 Jan.
    1836. Morgan. Shel.
Tavenner, Jesse & Cecelia Morris, dau. of Mahlon Morris, bm.
    8 March 1830. Shel.
Tavenner, John & Rebecca M. Nichols. Levi Tavenner attests bride's
    age, bm. 29 Dec. 1838. Shel.
Tavenner, John & Usee Drake, ward of John Hesser, bm. 11 Jan. 1830.
    Shel.
Tavenner, Jonah & Pleasant Warner. m. 1821-1822. Mines.
Tavenner, Jonah & Sarah Jane Baldwin, dau. of Ruth Baldwin.
    Isaac B. Baldwin, bm. 13 Aug. 1838. Shel.
Tavenner, Jonathan & Sarah Elizabeth Brown. m. 31 Oct. 1822. T.
    Littleton.
Tavenner, Levi & Susan Young. William Young, bm. 25 Feb. 1839.
    m. 28 Feb. 1839. Herndon. Shel.
Tavenner, Mahlon & Mary Ann Brown, dau. of James Brown. Jonathan
    Tavener attests groom's age. Fielding Tavenner, bm. 2 Nov.
    1831. m. 1 Nov. 1831. Gover. Shel.
Tavenner, Nimrod, son of Eli Tavenner & Sarah Grimes, dau. of
    George Grimes. Eli Tavenner, George Grimes, bm. 26 Nov.
    1838. Shel.
Tavenner, Richard & Catherine McCarty. m. 1821-1822. Mines.
Tavenner, Richard & Sidney Copeland. Eli Hunt attests bride's
    age, bm. 25 Oct. 1836. Shel.
Tavenner, Richard B. & Lucy E. Blaker. A. Francis attests bride's
    age. James A. Cox attests groom's age, bm. 1 Jan. 1844. Shel.
Tavenner, Samuel, son of Richard Tavenner & Sarah Jane McCray,
    dau. of James McCray. John Purcell, bm. 12 Nov. 1836. Shel.
Tavenner, Samuel H. & Ann Maria King, dau. of William King.
    James D. McPherson attests groom's age, bm. 7 Oct. 1844. Cam.
Tavenner, William & Alcinda Jane Silcott. 26 Aug. 1850. MarReg.
Tavenner, William, son of Richard Tavenner & Malinda Garner.
    Arthur Garner, bm. 18 April 1833. Shel.
Tawner, Jacob & Catherine Courtsman. m. 14 Feb. 1796. Littlejohn.
Taylor, Andrew J. & Emily E. French, dau. of Lewis French, who
    attests groom's age, bm. 9 Feb. 1850. Shel.
Taylor, Benjamin & May Owens. m. 14 Jan. 1805. Littlejohn.
Taylor, Benjamin F. & Nancy Taylor. Albert Heaton attests ages,
    bm. 14 Feb. 1829.
Taylor, Benjamin F. & Sarah Morris, dau. of Mahlon Morris, bm.
    13 Jan. 1835. Shel.
Taylor, Bernard, son of Timothy Taylor, late of New Town, Bucks
    County, Pa., deceased & Sarah Smith, dau. of Henry Smith,
    deceased. m. 15 Nov. 1792. FFMM.
Taylor, Charles N. & Sally W. Craven. Bride's father consents.
    3 May 1851. MarReg. m. 6 May 1851. Herndon.
Taylor, Daniel E., widower & Alsinda McKim, single. m. 1 March
    1832. ParReg A.

Taylor, Franklin, son of Jane Taylor, widow & Mary E. Davis, dau. of Elizabeth Davis, widow. Wit: William F. Davis. 5 Dec. 1853. MarReg. m. 8 Dec. 1853. Hirst.

Taylor, George W. & Ann Eliza White. m. 29 Nov. 1824. Tuston.

Taylor, Griffin & Susan Chilton. m. 18 Aug. 1827. McCan.

Taylor, Henry S. & Hannah I. Brown, dau. of William and Hannah Brown. m. 30 May 1827. FFMM.

Taylor, Ignatius & Mary Battson. m. 14 Dec. 1819. Williamson.

Taylor, James W. & Elizabeth Swart. John Moore attests ages, bm. 15 April 1839. Herndon. Shel.

Taylor, Jesse & Sarah Smith. m. 3 April 1811. Littlejohn.

Taylor, Jesse B. & Miranda Smith, dau. of James Smith, who proves groom's age, wit. 22 June 1852. MarReg. m. 24 June 1852. Bettinger.

Taylor, Jonathan & Lydia Brown. m. 20 Nov. 1822. FFMM.

Taylor, Joseph & Ann Fritts. William Fritts attests bride's age, bm. 13 Sep. 1847.

Taylor, Joseph & Elizabeth Skinner. m. 10 Sep. 1807. Littlejohn.

Taylor, Joseph & Margaret Ann Fritts. m. 13 Sep. 1847. Dulin.

Taylor, Lewis & Ruth W. Bradfield. Timothy W. Taylor attests bride's age, bm. 6 Nov. 1843. Shel.

Taylor, Mahlon & Amanda Gore, dau. of Thomas Gore, bm. 15 Dec. 1836. Shel.

Taylor, Samuel B. & Sarah E. Hogue, dau. of Elizabeth Hoge. Benjamin F. Taylor, bm. 15 Nov. 1834. Shel.

Taylor, Samuel E. & Alcinda McKim, dau. of James McKim, bm. 27 Feb. 1832. Shel.

Taylor, Stacy & Mary Hollingsworth. m. 29 May 1828. Tippett.

Taylor, Stacy & Ruth Beans. m. 23 Sep. 1802. Littlejohn.

Taylor, William & Ann Ansley. m. 18 Dec. 1798. Littlejohn.

Taylor, William & Elizabeth Violett. m. 19 Dec. 1816. Littlejohn.

Taylor, William & Euphamy Brown. Aaron Divine attests bride's age. Mahlon Bewley, bm. 3 June 1809. Littlejohn.

Taylor, William & Margaret Perry, dau. of Hezekiah Perry. Aaron Chamblin attests groom's age. Eskridge H. Torbert, bm. 3 March 1830.

Taylor, William & Mary R. Timms, dau. of Jesse Timms. Charles G. Eskridge, bm. 14 April 1832. Shel.

Taylor, Yardley & Hannah Brown, dau. of Richard Brown. m. 8 April 1818. FFMM.

Tebbs, Algernon S. & Julia E. Coleman. John A. Waggerman, bm. 23 Dec. 1835. White. Shel.

Tebbs, Charles B. & H. Fanny Cockerill. T. W. Edwards proves bride's age, wit. 18 Nov. 1850. MarReg.

Tebbs, Foushee & Maria Brown. Edwin C. Brown attests ages, bm. 13 Sep. 1847. Roszel. Shel.

Tebbs, Samuel I. & Hannah Binns. m. 17 March 1825. Burch.

Tebbs, Thomas F. & Margaret Hannah D. Binns. m. 6 Oct. 1818. Dunn. Shel.

Templar, John & Nancy Flanagan. m. 11 Feb. 1805. Littlejohn.

Templar, Stacy & Rachel Pettit. m. 30 Dec. 1806. Littlejohn.

Templar, William & Ann Taitipoe. m. 13 July 1803. Littlejohn.

Templer, James & Balsora Gregg, dau. of Thomas Gregg, who attests groom's age, bm. 3 April 1830. Shel.

Templer, Thomas, son of James Templer & Jane Lowe. Thomas Lowe
   attests bride's age, bm. 25 Dec. 1809. m. 1809-1810. Mines.
Terman, Samuel & Ann Elizabeth Dunn. William D. North attests
   ages, bm. 10 June 1833. Shel.
Thair, John & Sarah Russell. m. 1821-1822. Mines.
Thatcher, Daniel & Louisa Palmer, ward of George H. Alder, bm.
   Calvin Thatcher attests groom's age. 11 June 1829.
Thatcher, William & Mary Hewes. m. 1 Dec. 1807. Littlejohn.
Thomas, Aquila & Mary Broner. m. 12 Jan. 1802. Littlejohn.
Thomas, Chandler & Jane Ann Brady, dau. of Emily Brady. Joshua
   Nichols, bm. 12 Feb. 1849. Shel.
Thomas, Enoch & Laura Ellen Jennins (Jennings), free persons of
   color. Bride's brother consents "her next & only friend
   mother & father dead". 29 Dec. 1851. MarReg. m. 30 Dec. 1851.
   Smith.
Thomas, Fielder & Violet Gest, dau. of John Gist, who attests
   groom's age, bm. 2 Feb. 1809. Littlejohn.
Thomas, Griffith E. & Rebecca B. Wright. William G. Wright, bm.
   23 Nov. 1838. Shel.
Thomas, Herod & Mary Ann Robinson. Thomas Littleton attests ages,
   bm. 12 June 1832. m. 28 June 1832. Baker. Shel.
Thomas, Jefferson & Mary Bradfield. m. 29 April 1824. T. Littleton.
Thomas, Jesse & Eliza Williams. License: 22 Feb. 1814. T.
   Littleton.
Thomas, John & Margaret Dailey. m. 24 Sep. 1810. Littlejohn.
Thomas, John & Martha C. Carter, dau. of Samuel Carter, bm.
   17 Oct. 1849. Cam.
Thomas, John H. & Mary Fair. William Lacy attests bride's age.
   John Lowe attests groom's age, bm. 11 Aug. 1845. Shel.
Thomas, John W. & Emily Hamilton. Owen Hamilton proves bride's
   age, wit. 17 May 1851. MarReg. m. 22 May 1851. Leachman.
Thomas, Joseph & Ruth Janney. m. 21 June 1808. Littlejohn.
Thomas, Joseph & Sarah Worthington. Craven Osburn attests ages,
   bm. 28 Sep. 1829.
Thomas, Leonard & Elisabeth Heckmannin, dau. of Peter Heckmann
   and wife; both single. By license. m. 6 Aug. 1818. ParReg A.
Thomas, Leven & Rebecca Phillips, ward of John Graham, bm.
   Joseph Thomas attests groom's age. 25 May 1833. Shel.
Thomas, Maaziah & Elizabeth Furr, dau. of Enoch Furr. Jeremiah C.
   Furr attests groom's age, bm. 8 June 1829.
Thomas, Mahlon & Mary Carter. Bride's father consents, wit.
   5 Dec. 1850. MarReg. m. 10 Dec. 1850. Dodge.
Thomas, Moses & Ann Fox, dau. of Joseph Fox, bm. Benjamin D.
   Cockran attests groom's age. 1 Jan. 1835. Cam.
Thomas, Owen & Cecelia H. Beans. Wit: Humphrey Beans. 8 Dec.
   1852. MarReg.
Thomas, Philip & Sarah R. Bradfield. m. 21 March 1817. T.
   Littleton.
Thomas, Phinehas & Mary Carpenter. m. 15 June 1808. Fristoe.
Thomas, Robert W. & Rebecca J. Wright, dau. of Mahalah Burk,
   late wife of Joseph Wright, deceased. William Henry Thomas
   attests groom's age, bm. 4 Aug. 1849. Shel.
Thomas, Samuel & Elisabetha (Betsey) Mahoney (Mehonny). John
   Mahoney, bm. 19 May 1829. m. 21 May 1829. ParReg A.

LOUDOUN COUNTY MARRIAGES

Thomas, Silas & Elizabeth A. Nickens. m. 14 Feb. 1853. Smith.
Thomas, William & Elizabeth Hanley, dau. of David Hanley, who
attests groom's age and states he "is upward of 21 years of
age from the fact of his having been bound out and being
discharged from his apprenticeship and has for several years
been doing business for himself - ", bm. 25 Nov. 1840.
Cadden. Shel.
Thomas, William & Elizabeth Stewart. Richard Thomas, bm. 3 June
1840. Shel.
Thompkins, Benjamin & Sarah Rinker. m. 9 Oct. 1805. Littlejohn.
Thompson, Edward F., son of Alcano and Sarah Thompson, 22 years,
b. Loudoun & Annette Alexander, dau. of John and Annette
Alexander, 19 years, b. Prince William. Bride's father consents
in writing. David Alexander proves groom's age, wit. 3 Sep.
1853. MarReg. m. 8 Sep. 1853. Gover.
Thompson, George & Rebecca Wilson. m. 17 Jan. 1820. Williamson.
Thompson, George W. & Sarah Pursell. Benjamin Thompson, bm.
20 Dec. 1832. Shel.
Thompson, Hugh S. & Ruth H. Clendening. James H. Clendening
attests ages, bm. 23 Feb. 1848. Shel.
Thompson, Israel & Francis T. Wilson. m. 31 Dec. 1822. Williamson.
Thompson, Israel & Sarah Hogue, dau. of Francis Hogue. m. 2 July
1778. FFMM.
Thompson, Israel H. & Ann Hough. m. 29 Feb. 1804. FFMM.
Thompson, James & Emily Smith. Solomon Hibbs proves groom's age,
wit. 27 Jan. 1852. MarReg. Gover.
Thompson, John C. & Sarah Adams. Landon Worthington attests
bride's age, bm. Alfred Works, bm. 27 Oct. 1838. Shel.
Thompson, John E. & Mary Farris. m. 1807-1808. Mines.
Thompson, John F. & Lucinda Jones. James W. Jones attests ages,
bm. 13 Oct. 1845. Shel.
Thompson, John F. & Mary E. Kidwell. Joshua Kidwell attests ages,
bm. 29 Nov. 1843. Shel.
Thompson, John H. & Nancy Tavenner, dau. of Joseph Tavenner.
Elisha Janny attests groom's age, bm. 26 Dec. 1837. Shel.
Thompson, John L. & Lucinda Jones. m. 14 Oct. 1845. ParReg B.
Thompson, Lewis & Elizabeth Ann Burke. John Orrison attests
bride's age, bm. 28 Jan. 1839. Shel.
Thompson, Lorenzo D. & Mary Frances Feagins, ward of Wilfred F.
Feagins, bm. 9 Dec. 1839. Shel.
Thompson, Lorenzo D. & Ruth Ann Riley. Isaac Ryley proves bride's
age, wit. 10 Oct. 1851. MarReg. m. 9 Nov. 1851. ParReg A.
Thompson, Robert I. C. & Eliza Steadman. Parkerson L. Lott
attests ages, bm. 28 Jan. 1834. Shel.
Thompson, Samuel & Sarah Tribby. Jesse Tribby attests ages, bm.
5 Jan. 1829.
Thompson, Samuel P. & Elizabeth Hough. Bernard Hough attests
bride's age. Samuel Zimmerman attests groom's age, bm.
17 June 1839. Shel.
Thompson, Shadrack & Elizabeth Payne. John William Payne attests
ages, bm. 10 Oct. 1835. Shel.
Thompson, Thomas & Jemima Tracey. m. 22 Dec. 1796. Littlejohn.
Thompson, Thomas & Mary Hamilton. m. 14 Sep. 1816. Littlejohn.

Thompson, Thomas Edwin & Margaret M. A. Williams. m. 22 June
1832. Dorsey.
Thompson, Waters & Hulda A. Rusk. John James Rusk attests ages,
bm. 17 Jan. 1849.
Thompson, William M. & Mildred F. Ball. m. 26 Nov. 1820. Dunn.
Shel.
Thornton, Abraham & Eleanor Carter, dau. of Samuel Carter; free
people of colour. Thomas Littleton, bm. 11 June 1833. Shel.
Thornton, Bushrod Washington Muse & Louisa Jackson. Seth Smith,
bm. 10 Oct. 1843. Shel.
Thornton, Charles H. & Ann Eliza Adams, dau. of Henry Adams.
Meriweather T. Ashby, bm. 21 July 1835. m. 30 July 1835.
Morgan. Shel.
Thornton, James & Octavia Vanhorne. Jesse McConeaha attests
bride's age, bm. 4 Dec. 1832. Shel.
Thornton, James Madison & Sarah Catherine Hicks. James Philip
Thornton attests groom's age. Abraham Hiskett attests bride's
age, bm. 22 June 1833. Shel.
Thrasher, Archibald & Emily Jane Alder, dau. of Latimer Allder.
William Alder, bm. 30 Dec. 1837. Shel.
Thrasher, Elias, Jr. & Elisabeth Ritsche; both single. By license.
m. 5 Nov. 1818. ParReg A.
Thrasher, Luther A. & Elizabeth Margaret Cooper, ward of John
Souder, bm. 16 March 1839. Shel.
Thresher, Johannes & Herieta Gill; both single. By license. m.
31 Aug. 1824. ParReg A.
Thrift, Sanderson & Mary B. Shreve. John W. Thrift attests
groom's age. Benjamin Shreve, bm. 21 Oct. 1844. Shel.
Throckmorton, James B. & Eliza Jane Chamblin, dau. of Mason
Chamblin. Groom's guardian consents, wit. 12 May 1851.
MarReg. m. 2 June 1851. Herndon.
Throckmorton, John A. & Mary A. Tutt. N. C. Mason attests ages,
bm. 14 March 1839. Shel.
Thruston, Alfred B., Washington, D. C. & Fannie C. (B.) Gordon.
H. D. Magill, bm. 25 Aug. 1845. m., at house of Dr. Magill,
Leesburg. Adie. Shel.
Tidball, Josiah & Eliza Carter. m. 18 May 1809. Dunn.
Tigh, Tarrence & Anne Poston. Leonard Poston, bm. 7 Nov. 1796.
Tikes, Abner & Mary Nefus. m. 10 Jan. 1800. Littlejohn.
Tillet, James & Hannah Moss. m. 1 April 1805. Littlejohn.
Tillett, Edward & Elizabeth Pearson. Samuel A. Tillett states
groom's "in his 23rd year". John Pearson attests ages, bm.
18 July 1848. Shel.
Tillett, Edward & Susan Ball. John B. Ball attests ages, bm.
24 March 1830. Shel.
Tillett, Giles E. & Sarah Gregg. Samuel Lamb proves ages, wit.
18 June 1851. MarReg. m. 19 June 1851. Gover.
Tillett, John L. & Harriet Ann Poulton. Reed Poulton, bm.
13 Nov. 1841. Shel.
Tillett, John L. & Joanna M. Davis. Bride's mother consents in
writing. Edgar Jarvis proves groom's age, wit. 4 July 1853.
MarReg. m. 7 July 1853. Duncan.
Tillett, Samuel & Pleasant Acten. m. 7 Oct. 1815. Littlejohn.

LOUDOUN COUNTY MARRIAGES

Tillett, Samuel A. & Caroline S. Dennis. Elias Pool attests
   groom's age. Joseph S. Harden attests bride's age, bm. 1 June
   1841. Cam.
Timms, Henry & Castara Hesser, dau. of Nancy Marcus. John L.
   Parsons, bm. 19 Sep. 1836. Shel.
Timms, John & Elizabeth Emory. Jacob Arnold attests bride's age,
   bm. 14 Dec. 1833. Shel.
Timms, Joseph & Amelia (Emely) Presgraves. James Giles attests
   bride's age, bm. 21 Jan. 1799. Shel.
Timson, Henrich & Nancy Aellen; both single. By license. m.
   22 Feb. 1821. ParReg A.
Tinsman, Enoch & Elizabeth Alexander. Squire Lee attests ages, bm.
   6 May 1844. Shel.
Tinsman, Ludwell, son of Nancy Tinsman, who states groom's not of
   lawful age and has no father living & Geraldine Slack, dau.
   of Sigismunda Slack, who states bride's not of lawful age and
   has no father living. James Slack, bm. 2 July 1840. Cadden.
   Shel.
Tinsman, Samuel & Mary Triplett. 'George Tinsman attests bride's
   age, bm. 12 Aug. 1843. m. 17 Aug. 1843. Leachman. Shel.
Tintsman, Philip & Rebecca Huff. m. 8 Nov. 1810. T. Littleton.
Tippett, Samuel & Sarah Jane Ropp (Ross). Nelson Everhart proves
   ages, wit. 20 Dec. 1850. MarReg. m. 24 Dec. 1851. Chenoweth.
Tipton, Joshua & Harriet Lang. John Lang attests bride's age, bm.
   7 Feb. 1831. Shel.
Titus, Jeremiah & Susan Goodheart. John Goodheart attests ages,
   bm. 1 Oct. 1838. Shel.
Titus, Them & Catharine Smith. m. 1807-1808. Mines.
Titus, Tunis & Mary Ann Hunter. John Hunter attests bride's age.
   William Titus, bm. 15 Sep. 1840. Shel.
Titus, Tunis & Sarah Purdum. m. 15 Aug. 1803. Littlejohn.
Titus, William & Mary Jane Brown. Bride's mother consents. Joseph
   Cox, bm., body of bond. Tunis Titus, signs bond. 1 April
   1839. Shel.
Tolle, George & Sarah Crupper. m. 1 Dec. 1803. Williamson.
Tomlin, George Franklin & Susan Starkey, dau. of Isaac Starkey,
   wit. Groom's age taken for granted. 8 April 1852. MarReg.
Tomlinson, Phineas & Jemima Watts. m. 22 Dec. 1825. Dunn. Shel.
Tomlinson, Solomon & Sarah Silcott. m. 30 March 1816. Davis.
Tomlinson, Thomas & Achsah Iden. m. 16 Dec. 1807. Dunn.
Tomlison, William & Caroline Campbell. m. 14 Feb. 1822. Gilmore.
Torbert, James & Maria Humphrey. William Settle attests bride's
   age, bm. 27 Jan. 1835. Shel.
Torreyson, Isaac & Mary Baldwin. William Torreyson attests
   groom's age. John Baldwin attests bride's age, bm. 30 March
   1829. m. 2 April 1829. Williamson.
Torrison, John William & Rebeca Smith. m. 5 Dec. 1851. Chenoweth.
Torrison, Lewis & Rebecca Day. "The parties are widower & widow."
   Washington Jarvis, bm. 21 Feb. 1845. Shel.
Torrison, William & Mary W. Birkby. m. 23 Dec. 1828. Tippett.
Torry, James & Margaret Alexander W. Allen. m. 5 March 1801.
   Allen.
Touperman, John & Sarah Wilson. m. 15 July 1821. Harvey.

LOUDOUN COUNTY MARRIAGES

Towperman, Andrew & Elizabeth Moffett. Moses Wilson attests ages,
    bm. 24 June 1830. Williamson. Shel.
Tracy, George N. & Elizabeth A. Copeland. Thomas Tracy attests
    ages, bm. 29 Nov. 1844. Shel.
Trahern, James & Francis Ann Overfield, dau. of Anna Overfield.
    William McPherson, bm. 12 Dec. 1842. Shel.
Trail, Malotha & Martha Ann Saunders. Bride's mother consents in
    writing. Groom's age taken for granted. 29 April 1852. MarReg.
    Duncan.
Tramell, Gerrand & Ester Templar. m. 17 May 1808. Littlejohn.
Trammel, Thomas & Mary Catharine Jenkins. William Cooper attests
    ages, bm. C. C. McIntire, J.P., bm. 5 April 1839. m. 9 April
    1839. ParReg A. Shel.
Trayhern, James F. & Sally Ann Caldwell. Samuel B. T. Caldwell,
    bm. 7 June 1847. Shel.
Traysons, Silas H. & Sarah G. Wilden. m. 11 July 1842. Gover.
Trebee, Thomas & Mary Dodd. m. 23 April 1796. Littlejohn.
Trenary, James Francis & Letetia Chapell, dau. of James Chappel,
    under 21 years. W. G. Trenary attests groom's age, bm.
    24 May 1848. Krebbs. Shel.
Trenary, Richard & Matilda Settle. Nelson Settle attests ages.
    Robert Cunningham attests ages, bm. 2 Sep. 1834. Shel.
Trenay, Jonas & Nelly Wildman. Christopher Howser attests ages,
    bm. 12 Jan. 1830.
Tribby, Asahel & Catherine Statler. m. 21 Jan. 1813. Henkle.
Tribby, Thomas & Mary McFarlin. m. 2 Sep. 1813. Littlejohn.
Tribby, Townsend & Jane Ann Copeland. Reed Poulton, guardian of
    groom, attests bride's age, bm. 12 Feb. 1844. Shel.
Tridibo, William & Lowisa Venzel (Venzel); both single. m.
    14 Nov. 1830. ParReg A.
Tridipo, William & Louisa Winsel, dau. of George Winsel, who
    attests groom's age, bm. 8 Nov. 1830. Shel.
Trillett, John S. & JoAnna M. Davis. m. 7 July 1853. Duncan.
Trinay, Jonas & Nelly Wildman. m. 14 Jan. 1830. Tippett.
Triplet, Barr & Pamelia Chinn. m. 26 Nov. 1816. Williamson.
Triplett, Joel & Elizabeth Triplett. m. 17 Nov. 1820. Dagg.
Triplett, John & Elizabeth McIntire. m. 29 Nov. 1804. Littlejohn.
Triplett, Nathaniel & Mary Luckett, widow. William Butler, bm.
    21 Dec. 1809. Littlejohn.
Triplett, Nimrod & Susanna E. Saffer, dau. of William Saffer.
    John W. Saffer attests groom's age. William Gilmore, bm.
    14 May 1840. Cam.
Triplett, Reuben & Eleanor Williams. James Williams attests
    bride's age, bm. 16 March 1833. Shel.
Triplett, Richard & Sarah A. Tavenner, dau. of James Tavenner,
    who attests groom's age, bm. 19 Dec. 1836. Shel.
Triplett, Simon & Martha Lane, spinster. License: 20 April 1764.
    FeeBk 3.
Triplett, Uriel & Sarah Ann Fred, dau. of Elizabeth Fred. Joseph
    H. Fred, bm. 10 Feb. 1834. Shel.
Triplett, William & Frances Ann French. m. 1 Feb. 1820. Dagg.
Triplett, William & Mary James, widow. Edward Hammatt, bm.
    24 Oct. 1839. Roszel. Shel.

156

Trittapo, Thomas & Sarah Hiffner, in Maryland. m. 9 May 1833.
    ParReg A.
Trittepo, Michael & Margaret Fawley. m. 17 Jan. 1833. Hauer.
    ParReg A.
Trittipo, Michael & Margaret Fawley. Henry Fawley, bm. 14 Jan.
    1833. Shel.
Trittipo, John & Rachel K. Howell. m. 27 March 1845. ParReg A.
Trittipo, Samuel & Mary Frye. Andrew Frye attests bride's age,
    bm. 28 May 1836. m. May 1836. Campbell. Shel.
Troute, George & Sarah Fisher. Josiah Moffett, bm. 10 Dec. 1809.
    m. 1808-1809. Mines.
Trundle, Horatio & Sarah S. Craven, dau. of Sarah Craven, her
    guardian. Alfred Belt attests groom's age, bm. 1 Sep. 1830.
    m. 2 Sep. 1830. Littlejohn. Shel.
Trussel, Moses Buckner & Sarah Elizabeth Young. m. 5 Aug. 1847.
    Herndon.
Trussell, Baylis, son of Moses Trussell & Angelina Chamblin, dau.
    of Aaron Chamblin, bm. 19 Aug. 1834. Shel.
Trussell, Moses Buckner & Sarah E. Young. David Lewis Beall
    attests groom's age. George Young, bm. 31 July 1847. Shel.
Trussell, Nimrod & Susan Fleming. George Fleming attests ages,
    bm. 2 Nov. 1835. m. 2 Nov. 1835. Baker. Shel.
Tucker, Andrew & Elisebeth Niswanger. m. 28 Feb. 1810. T.
    Littleton.
Tucker, Benjamin & Peggy Kirby. m. 22 Oct. 1807. Littlejohn.
Tucker, Daniel & Rebecca Yound. m. 2 Jan. 1796. Littlejohn.
Tucker, John & Penelope Thompson. m. 21 July 1794. Littlejohn.
Tucker, John Randolph & Laura Holmes Powell, dau. of H. B. Powell.
    Henry L. Brooke attests groom's age, bm. 5 Oct. 1848. Cam.
Tucker, William & Ellen Underwood. m. 16 June 1825. Burch.
Tumblin, Reubin & Catharine Smallwood. Ezekiel Chambling attests
    ages, bm. 14 March 1809. m. 1808-1809. Mines.
Tuomey, Michael & Sarah E. Handy. George Adie, bm. 2 Oct. 1838.
    Cam.
Turley, Alexander & Susan Darne. m. 8 Dec. 1812. Littlejohn.
Turley, Edmond & Elizabeth Edelen. William Elgin, bm. 29 Nov.
    1799. Cam.
Tourmisteed, John Lewis & Amelia Garrett. Adam Cordell attests
    ages, bm. 28 Oct. 1843. Shel.
Turner, Jesse & Margaret Sanders. m. 12 Aug. 1805. Littlejohn.
Turner, John & Juliet Ann Wildman. David Brown attests ages, bm.
    13 Nov. 1840. Shel.
Turner, Michael, Jr. & Elizabeth Betts. Andrew Bell, bm. 29 Oct.
    1799. Littlejohn.
Turner, Reed & Sarah E. Dailey, dau. of Aaron Dailey, who proves
    groom's age, wit. 12 Jan. 1852. MarReg. m. 13 Jan. 1852.
    Smith.
Turner, Richard H. & Ann Eliza Simpson, dau. of Catharine
    Simpson. A. T. M. McCarty attests groom's age, bm. 15 Jan.
    1850. m. 17 Jan. 1850. Herndon. Shel.
Turnipseed, John L. & Amelia Garrot. m. 3 Nov. 1843. ParReg A.
Tutt, Charles & Ann M. Chichester. m. 14 April 1806. Littlejohn.
Tuttle, William & Elizabeth Breading. m. 8 June 1807. Littlejohn.
Ullum, Jacob & Elizabeth Water, dau. of Jacob Water. m. 21 Dec.
    1834. ParReg A.

Ullum, Samuel & Elizabeth Davis, dau. of Anthony Davis, who
    attests groom's age, bm. 10 Aug. 1849. m. 4 June 1849.
    ParReg A.
Ulum, Josiah & Elizabeth Waters, dau. of Jacob Waters. Samuel
    Waltman, bm. 15 Dec. 1834. m. 21 Dec. 1834. Hauer. Shel.
Umbaugh, George & Catherine Cross. Fielder Cross proves ages, wit.
    30 Oct. 1851. MarReg. Gover.
Underwood, Jackson & Caroline Tarlton. Burr A. Tarlton attests
    ages, bm. 21 Nov. 1844. Shel.
Underwood, Joseph & Harriett Scott. Jacob Ekman attests ages, bm.
    12 Jan. 1844. Shel.
Unglesbee (Ungleby), Thomas & Mahala Kendall (Kindle). John
    Smitley attests ages, bm. 10 Aug. 1849. m. 12 Aug. 1829.
    ParReg A.
Updike, Edon & Kezia Potts. George Purcell attests ages, bm.
    9 March 1829.
Updike, Enos, guardian of bride & Barsena White. Landon C.
    Carter attests groom's age. John Wornel, bm. 10 Aug. 1829.
Urton, John & Nancy Weadon. Horatio Drish attests ages, bm.
    22 Jan. 1841. Shel.
Urton, Nathan & Catherine Urton. m. 19 Jan. 1815. Williamson.
Usselmann, Michael & Elisabetha Palmerin. m. 17 May 1786.
    ParReg A.
Vail, Nathan & Ann Gregg. Smith Gregg attests ages, bm. 10 July
    1830. Shel.
Vananda, Lawson & Susan Clapper. Henry Clapper attests bride's
    age, bm. 28 Nov. 1831. Shel.
Vanderholf (Vanderhoof), Henry & Susan Ann Havenner. Wit: William
    Havenner. 21 June 1853. MarReg. m. 22 June 1853. Duncan.
Vandevanter, Armistead M. & Patience Taylor. Timothy Taylor, bm.
    5 May 1845. m. 6 May 1845. Massey. Shel.
Vandevanter, Fenton & Mary A. L. Saunders, dau. of Benton
    Saunders, bm. Washington Vandevanter attests groom's age.
    6 Dec. 1834. Shel.
Vandevanter, Gabriel, Col. & Jane Cecelia Heaton, sister of Dr.
    Decator Heaton. John T. W. Heaton attests bride's age, bm.
    10 April 1843. m. 12 April 1843, at house of bride's brother.
    Adie. Shel.
Vandevanter, Gabriel & Mary E. Braden, dau. of John Braden, bm.
    9 Nov. 1833. Shel.
Vandevanter, Isaac & Caroline S. Braden. John Braden, bm. 9 Sep.
    1839. Shel.
Vandevanter, John & Harriet A. Daine (Darne). Archibald Mains
    attests groom's age. Presley Saunders attests bride's age,
    bm. 29 Jan. 1831. m. Feb. 1831. Littlejohn. Shel.
Vandeventer, Joseph & Mary Elizabeth Greenlease, dau. of James
    Greenlease. Charles H. Greenlease, bm. 16 Feb. 1835.
Vandevanter, Washington & Cecelia E. Braden. Oscar S. Braden
    attests bride's age, bm. 11 April 1842. Shel.
Vanhorn, John & Sarah Carter, dau. of Richard Carter, who attests
    groom's age, bm. 27 July 1840. Cadden. Shel.
Vanhorne, Craven Osburn & Mary Emberson, dau. of Judson
    Emberson, bm. 17 May 1834. Shel.
Vanhorne, Garrett & Ann Whitcare. m. 29 Dec. 1807. Littlejohn.

Vanhorne, John & Eliza Titus. m. 30 July 1820. Dunn. Shel.
Vanhorne, John & Sarah Armstrong. m. 24 Dec. 1801. Littlejohn.
Vanpelt, Richard & Elizabeth Myres. m. 23 March 1793. Littlejohn.
Vansickler, William & Eunicy Coe, dau. of Robert Coe. Sampson
    Lickey attests groom's age. Hector Peacock, bm. 30 Dec.
    1844. Shel.
Varnes, John & Kitty Kirk. William Hart, bm. 28 May 1838. Shel.
Varney, William & Maria Cummings. George W. Noland attests bride's
    age, bm. 20 March 1843. Shel.
Varnum, Daniel & Rebecca Gibson. m. 19 May 1794. Littlejohn.
Vaughn, Jesse & Kessey Jinkins. m. 7 Feb. 1804. Littlejohn.
Vaunters, Philip A. & Eliza Jane Fling. Sanford Fling attests
    groom's age, bm. 4 Feb. 1839. Cam.
Veale, Alfred & Rebecca Jane Peacock. Elijah Peacock attests
    groom's age, bm. 26 March 1845. m. 27 March 1845. Gover. Cam.
Veale, Charles & Juliet Pratt. C. Binns, Jr., bm. 16 March 1799.
    Cam.
Veale, Elam C. & Mary E. Hough, dau. of Joseph Hough, bm. 24 Nov.
    1834. Cam.
Veale, William & Linny (Lenah) Horseman. William Horseman, Jr.
    attests bride's age, bm. 25 Feb. 1799. Cam.
Venander, George & Nancy Green. m. 2 Jan. 1794. Littlejohn.
Vermillen, Francis & Francis Downs. m. 26 Oct. 1816. Littlejohn.
Vermillian, Charles & Jane Tillett. m. 18 Dec. 1821. Gilmore.
Vermillion, James T. & Nancy Carruthers. Joel S. Nixon attests
    ages, bm. 28 Dec. 1840. Shel.
Vermillion, John & Hannah Pomroy, dau. of Burr Pomroy. James T.
    Vermillion attests groom's age. John Simpson, bm. 13 March
    1837. Shel.
Vermillion, John & Margaret Ellen Divine, dau. of William Divine,
    who attests groom's age. William Durne, bm. 16 Aug. 1834.
    Shel.
Vermillion, John & Phebe Webster. m. 2 July 1820. Dunn. Shel.
Vermillion, Philip L. W. & Jane W. Bazill. John C. Rose attests
    ages, bm. 6 Feb. 1846. m. 5 Feb. 1846. Herndon. Shel.
Vernon, James & Nancy Downs. m. 1807-1808. Mines.
Vernon, James & Nancy Johnson. m. 20 Oct. 1825. Dunn. Shel.
Verts, Joeph L. & Eliza Ann Baker, dau. of George Baker, bm.
    John Verts attests groom's age. 28 Jan. 1848. m. 3 Feb. 1848.
    Shuford.
Verts, Samuel & Duanna Harper. Truman Gore attests ages, bm.
    11 Dec. 1843. Shel.
Vertz, Jacob & Catherine Hutchenson; both single. By license.
    m. 18 May 1830. ParReg A.
Vestal, David & Mary Blinco. m. 23 Oct. 1817. Keyes.
Vickars, Aquilla & Anna Vickars. m. 15 June 1819. Williamson.
Vicker, William & Catharine Crimling. m. 1 March 1832. ParReg A.
Vickers, Abraham & Maria Richards. m. 13 Dec. 1827. Baker.
Vickers, Archibald & Pleasant Nichols, ward of Nathaniel Nichols,
    who attests groom's age, bm. 13 April 1829.
Vickers, William & Anna Reeder. m. 11 Aug. 1798. Littlejohn.
Vickers, William & Catharine Crim, dau. of Jacob Crim, who
    attests groom's age, bm. 27 Feb. 1832. Shel.
Vincel, George & Catharine Shoves, widow. Samuel Potterfield
    attests groom's age, bm. 13 Oct. 1837. Shel.

LOUDOUN COUNTY MARRIAGES

Vincel, George & Catherine Schneer, widow. m. 15 Oct. 1837. Larkine.
Vincel, George Tilghman & Susan Catharine Fry. m. 8 Dec. 1846.
    ParReg A. Shel.
Vincel, John & Elizabeth Ulam. m. 20 Jan. 1846. Shuford.
Vincel, Tilghman & Susan Fry, dau. of Peter Fry, who attests
    groom's age, bm. 8 Dec. 1846. Shel.
Vincell, John & Elizabeth Ulam, widow. John Davis attests groom's
    age, bm. 19 Jan. 1846. Shel.
Vincell, Solomon & Louisa Demory. Mahlon Demory attests ages, bm.
    28 March 1844. Shel.
Vinsel, Philip & Susan Everheart, dau. of Philip Everheart, who
    attests groom's age, bm. 31 Oct. 1829.
Vinson, Benjamin & Francis Johns. m. 28 March 1810. Littlejohn.
Vinson, William B. & Louisa M. Oxley. John T. Vinson attests ages.
    Charles Gassaway, bm. 27 Oct. 1843. Shel.
Violet, Elijah & Phebe Patterson. 29 Sep. 1799. Littlejohn.
Violet, James & Mary Samsele. m. 23 Oct. 1823. Dagg.
Virts, George P. & Martha E. Connor. James Thomas attests ages,
    bm. 27 Nov. 1843. Shel.
Virts, Henry & Esther R. Brown. John V. Brown attests ages, bm.
    12 Sep. 1842. Shel.
Virts, John & Christiana Verts. m. 1807-1808. Mines.
Virts, Samuel & Hannah Elizabeth Brown, dau. of Mary Brown. Joseph
    Cox attests groom's age and death of Jas. Brown, bm. 22 Jan.
    1838. Shel.
Virtz, John W. & Elizabeth C. Wells. James W. Nixon proves ages,
    wit. 15 Nov. 1851. MarReg.
Virtz, Peter & Mary Ann Alder. m. 27 May 1852. Startzman.
Wade, John & Hannah Myers. Thomas Myers attests ages, bm. 13 Sep.
    1809. m. 1808-1809. Mines.
Waddle, John & Sarah Crone. m. 12 Aug. 1813. McPherson.
Wade, John & Susan Wade. Martha Wade, widow of John Wade, consents
    and attests groom's age, bm. 3 Sep. 1843. m. 10 Oct. 1843.
    ParReg A. Shel.
Wade, Richard W. & Mary Elizabeth Myers. John F. Barrett, Robert
    Saunders, bm. 11 Jan. 1841. Gover. Shel.
Wade, Robert & Amelia Ann Myres. John F. Barrett attests groom's
    age. Robert S. Saunders attests bride's age, bm. 29 July
    1839. Shel.
Wade, Robert & Sarah Rowan. m. 1807-1808. Mines.
Wadsworth, Lawson & Catherine Gladden. m. 13 Oct. 1842. Hauer.
Waldtmann, David & Margretha Rapp; both single. By license. m.
    22 March 1812. ParReg A.
Walker, Benjamin & Elizabeth Kile. m. 13 April 1820. Dagg.
Walker, Burr Smith & Mary Ann Swart, dau. of James Swart, bm.
    3 May 1830. Shel.
Walker, Craven & Alice Cowgill. m. 22 July 1821. T. Littleton.
Walker, Garrett & Elizabeth Wiley. m. 22 June 1802. Dunn.
Walker, Garrett & Ruth Smith. m. 26 Aug. 1806. Littlejohn.
Walker, Garrett B. & Adaline B. Skinner. Lorenzo D. Walker attests
    groom's age, bm. 24 Feb. 1840. Cam.
Walker, Isaac, Frederick County, Va. & Susanna Talbott. m.
    8 April 1812. FFMM.

160

Walker, James G., son of Burr and Mareyan Walker, 22 years, b.
Loudoun & Harriet Ann Stephenson, dau. of James and Sarah
Stephenson, 21 years, b. Loudoun. Wit: William H. Stephenson.
18 Aug. 1853. MarReg. Gover.
Walker, John & Abigail Brook. m. 29 Jan. 1824. T. Littleton.
Walker, John & Letitia Humphrey. m. 13 Aug. 1811. Dunn.
Walker, Joseph & Mary Taylor. m. 28 April 1803. Littlejohn.
Walker, Lorenzo D. & Elizabeth Bemusdaffer. Ashford Weadon, bm.
7 Nov. 1842. Shel.
Walker, William & Ann Wiley, dau. of Hugh Wiley, bm. 12 June 1809.
Walker, William & Susanna Donaway. m. 13 Aug. 1798. Littlejohn.
Wallace, James M. & Adelaide Johnson, dau. of William Johnson, bm.
23 Nov. 1832. Shel.
Wallace, Joseph & Eliza. Rogers. Thomas Rogers, bm. 9 March 1786.
Waller, George & Melinda Lewis. m. 1820-1821. Mines.
Waller, Joseph & Priscilla C. Shores. B. B. Jeffries attests ages,
bm. 30 Dec. 1843. Shel.
Wallman, Jacob & Mary Sappington. m. 1821-1822. Mines.
Wallraven, Josiah & Lydia West. John West, bm. 25 Sep. 1809.
Walraven, Josiah & Elizabeth West. m. 25 Sep. 1809. Littlejohn.
Walter, John & Ruah Neale. John Murry, bm. 27 July 1830. Cam.
Walters, Jacob & Eva Waltmann, dau. of G. F. Samuel Waltmann;
both single. By license. m. 3 Nov. 1812. ParReg A.
Walters, James & Mary Wildman. m. 1806. Mines.
Walters, John & Ellen Dixon. m. 13 Dec. 1816. Littlejohn.
Waltman, Jacob & Sarah Birkirk. m. 13 April 1812. J. Littleton.
Waltman, Johannes & Sussana Stager; both single. By license. m.
20 July 1820. ParReg A.
Waltman, John & Margaret Waltman. m. 11 Aug. 1807. Littlejohn.
Waltman, Mortimer & Ellenor Fairfax. Samuel Wright proves ages,
wit. 6 Nov. 1851. MarReg.
Waltman, Samuel & Mary Ann E. Short, with Maryland license. m.
20 July 1834. ParReg A.
Waltmann, Jacob, widower & Rahel Thomas, widow. By license. m.
11 April 1811. ParReg A.
War, John & Caroline Emberson (Embuson). Judson Emberson, bm.
17 Sep. 1841. Shel.
War, John & Elizabeth Lightfoot. m. 24 March 1815. Littlejohn.
Ward, Charles Edward & Mary Esther Austin Wright. Edgar Jarvis
proves ages, wit. 2 Oct. 1850. MarReg.
Ward, Henry W. & Emily Dishman. Samuel Dishman, George Ward, bm.
9 April 1829. Williamson.
Ward, Hezekiah & Sarah Ann Towner. Wit: James F. Divine. 20 Dec.
1852. MarReg. m. 21 Dec. 1852. Duncan.
Ward, Thomas & Hannah Fox. Jacob Fox attests bride's age, bm.
25 Jan. 1836. Cam.
Ward, William N., Revd. & Mary Blincoe. m. 9 Aug. 1836, at house
of bride's mother, Leesburg. Adie.
Ward, William N. & Mary Blincoe. George Adie, bm. 9 Aug. 1836.
Warders, Livy & Sarah Deutch; both single. By license. m. 11 Nov.
1824. ParReg A.
Ware, Robert & Jane Nicholles. m. 29 April 1813. Dunn.
Ware, William P. & Amasa King. m. 28 May 1806. Littlejohn.

Warfield, R. L. & Mary E. Elgin, dau. of Francis Elgin, who
proves groom's age, wit. 8 Nov. 1852. MarReg.
Warford, Abraham & Elizabeth Piles. Francis Piles attests bride's
age, bm. 20 Dec. 1830. Cam.
Warnal, Thomas & Sarah Ryon. m. 24 Jan. 1797. Littlejohn.
Warner, Georg & Sarah Schumachern. m. 29 ____ 1789. ParReg A.
Warner, George, Jr. & Alcinda D. Loveless, dau. of Thomas
Loveless, bm. Mahlon Warner attests groom's age. 25 May 1835.
Shel.
Warner, Peter & Judith Schumachern. m. 14 Sep. 1785. ParReg A.
Warner, William & Christina Steinbrenner, dau. of Friderich
Steinbrenner and wife. m. 1817. ParReg A.
Warson, John & Frances Mills. m. 14 Feb. 1832. Green.
Warthin, Mickolaus & Elisabeth Sperling; both single. By license.
m. 9 Jan. 1817. ParReg A.
Washington, Bushrod C., Jefferson County, Va. & Maria P. Harrison.
Thomas B. Washington, bm. 27 Jan. 1835. m. 29 Jan. 1835,
St. James Church, Leesburg. Adie. Cam.
Washington, Edward S. & Ann E. Ellzey, dau. of Lewis Ellzey.
Mortimer McIlhany attests groom's age, bm. 14 April 1829.
Washington, George W. & Sarah Ann Wright, dau. of John Wright.
Alfred D. Offutt attests groom's age, bm. 18 Feb. 1833. Shel.
Washington, John A. & Amelia G. Sanders. m. 3 Dec. 1818. Griffith.
Washington, John Augustine, Fairfax & Eleanor Love Selden. W. C.
Selden, bm. 15 Feb. 1843. m. 16 Feb. 1843. Lippett. Shel.
Washington, Samuel E. & Sarah J. Everhart, ward of Jacob Shafer,
bm. Presly Saunders attests groom's age. 23 Jan. 1847. Shel.
Waters, Ellmore & Frances Kidwell, dau. of Elizabeth Kidwell,
who states bride was 21 years on 9 May 1838. John Coe, bm.
21 Jan. 1839. Shel.
Waters, Ishmael & Sarah Bradfield. m. 2 Nov. 1822. T. Littleton.
Waters, Jacob & Ellen Elizabeth Magaha. Presly Saunders attests
bride's age. John Mobberly, bm. 26 Oct. 1847. Shel.
Waters, John & Jane Neer, with Maryland license. m. 25 Dec. 1835.
ParReg A.
Waters, John Francis & Susan Niswaner. Christian Nisewanger,
Jacob Waters consent. Levi Waters, bm. 15 Jan. 1847. Shel.
Watkins, Bernard & Charlotte Littleton. John W. Littleton
attests ages, bm. 1 Sep. 1834. m. 4 Sep. 1834. Dorsey. Shel.
Watson, Lemuel & Lucy H. Birkby. Thomas Birkby, bm. 10 May 1832.
Shel.
Watson, Thomas & Elizabeth Havener. m. 4 Jan. 1813. Littlejohn.
Watson, Thomas & Luscinda Hickerson. m. 30 July 1808. Littlejohn.
Watt, John G. & Duanna Binns. m. 12 Nov. 1816. Littlejohn.
Watters, John & Mary Manken. m. 17 Oct. 1816. T. Littleton.
Wattman, Jacob & Elizabeth Ross. m. 29 Feb. 1808. Littlejohn.
Wattman, Mortimer & Elenor Fairfax. m. 11 Sep. 1851. Martin.
Watts, Monnze & Nancy Fouch. m. 6 Sep. 1815. Littlejohn.
Waugh, Alexander & Sussh. Binns. m. 31 Dec. 1798. Littlejohn.
Weadin, Francis & Sarah Jane Briscoe. m. 14 Nov. 1837. Tapler.
Weadon, John & Fanny Cowhe. m. 10 Oct. 1824. T. Littleton.
Weadon, John & Harriet Palmer. Albert D. Chamblin, bm. 24 Jan.
1837. m. 21 Jan. 1837. Morgan.
Weadon, John & Nancy Boland. James Daniel attests ages, bm. 28 Sep.
1842. Shel.

LOUDOUN COUNTY MARRIAGES

Webb, John W. & Sarah Ann Dorrell. Ashfield Vours, Jefferson
    County, attests groom was b. Feb. 1821. James Dorrell, bm.
    17 May 1842. m. 19 May 1842. Hauer. Shel.
Webb, John William & Amanda Jacobs. Nelson Chamblin attests ages,
    bm. 24 May 1847. m. 27 May 1847. Williard. Shel.
Weeden, John & Margaret Calaham. m. 30 Sep. 1813. Littlejohn.
Weedon, James & Nancy Mankins. m. 28 March 1817. T. Littleton.
Weedon, William & Lavina Wiley. David Brown attests ages, bm.
    7 Oct. 1837.
Weedon, William & Mary Wright. Benjamin Rust attests bride's age,
    bm. 28 June 1839. Shel.
Weeks, Burr & Ann Brent Gibson, dau. of H. Gibson. A. M. Gibson,
    bm. 10 Dec. 1839. Shel.
Weeks, Lewis & Susannah Hampton. m. 8 Feb. 1810. Williamson.
Weier, Peter & Sussana Frey, dau. of Peter Frey. By license. m.
    5 May 1812. ParReg A.
Wein, Johannes & Elisabetha Wenzel, dau. of Johannes Wenzel.
    By license. m. 12 March 1812. ParReg A.
Wein, Johannes, widower & Elisabeth Wentzel, single. By license.
    m. 26 Dec. 1826. ParReg A.
Weistman, Johannes & Sarah Morrison; both single. By license.
    m. 19 April 1821. ParReg A.
Welch, James & Mary Walker. Benjamin Walker, bm. 15 March 1813.
    Littlejohn.
Welcome, James & Theodosia Lucas. m. 11 Feb. 1797. Littlejohn.
Welford, John & Nancy Febbee. m. 9 Sep. 1815. Littlejohn.
Wells, Asa & Margaret Harrop. m. 28 Oct. 1824. Dunn.
Wells, Babell & Eliza Clendenen. m. 12 Nov. 1812. Littlejohn.
Wells, Henry, son of John and Catherine Wells, b. Fairfax, 23 years
    & Ann Hassman, dau. of Ann Horsman, b. Loudoun, 24 years.
    Barrett Check proves ages, wit. 8 Aug. 1853. MarReg. m.
    18 Aug. 1853, in Leesburg. Gover.
Welsh, B. W. & Alvina Craven. Joel Craven, bm. 3 May 1850. m.
    7 May 1850. Herndon.
Weltz, Johannes W., widower & Margretha Clausin, single. By
    license. m. 30 July 1820. ParReg A.
Wencil, Samuel & Elizabeth Keans. m. 5 March 1833. ParReg A.
Wenner, Jacob & Eliza. Ritchie. John Snow attests ages, bm.
    19 June 1833. m. 20 June 1832. Hauer. Shel.
Wenner, Johannes & Elisabetha Anna Waltman; both single. By
    license. m. 3 Feb. 1825. ParReg A.
Wenner, John & Sarah Everheart, Mrs. m. 2 Dec. 1832. ParReg A.
Wenner, John W. & Mary Jane Smith, dau. of Jacob Smith, who
    attests groom's age, bm. 21 Dec. 1847. m. 23 Dec. 1847.
    Shuford. Shel.
Wenner, Salomon & Margretha Ritsche, single. By license. m.
    18 Aug. 1825. ParReg A.
Wenner, Wilhelm, Reformed Schoolmaster, widower & Elisabeth
    Buschkirken, widow. Proclaimed. m. 28 Sep. 1788. ParReg A.
Wenner, Wilhelm, son of Wilhelm Wenner & Priscilla Schumacher,
    dau. of George Schumacher. m. 20 June 1784. ParReg A.
Wenner, William, son of William Wenner & Elisabetha Schart, dau.
    of Heinrich Schart; both single. By license. m. 15 April
    1813. ParReg A.

163

Wenner, William, son of William Wenner and wife & Maria Phale,
dau. of Jacob Phaly and wife; both single. By license. m.
21 Dec. 1817. ParReg A.

Wenner, William W. & Susan A. Waltman. Emanuel Waltman attests
ages, bm. 4 Jan. 1838. m. 9 Jan. 1838. Hauer. Shel.

Wentzel, Adam, son of Johannes Wentzel & Catharina Schlotzer, dau.
of Jacob Schlotzer, Jr.; both single. By license. m. 1 April
1813. ParReg A.

Wentzel, Adam, widower & Elisabeth Phale, dau. of Jacob Phale and
wife. By license. m. 22 Oct. 1818. ParReg A.

Wentzel, Johannes & Magdalena Hoffin. m. 24 July 1786. ParReg A.

Wentzel, Johannes, son of Johannes Wentzel and wife & Maria Fahle,
dau. of Jacob Fahle and wife. By license. m. 29 Jan. 1814.
ParReg A.

Wentzel, Phillip, son of Johannes Wentzel, Sr. and wife & Louisa
Eberhard, dau. of Phillip Eberhard; both single. By license.
m. 1 Nov. 1829. ParReg A.

Wenzel, Georg, Jr. & Barbara Kerns; both single. By license. m.
11 Dec. 1828. ParReg A.

Wenzel, Johannes, son of Georg Wenzel and wife & Anna Maria Boger,
dau. of late Michael Boger and wife; both single. By license.
m. 21 April 1825. ParReg A.

Wergman, Octavius T. & Mary Jane Ruse. m. 7 Jan. 1851. Chenoweth.

Wertenbaker, William J. & Sarah A. Thomas. Absalom R. Replor
attests groom's age, bm. 26 June 1838. Shel.

Werts, Conrad & Elizabeth Derry. m. 11 March 1819. Keyes.

Werts, Michael & Catherine Lees. m. 28 Nov. 1796. Littlejohn.

Werts, William & Philbina Werts. m. 1809-1810. Mines.

Wertz, Adam & Sussana Lilly; both single. By license. m. 28 Nov.
1826. ParReg A.

Wertz, Jacob, son of Peter Wertz & Elisabeth Slalcks, dau. of
widow Slalcks; both single. m. 7 April 1818. ParReg A.

Wertz, Jacob, son of William Wertz & Plassent Ana Jaius. By
license. m. 16 April 1818. ParReg A.

West, James & Judah Jackson. Charles Binns, bm. 15 Oct. 1835.
Shel..

West, John & Elizabeth Dawson. William Dawson, bm. 4 Feb. 1799.
Shel.

West, John & Elizabeth West. m. 26 Oct. 1796. Littlejohn.

West, Samuel & Elizabeth Rawlings. m. 6 March 1817. Williamson.

West, William, G. & Mary Ellzey, spinster. License: 17 Oct.
1761. FeeBk 4.

Wey, Peyton & Rachel Mink. Thomas A. Wey attests groom's age.
Lawrence Mink, bm. 3 Nov. 1829. m. 12 Nov. 1829. ParReg A.

Weyer, David & Catharina Elisabeth Sauder; both single. By license.
m. 17 June 1824. ParReg A.

Weyer, Michael & Maria Pottenfeld; both single. By license. m.
27 Sep. 1827. ParReg A.

Whaley, James & Mary Ann Whaley. Silas Hutchison attests bride's
age, bm. 11 May 1829.

Whaley, John G. & Lydia Presgraves. Melville B. Hutchison attests
ages, bm. 11 Dec. 1843. Cam.

Wheat, Benoni, Alexandria, parents dead & Matilda T. Fitzhugh,
dau. of Matilda Fitzhugh, widow. Wit: John S. Fitzhugh.
29 Oct. 1853. MarReg. m. 1 Nov. 1853. Hirst.

Wheatley, John & Elizabeth Rippon (Rappin), dau. of William
  Rippon, bm. 19 Feb. 1836. m. 21 Feb. 1836. Frye. Shel.
Wheeler, Johnson & Susannah Wright, ward of William Burk, bm.
  Sydnor B. Johnson attests groom's age. 12 Jan. 1846.
  m. 15 Jan. 1846. Massey. Shel.
Wheeler, Robert & Nancy Davis. m. 28 Sep. 1806. Littlejohn.
Wheeler, Thomas S. (T.), Genl., Maryland & Hester Ann McLeod,
  New York City. John M. Edwards attests bride's age. George M.
  Chichester, bm. 8 Aug. 1833. m. at house of John Edwards,
  Leesburg. Adie. Shel.
Wherry, Silas & Elizabeth Edwards. m. 30 March 1805. Littlejohn.
Whietly, Joseph & Sarah Sagel; both single. By license. m. 1 June
  1824. ParReg A.
Whitacre, Caleb & Phebe Gore. m. 31 Oct. 1776. FFMM.
Whitacre, James & Elizabeth Randall. William Randle, bm. 16 Nov.
  1799. Shel.
Whitacre, John & Nancy Hope, widow. Israel Dyer, bm. 20 June
  1833. Shel.
Whitacre, Robert, son of John and Naomi Whitacre & Sarah Roach,
  dau. of Richard and Hannah Roach. m. 28 May 1783. FFMM.
Whitacre, Thomas & Anna Howell. m. 21 Oct. 1805. Littlejohn.
Whitaker, Jas. & Elizabeth Randel. 14 Nov. 1799. Littlejohn.
White, Beriah & Francis Saunders. m. 14 Dec. 1816. Littlejohn.
White, Daniel T., son of S. N. C. White who states groom was b.
  11 March 1825 & Virginia Marlow (Mailow), dau. of George
  Marlow. Robert W. Gray attests groom's age, bm. 5 Dec. 1849.
  m. 11 Dec. 1849, at house of bride's father. Adie. Shel.
White, Hansford & Charlotte Grimes. Jesse Triplett attests ages,
  bm. 13 Aug. 1832. Shel.
White, J. & Mary Harrin. m. 17 Nov. 1803. Dunn.
White, James & Ann Catharine Poulton. Both fathers present and
  consent. C. Odin White, bm. 27 Feb. 1843. Shel.
White, James & Elizabeth R. Best. Enos T. Best attests bride's
  age, bm. 15 May 1833. Shel.
White, James & Elizabeth Lanckton. m. 22 Dec. 1809. Littlejohn.
White, James B. & Agnes B. White. John White consents. F. M.
  McIlhany attests groom's age, bm. 15 April 1834. Shel.
White, Jeremiah & Henrietta Wilson. m. 26 Feb. 1846. ParReg A.
White, Joel & Harriet Blaker. William Shields attests ages, bm.
  2 Jan. 1837. Shel.
White, John & Nancy Davidson. m. 6 Feb. 1808. Littlejohn.
White, John H. & Malinda S. George. John George consents. John
  George, Jr. attests groom's age, bm. 2 Dec. 1833. Shel.
White, John R. & Mary Cecelia Ellzey, dau. of Lewis Ellzey, bm.
  4 Jan. 1832. m. 10 Jan. 1832. Frye. Shel.
White, John Randolph & Sarah G. Janney. David Shawen attests
  ages, bm. 6 Dec. 1841. Shel.
White, Joseph & Margaret Braden. John Braden attests ages, bm.
  6 Feb. 1809. m. 1808-1809. Mines.
White, Josiah & Sarah Williams. m. 1807-1808. Mines.
White, Levi & Mary Holms. m. 14 Oct. 1805. Littlejohn.
White, Mahlon & Margaret Wynkoop. William Shields, bm. 3 Nov.
  1831. Shel.

White, Redmond F. & Maria L. Shumate, dau. of M. C. Shumate, bm.
Groom's brother proves his age. 18 Dec. 1848. m. 27 Dec. 1848.
Shel.

White, Richard & Mary Julia Nixon. Joel L. Nixon attests bride's
age, bm. 11 May 1850. Shel.

White, Robert & Mary Polston. m. 8 Dec. 1800. Littlejohn.

White, Thomas & Jane Nixon. m. 1807-1808. Mines.

White, Thomas & Kitty M. Hamilton. James H. Hamilton attests
ages, bm. 6 Jan. 1806.

White, Thomas & Margaret Hamilton. m. 1806. Mines.

White, Wesley & Jane Harden, dau. of Thomas Harding. Edward
Harding attests groom's age, bm. 2 Feb. 1837. Shel.

White, William & Ann Myres. m. 25 Dec. 1797. Littlejohn.

White, William & Christenia Mead. m. 9 May 1801. Littlejohn.

White, William & Elizabeth Yakey. Spencer Minor attests ages, bm.
13 Dec. 1841. Shel.

Whitenton, Benjamin & Darcus Reed. m. 5 Feb. 1793. Littlejohn.

Whiting, George W. Carlisle & Mary Ann Dulany. John P. Dulany
gives permission. Charles G. Eskridge, bm. 22 Dec. 1838. Shel.

Whiting, Pomphy & Rosand. Patrick. m. 1796. Littlejohn.

Whitmore, John H. & Elizabeth Ann Adams, dau. of Henry Adams, who
attests groom's age, bm. 25 Feb. 1850. Shel.

Whitmore, Michael W. & Louisa Duval, dau. of Harriet Duvall.
George Whitmore attests groom's age, bm. 12 June 1844. Shel.

Whitmore, William W. & Julia E. Beach. James D. McPherson attests
ages, bm. 11 Feb. 1849. Shel.

Wiard, Jonathan & Catharine Harper, dau. of James Harper, who
attests groom's age, bm. 22 Feb. 1834. m. 28 Feb. 1834.
Hauer. Shel.

Wiatt, James & Mary Wren. m. 14 Sep. 1816. Littlejohn.

Wickory, Solomon & Elisabetha Altemus; both single. By license.
m. 23 Jan. 1814. ParReg A.

Wicks, William K. & Virginia A. White. Jonah R. White attests
bride's age. Josiah P. White, bm. 3 June 1844. Shel.

Wickwis, Nimrod & Sussana Christy; both single. By license.
m. 11 March 1823. ParReg A.

Widdicombe, John & Louiza Tavenner, dau. of Eli Tavenner, bm.
18 Jan. 1834. Shel.

Wiehn, Michael & Rahel Williams; both single. By license. m.
7 May 1818. ParReg A.

Wiekly, Samuel & Anna Matteuis; both single. By license. m.
15 May 1821. ParReg A.

Wien, Johannes & Sarah Schlotzer, dau. of Jacob Schlotzer, Sr.
and wife. By license. m. 14 Dec. 1820. ParReg A.

Wiggengton, James & Margaret Rebecca McCoy. m. 25 March 1851.
Martin.

Wigginton, Benjamin & Mary Brooks. Mary Wiggington attests ages,
bm. 17 July 1849. Cam.

Wigginton, James & Martha R. McCoy. George M. McCoy proves ages,
wit. 24 March 1851. MarReg.

Wild, Georg & Susanna Bibern. m. 19 Nov. 1786. ParReg A.

Wildman, Charles & Henrietta Benjamin, dau. of Sarah Benjamin.
John Benjamin, bm. 11 May 1847. m. 12 May 1847. Gover. Shel.

LOUDOUN COUNTY MARRIAGES

Wildman, Charles William & Elizabeth A. Hamilton. John Moss
attests groom's age. H. M. Hardy attests bride's age, bm.
12 Aug. 1844. Shel.

Wildman, Enos & Jane Hamilton. m. 11 May 1815. Littlejohn.

Wildman, Jacob & Mary Lafever. m. 16 Feb. 1797. Littlejohn.

Wildman, John & Sarah Hawkins. m. 3 April 1811. Littlejohn.

Wildman, John W. & Anna Snowden Bentley, dau. of Robert Bentley.
Jared Chamblin, bm. 11 Jan. 1848. m. at home of bride's
father. Adie. Shel.

Wildman, Joseph & Charlotte Turner. John Turner attests ages, bm.
16 April 1841. Shel.

Wildman, Joseph & Hannah Nixen. m. 28 Dec. 1814. Littlejohn.

Wildman, Joseph & Sarah Carter. m. 26 Feb. 1811. Littlejohn.

Wildman, William & Eliza Girgin. m. 21 April 1823. Dunn.

Wildman, William & Mahala Carter. m. 9 Jan. 1815. Littlejohn.

Wiley, Harrison & Mary Elizabeth Green, dau. of Thomas Green,
who attests groom's age, bm. 27 March 1847. m. 28 March 1847.
Gover. Shel.

Wiley, John H. & Elizabeth S. Davis. Albert C. Davis attests ages,
bm. 5 March 1849. Shel.

Wiley, Joshua P. & Ruth H. Milburn. Wit: John Milburn. 3 Oct.
1853. MarReg.

Wiley, William & Charlotte E. Taylor. Joseph Taylor attests ages,
bm. 1 Feb. 1847. Shel.

Wiley, William & Rachel McMullan. m. 22 Dec. 1803. Dunn.

Wilkeson, William & Sydney Gibson. m. 3 Aug. 1820. Dagg.

Wilkins, James & Hannah Roberts. m. 14 Jan. 1808. Williamson.

Wilkinson, Joseph, son of Joseph and Barbary Wilkinson & Elizabeth
Gregg, dau. of William and Rebekah Gregg. m. 26 Nov. 1788.
FFMM.

Wilkinson, Joseph & Elizabeth Reed. m. 24 Sep. 1802. Littlejohn.

Wilkinson, William & Abigail Carter. George Rogers, bm. 29 March
1830. Shel.

Wilkinson, William & Rachel Butler. m. 23 May 1822. Gilmore.

Wicklaw (Wilklow), Jacob & Mary Ann Cooper. m. 11 March 1847.
Williard. ParReg A. Shel.

Wilklon, Jacob & Mary Ann Cooper. William Degroodt attests groom's
age. Wesley J. Saunders attests bride's age, bm. 8 March
1847. Shel.

Willard, Henry & Sarah Ellen Adlum, both of Jefferson, Frederick
County, Maryland. m. 28 July 1846. ParReg A.

Willcoxen, Levi & Catharine H. Harris, dau. of John A. Harris,
bm. 13 March 1809. Littlejohn.

Willett, George & Elizabeth Rhodes (Roads). Joseph Orrison
attests groom's age. Samuel Rhodes attests bride's age, bm.
6 Jan. 1835. m. 9 Jan. 1835. Baker.

Willfort, Georg & Nansy Teitus; both single. By license. m.
19 Aug. 1824. ParReg A.

Williams, Abner, son of William and Elizabeth Williams, the former
deceased & Mary Wood, dau. of Joseph and Abigail Wood. m.
30 Nov. 1796. FFMM.

Williams, Charles & Mary Steer. m. 10 April 1821. Gilmore.

Williams, Ellis & Lenah Smith. m. 13 May 1816. Littlejohn.

Williams, G. Washington & Sarah E. Skinner. Peter Skinner attests
groom's age, bm. 29 Aug. 1837. Cam.
Williams, Henry V. & Rebecca Johnson. Thomas S. Steadman attests
ages, bm. 8 Oct. 1840. Shel.
Williams, Hillary Wilson & Mary Washington Saunders, dau. of
Mahala Saunders. William W. Whitmore attests groom's age.
James D. McPherson, bm. 3 Jan. 1849. Shel.
Williams, Israel & Anna Milia Stautzenbergerin, dau. of Johannes
Stautzenberger; both single. By license. m. 25 April 1811.
ParReg A.
Williams, James & Ann Plummer. m. 8 Oct. 1793. Littlejohn.
Williams, John & Jane Geoley. m. 18 Jan. 1808. Littlejohn.
Williams, John & Margaret Browner. m. 3 Aug. 1815. Littlejohn.
Williams, John & Ruth Williams. m. 15 Nov. 1795. Littlejohn.
Williams, John A. & Matilda Spaytes. m. Oct. 1815. Littlejohn.
Williams, John C. & Elizabeth Spring. Henry Spring attests ages,
bm. 18 Sep. 1838. m. 20 Sep. 1838. Hauer. Shel.
Williams, John E., son of William and Mary Williams, b. Maryland,
26 years & Sarah E. Hains, dau. of Thomas and Margaret Haines,
21 years, b. Loudoun. William Dinzmore proves ages, wit.
8 Aug. 1853. MarReg. m. 11 Aug. 1853, Waterford. Gover.
Williams, Joseph & Betsy Ballenger. m. 12 Nov. 1807. Littlejohn.
Williams, Joshua & Jane Hixon. Stephenson Hixon attests bride's
age. Presley Williams, Stephen Hixon, bm. 2 May 1810.
Williams, Leonard & Sarah Scrivener. m. 17 Dec. 1814. Littlejohn.
Williams, Lilbourne & Phebe Smith. m. 20 June 1807. Littlejohn.
Williams, Presley & Jane Hixon. Stephen (Joshua) Hixon, bm.
2 May 1810. m. 1809-1810. Mines.
Williams, Samuel & Hannah Mellon. m. 16 March 1806. Fristoe.
Williams, Sydnor & Eleanor V. Craven. Charles Williams attests
bride's age, bm. 16 May 1836. m. 17 May 1836. Hauer. Shel.
Williams, Sydnah & Mary Catherine Waltman. Mortimer Waltman
proves bride's age, wit. 21 Aug. 1851. MarReg.
Williams, Thomas & Hannah Brent. m. 26 Feb. 1794. Littlejohn.
Williams, Tobias R. & Sarah Ann Amich (Amick). Jacob Smith
attests ages, bm. 24 May 1847. m. 27 May 1847. Williard. Shel.
Williams, Topsom & Rachel Hewitt. m. 13 May 1806. Littlejohn.
Williams, William & Elizabeth Everett. m. 6 Sep. 1769. FFMM.
Williams, William, Waterford & Mary E. Walker. m. 18 June 1845.
FFMM.
Williamson, Jesse & Susanna Stayley, Mrs. George Survick attests
bride's age, bm. 22 Sep. 1848. m. 24 Sep. 1848. ParReg A. Shel.
Wills, Benjamin E. & Charity Furr, dau. of Enoch Furr, bm.
Samuel Berkley, bm. 10 April 1809.
Wills, Troy & Lucinda Hampton. m. 5 Nov. 1822. Dagg.
Willson, John & Sarah Johnston. m. 14 Dec. 1802. Littlejohn.
Willson, Moses & Tamer Burson. m. 29 May 1794. Littlejohn.
Willson, Thomas & Sarah Farst. m. 18 Dec. 1797. Littlejohn.
Wilmarth, Jason & Mary Ann Jane Rutter, ward of Hugh F. Rutter,
bm. Edmund R. Garrett, bm. 9 Oct. 1837. Shel.
Wilson, Amos & Cathrine Myres. m. 5 Nov. 1798. Littlejohn.
Wilson, Henery & Elizabeth Rhods. m. 9 May 1810. T. Littleton.
Wilson, James & Sarah Titus. m. 25 March 1825. McDowell.

Wilson, James A. & Harriet M. Kendall, dau. of Charles Kendall,
   bm. Groom's age is "upwards of 21 years from appearance".
   22 May 1847. m. 24 May 1847. Hayes. Shel.
Wilson, Moses & Margaret Lloyd. m. 6 Nov. 1828. Williamson.
Wilson, Moses D. & Ann Lloyd. Armistead M. Howell attests ages,
   bm. 6 Sep. 1832. Cam.
Wilson, Nelson B. & Rebecca B. Hoskinson. Thomas L. Hoskinson
   attests bride's age, bm. 20 Feb. 1837. m. 21 Feb. 1837.
   Newman. Cam.
Wilson, Stephen, son of Samuel and Sarah Wilson & Martha Scott,
   dau. of Jacob and Elizabeth Scott, the former deceased. m.
   13 May 1789. FFMM.
Wilson, Tholemiah R. & Maria L. Boley. James D. McPherson attests
   ages, bm. 27 July 1848. Shel.
Wilson, Thomas & Alice Myres. m. 18 Sep. 1804. Littlejohn.
Wilson, Thomas & Mary Baracraft. m. 7 April 1814. Littlejohn.
Wilson, Thomas & Mary Oran. m. 10 Feb. 1808. Littlejohn.
Wilson, Thomas L. & Alice Powell. m. 18 Dec. 1828. Tippett.
Wilt, Georg & Catharina Wertz; both single. By license. m.
   25 March 1830. ParReg A.
Wilt, Jonathan & Mariah Tribble. m. 13 Jan. 1839. ParReg A.
Wilty, Frederick & Elizabeth Everhart. m. 1809-1810. Mines.
Win, John W. & Mary A. Derry. Michael Derry attests ages, bm.
   1 Jan. 1842. Shel.
Wince, Henry & Sarah Frye. m. 3 June 1824. Roszel.
Wince, Philip & Catherine Shaver. m. 25 April 1810. Littlejohn.
Wince, Philip & Elizabeth Strup. m. 24 March 1800. Littlejohn.
Wincil, Samuel & Elizabeth Kearn. m. 5 March 1833. Hauer.
Wine, Armistead J. & Mary E. Cassady. George H. Wine attests ages,
   bm. 19 Jan. 1848. m. 18 Jan. 1848. Shuford. Shel.
Wine, Edward & Ann Beach. Josephus Carr, bm. 24 Oct. 1846. Note
   on outside: "Never called again".
Wine, Edward & Ann Beach. James M. Carr attests ages, bm. 24 Oct.
   1846.
Wine, George H. & Ann C. B. Cassiday. John McGavack attests ages,
   bm. 7 Dec. 1849. Shel.
Wine, Washington & Ann Eliza Greenlease. John H. Greenlease
   attests ages, bm. 13 Feb. 1843. Shel.
Wine, Washington & Elizabeth Greenlease. 13 Feb. 1843. Mercer.
Winegardner, Adam & Reba. Jordon. m. 9 March 1807. Littlejohn.
Winegarner, Adam & Sarah Jorden. m. 14 March 1816. Littlejohn.
Winegarner, Henry & Patience Oxley. m. 29 Oct. 1801. Littlejohn.
Winegarner, Levi & Catherine Collins, dau. of Levi Collins, bm.
   8 Oct. 1832. Shel.
Winn, Josiah, son of William Winn & Margaret Moore. Samuel Moore
   attests bride's age, bm. 11 Dec. 1809.
Winn, Samuel & Barbary Warrenburg. m. 1 Dec. 1805. Fristoe.
Winn, Thomas M. & Nancy L. Violett, dau. of John Violett, who
   attests groom's age, bm. 9 Aug. 1831. m. 28 Aug. 1831.
   Williamson. Shel.
Winner, Jacob & Eliza Ritchie. m. 30 June 1833. ParReg A.
Winner, John & Elizabeth Wattman. m. 14 March 1808. Littlejohn.
Winner, John & Sarah Everheart, widow. Michael Whitmore, bm.
   27 Nov. 1832. m. 2 Dec. 1832. Hauer. Shel.

Winpigler, John & Rachel R. Taylor. Wit: David Monday. 6 July
1852. MarReg.

Winsell, Samuel & Elizabeth Keen, dau. of Jacob Keen, who attests
groom's age, bm. 26 Feb. 1833. Shel.

Wire, John & Susan Amick. George Amick attests ages, bm. 17 Feb.
1845. m. 20 Feb. 1845. ParReg A.

Wire, Peter & Mary Louisa Ann Stoneburner, dau. of Elizabeth
Stoneburner. Luther A. Thrasher, bm. 3 Feb. 1838. m. 6 Feb.
1838. Hauer. m. 8 Feb. 1838. ParReg A.

Wire, William & Catherine Potterfield. Jonathan Potterfield
attests bride's age, bm. 14 Nov. 1829. m. Nov. 1829.
Hutchinson.

Wirgman, Octavius P. & Mary Jane Ruse. Bride's father consents.
6 Jan. 1851. MarReg.

Wirts, Henry & Virginia Leslie, dau. of John Leslie,who attests
groom's age, bm. 11 Aug. 1845. Shel.

Wirts, Peter & Mary Ann Allder. Albert Allder proves ages, wit.
24 May 1852. MarReg.

Wirtz, Jacob, son of Peter Wirtz & Elisabeth Georg, dau. of
Johannes Georg; both single. By license. m. 21 April 1795.
ParReg A.

Wirtz, Johannes & Elisabeth Stedlerin. By license. m. 25 Sep.
1788. ParReg A.

Wirtz, Peter & Leah Battenfield, in Maryland. m. 27 March 1837.
ParReg A.

Wissinger, William & Elizabeth Parmer (Panner). Stephen Parmer
attests ages, bm. 22 Jan. 1842. m. 25 Jan. 1842. Hauer. Shel.

Wist, Jonathan & Maria Tribble. Adam Cooper attests ages, bm.
9 Jan. 1839. Shel.

Withers, James & Hannah Roberts. m. 14 Jan. 1808. Williamson.

Wodsworth, Lawson & Catharine Gladdin. Presley Davis attests ages,
bm. 12 Oct. 1842. Shel.

Wolfe, Adam & Sush. Stoneburner. m. 10 March 1796. Littlejohn.

Wolfe, John & Mary A. Ney. David Galleher attests ages, bm.
23 Nov. 1846. Shel.

Wolford, Asa R. & Martha E. Stone, dau. of John Stone, who
proves groom's age, wit. 12 May 1851. MarReg.

Wolford, Johannes & Jane Hough; both single. By license. m.
28 March 1822. ParReg A.

Wolford, John & Jane Covinson. John Hamilton attests ages, bm.
29 April 1845. Shel.

Wolford, John & Jane C. Orrison. m. 6 Dec. 1846. ParReg A.

Wolford, William & Reba. Hane. m. 22 Dec. 1798. Littlejohn.

Wood, Benjamin Thomas & Eliza J. Cornell. Alexander Keys, bm.
24 Dec. 1845. Shel.

Wood, David M., son of Joseph and Lydia Wood, 25 years, b.
Loudoun & Susan L. McLin (Melin), dau. of James and Mary
McLin, 26 years, b. Loudoun. Wit: John D. McLin. 25 Oct.
1853. MarReg. m. 27 Oct. 1853. Gover.

Wood, John & Molly King. m. 5 Oct. 1801. Littlejohn.

Wood, Joshua, Redstone, Fayette County, Pa. & Eleanor H. Stone.
m. 17 Nov. 1842. FFMM.

Wood, Richard, Jefferson County, Ohio, son of William and Mary
Wood & Lydia Steer, dau. of Isaac and Phoebe Steer. m. 17 June
1815. FFMM.

LOUDOUN COUNTY MARRIAGES

Wood, William & Mariah Robinson, dau. of Priscilla Robison.
John G. Hoge, bm. 14 Jan. 1841. Shel.
Wood, William S. & Mary Catharine Schooley. m. 18 July 1838. FFMM.
Woodey, William & Elizabeth Green. m. 25 Aug. 1808. Littlejohn.
Woodley, Benjamin & Elizabeth Richardson. m. 15 June 1796.
Littlejohn.
Woodley, William & Elizabeth Green. m. 25 Aug. 1808. Littlejohn.
Woody, James & Betsey Clifford. John A. Binns, bm. 9 May 1832.
Shel.
Woodyard, John N., son of Jabas and Nancy Woodyard, b. Prince
William, 31 years & Mary Ann Jones, dau. of Richard and
Catherine Jones, 25 years, b. Loudoun. 3 Oct. 1853. MarReg.
m. 4 Oct. 1853, in Leesburg. Gover.
Woodyard, William & Maria Ann Davis, dau. of Thomas Davis. 23 Oct.
1850. MarReg. Wills.
Woolard, Isaac & Phebe Banacraft. m. 13 Oct. 1803. Littlejohn.
Woolford, Joseph & Elizabeth Meeks. m. 4 Sep. 1796. Littlejohn.
Workman, Isaac & Margaret Smith. m. 1806. Mines.
Workman, Isaac & Sarah Mary Jane German. William L. Simpson
attests bride's age, bm. 24 June 1830. Shel.
Workman, Isaac & Susan. Peacock. m. 19 March 1808. Littlejohn.
Workman, James, son of Isaac and Sarah Jane Workman, about 23
years & Mary Elisabeth Cornell, dau. of Thompson and Mary
Cornell, about 22 years. m. 4 Sep. 1853. Martin.
Wornall, John & Rachel Wildman. m. 20 Dec. 1821. Gilmore.
Worsley, William & Virginia G. Edwards, dau. of Dr. Edwards.
Charles Gassaway attests bride's age, bm. 4 Nov. 1843. m.
7 Nov. 1843, at home of bride's father. Adie. Shel.
Worson, John & Frances Mills, dau. of George Mills. Henry Lacey,
bm. 11 Feb. 1832. Cam.
Wortenbaker, William & Sarah A. Thomas. m. 26 June 1838. Herndon.
Worthington, Joseph & Elizabeth Osborn. m. 25 Sep. 1795.
Littlejohn.
Worthman, James (See Workman, James, above.)
Wortman, George H. & Jane E. Snider. William Lafever, Jr. attests
ages, bm. 18 Dec. 1844. Cam.
Wortman, James W. & Mary E. Cornell. Wit: Thompson Cornell.
27 Aug. 1853. MarReg.
Wren, Samuel & Barbary Warrinburg. m. 1 Dec. 1805. Fristoe.
Wren, Thomas M. & Julia Cockerill. m. 8 July 1838. Trott.
Wrenn, James & Elizabeth Jacobs. m. 10 Aug. 1812. J. Littleton.
Wrenn, Sanford & Sally Dulin, dau. of William Dulin. Edward
Dulin, bm. 14 March 1799. Littlejohn.
Wrenn, Thomas M. & Julia Ann Cockerell. William Amber attests
bride's age, bm. 4 July 1838. Shel.
Wright, Albert & Elizabeth Ann Davis. Elias Davis attests ages,
bm. 26 Nov. 1838. m. 29 Nov. 1838. Hauer. Shel.
Wright, Anthony & Elizabeth Harper. m. 26 Oct. 1813. Littlejohn.
Wright, Bennett & Elizabeth Wine. Richard White attests ages, bm.
30 Oct. 1849. Shel.
Wright, Charles, father not known, about 32 years & Mary Catharine
Sanbower, dau. of Adam and Christena Sanbower, both deceased,
about 22 years. John W. Sanbower proves ages, wit. 11 Aug.
1853. MarReg. Martin.

171

Wright, Charles & Mary Violett. Ashford Violett attests bride's
   age. William G. Wright, bm. 14 March 1831. m. 15 March 1831.
   Baker. Shel.
Wright, Charles F. & Lydia J. Hamilton, dau. of John Hamilton,
   who attests groom's age, bm. 20 Feb. 1846. Shel.
Wright, Isaac & Susanna Mathias. m. 14 Dec. 1814. Littlejohn.
Wright, James P. & Elizabeth Cummins. m. 26 Nov. 1820. T. Littleton.
Wright, John & Catherine Quick, dau. of John Quick, bm. 7 May
   1799. Shel.
Wright, John & Elizabeth Stagg. m. 1 Feb. 1816. T. Littleton.
Wright, John & Margaret Brown. Thomas Young, bm. 16 Dec. 1844.
   Shel.
Wright, John H. & Elizabeth Hunt. John Hunt attests groom's age,
   bm. 19 Jan. 1850.
Wright, Joseph C. & Mahala Gibson. m. 7 Feb. 1821. Dagg.
Wright, Joseph H. & Catherine Rinker, dau. of Edward Rinker, bm.
   19 Sep. 1836. Shel.
Wright, Joseph L. & Margaret Orrison, dau. of Margaret Orrison.
   Jonah Orrison, bm. 19 Oct. 1846.
Wright, Moses & Dinah Ryan. 1793. Littlejohn.
Wright, Robert L. & Sarah C. Carter. R. R. Carter, bm. 17 May
   1843. Shel.
Wright, Samuel & Christian Clice. m. 12 May 1794. Littlejohn.
Wright, Thomas M. & Martha Brown. Hamilton Cross attests bride's
   age, bm. 9 April 1844. Shel.
Wright, William G. & Margaret Wilkeson. m. 21 Dec. 1820. Dagg.
Wrin, Samuel & Barbary Warrinburg. m. 1 Dec. 1805. Fristoe.
Writt, Thompson & Elizabeth Furr. John Iden, bm. 23 April 1831.
   m. 28 April 1831. Williamson. Cam.
Wyatt, Jacob & Morelles Derry. Michael Rimond attests bride's age,
   bm. 15 March 1799.
Wycoff, Cornelious & Elizabeth Riley. m. 13 Jan. 1812. J. Littleton.
Wykoff, Nicholas & Susan Riley. m. 29 July 1811. Littlejohn.
Wyncoop, Cornelius B. & Martha H. Harden. m. 26 Dec. 1852. Smith.
Wyncoop, George W. & Nancy Reese. Reed Poulton attests bride's
   age, bm. 31 Oct. 1836. Shel.
Wyne, William & Emily Carruthers. John Carruthers attests bride's
   age, bm. 17 June 1850.
Wynekoop, Jacob & Patsy McNabb. m. 16 Jan. 1820. Williamson.
Wyngrove, John & Maria Huldfish. John Divers attests bride's age,
   bm. 23 March 1809.
Wynkoop, Cornelius & Mahala Lacey, dau. of Israel Lacey, bm.
   14 Dec. 1843. Shel.
Wynkoop, Cornelius B. & Martha F. Harden. Wit: Henry Harden.
   25 Dec. 1852. MarReg.
Wynkoop, Garrett & Mary A. Hunt. John Wynkoop attests groom's
   age. Eli Hunt, bm. 6 June 1838. Shel.
Wynkoop, Garrett & Mary Lacey. Cornelius Wynkoop proves bride's
   age, wit. 2 Feb. 1852. MarReg. m. 3 Feb. 1852. Duncan.
Wynkoop, John & Mary Campbell. Garrett Wynkoop attests ages, bm.
   12 Oct. 1840. Shel.
Wynkoop, John J., son of Elizabeth W. Wynkoop & Matilda Jane
   Simmons. Landon Simons, bm. 28 July 1842. Shel.

Wynkoop, Joseph Thomas & Elizabeth Lowe, dau. of Jane Lowe.
Philip Henry Wynkoop attests groom's age, bm. 29 Nov. 1848.
Shel.

Wynkoop, Richard & Frances Thayer. Lorenzo D. Walker attests ages,
bm. 26 Dec. 1831. m. 29 Dec. 1831. Shel.

Wynkoop, Samuel C. & Susana Hunt. Garrett Wynkoop attests bride's
age, bm. 18 Sep. 1844. Shel.

Wynkoop, William & Catherine Clever. William Smith attests ages,
bm. 13 May 1833. Shel.

Wynkoop, William, son of Joseph Wynkoop & Mary Franklin. B. T.
Franklin attests bride's age, bm. Joseph Wynkoop, bm. 7 Jan.
1840. Shel.

Wynkoope, Philip & Elizabeth Cartwright. m. 30 Oct. 1805. Dunn.

Wynn, Josiah, son of William Winn & Margaret Moore. Samuel
Moore, bm. 11 Dec. 1809. Shel.

Yacky, Jacob & Harriett C. Neale, made ward of Richard Brown
"this day", bm. 8 Nov. 1830. Shel.

Yakey, John & Eliza Crumbaker. m. 30 Oct. 1838. Hauer.

Yaky, John & Mary Beemer. m. 6 Dec. 1832. Hauer.

Yaky, Martin & Amanda Russell. m. 1 Nov. 1836. Hauer.

Yates, Franklin A. & Emily Jane Griffith, dau. of Thomas Griffith,
wit. 20 Dec. 1853. MarReg. Hank.

Yeaca, Martin & Amanda Russell, dau. of Thomas Russell, bm. 31
Oct. 1836. Shel.

Yeaka, John & Mary Beamer. George Cooper, father, bm. 3 Dec.
1832. Shel.

Yeake, John & Mary Beemer. m. 6 Dec. 1832. ParReg A.

Yeakey, John & Eliza Crumbaker. Solomon Crumbaker attests groom's
age, bm. 26 Oct. 1838. Shel.

Yeaky, Simon & Barbera Cost. m. 4 May 1807. Littlejohn.

Yeates, William, Alexandria, D. C. & Sarah Caven, Waterford. m.
6 April 1814. FFMM.

Yellott, Coleman & M. Virginia Rust, dau. of General Rust, wit.
2 April 1851. MarReg.

Yerby, John & Mary M. Edwards. m. 27 Oct. 1810. Littlejohn.

Yocky, Martin & Amanda Russell. m. 1 Nov. 1836. ParReg A. Shel.

Young, Abraham & Susan B. Janney. John Janney affirms ages.
Charles F. Sangster, bm. 9 Feb. 1839. Shel.

Young, Alfred & Emily Worthington. Craven Osborne attests
bride's age, bm. 9 Sep. 1834. Shel.

Young, David & Elizabeth Hatcher. m. 11 Oct. 1800. Littlejohn.

Young, David & Phebe R. Donohoe. Stephen J. Donohoe, bm.
29 March 1836. White. Shel.

Young, George & Catherine Griffith. m. 20 June 1805. Dunn.

Young, Israel & Hanh. Philips. m. 3 Jan. 1806. Littlejohn.

Young, James & Louise Wyatt. m. 28 Aug. 1806. Dunn.

Young, Jerome B. & Mary E. Sterrett. Bride's mother consents.
R. H. Hoffman attests groom's age, bm. 18 Oct. 1843. Shel.

Young, John & Elizabeth Ann Gheen, dau. of Narcissa Gheen.
Leroy Gheen, bm. 16 March 1835. Shel.

Young, John B. & Eliza Aldridge, dau. of John Aldridge, bm.
20 March 1832. Shel.

Young, John M. & Teresa Allen. Samuel C. Allen attests bride's
age, bm. 2 Nov. 1829. Ogilvie.

Young, Samuel & Sophia V. Craven. Samuel Craven attests ages, bm.
30 Aug. 1838. Shel.
Young, Thomas & Martha A. Wright. Robert E. Beall attests ages,
bm. 9 Nov. 1844. Shel.
Young, Thomas Jefferson & Mercy Smith. Manly Mead attests ages,
bm. 16 Jan. 1836. m. 16 July 1836. White. Shel.
Young, William & Rebecca Nicolls. m. 2 April 1812. Dunn.
Zentbauer, Christian & Sarah Schart; both single. By license.
m. 28 Feb. 1822. ParReg A.
Zerwick, Christian & Elisabetha Derry, dau. of Jacob Derry; both
single. By license. m. 12 March 1812. ParReg A.
Ziegefuss, Johannes & Ana Philler, single. By license. m.
18 Aug. 1825. ParReg A.
Zimm, Jacob & Elizabeth Halley. William Ambler attests bride's
age, bm. 12 May 1833. Cam.

Section 2

Adams, Francis. His widow, Martha N. Adams, requests her dower
   in his estate. 18 April 1844. DB U, p. 54.
Adams, Gabriel. Exr., William Adams, moves his widow, Elizabeth
   Adams, be assigned her dower. 11 Nov. 1761. OB A, p. 531.
Alexander, Lorentz, J., of Baltimore City & Julia A. Hodgson, of
   Alexandria, dau. of Portia Hodgson, deceased, and sister of
   Cornelia Hodgson, deceased. Marriage contract. 19 April 1847.
   DB 4Y, p. 45.
Armistead, John B., of Caroline County, Va. & Anna Beale Carter,
   dau. of John Carter. 3rd parties: John Carter, Landon Carter.
   Marriage contract. 22 June 1796. DB X, p. 365.
Bagent, William, soldier in the Revolution. Died intestate
   leaving no widow but children: William; John; Jacob; Ellen;
   Catharine, wife of William Mahagon; Nancy, wife of Jacob
   Eckman; Sarah, wife of Washington Lewis; Mary, wife of
   Daniel Crim. John Bagant has since died leaving children:
   Mary; Catharine; Sarah; Lydia; Raynold; Thomas; Matilda.
   13 July 1846. MB 1846-1847, p. 116.
Bayly, Joseph. His widow, Elizabeth Bayly, relinquishes his will.
   14 Dec. 1789. OB L, p. 321. 22 Dec. 1789, DB R, p. 395.
Beans, James. His widow, Anna Beans, is alloted her dower. 7 Sep.
   1852. DB 5F, p. 335.
Beans, Matthew. His widow is alloted her dower. 2 April 1824.
   DB 3H, p. 180.
Benedict, William B., of Washington, D. C. & Henrietta Henderson,
   who holds 1/7th part of tract in Loudoun County. 3rd party:
   William H. Gray. Marriage contract. 18 May 1849. DB 5B, p. 263.
Berry, William, who has children by former marriage & Cynthia
   Triplett. Marriage contract. 10 Aug. 1810. DB 2N, p. 41.
Boggess, Henry. His widow, Mary Ann Boggess, is to be alloted her
   dower. 12 Dec. 1796. OB R, p. 32.
Brent, George. His widow, Joanna Brent, is to be alloted her
   dower. 12 April 1790. OB M, p. 4.
Bronaugh, William. His widow, Jane Bronaugh, renounces his will.
   12 Nov. 1827. MB 1826-1828, p. 323.
Broughton, William. His widow, Elizabeth Bayly late Elizabeth
   Broughton, requests her dower. 8 Feb. 1790. OB L, p. 339.
   Widow receives her allotment. 12 Sep. 1791. OB O, p. 10.
Boss, Peter. Widow, Mary Boss, receives allotment of her dower.
   15 June 1820. DB 3A, p. 290.
Brown, Daniel & Ann Watkins, widow of William Watkins. 3rd party:
   Mahlon Craven. Her children: Louisa; Bernard; Sarah Ann;
   Elender. Marriage contract. 25 May 1825. DB 3K, p. 306.

Bryerly, Samuel, of Frederick County, Va. & Elizabeth Taliaferro
Harrison, widow of Thomas Harrison, who has land in Prince
William County. 3rd parties: William C. Fitzhugh, Cuthbert
Powell. Her children: Ann; Frances. Marriage contract. 12 May
1827. DB 3-0, p. 78.

Burr, Charles, of Washington, D. C. & Mary A. Burr, his wife, dau.
of Cartwright and Elizabeth Tippett, the former deceased, of
Washington, D. C. 3rd party: Elizabeth Tippett. Marriage
settlement. 29 Nov. 1826. DB 3N, p. 98.

Butcher, Samuel. His widow, Susannah Butcher, requests her dower.
5 June 1778. OB G, p. 99.

Canby, Joseph & Mary Hughes, who holds real and personal property.
3rd party: Thomas Hughes. Marriage contract. 24 Feb. 1829.
DB 3R, p. 310.

Carney, William. Court attests Rosanna Carney is his widow and is
entitled to his pension. 13 Aug. 1839. MB 1836-1839, p. 323.

Carter, Addison B. & Lucy G. Burwell, of Winchester, Frederick
County, Va. Marriage contract. 15 Oct. 1849. DB 5C, p. 15.

Cavan, Patrick. His widow, Sarah Cavan, is to be alloted her
dower. 16 Sep. 1807. OB 1, p. 93. OB 2, p. 163.

Chick, William. His widow, Rebeckah Chick, is to be alloted her
dower. 13 Jan. 1801. OB U, p. 184.

Chilton, George. His widow, Ann Chilton, is to be alloted her
dower. 9 April 1771. OB E, p. 100.

Chittenden, W. B. & Ann Eliza Carter Richardson, sister of Peter
Lyons, deceased. She owns Richmond property from her parents.
Marriage contract. 27 Feb. 1843. DB 4V, p. 175.

Cleveland, William. His estate is to be divided between his widow,
Mary Cleveland, and her daughter, Darcus. 8 Feb. 1790. OB L,
p. 339.

Clowes, Joseph. His widow, Mary Clowes, asks his noncupative will
be presented at court and that Elizabeth Clowes, Thomas Clowes,
Mary Jane Clowes be summoned to show, if can, why it should
not be admitted to record. 11 Feb. 1833. MB 1832-1833, p. 337.

Combs, Samuel & Elizabeth Williams. Marriage contract. 3 April
1788. DB V, pp. 54, 55.

Conner, David & Ann Newton, who owns property. Her children:
John C.; Elizabeth Lee; Robert C.; Charles C.; Henry;
Alexander. Marriage contract. 27 Dec. 1821. DB 3D, p. 343.

Conrad, David. His widow, Elizabeth Conrad, is to be alloted her
dower. 18 Feb. 1851. DB 5F, p. 230. 9 Dec. 1850. MB 1850-
1852, p. 98.

Coutzman, Jacob. His widow is Catherine Coutzman. 14 Aug. 1780.
OB G, p. 256.

Craine, John & Elizabeth Wornal, widow of James Wornal, who owns
property from her father's estate. Marriage contract. 12 March
1836. DB 4F, p. 389.

Cridler (Crider), Frederick. His widow, Margaret Cridler, receives
her dower. 4 June 1822. DB 3E, p. 225.

Cummings, John, of Culpeper County, who has children by former
marriage & Margaret Emmingson (Emmison). Proved by Patrick
McGavack, Henry McGavack, Sarah McGavack. To be certified to
Culpeper Court. Marriage contract. 12 April 1813. MB 6, pp.
287, 304. DB 2Q, p. 256.

Damood, Jacob & Eleanor Marstellar. Marriage agreement. 22 Dec. 1826. MB 1826-1828, p. 51.

Denning, William, of Fairfax County & Margaret A. French, dau. of Lewis and Ann G. French, the former deceased. Marriage contract. 15 Dec. 1851. DB 5E, p. 246.

Donohoe, Cornelius. His widow, Margerett Donohoe, is alloted her dower. 11 April 1792. OB O, p. 260.

Dulin, ____. His widow, Nancy (Ann) Dulin, is alloted her dower. 1 Oct. 1840. DB 4-O, p. 299.

Dunn, ___. Power of attorney from Margaret Whalen otherwise Dunn widow, Winifred Whalen alias Phelan, wife of Jeremiah Phelan and Jeremiah Phelan to Edward Phelan presented to court under hand of --- consul of United States in the city of Dublin. 8 Dec. 1806. OB Z, p. 191.

Edward, Thomas W. & Sarah E. Chichester, of Leesburg. 3rd party: Robert Wright. Marriage contract. 27 Oct. 1843. DB 4T, p. 12.

Ellzey, William. His widow, Alice Ellzey, renounces his will. 12 Sep. 1796. OB Q, p. 479. His daughters: Elizabeth; Mary. 12 Sep. 1796. DB X, pp. 172, 174.

Ellzey, William & Rebecca Page, widow of Carter B. Page, of Richmond. 3rd parties: Burr William Harrison, John T. M. Harrison. Marriage contract. 20 April 1829. DB 3W, p. 462.

Emery, Jacob. His widow, Catharine Emery, is to be alloted her dower. 8 April 1816. MB 1816-1817, p. 138.

Evans, David. His widow, Elizabeth Evans, is to be alloted her dower. 9 July 1792. OB O, p. 285. 9 April 1793. OB P, p. 99. 12 April 1796. OB Q, p. 368.

Evans, David. His widow, Mary Evans, renounces his will. 9 July 1798. OB S, p. 95.

Evans, John. His widow, Mary Evans, is alloted her dower. 22 June 1772. OB E, p. 342.

Evans, Joshua. His widow, Martha Evans, is to be alloted her dower. 13 Dec. 1773. OB F, p. 296.

Evans, William. His widow, Martha Evans, renounces his will. 10 Feb. 1804. OB X, p. 24.

Ewers, Jonathan & Phebe Gregg, dau. of Joseph Gregg. 3rd party: Townsend J. Jury. Marriage contract. 20 Oct. 1836. DB 4L, p. 265.

Farrow, Joseph. His widow, Elizabeth Farrow, renounces his will. 13 April 1784. OB H, p. 227.

Fry, Nicholas. A pensioner, he died 23 March 1840. The court attests Margaret Fry is his widow. 11 Sep. 1840. MB 1840-1841, p. 137.

Fryer, James. His late relict, Abigail Self, appears in court. 12 Nov. 1771. OB E, p. 249.

Furr, Enoch. His widow, Sarah Furr, renounces his will. 9 April 1845. DB 4V, p. 52. MB 1843-1845, p. 346. She asks to obtain benefits of Congress of 17 June 1844. 9 Feb. 1846. MB 1846-1847, p. 19.

Garner, William & Ann Gover, dau. of Samuel Gover. Her son: Edwin Gover. Marriage contract. 19 Sep. 1833. DB 4B, p. 96.

George, John & Sarah Long. 3rd party: John Roof. Marriage contract. 15 May 1840. DB 4-O, p. 166.

Gibson, John. His widow, Elizabeth Gibson, is to be alloted her dower. 12 April 1814. MB 7, p. 208. OB 4, p. 139.

Gregg, George. Proved by oath of Timothy Nixon and affirmed by
William Gregg that his wife is Elizabeth Wilson, dau. of John
Wilson, deceased and granddaughter of Alexander Wilson, who
formerly resided this county, died in Pa. 8 Jan. 1809. OB 3,
p. 268. OB 4, p. 5.

Gregg, Samuel. His widow, Esther Gregg, renounces his will. 13 Feb.
1804. OB X, p. 21. Her dower is to be alloted. OB X, p. 107.

Griffith, Thomas, a Revolutionary War soldier. Court attests Mary
Griffith is his widow. 14 Oct. 1839. MB 1837-1839, p. 358.

Grubb, Ebenezer. His widow, Mary Grubb, renounces his will. 14 Feb.
1835. DB 4E, p. 33.

Gulick, John. His widow, Leanah (Lenah) Gulick, renounces his
will. 12 Sep. 1808. OB 2, p. 128. She is to be alloted her
dower. 12 Dec. 1808. OB 2, p. 229.

Gulick, Moses. His widow, Patsey Gulick, is to be alloted her
dower. 8 Jan. 1827. DB 3S, p. 231.

Halbert, Michael. His widow, Rosey Halbert, renounces his will.
11 April 1796. OB Q, p. 355.

Hamilton, David, a poor shoemaker. His widow, Catherine Hamilton,
is to be put on pension list. 10 April 1787. OB K, p. 92.

Hamilton, Robert. His widow, Jane Hamilton, is to be alloted her
dower. 14 Oct. 1800. OB U, p. 67.

Handley, David. His widow, Mary Handley, renounces his will.
13 Aug. 1850. MB 1850-1852, p. 40.

Hardage, Lane, of Montgomery County, Md., who owns "Fortune" and
"Mill Road" plantation there & Mary Greenfield. Marriage
contract. 23 Nov. 1799. DB 2A, p. 46.

Harris, Obed. His widow, Elizabeth Harris. 14 Aug. 1811. MB 5,
p. 75.

Harris, William. His widow, Hannah Harris, relinquishes admin.
of his estate in favor of Joseph Combs. 10 Nov. 1766. OB C,
p. 219.

Harrison, William Butler. Court certifies his wife, Penelope
Harrison, is sister and sole heir of Capt. Andrew Russell,
5th Va. Reg. in late war with Great Britain. 10 Dec. 1799.
OB T, p. 201.

Hawke, William, of Leesburg & Jane Perfect, dau. of Robert
Perfect. Marriage contract. 28 July 1821. DB 3D, p. 25.

Gordon, Robert. Court orders John Helm and Sarah, his wife, admr.
of Gordon, to make report. 9 May 1785. OB H, p. 484.

Hicks, Israel. His widow, Rachel Hicks, is to be alloted her
dower. 14 Aug. 1815. MB 1815-1817, p. 6.

Hodgson, William, of Alexandria & Portia Lee, dau. of late
William Lee, James City County and ward of Richard Bland Lee.
Couple m. 2 May 1790. Marriage contract. 28 June 1816.
DB 2U, p. 190.

Holyfield, Valentine. His widow, Eleanor Holyfield, relinquishes
admin. of his estate. 13 July 1762. OB B, p. 3.

Hooff, Philip H. & Elizabeth Blincoe, dau. of late Sampson
Blincoe. 3rd party: Martha S. Blincoe. Marriage contract.
10 Feb. 1847. DB 4X, p. 263.

Hough, John. His widow, Elizabeth Hough, is alloted her dower.
15 Feb. 1825. DB 3I, p. 266.

LOUDOUN COUNTY MARRIAGES

Humfrey, Isaac. His widow, Jane Humfrey, is alloted her dower.
10 June 1799. OB T, p. 17.

James, John. His widow, Sarah B. James, is to be alloted her
dower. 9 Dec. 1847. DB 4Y, p. 394.

James, Thomas. His widow, Mary James. Deed from James Matson.
9 May 1840. MB 1840-1841, p. 151.

James, William. His widow, Abigail James, relinquishes admin. of
his estate. 8 Nov. 1813. MB 7, p. 69.

Johnson, Daniel C. & Britania S. Loman (Lomax), widow of Lawson
Loman. Marriage contract. 14 Feb. 1822. DB 3F, p. 61.

Johnston,____, Colo. His widow, Henrietta Eskridge late Johnston,
is to be alloted her dower. 10 Aug. 1812. MB 6, p. 74.

King, William & Tacey Daniel, dau. of Thomas Humphrey, deceased,
and widow of Joseph Daniel. 3rd party: John M. Young.
Marriage contract. 15 Sep. 1831. DB 3W, p. 474.

Kyst, John. His widow, Catharine Kyst, to receive her dower and
his estate to be divided. Children: Frederick; Henry;
Christian; Jacob; John; George; Elizabeth; Molly and Anthony
Connard her husband; and Christianna and Samuel Wright, her
husband. 9 March 1801. OB U, p. 245.

Lacey, David. His widow, Sarah Lacey, renounces his will. 5 Dec.
1818. DB 2Y, p. 197.

Lambert, Francis & Mary Louisa Saffer, dau. of William and
Susan Saffer, the former deceased. 3rd party: Susan Saffer.
Marriage contract. 20 May 1846. DB 4X, p. 346.

Lane, John. His widow, Catharine Lane, is to be alloted her
dower. 14 April 1763. OB B, p. 111.

Lane, William Carr. His widow, Ann Lane, renounces, his will.
10 June 1771. OB E, p. 151. 6 April 1771. DB H, p. 159.

Leadbeater, John, Baltimore City, Baltimore County, Md. &
Mary P. Stabler, of Alexandria, dau. of the late Edward
Stabler. Her sister: Caroline Stabler, deceased. 3rd party:
William Stabler. 19 June 1835. DB 4E, p. 70.

Lee, George & Evelyn B. Beverly, dau. of Robert Beverly, Essex
County. 3rd party: Carter Beverly. Marriage contract. 12 Oct.
1798. DB Z, p. 221. OB T, p. 1.

Leedom, Thomas & Hannah Williams. Marriage contract. 24 Oct.
1814. DB 2S, p. 55.

Littleton, Eli, of Clarke County, Va. & Emily Ward. 3rd party:
William D. Settle. Marriage contract. 19 Nov. 1851. DB 5E,
p. 282. 9 Feb. 1852. MB 12, p. 295.

Love, James. His widow, Susanna Love, is to be alloted her dower.
His other heirs: Thomas B.; James D.; Fenton M.; Mary R.
4 May 1846. DB 4W, p. 308.

Love, Richard H. His wife, Eliza Matilda Love, relinquishes her
dower in conveyance by Richard H. Love and wife to Richard H.
Ludwell and Ann C. Lee. 13 March 1815. MB 7, p. 394.

McClellan, William. His household estate is divided between his
widow, Sarah Wilson McClellan and his son, Robert McClellan.
12 May 1778. OB G, p. 96.

McCray, James, a pensioner, d. 25 July 1840. Court attests Mary
McCray, his widow, now resides in Loudoun. 9 May 1840.
MB 7, p. 151.

LOUDOUN COUNTY MARRIAGES

McGeath, William. His widow, Lydia Henry, formerly Lydia
    McGeath, is to be alloted her dower. 15 Dec. 1807. OB 1,
    p. 226.
McKnight, William. His widow, Margaret McKnight, is to be
    alloted her dower. 12 March 1812. MB 5, p. 289.
Miller, George. His widow, Mary Miller, renounces his will.
    27 Feb. 1849. DB 5B, p. 33.
Mills, John. His widow, Elizabeth Mills, is to be alloted her
    dower. His other heirs: Elizabeth Mills, deceased; William
    Mills. 13 Nov. 1846. DB 4Y, p. 395.
Monday, Aaron, Revolutionary pensioner of the U. S., d. 8 Sep.
    1834. His widow, Ann Monday, proved by Thomas R. Saunders.
    14 Oct. 1834. MB 1834-1836, p. 64.
Monkhouse, Jonathan. His widow, Mary Monkhouse, receives her
    dower.10 Aug. 1778. OB G, p. 115.
Mullen, Samuel & Barbara Oden, who has dower interest in lands of
    Jacob Stoneburner. 3rd party: Charles B. Ball. Marriage
    contract. 30 Dec. 1844. DB 4U, p. 252.
Neale, Thomas. His widow to be alloted her dower. Index - "Ann
    Neale's Dower to be alloted." 11 Oct. 1790. OB N, p. 4.
Neer, David. His widow, Susannah G. Neer, to be alloted dower.
    13 April 1832. DB 3Z, p. 340.
Newton, John, of Leesburg & Harriet McCabe, dau. of Henry
    McCabe and ward of Charles Binns. Marriage contract. 21 Jan.
    1808. DB 2I, p. 309.
Noland, Philip, Junior. His widow, Mary Noland, renounces his
    will. 13 June 1785. OB I, p. 28.
Oden, Thomas & Barbara Drish, widow of William Drish, who has
    dower rights in estate of Jacob Stoneburner, a former
    husband. 3rd party: Samuel M. Edwards. Marriage contract.
    31 May 1832. DB 3Y, p. 43.
Orange, James & Susan Fichter. 3rd party: George Turner.
    Marriage contract. 26 Nov. 1834. DB 4C, p. 229.
Osborne, Richard. His widow, Hannah Osborne, requests her dower.
    10 April 1797. OB R, p. 98.
Oswald, Henry. His widow, Martha Oswald, to tell court why she
    will not admin. his estate. 17 Aug. 1810. OB 4, p. 169.
Page, Thomas I. & Benjamina Price. 3rd party: Benjamin King.
    Marriage contract. 7 Nov. 1838. DB 4L, p. 212.
Palmer, Samuel, Sr. & Mary Porter. 3rd party: Mason Chamblin.
    Marriage contract. 30 June 1835. DB 4D, p. 363.
Palmer, Samuel L., of Philadelphia, who does not now reside in
    Va. & Nancy Thrift, who has property in Fairfax. 3rd party:
    Mason Chamblin. Marriage contract. 8 May 1842. DB 4Q, p. 331.
Patterson, Fleming. His widow, Elizabeth Patterson, requests her
    dower. 8 Feb. 1779. OB G, p. 140.
Payne, Jonah. His widow, Valinda Payne, is to be alloted her
    dower. 11 Jan. 1790. OB L, p. 326.
Payne, Josiah. His widow, Verlinda Skinner late Verlinda Payne,
    requests her dower. 9 April 1793. OB P, p. 98.
Potter, John, of Leesburg & Elizabeth Green, who is possessed of
    considerable property. 3rd parties: William Ellzey, Syner
    Bayly. Marriage contract. 2 Sep. 1814. DB 2S, p. 289.

Potts, Edward. His widow, Mary Potts, is to be alloted her dower.
9 Sep. 1845. DB 4W, p. 57. 8 Sep. 1845. MB 9, p. 444.

Powell, Cuthbert. His widow, Catherine Powell, is to be alloted
her dower. 14 Aug. 1850. DB 5F, p. 329.

Powell, Elisha. His widow, Ann Powell, is to be alloted her dower.
9 Oct. 1810. OB 4, p. 195.

Powell, Leven. His wife, Sarah Powell, relinquishes her dower in
certain lands conveyed by her husband to Christopher Perfect.
10 Nov. 1766. OB C, p. 219.

Pugh, Samuel. His widow, Charity Pugh, to receive her dower.
10 April 1780. OB G, p. 234.

Pugh, Spencer & Mary Hopewell. Marriage contract. 9 April 1803.
DB 2C, p. 462.

Ramey, Jacob. His widow, Deborah Ramey, is to be alloted her dower.
13 April 1801. OB U, p. 302. 14 June 1802. OB V, p. 293.

Rawlings, John. His widow, Susanna Rawlings, to be summoned to
take admin. of his estate. 9 Feb. 1796. OB Q, p. 333.

Redmond, Andrew. His widow, Ann Redmond, renounces his will.
14 Dec. 1807. OB 1, p. 2193. 11 April 1808. OB 1, p. 344.

Reed, Reuben. His widow, Sarah Reed, is to be alloted her dower.
11 July 1791. OB N, p. 242. 1 Oct. 1791. OB O, p. 49.

Reid, James. His widow, Rebecca Reid, receives her dower.
10 June 1815. MB 1815-1817, p. 166.

Richardson, Robert P. & Ann Eliza Carter Lyons. Marriage contract.
Proved in Court of Hastings, Richmond. 12 Nov. 1838. MB 1837-
1839, p. 175. DB 4L, p. 151.

Robertson, John & Elizabeth Purcell. Marriage contract. 20 March
1806. DB 2G, p. 211.

Rolls, George, late of county, captain U. S. Navy, Revolution,
d. 1795. John Dunkam and Margaret A. (formerly Rolls) Dunkam
attest service and that he left children: George N.; Charles;
Margaret A. George N. d. intestate, unm. Charles left
children: Sarah E. m. William Smith; John W.; Alexander P.;
Edward O.; Nathaniel S.; George N.; Margaret S. (last 6 under
21 years). 9 Nov. 1835. MB 1834-1836, p. 315.

Rose, Robert T. & Harriet M. Swart, dau. of James Swart. Elizabeth Taylor, wife of James W. Taylor, formerly widow of
James Swart the Elder. Marriage contract. 1847. DB 4Y, p. 251.

Rozell, Peter. His wife, Anna Rozell, relinquishes her dower in
certain lands conveyed by her husband to Jeremiah Foster.
11 Nov. 1766. OB C, p. 222.

Rust, William. His widow, Monacha Rust, to be alloted her dower.
11 Feb. 1801. OB U, p. 220.

Sands, Isaac. His widow, Mary Dunscomb late Mary Sands, asks
her dower be assigned. 14 Dec. 1795. OB Q, p. 312.

Sanders, Henry. His widow, Patience Sanders, renounces his will.
28 Nov. 1823. DB 3G, p. 262.

Sanders, Nicholas. His widow, Mary Sanders, to be alloted her
dower. 9 May 1803. OB W, p. 134.

Saunders, Brittan & Ann Eckart, late wife of Casper Ekart.
3rd parties: Charles Gullatt, Samuel M. Edwards. Marriage
contract. 7 March 1825. DB 3K, p. 51.

Scott, Joseph. His widow, Hannah Fox late Hannah Scott, to be
alloted her dower. 14 April 1778. OB G, p. 82.

Scott, Robert. His widow, Charity Furr, to have her dower in
lands sold by her late husband. 14 Sep. 1784. OB H, p. 382.

Shreve, William. His widow, Freelove Shreve, to have her dower
alloted on motion of William Shreve, his heir. 14 March 1759.
OB A, p. 217. Her dower alloted. 8 May 1759. DB A, p. 290.

Sinclair, ____. His widow, Edith Sinclair, to receive her dower.
15 Aug. 1817. MB 1815-1817, p. 415.

Sinkler, Wayman, of Prince William County, Dittengen Parish &
Hester Linton, widow, Cameron Parish. 3rd party: David Flynt.
Marriage contract. 19 Nov. 1760. DB B, pp. 92, 93.

Slacht, Cornelius, died in the Continental Service. His widow is
Amey Slacht, attested to by oath of Jacob Slacht. 12 April
1785. OB H, p. 463.

Slaughter, Arthur & Sarah D. H. Fowke, dau. of Robert D. Fowke.
Marriage contract. 28 May 1811. DB 2-O, p. 194. 13 Jan. 1812.
MB 5, p. 197.

Slopewell, John. His widow, Hannah Talbert, to administer his
estate. 13 June 1769. OB D, p. 225.

Smart, John P. & Mary E. Wherry. 3rd party: Hamilton Rogers.
Marriage contract. 6 Oct. 1841. DB 4P, p. 397.

Smith, James & Nancy James, dau. of William and Abigail James.
Her brother, William James, deceased. 3rd parties: Dean
James, John James. 22 Feb. 1825. DB 3I, p. 343.

Smith, John, of Montgomery County, Md. & Maria Vermillion, widow
of Benjamin Vermillion. 3rd party: Michael William Whitmore.
Marriage contract. 14 March 1844. DB 4T, p. 294.

Smith, Seth. He produces memo by sister, Mary Smith, during her
last illness, died 6th Inst. in the presence of Mary Galleher,
widow of William Galleher and Sarah Galleher, widow of John
Galleher. Mary Smith wished her brother to have all property
including Ohio land. Next of kin: Jacob Smith; Amos Smith;
John Smith; Samuel Smith; Aaron Halloway and Rachel his wife
(late Smith); James McPherson and Kezeah his wife (late
Smith), all of whom reside out of the Commonwealth. 14 May
1832. MB 1832-1833, p. 73.

Snyder, Peter. His widow, Sarah Dawson late Snyder, to be alloted
her dower. 10 Oct. 1843. DB 4S, p. 394.

Stephens, Joseph. His wife, Elizabeth Stephens, comes into court
and relinquishes her dower. 14 Nov. 1771. OB E, p. 252.

Stephenson, James. His widow, Elizabeth C. Stephenson, to be
alloted her dower. Jan. 1843. DB 4S, p. 74.

Stukesberry, Robert. His widow, Jane Parks, as attested by her
husband, Andrew Parks, in petition to court. 10 Oct. 1774.
OB F, p. 505.

Sullivan, George & Elizabeth James, dau. of Benjamin James,
deceased. Marriage contract. 1 March 1848. DB 5A, p. 283.

Surghnor, James & Harriet P. Harrison, dau. of Valentine Harrison,
who owns some Kentucky land. 3rd party: Selden Harrison.
Marriage contract. 24 Nov. 1808. DB 3L, p. 244.

Swart, James. His widow, Elizabeth Swart, renounces his will.
11 Nov. 1833. MB 1833-1834, p. 201. She receives her dower.
Feb. 1834. DB 4B, p. 372.

Taylor, William. His widow, Sarah Taylor, claims her right of
dower. 14 Sep. 1789. OB L, p. 269.

Thompson, Eleanor & Jemima Pettit, widow of George Pettit.
3rd party: Mahlon Baldwin. Marriage contract. 28 Aug. 1843.
DB 4S, p. 360.

Tillett, Samuel. His widow, Eleanor Tillett, renounces his will.
23 Oct. 1839. DB 4N, p. 111.

Tillett, Edward. Dower of his widow, Elizabeth Tillett, recorded.
13 July 1807. OB Z, p. 422.

Tramell, Samson, Jr. His widow, Caron Tramell, asks for her dower.
16 Sep. 1795. OB Q, p. 254.

Tyler, Edmund. His widow, Mary K. Tyler, receives her dower.
16 Sep. 1844. DB 4U, p. 213.

Vandevanter, Isaac. His widow, Mary Vandevanter, renounces his
will. 13 April 1835. DB 4D, p. 79. MB 1834-1836, p. 171.

Wade, Jesse. His widow, Mary Wade, renounces his will. 10 Dec.
1810. OB 4, p. 257.

Walrond, John. Court certifies his widow is Elizabeth Walrond
and that he d. in the Continental Army. 9 Oct. 1786. OB I,
p. 346.

Waters, Diah. His widow, Catherine Waters, receives her dower.
12 May 1817. DB 2W, p. 365.

Watson, Thomas. Court orders his estate divided between his
children and Jacob Gardner, who intermarried with his widow.
8 Sep. 1783. OB H, p. 141.

Watts, Richard Key, Jr. & Helen G. Rose. 3rd party: John Rose.
Marriage contract. 6 Dec. 1820. DB 3B, p. 278.

Weadon, William & Mary Wright, widow of Charles Wright. 3rd
party: Benjamin Rust. Marriage contract. 25 June 1839.
DB 4M, p. 296. MB 1837-1839, p. 312.

West, John, Revolutionary pensioner, d. 19 Dec. 1835. His widow,
Hannah West, proven by Mahlon Morris. 14 March 1836. MB 1836-
1837, p. 29.

West, William. His widow, Mary West, named in his will and is to
be joined with the other executors in the probate. 15 Nov.
1769. OB D, p. 299.

Whaley, James. His widow, Ann Whaley, renounces his will. 8 Aug.
1785. OB I, p. 57.

Wigginton, Benjamin, pensioner, d. 2 Dec. 1845. He left no widow
but children: Presly; John; daughter believed to be named
Jane. 9 Feb. 1846. MB 1846-1847, p. 21.

Wildman, John. His widow, Eleanor Wildman, renounces his will.
18 March 1826. DB 3N, p. 73.

Williams, William. His wife, Elizabeth Williams, relinquishes her
dower to Ellis Williams. 13 May 1816. MB 1815-1817, p. 140.

Wills, Thomas William. His widow, Hester Wills, to be alloted
her dower and slaves and personal estate of Jacob Smith to be
divided and alloted to Jacob Smith, the heir, his part.
12 June 1764. OB B, p. 361.

Wood, Joseph. His widow, Lydia Wood, renounces his will. 1 April
1844. DB 4T, p. 353. She receives her dower. 1 June 1844. DB
4U, p. 56.

Woodford, William. His widow, Elizabeth Hill, wife of James Hill,
is to be alloted her dower. 10 Jan. 1831. DB 3W, p. 199.

Woodford, William. His widow, Susanna Woodford, is to be alloted
her dower. 18 June 1808. OB 2, p. 84. 12 March 1812. MB 5,
p. 289.

Wright, Anthony. His widow, Elizabeth Wright, is to be alloted her dower. 9 Nov. 1818. DB 2X, p. 201.

Wright, William. His widow, Ann Wright, is to be alloted her dower. 12 Aug. 1817. MB 1815-1817, p. 405.

Young, William. His widow, Rebecca Young, is to be alloted her dower. His heir, William Young. 14 Oct. 1851. MB 1850-1852, p. 257. 15 March 1853. DB 5G, p. 214.

Addenda

Bailey, John, Jr. & Lucy Hutchison. Chapin Bailey attests bride's age, bm. 7 Dec. 1835. Cam.

Ballenger, William, son of Henry Ballenger, Frederick County, Maryland & Cassandra Plummer, dau. of Samuel Plummer, Prince George's County, Maryland. m. 3 Aug. 1751. Monoquisy Meeting House. FFMM.

Beverdige, William & Lucy Chinn, dau. of Rawleigh Chinn. Jas. Pickett, bm. 6 Nov. 1799.

Birdsall, William & Hannah Steer. m. 1 March 1809. FFMM.

Brown, John, son of Isaac and Margaret Brown, deceased, Frederick County, Va. & Elizabeth Richardson, dau. of Richard and Mary Richardson, of Frederick County, Maryland. m. 29 Jan. 1795. At Richard Richardson's house. FFMM.

Donaldson, John & Jane Wigington. License: 21 Dec. 1761. FeeBk 4.

Drinker, George, Alexandria, Va., son of Joseph and Hannah Drinker, of Philadelphia, Pa. & Ruth Miller, dau. of Warwick and Elizabeth Miller, deceased, of Chester County, state aforesaid. m. 9 July 1795, Alexandria. FFMM.

Elgin, Ignatius & Mary Ann Lee, dau. of Joshua Lee, bm. 7 Nov. 1831. Cam.

Everheart, Israel & Maria Ropp, dau. of Nicholas Ropp. Solomon Ritchie, bm. 29 Nov. 1836. Shel.

Fox, Jesse & Sarah Poukens, dau. of John Poppens. Asa Fox, bm. 12 April 1796.

Gille, Beverly T. & Emily E. Saunders (Summers). John Surghnor, bride's guardian, attests groom's age, bm. 31 Aug. 1841.Shel.

Gipson, Gideon, of Linganore, Frederick County, Maryland & Hannah Unkles, of Pipe Creek, county proved aforesaid. m. 12 Dec. 1770, Pipe Creek. FFMM.

Goings, Elihu & Susannah Lucas. m. 19 April 1813. Henkle.

Green, Andrew & Mary Lucas, dau. of Thomas Lucas. Joseph Grove, bm. 5 March 1799.

Harper, Washington & Emily Ryan (Cross). John Cross proves bride's age, wit. 12 Jan. 1852. MarReg. m. 13 Jan. 1852.Gover.

Harvey, Fielding (Fielden) & Ruth Trayhorn (Treyhorn), ward of Stephen McPherson, bm. 15 March 1832. Green. Shel.

Hewes, Abraham, Alexandria & Rachel Miller. m. 14 July 1796, at Alexandria. FFMM.

Hixon, Stephen & Mary Rawlins. m. 1809-1810. Mines.

Hixon, Timothy & Leher Hanks. m. March 1797. Littlejohn.

Hixon, Timothy & Patience Wiatt. m. 2 Dec. 1796. Littlejohn.

Hixon, Timothy & Sarah Patterson. m. 20 Sep. 1803. Littlejohn.

LOUDOUN COUNTY MARRIAGES

Hixon, William & Rachel Lacey. m. 26 May 1804. Littlejohn.
Hole, William P. & Eleanor Harrison. 12 July 1810.
Hough, Joseph & Sarah Gray. m. 15 April 1812. T. Littleton.
Howell, John & Patty Reed. James Reed, bm.26 Dec. 1809.24 Dec.
    1809. Littlejohn.
Howell, Townsend & Ann C. Frye. Joseph Frye attests ages, bm.
    19 Nov. 1845. Torrence. Cam.
Janney, Jonas, Gent. & Pleasant Smith. m. 23 May 1825. Janney,
    Clerk.
Lamb, Samuel & Lucy Orrison. m. 9 June 1853. Rodgers.
Landrie, Thomas & Amelia Carr. m. 27 Dec. 1802. Littlejohn.
Lane, Arthur F. & Catharine L. Crain. Peter Gregg, bm. 10 Jan.
    1833. m. 20 June 1833. Furlong.
Lane, Jefferson & Milly Gante, dau. of Lucy Gant. Presly Saunders,
    bm. 29 June 1842. Shel.
Lane, Lewis & Rachel Lane, dau. of William Lane, bm.; free people
    of colour. 14 Dec. 1831. Shel.
Lane, Lyman L. & Nancy Cost. Jacob Cost attests ages. Samuel
    Purcell, bm. 6 Jan. 1834. Shel.
Lane, William & Elizabeth Gregg. m. 15 Sep. 1840. Gover.
Lanen, James & Elisabeth Jane Webb, dau. of Elizabeth Webb, widow
    of Elisha Webb. John W. Webb, bm. 19 June 1848. Shel.
Lang, Claiborne & Elizabeth A. Richards. Samuel R. Newlon attests
    ages, bm. 10 Nov. 1834. Shel.
Lang, Conrad & Anna Maria Fuhrerin. m. 30 May 1786. ParReg A.
Lang, Johannes & Catharine Mill; both single. By license. m.
    9 May 1826. ParReg A.
Lang, Johannes, son of Johannes Lang and wife & Sussana
    Steinbrennerin, dau. of Daniel Steinbrenner and wife. By
    license. m. 17 May 1818. ParReg A.
Lang, John & Hannah Andrews. m. 15 Jan. 1813. Littlejohn.
Lang, Michael & Elianora Lilly; both single. By license. m.
    9 May 1826. ParReg A.
Lockheart, Jefferson & Margaret Waltman. m. 27 Oct. 1836.
    ParReg A. Shel.
Love, Thomas & Leah White. m. 13 Feb. 1821. Gilmore.
Lovett, David Harrison, Dr. & Jane Laurens Green, dau. of John C.
    Green. James H. Bennett, bm. 3 Jan. 1835. Shel.
Megrew, James, Monalen Township, York County, Pa. & Mary
    Ridgeway, of Pipe Creek, Frederick County, Maryland. m.
    11 Dec. 1760, Pipe Creek. FFMM.
Miller, Mordecai, Alexandria, Va., son of Warwick and Elizabeth
    Miller, deceased, of Chester County, Pa. & Rebecca
    Hartshorne, dau. of William and Susannah Hartshorne, of
    Fairfax County. m. 8 Nov. 1792, Alexandria. FFMM.
Osborn, Nicholas & Elizabeth S. Currell. m. 30 Oct. 1804.
    Littlejohn.
Page, Mann, Gent. His widow, Mrs. Seldon, asks for her dower and
    division of his estate between her and her son, William Page.
    18 Aug. 1786. OB I, p. 323.
Pidgion, William, son of Charles Pidgion, of Menallen Township,
    York County, Pa. & Rachel Everett, dau. of John Everett, of
    Hamiltons bans Township, county aforesaid. m. 9 Oct. 1760.
    FFMM.

LOUDOUN COUNTY MARRIAGES

Pleasants, John Scott, son of Jacob and Sarah Pleasants, the
former deceased, of Henrico County & Sarah Lownes, dau. of
James and Sarah Lownes of Alexandria. m. 29 April 1790,
Alexandria. FFMM.
Plummer, Joseph West, son of Joseph and Sarah Plummer & Mary
Taylor, dau. of Thomas and Cabel Taylor, both of Frederick
County, Maryland. m. 4 Jan. 1775, house of Thomas Taylor, of
Menoquesy. FFMM.
Plummer, Samuel, Frederick County, Maryland, son of Samuel and
Sarah Plummer, Prince George's County, Maryland & Mary
Tucker, same place, dau. of Robert and Lydia Tucker, Bucks
County, Pa. m. 18 Feb. 1764, Bush Creek, Frederick County,
Md. FFMM.
Richardson, Richard, son of Richard ___ Richardson & Mary
Pierpoint, dau. of Francis Pierpoint, both of Frederick
County, Maryland. m. 13 Sep. 1762. Monococy. FFMM.
Robey, Alexander & Mary Jane Ross. m. 11 March 1847. Dodge.
Robey, Colbert & Nancy Ross, dau. of John Ross. William Ross
attests groom's age, bm. 31 Dec. 1844. m. 9 Jan. 1845. Dodge.
Robey, Thompson B., son of Jane Robey, who states groom's under
21 years & Mildred A. Nalls, dau. of Carr B. Nalls, bm.
29 Jan. 1848. Shel.
Ross, Joseph & Mary Web. m. 17 Nov. 1798. Littlejohn.
Ross, Nicholas & Elizabeth Waltman, ward of Jacob Waltman, who
attests groom's age, bm. 11 Dec. 1809.
Ross, Samuel & Rachel Beamer. m. 10 Nov. 1842. Hauer.
Ross, Samuel C. & Lydia Price. m. 2 Jan. 1822-21 March 1822.
Mines.
Rossett, Ransalaer & Eliza Ann Cromwell. m. 11 March 1845. Gover.
Roszell, Stephen C. & Anna Don. m. 15 Feb. 1812. Dunn.
Rouse, John & Mary Fitzgerald. m. 11 Jan. 1808. Littlejohn.
Roust, James W. & Margaret Hickman. m. 30 Jan. 1845. ParReg A.
Rowan, George & Saria Thompkins. m. 20 Sep. 1798. Littlejohn.
Royston, Matthew W. & Minerva C. Carpenter, dau. of Harriet F.
Carpenter, who states bride was b. 17 Nov. 1820. Robert
Carpenter attests ages, bm. 5 Sep. 1842. Shel.
Rozel, S. A. & Louisa D. Tebbs. Charles G. Eskridge, bm. 2 Nov.
1841. Shel.
Roszel, Stephen Wesley & Catharine Triplet. m. 16 Jan. 1806.
Smith. Shel.
Ruff, Friderich & Rebecca Schambers; both single. By license. m.
5 Sep. 1811. ParReg A.
Ruff, Johannes & Elisabeth Deh; both single. By license. m.
20 Nov. 1828. ParReg A.
Rutter, Mason & Ann Andrews. Jonathan Andrews attests ages, bm.
31 Aug. 1833. Shel.
Scholfield, Jonathan, Alexandria & Eleanor Brown, Frederick
County, Va. m. Oct. 1806, Fairfax. FFMM.
Thompson, Eleanor & Jemima Pettitte. John Clear attests bride's
age, bm. 22 Aug. 1843. Shel.
Thompson, Thomas Edwin, son of Richard Thompson & Margaret M. A.
Williams. Notley C. Williams, bm. 22 June 1832. Shel.
Wanton, Phillip, Alexandria, Fairfax County, Va. & Mary Saunders,
Alexandria. m. 31 May 1792, Alexandria. FFMM.

Waters, Samuel, Frederick County, Maryland, son of Samuel and
Artrage Waters, of Prince George's County, Maryland &
Susannah Plummer, dau. of Joseph and Sarah Plummer, Frederick
County, Maryland. m. 31 Dec. 1772, Bush Creek. FFMM.

Wright, Joel, son of John and Elizabeth Wright of Monallen Township, York County, Pa. & Elizabeth Farquhar, dau. of William
and Ann Farquhar, Pipe Creek, Frederick County, Maryland. m.
1 July 1772, Pipe Creek. FFMM.

Wright, Joseph, son of John and Elizabeth Wright, Menallen Township, York County, Pa. & Mary Farqhar, dau. of William and
Ann Farqhar, Pipe Creek, Frederick County, Maryland. m.
9 April 1761, Pipe Creek. FFMM.

LOUDOUN COUNTY MARRIAGES

Appendix

Names On Minister's Returns

Where noted, ministers gave bonds to the Governor in order to
perform the rite of matrimony. The bonds are on file in the
Office of the Circuit Clerk, Leesburg, Va.

Adie, George. Protestant Episcopal. Deacon. MB 1832-1833, p. 148.
Allen, William. Presbyterian. Dec. 1800. Bond.
Alomory, John. Methodist Episcopal.
Baker, ____.
Benton, Benjamin H. Baptist. Aug. 1845. Bond.
Bettinger, B. F. Presbyterian.
Birkby, Thomas K. Methodist Episcopal.
Blackwell, John D.
Boyd, Andrew Hunter Holms. Presbyterian. May 1838. Bond.
Broaddus (Broadus), William.
Brooke, George H. Methodist Episcopal.
Bryan, Thomas M.
Burch, Robert. Methodist Episcopal. Elder. May 1823. Bond.
Burton, Theophilus. Methodist Protestant. May 1850. Bond.
Cadden, Robert. In Middleburg.
Campbell, M. W. Presbyterian.
Carter, George W.
Chapman, Robert M.
Chenoweth, Alfred G.
Coombs, John N.
Cross, William G.
Cushing, Henry C.
Cutler, Benjamin C. Episcopal. Dec. 1830. Bond.
Dagg, John L.
Dashiell, R. L. In Middleburg.
Davis, John. Methodist Episcopal. Elder.
Davis, William F. R.
Dodge, H. W. Baptist. In Upperville.
Dorsey, Edwin
Dorsey, Thomas J.
Doup, Jacob. Methodist Episcopal.
Dulin, E. L.
Duncan, James A. Methodist Episcopal. Jan. 1832. Bond.
Dunn, John. Protestant Episcopal.
Eggleston, W. G.
Eidson, W. H.
Evans, French S. Methodist. May 1825. Bond.

Fowles, John
Fristoe, William
Frye, Christopher. Methodist. May 1807. Bond.
Frye, George M.
Frye, Joseph
Furlong, Henry
Gilmore, William. Baptist. March 1807. Bond.
Gover, Samuel. Methodist Episcopal.
Green, John C. Methodist Episcopal.
Greer, T. W.
Griffith, Alfred. Methodist. June 1818. Bond.
Grubb, William D.
Hank, J. N.
Hargraves, John T. Presbyterian. Dec. 1832. Bond.
Harvey, Enoch
Hauer, Daniel. Evangelical Lutheran. In Lovettsville.
Hayes, Thomas C. Methodist Episcopal.
Helm, Joseph. Methodist South. Dec. 1852. Bond.
Hemphill, Andrew
Henkle, Eli
Herndon, H. B.
Herndon, R. N. Left for Richmond Co., Va. 1843.
Herndon, Thadeus. Baptist. March 1835. Bond.
Hirst, William. Methodist Episcopal.
Holland, Horace
Hoskinson, Josiah
Humphreys, G. W.
Hutchinson (Hutchison), Eleazer C. Presbyterian. Oct. 1829. Bond.
Hutt, John
Jefferson, Hamilton. Shelburne Parish.
Jones, Joseph H. Baptist. June 1835. Bond.
Kennerly, Samuel. Methodist Episcopal.
Keppler, Samuel
Keyes, Thomas
Krebbs, William. Methodist Episcopal.
Larkin, J. (L.). In Hillsboro.
Leachman, Robert C.
Lippett, E. R. Protestant Episcopal.
Littlejohn, John. Methodist Episcopal. June 1786. Bond.
Littleton, Oscar. Methodist Episcopal. Nov. 1852. Bond.
Littleton, Thomas
Luckett, Henry F. Methodist. April 1833. Bond.
Marders, S. L.
Martin, G. H.
Massey, John E.
Massey, Joseph T. Baptist Church (Ketockton).
McCan, James
McDowell, William P. Methodist. Nov. 1824. Bond.
McGee, Thomas
McPherson, John
Mines, John
Monroe, Thomas H. W.
Mercer, William
Moore, Francis
Morgan, Gerard

LOUDOUN COUNTY MARRIAGES

Newman, Theron W.
Nixon, Lorenzo D.
Nixon, R. T.
Ogilvie, John
Phelps, Elisha P. Methodist Episcopal. April 1837. Bond.
Plunkett, Joseph H.
Raymond, Moses
Richey, F. H.
Ridgeway, H. B. Methodist Episcopal.
Rodgers, Samuel. Methodist Episcopal.
Roszell, S. A. Methodist. March 1841. Bond.
Roszell, Stephen S. Methodist. March 1841. Bond.
Sanders, Ramey G.
Saunders, James. Methodist Episcopal. Oct. 1807. Bond.
Shaull, ____
Sheras, ____
Shuford, Mortimer L. German Reformed. In Lovettsville. June 1844.
    Bond.
Smith, Henrie R. Presbyterian. Jan. 1850. Bond.
Startzman, Christian. Evangelical Lutheran. In Lovettsville. Aug.
    1849. Bond.
Tapler, ____
Tippett, Charles B.
Torrence, Irvin H. Methodist Episcopal.
Trone, John S.
Trott, Samuel. Baptist. Centreville, Fairfax Co., Va.
Tuston, Septimus. Presbyterian. Nov. 1824. Bond
Villiger, George
Ward, William N. Protestant Episcopal.
Watt, John G.
Whaley, ____
White, Joseph. Methodist Episcopal.
Whittle, Francis. Protestant Episcopal.
Wicks, William. Methodist Episcopal. Hillsboro Circuit. Nov. 1830.
    Bond.
Willard, Philip. Evangelical Lutheran. In Lovettsville.
Williamson, William
Wills, D. P.
Wilmer, Richard H. Protestant Episcopal.

The following clerks returned marriage records for the Society
of Friends:

Bond, Robert. Goose Creek Monthly Meeting.
Brown, Thomas S.
Mendenhall, Jacob. Fairfax Monthly Meeting, Waterford.
Taylor, ____. Goose Creek Monthly Meeting.

Beatey (cont.)
  Jane 146
Beaton, Mary 84
Beatty, Catharine 86
  Cora Ann 34
  David 8
  Eliza 148
  Elizabeth 10, 24, 140
  John 78, 140
  John H. 148
  Mary 8, 100
  Mary Jane 101
  Susan 24, 78
  William 34, 57
  William H. 148
Beaty, Cora Ann 34
  Mary 121
  Sally 26
Beavers, Abraham H. 21
  Eliza 55
  Elizabeth 90
  Harriet 126
  James 124
  John 11, 105, 119
  John A. 4
  John Asbury 11
  Joseph 11
  Julia Ann 88
  Samuel 11, 51
  Sarah 124
  Susan 3
  Washington 11
Bebbely, Minta 107
Beck, Ann 19
  Ann (Mrs.) 19
  Catharina 112
  Edward 19
  Philip 112
Beckham, Ann 90
Beemer, Mary 173
Beerley, Elizabeth 100
Beil, Jacob 125
Bell, Andrew 157
  Everline 123
  Nancy 37
  Susan 82
  Thomas 65
Bellard, John 129
  Rachel 129
Belt, Alfred 69, 100,
  135, 139, 157
  Ann E. 135
  Mary Eleanor 69
  Ratha Ann 139
Beltz, Maria 104
  Maria Margretha 32
  Peter 32
Belz, Andreas 40
  Ann Maria 40
Bemusdaffer, Elizabeth
  161
Benedum, Henry 74
  James H. 33
  Maria 122
  Sarah Ann 74
Benjamin, Henrietta 166
  James 65
  John 166
  Sarah 166
  Warner 65
Bennet, Elizabeth 63
  Sanny 2
Bennett, Dewanner S. 26
  Elizabeth 44
  James H. 186
  Mary W. 117
  Susan W. 57
  Sydnor 108, 117, 135

Bentley, Anna Snowden
  167
  Mary Elizabeth 59
  Robert 59, 107, 167
  Virginia L. 107
Benton, Eliza H. 7
  Mary Ann 6
  Richard H. 7
  Sarah S. 97
  William 6, 12, 97
Berg, Sarah 132
Berkeley, Elizabeth 135
  Mary Lewis 32
Berkley, Ann 90
  Samuel 168
Best, Elizabeth R. 165
  Enos T. 165
  Frances 63
  Martha 39
Bett, Elizabeth 142
Betts, Elizabeth 157
Betzer, Catharine 37
  Harmon 37
Beveridge, Andrew 38,
  107
  Margaret 41
  Noble 136
  Susan 107
Beverly, Carter 179
  Evelyn B. 179
  Robert 179
Bewley, Mahlon 151
Bezella, Rachel 90
Bibern, Susanna 166
Biegel, David 13
Bikit, John 123
Bilzer, Harman 148
  Mary 146
  Susah. 29
Binns, Ann Louisa 89
  C. 78, 107
  C. (Jr.) 23, 57, 135,
    136, 159
  C. W. 61
  C. W. D. 93
  Catey A. 41
  Charles 5, 6, 37, 50,
    51, 80, 97, 113,
    139, 146, 164, 180
  Charles (Jr.) 58
  Duanna 162
  Elizabeth 74
  Hannah 151
  J. 37
  J. A. 7, 82
  Jn. A. 129
  John A. 20, 40, 41,
    48, 79, 81, 91, 95,
    105, 125, 171
  Margaret Hannah D. 151
  Simon A. 76
  Sussh. 162
Birch, Barbary 82
Birchett, Nancy 53
Birdsall, Ann 58
Birdshal, Ruth 131
Birkby, Hannah Sophia
  112
  Lucy H. 162
  Mary W. 155
  Richard B. 129
  Thomas 77, 112, 162
Birkett, Margaret E. 3
  William 3
Birkirk, Sarah 161
Birkit, Susan Ann 39
Birkitt, Margaret E. 3

Birkitt (cont.)
  William 3
Birkly, Sarah 129
Biscoe, Elizabeth R. 6
  James B. 6
  Mary 110
Bishop, Henderson 17
  John 63
  Sarah 79
Bitzer, Ann 114
  James Harvey 13
  Lydia Ann 6
  Mary 70
  William 6, 149
Bitzon, Ann 40
Blackwell, Benjamin 126
  Elizabeth F. 126
Blahn, Maria 1
Blakeley, Emily A. 80
Blakely, Elizabeth 57
  Nancy 44
  William 57
Blaker, Harriet 165
  Icey 50
  John 99
  Lucy E. 150
  Mary Catherine 131
  Matilda 89
  Sarah 97
  Susan 136
Blakley, Sarah 1
Blashill, Elisabetha 145
Blatscher, Elisabetha
  146
Bleakley, Elizabeth 57
  Susan 81
Blemar, Sarah A. E. 141
Bletscher, Henrich 13,
  144
  Maria 144
Blieker, Nanzy 1
Blinco, Mary 159
  Sarah 47
Blincoe, (?) (Mrs.) 49
  Charles W. 73
  Elizabeth 73, 75, 178
  Francis 42
  Joseph (Jr.) 47
  Martha I. 72
  Martha J. 73
  Martha S. 178
  Mary 161
  Sampson 178
  Sarah 47
Blotzer, Sussana 21
Bloxham, James A. 70
Blundon, Susan 86
  W. 86
Bocker, Clare (Mrs.) 14
  Samuel 6, 14
Bockern, Christina 6
Bodine, John 56
  Joseph H. 33, 43, 90
  Mariah 90
  Mary 34
  Mary Jane 90
  Winifred 56
Boger, Anna Maria 164
  Friedrich 14
  Joseph 69
  Michael 164
  Michal (Sr.) 14
  Philip 15
  Regina 69
Bogerin, Joseph 69
  Regina 69
Boges, Catherine 4
Boggess, Lydia Jane 3

Brown (cont.)
  Mary Ann 4, 124, 150
  Mary E. 146
  Mary Jane 155
  Matilda 34, 79
  Nancy Ann 101
  Rebecca K. 111
  Richard 18, 74, 118,
    120, 151, 173
  S. (Mrs.) 111
  Sarah 11, 18, 64, 81,
    116
  Sarah (Mrs.) 118
  Sarah Elizabeth 150
  Sarah Jane 125
  Sidney 27, 31
  Susan J. 146
  William 19, 61, 81,
    151
  William H. 34
  William P. 4
Browner, Margaret 168
Brumley, Rachel 10
Buchhanan, Jean 87
Buckhannan, Tamison 31
Buckley, Elizabeth 58
Buckner, Ariss 13
  Caroline R. 13
  S. Ans' 18
  Spencer A. 13
Buffington, Hanh. 119
  Jane 144
  Samuel 149
Bugel, David 13
Bulick, Huldah 149
Bumcrotz, John 143
  Mary 143
Bumerouts, John 31
Bunnell, Jonathan 20
Burch, Barbary 20
  James 20
  Julia 82
  Lewis D. 82
Burchett, Kitty 121
  Sarah Ann 20
  William 20, 121
Burgess, Elizabeth 34
  Margaret 146
  Roxanna 146
  William 146
Burgoine, Martha 98
  Sarah 5
Burk, Mahalah 152
  William 165
Burke, Ann Virginia 142
  Elizabeth Ann 153
  Joseph D. 63
Burket, John (Jr.) 55
Burkett, John 123
  Rosanah 123
  Sarah 86
Burnhouse, Youlyanna 85
Burr, Mary A. (Mrs.) 176
Burson, Cyrus 47, 83
  Edeth G. 65
  George 21
  Jane 128
  John 47
  Joseph 21
  Kitty 21
  Laban 47
  Lydia 19
  Margaret M. 113
  Mary 90
  Mary Ann 47
  Sarah 18
  Sarah (Mrs.) 21
  Tamer 168

Burwell, Lucy G. 176
Buschkirken, Elisabeth
  (Widow) 163
Bussell, Winney 148
Bussey, John T. 125
  Martha 125
Busson, Aaron 137
  Benjamin 137
  James 137
  Sarah 137
Butcher, Amanda M. 78
  Catherine 4
  John 142
  John H. 78
  Martin O. 78
  Susannah (Widow) 176
Butler, Ann 87
  Ann Lawson 20
  John 3, 142
  Rachel 167
  William 53, 156
Buttler, Ruth 93
Butts, Oliver G. 123
Byrne, George F. 140
Cadel, Margretha 123
Cadwalader, Sarah 79
Calaham, Margaret 163
Caldwell, Phobe W. 18
  S. B. T. 88
  Sally Ann 156
  Samuel B. F. 11
  Samuel B. T. 18, 156
Calir, Nanzy 102
Callason, Reynolds 135
Calleson, Henrietta 143
Callison, Jeremiah 143
Calor, Hannah (Widow)
  148
Calvert, Jesse 147
  Sarah M. 147, 148
  Vincent 21
Camble, Reba. 42
Cammee, Elizabeth 105
Campbell, Andrew 22
  Caroline 155
  Colin C. 21
  Delila 69
  Eliza Ann 143
  Elizabeth 13, 70
  Emily 9
  Hugh 126
  Jane 147
  John 6, 9, 22, 69, 70,
    108
  Lydia 101
  Mahala 6
  Margaret 105
  Margret 22
  Martha A. 20
  Martha Ann 22
  Mary 172
  Mary A. 108
  Samuel 91
  Sarah 22, 63, 143
Cample, Sarah 105
Campher, Elizabeth
  (Mrs.) 22
  Margretha 132
  Samuel 22
  Sarah 95
Canby, Elizabeth T. 73
  John 136
  John H. 107
  Samuel P. 96
Canter, Edy (Widow) 107
  Elizabeth 117
Card, William (Jr.) 26
Carlisle, David 33, 138

Carlisle (cont.)
  Lydia 36
  Mary 33
  Mary Anne 3
  Robert 36
Carnacle, Elizabeth 147
Carnell, William 71
Carnes, Charlotte 144
  Margaret 54
  Margaret H. 142
  Sarah 136
Carney, Rosanna (Widow)
  176
Carnickel, Cathrine 57
Carnine, Eden 92
  Mary Jane 147
  Sarah C. 92
Carns, Elizabeth 146
Carpenter, Amanda M. 4
  Elizabeth 4, 103
  Harriet F. 187
  Louisa 145
  Mary 152
  Minerva C. 187
  Robert 187
Carr, Amelia 186
  Amos 87
  Ann E. 96
  David 101
  Elizabeth 21
  Harriet J. 101
  James 87
  James M. 4, 23, 32,
    82, 169
  Jane 53, 140
  Jane S. 140
  Josephus 169
  Margaret 27, 130
  Martha Ann 23
  Mary 100
  Mary Ann 130
  Mary E. 69
  Nancy 87
  Peter 140
  Rachel 111
  Thomas 23, 27
  William 69
Carrico, Eleanor 79
  James 79
Carrin, Eden 92
  Sarah C. 92
Carrington, Margaret 57
Carrol, Elizabeth 108
Carroll, Andrew 113
  Mary F. 49
  Sarah 123
  William 33, 100, 123
Carruthers, Christian 93
  Emily 172
  Joanna 102
  John 172
  Nancy 159
Carson, Mary 91
Carter, Abigail 167
  Alice 56
  Anna Beale 175
  Catharine 51
  Charles 24
  Eden 85, 110
  Edmonia R. 26
  Edward 24, 91
  Eleanor 154
  Eliza 154
  Elizabeth 108, 127,
    140
  Emily 91
  Francis M. 43, 85
  Hannah 57

Cockerille, Amanda F. 110
　Sanford W. 110
Cockran, Benjamin D. 152
　Marion V. 27
　Mary R. 60
　Sarah Ann 140
　Tholemiah 60
Cockrel, Isabella 101
　Joseph 101
Cockrill, John 32
　Joseph Marmaduke 91
　Kelly 91
　Kitty 91
　Martha Ann 32
　Sarah 59
Cockrille, Elias 28
　Janet 124
Coe, Catharine Sarah 6
　Catherine 28
　Elijah 129
　Elizabeth 28
　Emily Jane 97
　Emley 141
　Esther Ann 129
　Eunicy 159
　John 162
　Mary 28, 97
　Mary E. 28
　Mary Jane 7
　Peter 7
　Robert 159
　Susannah 62
Coffer, Thomas 34
Cogill, Rachel 115
Cohagen, Elizabeth 120
　Mary 67
Cohages, Mary 67
Cohl, Prissila 87
Coist, Eve 91
　John 109
Colbert, Catharine 119
Cole, Catharine Sarah 6
　Eliza Jane 128
　Elizabeth 28
　Mary Jane 7
　Matilda 121
　Nancy 124
　Peggy 28
　Peter 7, 124
　Priscilla 121
Coleman, Julia E. 151
Collett, Elizabeth 104
　William 28
Collings, Elizabeth 2
　Levi 2
Collins, Catherine 169
　Chloe 92
　Elizabeth 2
　John A. (Rev.) 142
　Levi 2, 169
　Nancy 51
　Prudence 23
　Sarah 117
　Sarah (Mrs.) 37
　Tabitha Ann 35
Combes, Joseph 46
　Malinda 70
　Violet 46
Combs, Ann 48
　Elizabeth 101
　Emily 24
　Jane 42
　Joseph 49, 178
　Martha 32
　Nancy 40
　Tamer 28
Commerell, Susanna 31

Commerell (cont.)
　William 31
Compher, Abigail 1
　Catherine 76
　Cathrine 147
　Christian 22
　Elizabeth 45
　John 8, 45, 136, 145, 147
　Lydia Ann 145
　Margaret 136
　Margaret A. 5
　Mary 59
　Peter 59, 76
　Sarah 8
Comstock, Cynthia 134
Conard, Abner A. 147
　Charlotte E. 147
　David 35, 72
　Delila 72
　John 95
　L. C. 95
　Leah Ann 35
　Leanna 95
　Mary Carolina 95
　Nancy Carolina 95
Conden, Elizabeth (Widow) 125
Condon, Elizabeth 130
Connalley, Peggy 15
Connard, Anthony 179
　Edward (Jr.) 77
　Elizabeth 27, 70
　Guely 114
　Molly (Mrs.) 179
　Sarah 30, 109
Conner, Alexander 176
　Amelia 32
　Charles C. 176
　Elizabeth Lee 176
　Henry 176
　John 112
　John C. 176
　Joseph 113
　Nancy 13
　Robert C. 176
Connor, Anne 106
　Hugh 121
　John 105
　Martha E. 160
　Mary 121
Conrad, Barbara A. 111
　David 78
　David P. 42
　Elisabeth 41
　Elizabeth (Widow) 176
　John M. 111
　Jonathan 97
　Mary A. 78
　Sarah E. W. 42
Conwell, Isaac 30
　Loveless 30
Cook, Levi 66
Cooke, Priscilla E. 66
Cooksey, Simpson 130
Cookus, Julietta 22
Cool, Emily 24
Cooley, Ann 74
Coombes, Jno. 49
　Sarah 49
Coombs, Jno. 49
　Martha 74
　Sarah 49
Cooper, Adam 170
　Ann 146
　Catharine 20
　Catherine 31, 113
　Civilla 94

Cooper (cont.)
　Eliza Ann 31
　Elizabeth Margaret 154
　George 31, 173
　Jane W. 57
　John W. 56
　Margaret 31, 109
　Mary 31
　Mary Ann 167
　Peter 31
　Samuel 35
　William 156
Cooperin, Christina 52
Copeland, Andrew 21
　Craven A. 26
　David 96
　Elizabeth 28
　Elizabeth A. 156
　J. R. 121
　Jane 31
　Jane Ann 156
　John 116
　Mary Ann 116
　Rebecca (Widow) 123
　Rebecca C. 96
　Sidney 150
　Zillah 26
Cordell, Abraham 32
　Adam 45, 46, 145, 157
　Aryann Catherine 45
　Catharine 46
　Elizabeth 46
　Helen A. 77
　M. E. 15
　Mary Martha 52, 145
　Presley 15, 77
　Samuel 2, 10
　Susan 143
　Susannah (Mrs.) 32
Core, Samuel 110
Cornell, Eliza J. 170
　Mary (Mrs.) 171
　Mary E. 171
　Mary Elizabeth 171
　Nancy 3
　Thompson 171
Cornelle, Thomas 25
Cornine, Eden 147
　Mary Jane 147
Cornwell, Benson 134
Corry, John 48
Corwin, Cynthia 136
Cost, Barbara 173
　Cornelia Ann 69
　Jacob 186
　Nancy 186
Costello, James 32
　John H. 89
　Margaret F. 89
Costrolow, Jane 12
Costs, Betsey 34
　Cornelia Ann 69
　Elizabeth 23
　Jonathan 69
　Mary 23
　Peter 23
Counard, Amelia 79
Couper, Alexander 27
　Betsy 27
Courtsman, Cathcrine 150
Coutsman, Clarissa 122
Coutzman, Catherine (Widow) 176
　Rosah. 116
Covinson, Jane 170
Cowgill, Alice 160
　Rebecca 69
　Sarah 70

Cowgill (cont.)
  Tamer 138
Cowhe, Fanny 162
Cowper, Alexander 27
  Betsy 27
Cox, Henrietta M. 96
  James A. 150
  John W. 96
  Joseph 19, 155, 160
  Mary 62
  Mary E. 28
  Patty 63
  Polly (Widow) 65
  Sally 63
  Samuel 28, 90, 96
  Sarah 19
  Sarah (Mrs.) 19
  Virginia Ann 90
Coxen, Nancy 49
Crabel, Sophia 24
Craig, George 19
  Harriet 27
  Jane 84
  Nancy 62
  Norval 70, 87, 123
  Rapha 116
  William S. G. 32
Crain, Catharine L. 186
  Emily 61
Cranmer, Andreas 135
  Hannah 135
Cranwell, Eliza A. 9
  Jane S. 2
  John 2
  Susan 9, 137
  Susan M. 137
Crates, Mary 70
Cravans, Abigail 55
Craven, Alvina 163
  Edith 100
  Eleanor H. 33
  Eleanor V. 168
  Elenor 114
  Elizabeth 93
  James 83, 100
  Joel 163
  Lavina 24
  Mahlon 175
  Maranda 83
  Margaret 43, 139
  Mary 142
  Miranda 82
  Sally W. 150
  Samuel 174
  Sarah 157
  Sarah E. 100
  Sarah S. 157
  Sophia V. 174
Crawford, Daniel T. 44,
    77
  Mary E. 44
Cremor, Cathrine 39
Crider, Emily 53
Cridler, Andrew M. 90
  Ann Elizabeth 61
  John 61
  Margaret (Widow) 176
Crim, Catharine 159
  Charles 24
  Christena 24
  Christiana 24
  Daniel 175
  Elizabeth 132
  Jacob 159
  John 31, 132
  John H. 52, 97
  Mary (Mrs.) 175
  Peter 89

Crim (cont.)
  Sarah Ann 144
  Susan 52
  Susanna 52
Crimling, Catharine 159
Crimm, Barbara 65
  Carl 33
Criss, Eleanor 100
Crombacker, Eve (Widow)
    135
Cromwell, Eliza Ann 187
Crone, Sarah 160
Crookes, Peggy 33
Crooks, Lucinda 92
Cross, Alice Ann 127
  Catherine 158
  Catherine Ann 35
  Elizabeth 42, 140
  Emily 185
  Fielder 158
  Hamilton 172
  Harrison 35, 118, 127
  James 42
  John 185
  Julia Frances Ann 118
  Lewis 48
  Minto 126
  Susan 34
Crowell, Isabella 128
Crowen, Isabella 128
Crumbacker, Catherine 46
  Jacob 46
Crumbaker, Eliza 173
  Solomon 173
Crupper, Eli 8
  Mary 21
  Mary Ann 50
  Sarah 155
Crusin, Jacob 34, 116
Crusur, Nancy 37
Crusus, Nancy 37
Cruthers, Rachell 93
Culin, Caty 33
Cullison, Elizabeth 128
  Heneritia 143
Cumming, Nancy 6
Cummings, Ansey 34
  Delilah 90
  Jane 41
  John 126
  Maria 159
  Mary 71
  Sarah 126
  Susan 90
  Thomas 90
Cummins, Ann E. 4
  Elizabeth 172
  Minrod 57
  Rebecca 9
Cumpton, Ann 59
Cunard, Jonathan 95
  Luther C. 54
  Sarah 34
Cunnard, Ann 9
  Betsey 47
  Cynthia M. 31
  Jane 109
  L. C. 42
Cunning, Nancy 11
Cunningham, Ann 1
  Mahalda 102
  Robert 156
Curl, Elizabeth 42
Currell, Elizabeth S.
    186
  Margaret Elizabeth 42
  Nancy H. D. 94
  Parmelia 94

Currell (cont.)
  Polly 126
Curry, Elizabeth Ann 30
  John 48
  Laura Jane 46
  Martha 97
  Martha Ellen 22
  Robert 22, 46
Curtis, Mary 46
  Polly 98
Cushman, Charles 73
Custor, Polly 26
Dagg, Clarissa P. 98
  Mary Jane 3
Dailey, Aaron 157
  Ann 98
  Harriet 21
  John 30
  Margaret 152
  Mary 99
  Mary E. 41
  Mary J. 41
  Pleasant R. 30
  Sally 148
  Sarah E. 157
  William 41
Daine, Harriet A. 158
Dakins, Sarah W. 121
Daliham, Leticia 57
  Lettia 57
Daniel, David 85, 147
  Hannah L. 142
  Hester 40
  James 162
  Jane 21
  Joseph 179
  Lemuel 112
  Lucy H. 81
  Mary 62, 134, 142
  Mary Ann 112
  Matilda J. 147
  Rachell 139
  Sarah 143
  Tacey (Widow) 53, 179
  Tacy 87
  Tacy H. 81
  William 35
Darflinger, Elizabeth 38
  Frederick 38
Darley, Jane 63
Darne, Elizabeth 139
  Gunnell 139
  Harriet A. 158
  James 59
  James W. 59
  Malinda 59
  Susan 157
Darr, Barbara 67
  Elizabeth 134
  Rachel A. 144
  Sarah 48, 92
Darry, Jacob 102
  Nansy 102
Davidson, Frederick A.
    104
  Nancy 165
Davis, Albert C. 167
  Amanda 32
  Ann 106
  Anna 7
  Anthony 142, 158
  Benjamin 36, 120
  Betty (Mrs.) 108
  Catherine 12, 20, 143
  Darcus S. 65
  Elias 71, 171
  Eliza 26
  Elizabeth 1, 19, 20,

Davis (cont.)
  66, 109, 158
  Elizabeth (Widow) 151
  Elizabeth Ann 171
  Elizabeth S. 167
  Gary 37
  George 7
  H. M. 135
  Harriet Ann 57
  Howell 36
  James 7
  Jemima 108
  Jeremiah 65
  JoAnna M. 156
  Joanna M. 154
  John 66, 74, 160
  John L. 37
  Joseph 20
  Julia Ann 91, 135
  Lucinda 20
  Malinda 36, 92
  Margaret A. 37
  Margeret 19
  Maria 145
  Maria Ana 133
  Maria Ann 171
  Mary 25
  Mary Ann 101, 142
  Mary C. 100
  Mary E. 100, 151
  Mary Jane 103
  Nancy 49, 165
  Presley 36, 170
  Rachel 109
  Sahra 43
  Sally 74
  Samuel 20, 25
  Samuel T. 85
  Sarah (Widow) 62
  Sarah D. 92
  Susanna 53
  Susanna E. 120
  Susannah 65
  Thomas 7, 35, 36, 108,
    136, 147, 171
  Thomas S. 92
  William 7, 21, 55, 57
  William F. 151
Davison, Theodore N. 101
Dawes, John E. 8
  Mary Ann 8
Dawson, Ann 50, 93
  Eguenia S. 75
  Eguenia T. 75
  Elizabeth 122, 145,
    164
  Harriet A. 116
  Hortensia 68
  Mary F. 37
  Monecai 138
  Richard 93
  Samuel 121
  Samuel (Mrs.) 75
  Sarah 21
  Sarah (Widow) 182
  Sarah Ann 68
  Tamer 57
  Theodore N. 49
  William 164
Day, Jane 52
  Rachel 41
  Rebecca 155
Daymude, James 87
  Sophena 87
DeButts, Mary 24
  Richardetta T. 24
  Samuel W. 24
Deakins, Catharine 44

Debell, Mary (Widow) 83
Dedricks, Daniel 88
Deemer, Mary 173
Degroodt, William 167
Deh, Elisabeth 187
Demery, Catharina 147
  Margretha 32
  Maria 147
Demmerich, Eva 61
Demory, Louisa 160
  Mahlon 160
  Mary 40
Denges, Isabella 142
  Mary 56
Denham, Amey Ellen 11
  Charles T. 11
  Charles Thomas 91
  David B. 25
  Margaret A. 74
  Mary Jane 25
  Oliver 74
Dennis, Caroline S. 155
  Catharine 146
  Frances Jane 65
  Henry 65
  Louisa 85
  Mary J. 6
  Matilda 24
  Oliva F. 38
  Sophronia Eveline 79
  William A. 38, 79
Derri, Baltaser 108
  Catharina 108
Derry, Barbara 122
  Christian 1
  Elisabetha 174
  Elizabeth 164
  Hanson 131
  Jacob 38, 121, 174
  Lewis W. 38
  Lidia A. 109
  Lydia Ann 109
  Magthalena 121
  Margaret J. 1
  Maria 38
  Mary 38
  Mary A. 169
  Michael 109, 169
  Morelles 172
  Philip 86
  Sarah 3
  Solomon 127
  Susanna 94
  William 38, 128
Detro, Catherine 105
Deutch, Sarah 161
Dewar, Elizabeth 16
  Lucinda 72
Dewis, Ester 67
Dickens, Sarah W. 121
Dickey, John P. 12
  Mary Ann 145
Dickson, Sarah 42
Dicky, Thomas N. 69
Diedericks, Caroline 88
  Daniel 88
Diewer, Margretha 106
Dillehay, Lydia 123
Dillon, Ann 148
  Mary 108
  Reba. 20, 145
  Ruth 10
Dinzmore, William 168
Dishman, Emily 161
  Samuel 161
  Susanna 140
Divers, John 172
Divine, Aaron 39, 151

Divine (cont.)
  D. M. 123
  Emily Ann 47
  Jacob 39
  James F. 161
  Juliet F. 47
  Margaret Ellen 159
  Martha Ann 55
  Robert E. 39
  William 47, 55, 92,
    159
Dixon, Elizabeth 10, 11
  Ellen 161
  Mary 52
  Samuel 77
Dodd, Elizabeth 39
  John (Jr.) 39
  L. 39
  Mary 156
  Samuel 39
  Sarah 48
Doe, Mary 8
Doman, Margretha 72
Don, Anna 187
Donahoe, Margaret 122
Donaldson, Bailey 12
  Elizabeth C. 98, 108,
    109
  George R. 84, 103
  Harriet H. 98
  Julian 114
  Margaret 103
  Mary Hannah 109
  Stephen 52
  Susan H. 108
Donaway, Susanna 161
Donohoe, Elizabeth 108
  John 54
  Margaret Ann 79
  Margerett (Widow) 177
  Mary 112
  Phebe R. 173
  Sarah 75
  Stephen J. 173
Dorman, Thomas W. 144
Dornell, Thomas S. 86
Dorrell, Catharine 130
  Elizabeth 33
  George W. 17, 148
  James 163
  Sarah Ann 163
  Thomas 135
Dorsey, Alfred I. 105
  Allen M. 40
  Presley K. 109
Dorstimer, Elizabeth 141
Doughstiner, Mary 146
Douglass, Reba 149
Dove, Caroline 143
  Elizabeth 82
  Mary 42
  William 42, 82, 143
Dowdel, Lucinda 93
Dowdell, Elizabeth 112
  Elizabeth E. 112
  John 107
  Moses 19
  Sampson G. 81
  Thomas G. 113
Dowdle, Thomas G. 113
Dowell, Ann C. 112
  C. 40
  Conrad 115
  Jane Ann 115
  Lucretia 109
Dowlan, Rachel 120
Dowling, Mary (Widow)
  120

Emmingson, Margaret 176
Emmison, Margaret 176
Emory, Elizabeth 155
Emrey, Stephen 49
Emrich, Jacob 43
Engelbrecht, (?) 52
Ernst, Elisabetha 103
Erskins, John 53
Eskeridge, Charles G. 91
Eskridge, Alfred A. 120
  C. W. C. 135
  C. W. G. 122
  Charles G. 2, 15, 16,
    25, 36, 42, 63, 69,
    73, 112, 141, 151,
    166, 187
  Henrietta 179
Etcher, Mary E. 16
  Peter 145
  Sophia F. 145
Evans, Adan 87
  Ann Catharine 109
  Cathrine 128
  Elizabeth 43, 87
  Elizabeth (Widow) 177
  Harvey 109
  Jemima 26
  Jesse 28, 44
  Martha (Widow) 177
  Mary 43, 65
  Mary (Widow) 177
  Nancy 28, 101
  Penelope 34
  Sarah Ann 28
  Susanna 84
Eveland, Elizabeth 21
  Mary 109
  Rachel 108
Evelina, Ann 48
Evence, Elizabeth 87
Everett, Elizabeth 168
  John 118, 186
  Rachel 118, 186
Everhard, Catharine 33
Everhart, Ann Eliza 71
  Ann Elizabeth 23
  Anna E. 22
  Charlotte 36
  David 100
  Elizabeth 8, 121, 125,
    143, 169
  Israel 44
  Margaret 38
  Mary 86
  Mary C. 21, 100
  Mary E. 100
  Matilda A. 44
  Michael 22
  Nathaniel W. 149
  Nelson 71, 121, 129,
    155
  Nelson B. 21
  Philip 36
  Sarah J. 162
  Solomon 44, 102
  Solomon (Jr.) 44
  William N. 121
Everheart, Ann Eliza 71
  Charlotte 36
  John 55
  Martha 71
  Nelson 71, 86, 125
  Philip 36, 44, 56, 71,
    160
  Sarah (Mrs.) 163
  Sarah (Widow) 169
  Sarah Ann 56
  Solomon 56

Everheart (cont.)
  Susan 160
Everitt, Ann 146
  Elizabeth 120
Evins, Elisabeth 86
Ewers, Ann 106
  Franklin 117, 122
  Hannah 48, 106
  Helen 23
  Isabella 66
  Levi G. 10, 30, 47, 97
  Margaret 129
  Mary 84, 122, 149
  Reba. 132
  Robert 66
  William 44, 122
Fadely, Ann 98
  Jacob 98, 122
  Sarah D. 122
Fadley, Mary 105
Fadly, Ann 98
  Jacob 98
Fahle, Jacob 164
  Maria 164
Fahly, Johannes 45
Fair, Mary 152
Fairfax, Catharine 130
  Elenor 162
  Ellenor 161
  George William 113
Fairhurst, Elizabeth 139
Falley, John 53
Fally, John 45
Faraught, Elizabeth 124,
  125
Farish, Rachel 72
Farnsworth, Enos 146
Farqhar, Ann (Mrs.) 188
  Mary 188
  William 188
Farquhar, Ann (Mrs.) 188
  Elizabeth 188
  William 188
Farr, Martha V. 144
Farrel, Matilda T. 147
Farrey, William 50
Farris, Betsey 112
  Mary 153
  Nancy 89
Farrow, Elizabeth
  (Widow) 177
Farst, Sarah 168
Fawley, Christena 138
  Christena (Mrs.) 32
  Christina 138
  Elizabeth 28, 52
  Hannah 69
  Henry 29, 32, 52, 69,
    157
  Jacob 138
  John 52, 53, 57, 93
  Joseph 32
  Margaret 53, 157
  Mary 29
  Polly 57
  Sarah Ann 32
  Susan 29
  Susanna 29
Feagans, Huziah 14
Feagins, James 46
  Mary Frances 153
  Wilfred F. 153
Febbee, Nancy 163
Fechter, Sarah Ann 82
Fectehler, Ann 125
Feggins, Jane 14
  Sarah Ann 14
Feitchter, Sarah 44

Felby, Sally (Widow) 101
Felckner, Martin 135
Fenandis, Sarah 127
Fernandis, Sarah 126
Ferrill, Amanda 49
  Dorcas (Mrs.) 49
  Joseph 49
  Nelson 49
Ferry, William 50
Fichter, Amanda 99
  Caroline 26
  George 26, 99
  Sarah Ann 82
  Susan 180
  Susan (Widow) 113
Fictcher, Mary 21
Fiechter, George 40
  Nancy 40
Field, Margaret 113
Fields, Bitha Ann 136
  James 93, 107
  Luke 136
  Martha 46
  Mary 107
  Sarah Catharine 76
Figgans, Emza A. M. 136
Figgins, Emza A. M. 136
  Huziah 14
  Jane 14
  Safronia 93
  Sarah Ann 14
  Sufronia 93
Filler, Emeline 5
  Henry 17
  Jacob 5, 30, 33
  John 38
  Margaret A. 46
  Mary 107
  Mary Ann 46
  Mary M. 143
  Matilda 33
  Michael 46
  Rebecca 104
  Sally (Mrs.) 17
  Samuel 46
  Sarah Ann 26
Fillinggim, Mary 131
Finch, Malvina F. 90
  Marshall 90
Finnacom, Dianna 101
Fioccoats, Catherine 4
Firestone, Christianna
  135
  Eve 37
Fisher, Mary 59
  Sarah 157
Fitcher, Amanda 99
  George 99
Fitchter, Edney 102
  George 102
  Harriet F. 94
Fitzgerald, Mary 187
  Sarah 131
Fitzhugh, Ann M. 9
  John S. 164
  Lucian 12, 139
  Mary J. 107
  Matilda (Widow) 164
  Matilda T. 164
  William C. 176
  William H. 55
Flanagan, Nancy 151
Fleming, Dinah 123
  Eveline 123
  George 123, 157
  Jesse 32
  Rebecca G. 123
  Rebecca J. 123

Gardner (cont.)
 Elizabeth (Mrs.) 138
 Elizabeth E. 98
 Jacob 183
 Margaret 146
 Martha A. 138
Garett, Catharine 25
Garner, Arthur 150
 Elizabeth 20
 Lydia 32
 Malinda 150
 Mary 78
 Mary Ellen 122
 Rachel 130
 Sarah 99
Garret, Betsey 35
 Emily 93
Garrett, Abigail 88
 Amelia 157
 Benjamin 55
 Catharine 130
 Edmund R. 54, 168
 Eliza 119
 Enos 119
 Margaret 55
 Mary 14
 Rebecca 80
 Samuel 80
 Sarah 35
 Sarah E. 55
 Silas 3, 101
Garrison, Patsey 65
Garrissen, Elizabeth 130
Garrot, Amelia 157
Garvick, Pleasant M.
 (Widow) 148
Gasaway, Charles 119
Gassaway, Charles 119,
 160, 171
Gaunt, Elizabeth 37
 John 37
 Rachel Ann 37
 Samuel 37
Gear, Mary Ann (Widow)
 50
Geaslin, Amanda M. F.
 136
Geddy, Elizabeth 58
Geist, Catharina 1
 Sarah 44
Geists, Sarah 44
Geoley, Jane 168
Georg, Elisabeth 170
 Johannes 57, 170
 Lydia 57
George, John 165
 John (Jr.) 165
 Malinda S. 165
German, Sarah Mary Jane
 171
Gest, John 152
 Violet 152
Gheen, Amey 56
 Anna 39
 Arminda 120
 Elizabeth Ann 173
 Leroy 173
 Margaret 53, 91
 Narcissa 173
 Sally 144
Gibbins, Rebecca 33
Gibbons, Mary 93
Gibbs, James 87, 89, 145
 James Lewin 107
 John H. 117
 Patty 107
 Rebecca 89
 William 89

Gibert, Phebe 79
Gibson, A. 124
 A. M. 9, 124, 163
 Aaron 86
 Abner 63
 Alcinda M. 73
 Almedia 94
 Alpheus (Dr.) 73
 Amelia 86
 Ann Brent 163
 Eliza Bruce 18
 Eliza H. 92
 Elizabeth 16
 Elizabeth (Widow) 177
 Elizabeth Ann 7
 Emily J. 114
 George W. 1
 H. 163
 Harriet Ann (Mrs.) 73
 Israel 114
 Julia A. 1
 Lucelia C. 124
 Luclemma E. 10
 Mahala 172
 Mahlon 18
 Maria S. 63
 Moses 56
 Phebe 41, 53
 Rebecca 10, 159
 Rebecca Ann 116
 Rebekah 111
 Rosetta 83
 Rozilla 129
 Ruth Hannah 4
 Sarah 47
 Solomon 7, 56, 94
 Sydney 167
 Thomas E. 140
 Thurza 83
Giddion, Catherine 107
Gideon, Mary 43
 Peter 43
Gilasby, Sarah 63
Gilbert, Ann 79
Giles, James 155
Gill, Herieta 154
 John L. 53
 Rutha 2
 Susan E. 53
Gillow, Polly 31
Gilmore, James 80
 William 87, 156
Girgin, Eliza 167
Gist, Charles W. 79
 John 152
 Mary Ellen 79
 Violet 152
Gladden, Catherine 160
Gladdin, Catharine 170
Glade, Mathey 144
Gladhill, Mary Ann 36
 Milly 39
Glascock, (?) 145
 Caroline 136
 Delila (Widow) 118
 Enoch 67
 Hannah 16
 Uriel 16
Glasgow, Catharine 26
 Mary Ann 26
Glasscock, Mary E. 50
 Uriel 50
Gochanauer, Mary J. 13
Gochenauer, Mary J. 128
Gochnauer, David 13
 Elizabeth 140
 Mary J. 128
 Mary Jane 13

Gochnauer (cont.)
 Sarah E. 140
Goins, Molley 61
Golden, Jane 43
 Phoebe 53
Gooden, Maria 10
Goodhart, Elizabeth 121
 J. W. 10
 Mary Elizabeth 10
Goodheart, Elizabeth 12
 Jacob 12
 John 155
 Susan 155
Goodin, Catharine Ann
 123
Goodwin, Martha 32
Goram, Jas. 137
 Samuel 69
 Sarah J. 69
Gordon, Catharine 118
 Fannie B. 154
 Fannie C. 154
Gore, Amanda 151
 Ann 149
 Joseph 102
 Mahlon 98
 Mark 149
 Massa 74
 Peter 58
 Phebe 165
 Sarah E. 53
 Thomas 151
 Tilghman 50, 90
 Truman 159
 William 32
Goslin, Bernard 141
Gossett, Elizabeth 136
Gouchehaur, Frances A.
 35
Gouchenour, Elisabeth 35
 Frances A. 35
Gouchnauer, Catharine A.
 70
 Jacob 50, 70
Gouchonouer, Nancy Ellen
 50
Gourley, Hanah 124
 Joseph B. 83
Gover, Ann 55, 177
 Carey C. 137
 Edwin 177
 Edwin R. 68
 Hannah 68
 Jesse 96
 John W. 64
 Mary Sophia 69
 Miriam (Mrs.) 96
 Polly 68
 Robert 68
 Robert A. 104
 Samuel 39, 177
 Sarah H. 96
 Sarah Virginia 68
Gower, Elizabeth 137
Gr---, Mary 85
Grady, E. B. 120
 Frances T. 98
 Maria Louisa 120
 Mariah Louisa 120
 Mary 26
Graham, Andrew 35
 David E. 17
 Elizabeth 35
 James 93
 John 17, 152
 Malinda 19
 Mary Ann 93
 Permilia 63

205

Hamilton (cont.)
Duannah 70
Eleanor E. 141
Eliza 93
Elizabeth 121
Elizabeth A. 167
Emily 152
James 27, 34, 42, 58,
74, 103
James H. 166
Jane 50, 167
Jane (Widow) 178
John 170, 172
Kitty M. 166
Louisa J. 65
Louise Jane 99
Lydia J. 172
Margaret 166
Martha 117
Mary 127, 153
Mary B. 94
Nancy 113
Owen 152
Sarah 21
Susan 119
Susannah 148
William A. 107
Hamm, Philip 66
Hammat, E. 132
Edward 64, 79, 100
Mary R. 64
Hammatt, Edward 12, 156
Sarah A. 12
Hammer, George 116
Hammerley, Salley W. 90
Hammerly, Ellen 58
Jane 110
Jane A. 5
John W. 52
Magden 110
Magdin 110
Sally W. 88
Hammett, Edward 41
Nancy 91
Hampton, Lucinda 168
Nancy 104
Sarah 36
Susanna 122
Susannah 163
Vise 64
Hancock, C. F. 142
Edmonia 142
George 142
Martha Virginia 73
Hand, Margaret 60
Handley, Daniel 83
David 111
Harriett 111
Mary (Widow) 178
Nancy 103
Handy, Jane E. 130
Mariah 63
Mary Ann 99
Sally E. 143
Sarah E. 157
Hane, Reba. 170
Hanes, Abraham H. 125
Mary 51
Mary Ann 51
Thomas I. 113
Hanking, John W. 138
Hanks, Abigal 76
Leher 185
Hanley, David 111, 153
Elizabeth 153
Harriett 111
Hann, Elizabeth 150
Matthias 150

Hann (cont.)
Susannah 23
Hansford, Emsey 17
Hanson, Sarah (Widow) 47
Harden, Albert 65
Elizabeth 55, 141
Henry 172
Jane 166
Joseph 141
Joseph S. 155
Martha F. 172
Martha H. 172
Thomas 141, 166
Hardey, Margeret 97
Hardin, Kitty 1
Harding, Edward 40, 78,
166
Elizabeth 141
Harriet 120
Jane 166
John J. 120
Rachel 78
Sarah Jane 58
Thomas 78, 166
William H. 50
Hardy, Ann Wilson 12
Barbara 20
H. M. 167
Henry M. 137
Hiram 139
John 11
Mary E. 11
Harkin, Mary Ann 6
Harned, William 20
Harper, Ann 74
Catharine 65, 82, 149,
166
Catherine 7, 82
Cathrine 99
Daveus (Widow) 122
Duanna 159
Effamah 29
Effannah 29
Elizabeth 53, 76, 171
Enoch 17
James 166
Jonathan 66
Mahala 17
Margaret 65
Margaret A. 34
Margret 65
Mary A. 7
Rachel 39, 149
Sampson 36
Samuel 66
Sarah 55, 63
Stasee 65
Thomas 29, 63
Washington 82
William 34, 66
Harra, Margaret 2
Harriman, Francis 91
Harrin, Mary 165
Harris, Ann Sophia 148
Catharine H. 167
Eleanor I. 1
Eliza H. 17
Elizabeth 113
Elizabeth (Widow) 178
George 66
Hannah (Widow) 178
Hannah Ann 95
Isac 42
John A. 167
Mary M. 69
Ruth 63
Sally L. 74
Samuel 74

Harris (cont.)
Samuel B. 1, 69
Susanna (Mrs.) 66
William A. 112
William P. 66
Harrison, Ann 176
Burr William 177
E. T. 19
Eleanor 186
Elenor 74
Eliza Jane 70, 77
Elizabeth Taliaferro
(Widow) 176
Frances 176
Harriet 135
Harriet P. 182
James 24, 66, 67, 70
Jane C. 66
John T. M. 177
Margaret L. 30
Maria P. 162
Mary Ann 24
Mary L. 93
Penelope (Mrs.) 178
Sarah 123
Selden 182
Thomas 176
Valentine 182
William 46, 139
William S. 98
Harrop, Catherine 56
James 56
Margaret 163
Nancy 56
Hart, Amanda Malvina 72
Daniel 72, 97
Eliza 134
Jonathan 26, 64, 72
Lydia Ann 21
Martha J. 26
Sarah 64, 92
Thomas W. 51
William 159
Hartman, Ellen Amanda
129
Margeret 105
Hartshorne, Rebecca 186
Susannah (Mrs.) 186
William 186
Harvey, Amos 27
Harvin, Ann 144
Haslett, Harriet J. 40
Hassman, Ann 163
Ann (Mrs.) 163
Hatcher, Ann 38
Elizabeth 98, 173
Sallie A. 30
Thomas 7
Hatchison, Sarah E. 78
Hatton, Benjamin 43
Elizabeth 43
George 140
Henry 144
Haushalter, (?) (Widow)
103
Adam 67
Daniel 67
Haushaltern, Elisabetha
41
Havener, Bazil 68
Catherine 103
Elizabeth 162
Emily 77
Harriet E. 71
James 71
Joseph 77
Lucindy (Mrs.) 71
Mary Jane 35

Havener (cont.)
Michael H. 108
Sarah Ann 95
Silas 77
Sydney Jane 108
Thomas A. 35, 71
William 103
William D. 95
Havenner, Harriet E. 71
James 71
Joseph 68
Lucindy (Mrs.) 71
Penelope M. 132
Philip F. 103
Rebecca J. 5
Susan Ann 158
Thomas A. 132
William 158
William A. 68
Hawes, Asa 32
Harriet Ann 32
Hawkins, Elizabeth L. 70
Rebecca 85
Sarah 167
Hawling, Isaac 132
Isaac (Jr.) 132
Isaac W. 53
Jane S. 67
Martha 53, 127
Mary 127
Sarah 49
Sarah Francis 132
Haws, Asa 68
Elizabeth 68
James 68
Hay, George 127
Hortensia M. 127
Hazard, Leah 146
Head, George 55, 75
George R. 69
Heater, Nancy 138
Solomon 138
Heath, Andrew 80
Andrew (Sr.) 63
Catherine 63
Hannah (Mrs.) 80
John 69
Ruhannah 99
Sarah 80
Heaton, Albert 150
Amanda Mary Ann 148
Decator (Dr.) 158
James 63, 69, 114
Jane Cecelia 158
John T. W. 158
Jonathan 148
Virginia 63
Hechus, Maria 131
Heckman, Margretha 14
Maria 52
Peter 14, 69
Rahel 95
Heckmanin, Margretha 14
Peter 14
Heckmann, Conrad 69
Peter 152
Heckmannin, Elisabeth
152
Magdalena 86
Peter 86
Heffner, Catharine E.
125
Hefner, George 99
Hehir, Stephen 45
Helaffer, Jane 36
Helbringle, Rebecca
Elizabeth 137
Hellnigle, Rebecca

Hellnigle (cont.)
Elizabeth 137
Helm, John 178
Sarah (Mrs.) 178
Hemrich, Jacob 4
Maria 4
Henderson, Andrew 34
Annie 59
Henrietta 11, 175
Margaret 99
Richard H. 59
Sally M. 89
William H. 70
Hendrick, Elizabeth 2
Nancy 81
Henley, Daniel 83
Henning, Elizabeth 60
Henrich, Anna Maria
(Widow) 134
Maria 125
Henry, Lydia (Mrs.) 180
Malinda 85
Hensen, Nancy 136
Hensey, Thomas 5, 98
Henton, Elizabeth
(Widow) 110
Hepburne, Delilah 28
Herbert, Elenor 72
Mary 131
Hereford, Elizabeth 114
M. 1
Thomas A. (Sr.) 70
Herford, Francis 50
Herndon, T. D. 1
Herod, Mary 149
Herrick, Mary 5
William M. 8
Herron, Elizabeth 28
Heskett, Catharine 42
Catharine D. 42
Mary S. A. 126
Heskit, Rosanna R. 83
Hess, Elizabeth 36
Hesser, Andrew 86
Castara 155
Creighton 16
James E. 96
John 10, 150
Lucinda 120
Mary A. 16
Mary M. 16
Sarah 114
Sarah Ann 96
Hessner, Sarah Ann 96
Hessor, Ann 20
Hessos, Ann 20
Hewes, Mary 152
Hewett, Abraham 64
Hewit, Mary 37
Hewitt, Abraham 108
Rachel 168
Heyold, Elizabeth 77
Hiatt, Sarah 10
Hibbs, Cathrine 139
John R. 35
Mary 126, 127
Rachel (Widow) 48
Rachell 72
Solomon 153
Hickerson, Luscinda 162
Hickman, Catharine E. 89
Catherine 10
Columbus 28
Elizabeth 113
John 130
Margaret 130, 187
Mary 33, 81
William 113

Hicks, Abegail 40
Rachel (Widow) 178
Sarah Catherine 154
Hieronymous, Nancy B. 94
Hiffner, Sarah 157
Higdon, James 71, 88
Susan A. E. 9
Higgins, Eliza (Mrs.) 71
Thomas 71
Hilburn, Mary 95
Hildfish, Maria 172
Hile, Sarah 98
Hill, Anna 118
Elizabeth 79
Elizabeth (Mrs.) 183
James 50, 96, 183
Mary Ann 2
Olivia 96
Hilliard, Anne E. 87
Emely 141
Emily 141
Joseph 87, 141
Sally 78
Hines, Hester 27
Lucy Ann 27
Mary 46
Hinton, C. 60
Hirst, Daniel 121
Hannah S. 81
John 71
Martha (Mrs.) 121
Mary (Mrs.) 71
Sarah 142
Hiskett, Abraham 154
Sarah 45
Hitaffer, John 71
Sarah (Mrs.) 71
Hite, Sarah 85
Hixon, Benjamin 79, 135
Eleanor 4
Elizabeth 127
Isabella L. 135
James 72, 76
Jane 168
John H. 94
Joshua 168
Mary 60, 87
Rachel 36
Sarah 76
Stephen 168
Stephenson 168
Sussanah 122
Hixson, Benjamin 54, 78
Mary P. 78
Parmelia 79
Sarah R. 89
Stephenson 130
Susan Mary 130
Tacey Jane 54
Hobbs, Amelia 142
Cath. 134
Nancy 35
Hodgson, Cornelia 175
Julia A. 175
Portia 175
S. L. 118
S. S. 35
Hoe, Mary Dale 29
Hoffer, Elisabetha 128
Hoffin, Magdalena 164
Hoffman, Catharina
(Widow) 116
Catherine 87
John 82
R. H. 173
Sarah C. 82
Hoge, Ann (Mrs.) 72
Anne (Mrs.) 72

Hoge (cont.)
Elizabeth 151
James 72, 99
John 72
John G. 73, 171
Mary (Mrs.) 111
Rachel 33
Sarah E. 111, 151
Solomon 72
W. 111
William 111
Hogeland, Jackson 72
James 72
John J. 6, 17, 53
Mary C. 6
Hoggins, Nelly 144
Hogue, Anne (Mrs.) 72
Elizabeth 151
Francis 72, 153
James 99
John 72
John G. 22
Joshua G. 90
Pleasant 75
Sarah 153
Sarah E. 151
Hollam, Nancy 138
Hollingsworth, Harriet
(Mrs.) 73
Isaac 73
Lydia 75
Mary 151
Holmes, Elijah 79
Elizabeth 66
Emily 111
John 72
Mary 81
Mary (Mrs.) 133
Phila 72
Priscilla 8
Rachel 133
Sophia 82
William 72, 133
Holms, Elizabeth 62
Mary 165
Nancy 19
Holyfield, Eleanor
(Widow) 178
Homan, Hannah 61
Hood, Sarah 61
Hooe, Howson L. 29
Jane E. 87
Mary D. 29
Hooff, Catharine 100
Hooper, Edward 15
Hope, Elizabeth Ann 114
John 114
Joseph 19
Lydia Virginia 128
Mary 74
Nancy (Widow) 165
Hopewell, Mary 181
Hopkins, Elizabeth
(Mrs.) 74
John 74
Horner, Catharine J. 96
Horseman, Ann 135
Lenah 159
Linny 159
William 91
William (Jr.) 159
Horsman, Ann 163
Ann (Mrs.) 163
Julia A. 97
Hoskins, Eliza 15
Elizabeth 104
Hoskinson, Ann 74
Rebecca B. 169

Hoskinson (cont.)
Thomas L. 14, 42, 98,
169
Hough, Ann 153
Ann Eliza 71
Ann Eliza. 116
Armistead T. M. 63
Benjamin 4, 75, 115,
116
Bernard 82, 153
Deborah B. 13
Eleanor 115
Eleanor (Mrs.) 74
Eleanor J. 138
Eliza 39
Elizabeth 22, 75, 133,
153
Elizabeth (Widow) 178
Ester 103
Garrett 38, 75, 133
George W. 39
Hannah 133
Harriet E. 100
Harriet Ellen 105
Henrietta C. 116
Jane 170
John 75, 104
Joseph 11, 75, 100,
159
Leven W. S. 49
Louisa 82
Louisa Jane 82
Mahlon 19
Mary 49, 133, 134
Mary (Mrs.) 19
Mary E. 159
Mary Frances 4
Mary M. 75
Mary Margaret 49
Phebe Ellen (Mrs.) 75
Rachel A. 51
Roseanah 32
Samuel 75
Sarah 11, 38, 67, 131,
147
William 74, 105
William H. 61, 75
William T. 13
Hougue, Mary 75
Householder, Caroline A.
63
Gideon 63, 70, 100
Houser, Abraham 147
Ann 128
Christopher 93
Jacob 147
Mary 138, 147
Mary E. 5
Rd. 74
Rebecca J. 138
Richard 138
Housholder, Haml. 138
Jacob 143
Howard, Caroline 148
Cathrine 71
Howel, Wineford 64
Howell, Anna 165
Armistead M. 169
Daniel 53
Edah 82
Emily 70
Jesse 82
John 51
Mary 23
Nancy 51
Rachel K. 157
Howewell, Mary 117
Howser, Christopher 156

Howser (cont.)
Mary 147
Matilda 79
Rebecca 138
Rebecca J. 138
Richard 100, 138
Huff, Elizabeth 62
Rebecca 155
Huffman, Emily 11
Jacob 87
John 11, 76
Martha C. 76
Hugeley, Jacob 43
Hughely, Mary 8
Hughes, Ann 36
Catharine 98
Elias 65
Elizabeth (Mrs.) 76,
77
Hannah 18
J. 77
Jane P. 96
John H. 106
Mary 22, 23, 176
Mary Ann 60
Matthew 76, 77
Thomas 176
Hughs, Hannah 18
John A. 96
Martha 3
Mary 32
Hume, Patrick 40
Humfrey, Jane (Widow)
179
Hummer, Abigal 70
George W. 13
John W. 52
Martin B. 21
Mary 77
Matilda 9
Nancy 17
Sarah C. 9
Thomas 9
Washington 117
Hummings, Rachel 138
Humphrey, Abner 72
Ann 136
Armelia 35
Hannah 10
Jacob F. 24
John 42
John G. 57, 84, 99
Letitia 161
Maria 155
Mary 71, 117
Mary P. 101
Nancy 42
Polly 21
Rachel 66
Tacey 72, 179
Tacy 35
Thomas 179
Thomas G. 54, 101
Humphreys, John 42
Nancy 42
Humphries, John 42
Nancy 42
Hunt, Eli 150, 172
Elizabeth 172
Emily 63
Joel 95
John 63, 172
Jonathan 26
Lucinda 70
Martha J. 26
Mary 39
Mary A. 172
Mary Eleanor 78

210

Linch (cont.)
  Mary Ann 90
Linck, Mary Ann 90
Linton, Hester (Widow)
  182
  John 12
Little, Elizabeth 123
  Sarah (Widow) 107
Littlejohn, John 54
Littler, Ann (Mrs.) 66
  John 66
  Rachel B. 15
  Sarah Ann 66
Littleton, Amanda 97
  Charles M. 119
  Charlotte 162
  Emma 64
  Fielding 78, 91, 121,
    127
  J. K. 50
  John T. L. 51
  John W. 162
  Marcus D. 91
  Margaret 91
  Nancy 39, 95
  Nancy E. 50
  Oscar 91
  R. C. 51
  R. K. 23
  Richard 23
  Sarah Elizabeth 51
  T. 3, 7
  Thomas 21, 64, 152,
    154
Livingston, Mary B. 124
Lloyd, Ann 169
  Margaret 169
Locker, Garrett 61
  George 43
  Gerard 2
  Louisa E. 43
  Mary Catharine 2
  Rachel Ann 61
Lockheart, William 92
Lodge, Elizabeth 27
  Emily 138
  Joseph 77, 92
  Laban 71
  Marsha A. 92
  Mary 77
  Mary C. 77
  Nathan 27
  Susanna 104
  William 138
Logan, Samuel 92
Loman, Britania L.
    (Widow) 179
  Lawson 179
  Mary E. 102
Lomax, Britania S.
    (Widow) 179
  Britannia 82
  Lawson 179
Long, Ann Eliza 114
  Conrad 114
  Phillip 50
  Sarah 55, 177
Longly, Joseph 54
  Permelia 36
Lott, Elizabeth 141
  Francis 92
  P. L. 139
  Parkerson L. 110, 153
Love, A. E. 75
  Eliza Matilda (Mrs.)
    179
  Fenton M. 179
  Hannah 118

Love (cont.)
  James D. 179
  James J. 16
  Mary R. 179
  Richard H. 179
  Sarah N. 75
  Susan A. 18
  Susanna (Widow) 179
  Susannah 30
  Thomas B. 179
Lovelace, John T. 144
  Sarah Ann 144
Loveless, Alcinda D. 162
  Catherine 8
  Elizabeth 42
  John 93, 136
  Mary 43
  Mary Ann 136
  Thomas 162
Lovett, Amanda C. 13
  Daniel 60
  Daniel W. 54
  David 123
  Evelina 54
  James P. 93
  Martha 60
  Mortimer C. 13
Lowe, Catherine 105
  Elizabeth 33, 148, 173
  Elizabeth Ann 12
  Henry 33, 85, 100
  Jane 93, 152, 173
  John 152
  Louisa A. 85
  Margaret O. 17
  Mary 100
  Mary Jane 50
  Rector 50
  Thomas 152
  William 93
Lownes, James 187
  Sarah 187
  Sarah (Mrs.) 187
Lowry, Eliza (Mrs.) 10
Lucas, Cascy 102
  James 120
  Mahala 120
  Martha Ann 24
  Mary 120, 185
  Sarah Ann 49
  Susannah 185
  Theodosia 163
  Thomas 102, 185
Luck, Drusilla Ann 106
  Emily M. 139
  Jordan B. 106
  Jordon B. 139
Luckett, Francis W. 17,
    59
  Horace 7, 35
  L-- 77
  Ludwell 39
  Maria Louisa 7
  Martha L. 59
  Mary (Widow) 156
  Samuel C. 7
  Sarah 62
  Sarah Frances 35
Ludwell, Richard H. 179
Luke, Catherine 43
Lum, Hester Ann 120
  John 120
Lumm, John 47
  Mary Ann 47
Luntz, William 94
Lupton, Hannah M. 122
  Isaac 122
  Sarah Ann 81

Lupton (cont.)
  Tamson (Mrs.) 122
Lush, Jane 107
Lybough, Joseph 53
  Susannah 53
Lyden, Margret 34
Lyder, Mahala 126
Lyders, Eleanor 80
Lynch, Jane 124
  Margaret 83
Lynd, Caroline Amanda 90
Lyne, Mary 106
  Susan 30
  William 106
Lynn, Joseph R. 94
  Maria V. 72
  Michael 94
  Parmelia C. 42
  William M. 71, 72, 94
Lynnd, Caroline Amanda
    90
  Nicholas 90
Lyon, Alexander 47
  Sarah E. 47
Lyons, Ann Eliza 176
  Ann Eliza Carter 181
  Elizabeth 119
  John 94
  Peter 176
  William 34
Maberry, Nelly 85
Mack, Elisabetha 117
  Nanzy 96
Macpherson, Sarah 94
Maddux, Evelina B. 25
Magaha, Ann 139
  Elizabeth 45
  Ellen Elizabeth 162
  John 45
  Joseph 88
  Margaret 79, 94
  William 94
Magahy, Ann 139
  Duana 1
Magill, (?) (Dr.) 154
  H. D. 154
Mahagon, Catharine
    (Mrs.) 175
  William 175
Mahaney, Stephen 45
Mahany, Eliza Ann 33
Mahoney, Betsey 152
  Elisabetha 152
  John 152
Mahonner, Mary 75
Mahonny, Elvina 65
Mahony, Eliza Ann 33
Mailow, George 165
  Virginia 165
Mains, Archibald 158
Major, Elizabeth 78
  James 95
  Margaret 111
Maker, Mary 143
Manken, Mary 162
Mankins, James W. 38, 47
  Nancy 163
Manley, Dorcas 64
Manly, John S. 64
Mann, Catharina 105
  Johannes 95, 105
  Magdalena (Mrs.) 95
  Sarah 86
Mannin, Elisabeth 146
Mansfield, Rebecca 71
  Rebekah 71
March, Rachel 58
Marchant, Mary 141

213

215

217

218

Peugh (cont.)
  Leonidas 44
  Margaret E. 26
  Mary (Widow) 5
  Rebecca J. 134
Peyton, Elizabeth 51,
  117
  Lucinda B. 97
  Margaret M. 89
  Susanna T. 90
  William 90
Phahle, Margretha 55
Phale, Catharina 62
  Elisabeth 164
  Jacob 62, 148, 164
  Johannes 117
  Margretha 52
  Maria 164
  Sussana 148
Phaley, Elizabeth 52
Phaly, Christina 141
  Jacob 164
  Johannes 141
Phelan, Edward 177
  Jeremiah 177
  Winifred (Mrs.) 177
Philips, Elizabeth 109
  Hanh. 173
  Huma 127
  Israel 131
  Jesse 114
  Margaret 19
  Sarah 115
Philler, Ana 174
  Elisabeth 95
  Margretha 3, 103
  Nanzy 134
  Sarah 134
Phillern, Catharina 22
Phillips, Amy 145
  Amy Ann 102, 103
  Charles Fenton 117
  David 118
  Edmund 19, 145
  Israel 45, 51, 117,
    149
  Margaret 105
  Margaret L. 107
  Philip L. 107
  Rachel (Mrs.) 103
  Rebecca 152
  Sarah A. 19
  Thomas 24, 103
  William F. 142
Phinety, Sarah 135
Pickerill, Elizabeth 31
Pickett, Jas. 185
  William 27
Pickings, Margaret 49
Pidgeon, Rachel (Jr.) 28
Pidgion, Charles 118,
  186
Piecock, Anna (Widow) 70
Pierce, Carey 107
  Hannah 50, 51
  Sarah Ann 17, 50
  William 50
Pierpoint, Eli 40, 62
  Elizabeth 91
  Esther (Mrs.) 91
  Francis 187
  Joseph 18
  Mary 71, 187
  Mary Esther 18
  Obed 71, 91
  Rue Ann 18
  Sarah 92
Piggott, Elizabeth 19

Pile, Nancy 4
Piles, Elizabeth 162
  Francis 118, 162
  Mary 17
  Sarah 40
  Sarah A. 9
Pinn, William 118
Piott, Mary 76
Plaster, David H. 72
  Henry (Jr.) 72, 90
  Susan H. 72
  Susan R. 80
  Susannah 78
  Veturia Ann 90
Pleasants, Jacob 187
  Sarah (Mrs.) 187
Plummer, Ann 168
  Cassandra 185
  Joseph 187, 188
  Samuel 81, 185, 187
  Sarah 81
  Sarah (Mrs.) 81, 187,
    188
  Susannah 188
Poland, Alexander 46,
  147
  John 118
Polen, Dicey 10
  John 118
Poling, Edward 118
Polston, Mary 166
Pomeroy, Jane 93
Pomroy, Burr 159
  Hannah 159
Pool, Elias 106, 155
  Fanny 5
  Harrison 6
  Mary 62
  Susannah 106
Popkins, Ann M. 69
  Elenor 60
  James H. 69
  Mary 63
Poppens, John 185
  Sarah 185
Pordom, Ehry 115
Porter, Mary 115, 180
  Mary Ann 30
Poston, Anne 154
  Benajmin J. 128
  Elizabeth 40
  John F. 63
  Joseph W. 123
  Leonard 154
  Leonard R. 128
  Susan M. 128
  William W. 119
Pottenfeld, Catharina
  133
  Maria 164
Potter, Hannah 103
  John 30
Potterfield, Catherine
  170
  Jonathan 170
  Priscilla 137
  Samuel 159
Pottet, Rachel 19
Potts, David 30, 34
  Elizabeth 34
  Elizabeth (Widow) 94
  Emma F. 64
  Ezekiel 29
  Hannah 12
  Jane 30
  Jonas 111, 120
  Kezia 158
  Lydia H. 83

Potts (cont.)
  Martha 122
  Mary (Widow) 181
  Mary J. D. 29
  Sarah 45
  Susan Ann 111
  Tamer 79
  William 64
Poukens, John 185
  Sarah 185
Poulson, Elizabeth 76
  Susanna 117
Poultney, Elenor 118
Poulton, Catharine 165
  Charles 120
  Harriet Ann 154
  Reed 12, 22, 120, 147,
    154, 156, 172
  Thomas 83
  William H. 44
Powell, Alice 169
  Amey 36, 91
  Ann (Widow) 181
  Ann Maria 120
  Ann W. 112
  Burr 30
  Catherine 123
  Catherine (Widow) 181
  Cuthbert 2, 59, 176
  Elisha 53
  Elizabeth W. 30
  Ellen D. 59
  Fars. A. 58
  George C. 30
  George Cuthbert 101
  Gertrude Ann 29
  H. B. 73, 157
  Hannah 9
  Jane Serena 59
  John Calrymple 113
  John D. 91
  Josephus 88
  Laura Holmes 157
  Leven H. 91
  Lucy Lee 91
  Margaret 122
  Mary E. 120
  Mary E. (Mrs.) 2
  Mary P. 32
  Peyton 36, 120
  Polly 134
  Rebecca Louisa 73
  Rosalie D. 127
  Sally E. 47
  Sally Pendleton 66
  Sarah 53, 66, 95
  Sarah (Widow) 181
  Susannah E. 56
  Thomas 24
  William 5, 95
  William A. 127
  William L. 73
  Winefred 88
Power, Margaret Ann 14
  Mary Jane 3
  Robert 14, 56
  Walter 120
Prall, Virginia L. 18
Pratt, Juliet 159
Presgraves, Amelia 155
  Emely 155
  Lucinda 78
  Lydia 164
  Mary Ann 121
  Richard H. 47
Preston, Ann 31
  Darcus 37
  George 31

220

221

Simpson (cont.)
  William L. 171
Sims, Richardetta 124
  William 124
Simson, Mellion 48
  Richard 48
Sinclair, (?) (Mrs.) 25
  Craven 33
  Edith (Widow) 182
  Eleanor 62
  Esther 38, 56
  Fanny 35
  George 33, 62
  James 60, 75, 87, 92,
    98, 111, 131
  Jane 141
  John 140
  Mary 18
  Mary E. 25
  Samuel 33
  Sarah 33
Sinclear, Ann 60
  James 60
  Mary (Mrs.) 60
Sinkfield, Abraham 108
Sinnis, Emeline 86
Sixlin, Elizabeth 15
Skillman, Abraham 94,
  140
  Martha Ann 12
  Violinda Ann 94
Skinner, Adaline B. 160
  Alexander 42
  Amos 47
  Ann Eliza 97
  Benjamin F. 37
  Catherine L. 47
  Elizabeth 75, 151
  Gabriel 42, 97, 140
  John R. 21
  Lauretta C. 110
  Martha 48
  Mary 87
  Nancy 42, 127
  Nathaniel 48
  Peggy 75
  Peter 140, 168
  Rebecca 42
  Roberta Ann 119
  Sarah 37
  Sarah E. 168
  Thomas 110
  Verlinda 180
Slacht, Amy (Widow) 182
  Jacob 182
Slack, Fenton 116
  Geraldine 155
  James 155
  Mary 42
  Sigismunda 155
  Susan 25
  Tunis 25
Slalcks, (?) (Widow) 164
  Elisabeth 164
Slater, Airy Ann 75
  Ary Ann 75
  Elizabeth 144
  Ellen H. 84
  Jacob 144
  Samuel 75
  William 84
Slates, Scivilla (Widow)
  143
  Sevilla (Widow) 143
Sly, Nelly 125
Slytes, Horatio 71
Smale, Mary 92
  Simon 92, 125

Smallwood, Adaline 28
  Amanda 123
  Amelia 93
  Bayn 61
  Catharine 157
  Eleanora 40
  George 115
  John 83
  John Wesley 5
  Lucretia 58
  Mary 25, 61, 141
  Mary Agnes 5
  Polly 141
  Rachel J. 32
  Rachel Jane 33
  Sarah Jane 112
  Susnh. 58
  Wesley 112
  William 28
Smarr, Anna 124
  Sarah (Widow) 140
Smart, John P. 109
  Samuel 65
Smith, Abraham 135, 142
  Alice 140
  Amanda Davis 121
  Amos 182
  Ann 71
  Benjamin 112
  Catharine 155
  Catherine 39, 136
  Catherine Eliza 10
  Datherine 76
  Elizabeth 5, 35, 73
  Elizabeth (Mrs.) 141
  Elizabeth M. 137
  Elizabeth W. 112
  Emily 153
  Emily Ann 17
  Emily R. 135
  Febe 59
  George D. 79
  Hannah 50, 120
  Henry 150
  Hugh 141
  Jacob 5, 10, 26, 29,
    136, 163, 168, 182,
    183
  James 8, 151
  Jane K. 54
  Janthy 111
  John 18, 24, 33, 182
  John F. 121
  John S. 104
  Kezeah 182
  Kezia T. 61
  Leannah 143
  Lenah 167
  Louisa 115
  Lucy 131
  Margaret 48, 56, 84,
    171
  Margaret E. 25
  Martha A. 82
  Mary 2, 37, 63, 84,
    93, 182
  Mary Ann 137
  Mary F. 2
  Mary Jane 163
  Mary S. 2
  Mercy 174
  Middleton 39
  Miranda 151
  Nancy 139
  Phebe 168
  Pleasant 186
  Priscilla D. 8
  Rachel 110, 182

Smith (cont.)
  Rachel (Mrs.) 71
  Rebeca 155
  Rufus 25
  Ruth 160
  Samuel 182
  Sarah 12, 60, 123,
    150, 151
  Sarah Ann 18
  Sarah E. (Mrs.) 181
  Sarah N. 56
  Sebella 109
  Seth 4, 50, 154
  Solomon 69, 142
  Stephen P. 82
  Susan 29
  Susanna 1
  Thomas 71
  William 60, 73, 97,
    105, 173, 181
Smither, Ann 27
  Rachel 65
Smithers, Priscilla 29
Smithey, Peggy 85
Smitley, Eliza 39
  Elizabeth 39
  Jane 39
  John 158
Smitson, James 61
  Thomas 22
Smyth, Elizabeth 50
Snider, Jane F. 171
Snoots, John 95
  John (Jr.) 98
  Mary 22
  Sarah 20, 95
  Susan 22
Snow, John 163
Snowden, Maria 82
Snutts, Catherine 45
Snyder, Catherine S. 140
  Lydia 120
Soloman, Susan 106
Solomon, Catherine
    Eugenia 105
  Emeline 130
  Henrietta D. 128
  James 78
  Mary Ann 13
  William 13
Solston, Fielding 68
Sopher, Ruth 131
Sorrell, Ann 135
Souder, Elizabeth C. 5
  George P. 5
  John 154
South, Henrietta 21
Sowers, William 144
Spates, Alfred 130, 139
  Amy Ann 52
  Ann 15
  Elenor 74
Spaytes, Matilda 168
Speaks, Boly 43
  Charles 80
  Charles E. 3
  Emily Violette 35
  Nancy 43
Specht, Catherine 34
Speck, Catherine 88
Speckt, Catherine 34
Spence, Catharine 64
Spencer, Elizabeth 62
  Hannah 21, 69
  John M. 128
  Margaret 111
  Mary C. 41
  Sarah 11, 142

224

Vandevanter (cont.)
Joseph 99
Mary (Widow) 183
Washington 158
Vandevender, Leannah 139
Vandeventer, Duanna 25
Eliza A. 16
Gabriel 16
Joseph 81
Sarah 25, 81
Vandivender, Joseph 99
Vanhaun, Elizabeth 23
Vanhorn, Elizabeth 23
Mary 17
Sarah 20
William 15
Vanhorne, Ann Elizabeth
116
Bernard 20
Ishmael 70
Jane 40
Margaret 4
Mary 4, 7
Nancy 109
Octavia 154
Polly 7
Sarah 61
Vanpelt, Betsey Ann 88
Elizabeth 77
Julian 83
Sarah 73
Vansickle, Lydia 73
Vansickler, John 72, 91
Philip 132
Sarah 132
Vanskiver, Elizabeth 42
Mary 114
Ruth 56
Varnes, John 67
Vaughters, Betsey 76
Richard 76
Vauters, Margaret
Virginia 66
William 66
Veal, John 132
Veale, Elam C. 123
Venander, Catharine 15
Jane 6, 115
Margaret 149
Nancy 50
Venzel, Lowisa 156
Vermillian, Lettice 58
Vermillion, Amelia 149
Benjamin 182
Garrison 129
Henson 123
James 122
James T. 159
Letty 10
Maria (Widow) 182
Sarah 129
Vernon, Mary 79
Verts, Adalade 96
Christena 28
Christiana 160
Conrad 15
Jacob 28
John 96, 159
Margaret Jane 15
Sarah 118
Sarah J. 27
Sarah Jane 28
Susan Ann (Mrs.) 28
William 118
Vertz, Adalade 96
John 96
Vickars, Anna 159
Vickers, Ann 57

Vickers (cont.)
Elizabeth 41
Leah 110
Margaret 124
Ruth 56
Sarah 141
Vincel, Caroline 103
Eliza 93
Vincell, George 137, 142
John 36
Vinsel, Louisa Virginia
71
Vinsell, Georve 17
Vinson, John T. 160
Violet, Sarah 139
Violett, Ashford 172
Elizabeth 151
Jemima 13
John 38, 169
Mary 172
Mary Ann 38
Nancy L. 169
Virts, Conrad 15, 144
Elisabeth 7
Elizabeth C. 144
Henry 116
Jane 45
John W. 6
Jona. 33
Margaret Jane 15
Sarah 118
William 45, 118
Virtz, Catharine 53
Conrad 53, 84
John 94
Mary 94
Mary Eliza 84
Vours, Ashfield 163
Wade, Elenor 89
Hezekiah 89
John 160
Martha (Widow) 160
Mary 112, 148
Mary (Widow) 183
Mary C. 29
Priscilla 23
Robert 23
Susan 160
Waggerman, John A. 151
Waggle, Dolly 59
Wagley, Ann 54
Waird, Louisa Ann 143
Michael 143
Waldtman, Elisabetha 102
Waley, Lewis D. 133
Walker, Barbara 145
Ben 92
Benjamin 163
Burr 161
Burr S. 38
Elizabeth 49, 123, 145
Garrett 134
Lorenzo D. 140, 146,
160, 173
Mareyan (Mrs.) 161
Mary 163
Mary Ann 92
Mary E. 168
Rachel 46
Rebecca Jane 81
Ruth Sarah 146
Sarah (Mrs.) 145
William 145
Waller, Elizabeth 96
George 20, 96
Sarah Ann 20
Walrond, Elizabeth
(Widow) 183

Walter, Eunus 120
John 68
Sarah A. 68
Walters, Eliza J. 94
Maria 42
Sarah 19, 100
Waltman, Elisabetha Anna
163
Elizabeth 187
Emanuel 143, 164
Jacob 80, 187
Margaret 92, 161, 186
Maria Anna 103
Mary Anna 103
Mary Catherine 168
Mortimer 168
Samuel 158
Sarah Ann 80
Susan A. 164
Waltmann, Eva 161
G. F. Samuel 161
Wampler, Ann B. 97
Ann R. 96
War, John 123
Lucinda 124
Mary E. 123
Ward, Emily 91, 179
George 191
Ware, Charles A. 39
Warford, Abraham 90, 138
Catherine 138
Hannah 60
Theodosia 90
Warner, George 24
Hannah 24
Israel 53, 80
Mahlon 162
Mary C. 117
Mary Catharine 117
Massey 53
Pleasant 150
Sarah 80
Warr, Eveline 22
Warrenburg, Barbary 169
Warrick, Betsy 26
Warrinburg, Barbary 171,
172
Wartman, Nancy 36
Washington, Edward S.
113
Elizabeth C. 113
Mary S. 41
Samuel E. 45
Thomas B. 162
Water, Eliza 68
Elizabeth 157
Jacob 157
Sophia 64
Susannah 33
Waterman, A. G. 69, 85
Waters, Artrage (Mrs.)
188
Catherine (Widow) 183
Elizabeth 158
Helen 106
Jacob 68, 148, 158,
162
Levi 9, 162
Libbe 145
Maria Louisa 9
Mary 110
Mary Ann 148
Samuel 188
Watkins, Ann (Widow) 175
Bernard 2, 175
Catharine 51
Eleanor 2
Elender 175

228

Watkins (cont.)
James 48
Louisa 175
Margaret (Mrs.) 48
Sarah 97
Sarah Ann 55, 175
William 175
Watson, Elisa 36
Frances Ann 83
Maria 130
Rachel Ann 126
Wattkins, James 48
Margaret (Mrs.) 48
Wattman, Elizabeth 128,
169
Watts, Jemima 155
Nancy 102
Susanna 88
Waugh, Alexander 54, 137
Weadon, Ashford 161
Ashton 36
Catharine 36
Elizabeth 40
F. M. 26
Frederick 40
John 46
Nancy 158
Weatherill, Mary Eleanor
61
Nancy C. 73
Weatherly, David 81
Weaver, Rachel 118
Web, Mary 187
Webb, Elisabeth Jane 186
Elisha 186
Elizabeth (Widow) 186
Elizabeth Jane 89
John W. 186
Mary Ann 58
Reba. 146
Webster, Phebe 159
Weeden, Mary 142
Sarah 105
Weedon, Ashton 36
Catharine 36
Mary 143
Weekes, Elizabeth D. 36
Weiert, Rahel 128
Wein, Elisabeth 72
Welch, James 86
Sophia M. 86
Weldon, Mary 113
Wellford, Parke F. 127
Wells, Catherine (Mrs.)
163
Elizabeth C. 160
John 163
Julia Ann 6
Wenner, Carlotta 132
Caroline M. !$@
Charlotte 135
John W. 94, 142
Jona. 135
Jonathan 103
Margaret 94
Maria (Widow) 50
Mary 1
Mary Ann 44
Wilhelm 163
William 44, 53, 163,
164
William (Jr.) 53
Wentzel, Catharina 14
Catharina (Mrs.) 86
Catharine 41
Elizabeth 163
Georg 14, 86
Johannes 14, 41, 164

Wentzel (cont.)
Johannes (Sr.) 164
Magdalena 86
Maria 14
Sarah 117
Wentzeln, Catharina
(Mrs.) 86
Georg 86
Magdalena 86
Wenzel, Elisabetha 163
Georg 164
Johannes 133, 163
Susanna 133
Werts, Philbina 164
Wertz, Catharina 169
Elisha 38
Jacob 30, 38, 62
Leah 62
Peter 14, 78, 164
Sibila 78
William 164
Wertzin, Ann 14
Elisabetha 30
West, Elizabeth 99, 161,
164
Hannah (Widow) 183
John 161
Jonathan 79
Lydia 161
Maria 78, 136
Mary (Widow) 142, 183
Samuel 24
Westwood, Francis H. 43
William 43
Wetherile, Nancy C. 73
Wey, Thomas A. 164
Weynt, Margretha 128
Whalen, Ann (Widow) 183
Margaret 177
Winifred 177
Whaley, Ann 82
Ann M. 82
Elizabeth 40
Hannah 74
Harriett 88
James 113
Jane E. 113
John G. 113
Levi 28
Mary Ann 164
William 40, 74
Wheatley, Jane 149
Joseph 20
Mary Ann 20
Nancy Ann 20
Wherry, Mary E. 141, 182
Whistleman, Mary 148
Whitacker, John 7
Whitackre, Naomia 60
Whitacre, Amos 15
James 16, 51, 77, 90
John 165
Lydia 77
Mary Ann 15
Naomi (Mrs.) 165
Ninia 138
Sarah 101
Whitcare, Ann 158
White, Adin 23
Agnes B. 165
Amanda 33, 34
Ann Cecelia 104
Ann Eliza 151
Barsena 158
C. Odin 165
Celia 33
Elizabeth 81, 110
Henry 104

White (cont.)
Jane 83
John 101, 165
John H. 55
John R. 12
Jonah R. 166
Joshua 93
Josiah (Jr.) 47
Josiah P. 166
Lean 186
Levi 36, 48, 73, 110,
111
Louisa 23, 111
Margaret H. 93
Margeret 92
Maria 110
Mary 95, 111
Mary Ann 88, 120
Mary E. 101
Mary Isabella 12
Nancy 149
Nathan 120
Rachel 81
Richard 93, 171
Robert J. T. 86
Rosanna M. 55
Ruth 127
S. N. C. 165
Sarah 36
Sarah E. 18
Thomas 34, 110, 111
Virginia A. 166
Wesley 65
Whiteley, Margaret 142
Nancy 140
Whiting, Louisa 19
Margaret 19
Whitmore, Catharine 67
Elizabeth 136
George 95, 134, 142,
166
Margaret 13
Michael 13, 67, 169
Michael William 182
William W. 168
Whittacre, Masey 109
Whitter, Eliza 135
Wiatt, Patience 185
Wickes, Eliza D. 37
William 37
Wicuff, Sush. 16
Wierd, Michael 128
Wiggenton, Benjamin 48
Wiggington, Mary 166
Wigginton, Benjamin 6
Jane 183
John 183
Presley 183
Sarah 6
Wigington, Jane 185
Wild, Magreth 37
Wilden, Sarah G. 156
Wilder, Henry 45
Sarah J. 45
Wildman, (?) (Mrs.) 96
Agnes 76
Amelia 16
Ann 100
Catherine 4
Cathrine 75
Charles B. 144
Dewanner 139
Eleanor (Widow) 183
Eleanor A. 17
Frances 107
Jacob 100
Jane D. 17
Joseph 16, 76

Wildman (cont.)
Juliet Ann 157
Mary 161
Nancy 35
Nancy A. 16, 17
Nelly 156
Rachel 105, 171
William 107
Wildt, Rahel 128
Wiley, Ann 161
Catherine 37
Deborah Ann 137
Elizabeth 160
Emily 22
Hugh 161
James 5
James W. 90
John 22
Kezziah 18
Lavina 163
Mary 68
Thomas H. 137
Wilkeson, Margaret 172
Wilkins, Jane 22
Wilkinson, Barbara
(Mrs.) 72
Barbary (Mrs.) 167
Elisabeth 81
Elisabetha 118
Joseph 72, 167
Sarah 72
Susannah 110
Thomas 81
Wilkison, Evan 110
Sarah 45
Susannah 110
William 140
Will, Mary 6
Willd, Christina 148
Willemanin, (?) (Widow)
52
Willet, Linney 2
William 2
Willett, Nancy A. 70
William, George 40
Williams, Alice 21
Amelia A. 143
Catharine H. 17
Charles 112, 168
Eleanor 156
Eliza 152
Elizabeth 122, 176
Elizabeth (Mrs.) 88,
167, 183
Ellis 183
Hannah 29, 88, 179
Hannah Ann 75
Henry S. 39, 143, 149
Hiram Opie 17
Israel 29
James 23, 156
Jane 117
John 144
Julia Ann 88
Lyddnah 104
Margaret M. A. 154,
187
Martha 30
Mary (Mrs.) 168
Mary C. 149
Mary Catherine 149
Mary E. 104
Notley C. 187
Presley 168
Rahel 166
Ruth 168
Sarah 165
Sarah Ellen 143

Williams (cont.)
Syddnah 75
T. R. 62
William 49, 88, 167,
168
Willis, Elizabeth 21
Sally (Widow) 136
William 21
Wills, Hester (Widow)
183
Jane 134
Willson, Nancy 73
Wilsen, Dienna 25
James 25
John 41
Wilson, Alexander 178
Ann 2
Anna Bell 55
Archibald 47
Charlotte 55
Charlotte F. 12
Darcus 137
Dienna 25
Edward 2
Eleanor 74
Elizabeth 41, 51, 60,
74, 178
Ellen 78
Evelina 47
Fornetta 40
Francis T. 153
Gustavia B. 2
Hannah 70
Hannah P. 19
Harriett H. 64
Helen Mary 12
Henrietta 165
James 25, 46, 74
Jane 46
John 47, 178
John M. 48
Julia A. H. 15
Lucy J. 33
Mary 24, 78, 97
Moses 21, 156
Nancy 148
Phebe 143
Polly 23
Rebecca 153
Rebekah 48
Ressy 32
Robert 48
Samuel 169
Sarah 149, 155
Sarah (Mrs.) 169
Susanna 74
William 19
Wilt, George W. 79
Wince, Lucinda E. 126
Wine, Catharine A. 125
Catherine 14
Daniel 61
Elizabeth 171
George H. 99, 169
George Henry 125
John 46
Sarah Ann 99
Winecoop, Maranda 123
Winegardner, Adam 106,
130
Mary 106
Sarah 130
Winegarner, Levi 1
Winn, Sophia 101
Sophiah 108
Thomas M. 38
William 169, 173
Winner, John 135

Winner (cont.)
Jona. 135
Mary 135
Winsel, George 156
Louisa 156
Winters, Eliza 135
Wire, Elizabeth 78
Sarah Ann 43
Wirtz, Christiana 1
Christinia 44
Peter 1, 170
Wise, Jane 113
William 113
Wisener, Nathan 16
Wissinger, Julian M. 141
Wit, (?) (Mrs.) 80
Wittman, Elisabeth 132
Wnykoop, Cornelius 172
Wock, George W. 104
Wolf, Adam 45
Barbara 149
Catherine 80
Elizabeth 129
Mary 45
Susan 89, 93
Wolfe, Mary 33
Wolff, Barbara 149
Wolford, Elizabeth 118
John 147
Mahala 2
Maria Ann 134
Maria Anna 134
Mary Ann 134
Mary Anna 134
Rebecca 147
William 2, 134
Wollford, Maria Ann 134
Maria Anna 134
Mary Ann 134
Mary Anna 134
Wood, Abigail (Mrs.) 167
Elizabeth 70
Joseph 12, 167, 170
Lydia (Mrs.) 170
Lydia (Widow) 183
Mary 167
Mary (Mrs.) 170
William 170
William S. 51
Woodard, Julia Ann 79
Wooddy, Isabel 70
John 70
Woodey, Sally 69
Woodford, Elizabeth
(Widow) 183
Susanah 24
Susanna (Widow) 183
William 53
Woodley, Mary Jane 79
Woodward, J. 65
Jabez 65
Jane 65
Prudence 67
Woody, Mary Jane 79
Woodyard, Jabaz 171
Nancy (Mrs.) 171
Walter 55
Woolf, John 57
Woolford, Elizabeth 118
Workman, Charlotte 68
Isaac 68, 146, 171
Matilda 146
Sarah Jane (Mrs.) 171
Works, Alfred 153
Wornal, Elizabeth
(Widow) 176
James 176
John 16, 24, 70, 112

Wornall, James 8
  John 4, 32, 88
  Sarah 8
Wornel, John 158
Wornell, Elizabeth 32
Worseley, Mary Ann 101
  William 101
Worsley, Mary Ann 101
  William 74, 101
Worthington, Emily 114,
    173
  Joseph 114
  Landon 85, 153
  Landon W. 35
  Sarah 152
Wortman, Ann Amanda 65
  Isaac 65
Wren, Elizabeth 66
  Margaret 109
  Mary 166
  Sarah 66
Wrenn, Jane 63, 66
Wright, Alfred 5, 10
  Amy 109
  Ann (Widow) 184
  Ann E. 134
  Anthony 58
  Catharine 91
  Charles 183
  Charles F. 59
  Christianna (Mrs.) 179
  Effee 107
  Elizabeth (Mrs.) 188
  Elizabeth (Widow) 184
  James P. 10
  John 162, 188
  John E. 134
  Jonathan 73
  Joseph 152
  Mahala 20
  Martha 99, 115
  Martha A. 174
  Mary 99, 163
  Mary (Widow) 183
  Mary Esther Austin 161
  Mary Jane 116
  Nancy 83, 106
  Rachel 41
  Reba. 97
  Rebecca 147
  Rebecca J. 152
  Rebecca M. 23
  Rebecca W. 152
  Robert 177
  Robert L. 23
  Samuel 129, 161, 179
  Sarah Ann 162
  Susan 10
  Susannah 165
  Thomas 130
  Uriah 16
  William 18, 35, 83
  William G. 20, 152,
    172
Wunder, Caroline H. 69
  Henry S. 56
  Hy. S. 69
Wyard, Michael 128
  Rachel 128
Wyatt, Elizabeth 44
  Louise 173
Wylie, Mary 108
Wynkoop, Alcinda 79
  Catharina A. 9
  Catharine 129, 140
  Cornelius 22
  Elizabeth 84, 140
  Elizabeth W. 172

Wynkoop (cont.)
  Garrad 22
  Garret 84
  Garrett 172, 173
  George W. 129
  Jane 22
  John 172
  Joseph 22, 173
  Leva Jane 109
  Margaret 22, 165
  Nancy E. 106
  Philip Henry 173
  Samuel C. 9, 22, 143
  Sarah E. 84
  Thomas 140
Wynn, John 18
Yabower, Elizabeth 124,
    125
  John 124
Yakey, Elizabeth 166
Yantus, Elizabeth 12
Yates, Alice (Jr.) 108
  Franklin A. 61
  Johanah 89
  Malinda Jane 61
Yeaky, Amanda 134
Yearnest, Mary 130
Yoates, Verlinda 117
Yound, Rebecca 157
Young, Ann 16
  David 12, 18, 55
  Edith 18
  Elizabeth 13
  George 157
  Hannah 21
  Henry 56
  Hercules 21
  John 18, 39, 79
  John B. 113
  John M. 179
  Latitia 136
  Louisa 144
  Lucy M. 79
  Mary 53, 55
  Nancy 12, 83
  Rachel 39, 56
  Rebecca (Widow) 184
  Sarah (Mrs.) 21
  Sarah E. 157
  Sarah Elizabeth 157
  Susan 150
  Thomas 172
  William 16, 150, 184
Zeller, John 108
  Lydia Ann 108
Zenbauern, Magdalena 128
Ziegenfussin, Magdalena
    113
Zillers, Catharine Ann
    64
Zillus, Catharine Ann 64
Zimmerman, Samuel 153

231